Turks & Caicos Islands

the Bradt Travel Guide

Annalisa Rellie & Tricia Hayne

edition
I

www.bradtguides.com

Bradt Travel Guides Ltd, UK
The Globe Pequot Press Inc, USA

MW01004283

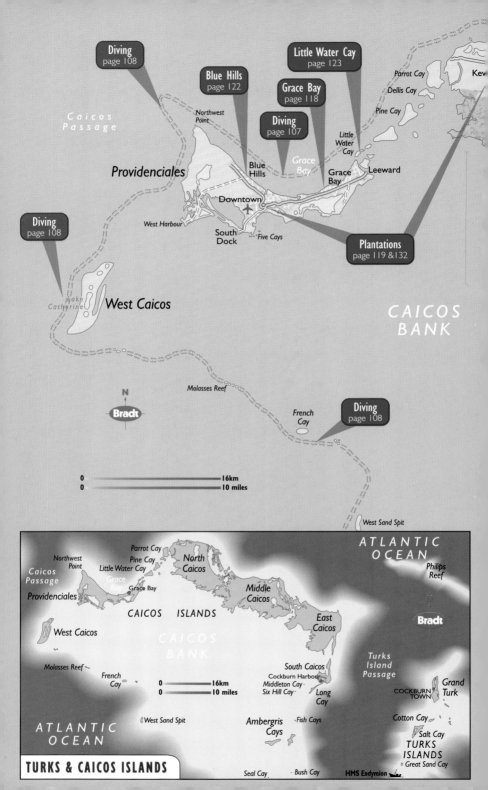

Diving page 108

Blue Hills page 122

Little Water Cay page 123

Grace Bay page 118

Diving page 107

Caicos Passage

Parrot Cay

Dellis Cay

Kev

Pine Cay

Northwest Point

Little Water Cay

Blue Hills

Grace Bay

Providenciales

Grace Bay

Leeward

Downtown

West Harbour

South Dock

Five Cays

Diving page 108

Plantations page 119 & 132

Lake Catherine

West Caicos

CAICOS BANK

N
Bradt

Molasses Reef

French Cay

Diving page 108

0 — 16km
0 — 10 miles

West Sand Spit

ATLANTIC OCEAN

Northwest Point

Parrot Cay

Pine Cay

North Caicos

Philips Reef

Caicos Passage

Little Water Cay

Grace Bay

Grace Bay

Bradt

Providenciales

CAICOS ISLANDS

Middle Caicos

West Caicos

CAICOS BANK

East Caicos

Turks Island Passage

Molasses Reef

French Cay

South Caicos

Cockburn Harbour

Middleton Cay

Six Hill Cay

COCKBURN TOWN

Grand Turk

0 — 16km
0 — 10 miles

Long Cay

Cotton Cay

Salt Cay

Fish Cays

TURKS ISLANDS

Ambergris Cays

Great Sand Cay

ATLANTIC OCEAN

West Sand Spit

Seal Cay

Bush Cay

HMS Endymion

TURKS & CAICOS ISLANDS

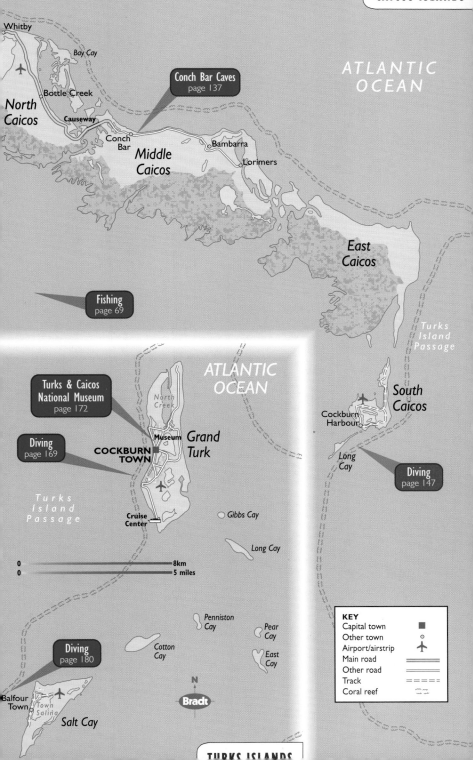

ATLANTIC
OCEAN

Whitby

Bay Cay

Conch Bar Caves
page 137

Bottle Creek

**North
Caicos**

Causeway

Conch
Bar

Bambarra

*Middle
Caicos*

Lorimers

*East
Caicos*

Fishing
page 69

*Turks
Island
Passage*

ATLANTIC
OCEAN

Turks & Caicos
National Museum
page 172

*North
Creek*

*South
Caicos*

Cockburn
Harbour

Diving
page 169

Museum

*Grand
Turk*

**COCKBURN
TOWN**

*Long
Cay*

Diving
page 147

*Turks
Island
Passage*

**Cruise
Center**

○ *Gibbs Cay*

0 ——————— 8km
0 ——————— 5 miles

Long Cay

*Penniston
Cay*

*Pear
Cay*

Diving
page 180

*Cotton
Cay*

*East
Cay*

N

Bradt

KEY
Capital town ■
Other town ○
Airport/airstrip ✈
Main road ═══
Other road ───
Track ════
Coral reef ⌐⌐

Balfour
Town

*Town
Salina*

Salt Cay

TURKS ISLANDS

Turks & Caicos Islands
Don't miss...

Diving
Diver at Spanish Anchor,
off West Caicos (JFC) page 63

Birdlife
Flamingoes *Phoenicopterus ruber*
(SP) page 23

Beaches
Whitby, North Caicos
(TH) page 132

Natural world
Conch Bar Caves,
Middle Caicos
(SP) page 137

Heritage
Turks & Caicos
National Museum,
Grand Turk
(BH) page 172

top	**Flamingo tongue** *Cyphoma gibbosum* (JFC) page 29
left	**Shoal of silversides** (JFC)
below	**Hawksbill turtle** *Eretmochelys imbricata* (JFC) page 26

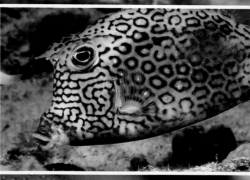

top   Juvenile queen angelfish
              Holacanthus ciliaris (JFC) page 28

above left   Social feather duster *Bispira
              brunnea* (JFC)

above middle Trunkfish *Lactophrys trigonus*
              (JFC) page 28

above   Coney *Epinephelus fulvus*
              (JFC) page 28

left   French grunt *Haemulon
              flavolineatum* (JFC) page 28

top **Kayaking, North Caicos**
(SP) page 131

left **Fluke of humpback whale**
Megaptera novaeangliae
(SP) page 27

below **Fools' Regatta, Providenciales**
(SP) page 56

AUTHORS

Annalisa Rellie Following her childhood education in a seaside convent, Annalisa Rellie studied theatre at the Guildhall School of Music and Drama in London, after which the casting couch of early marriage spared her an actor's breadline and led to a quarter of a century happily exploring the world with her diplomat husband. When they settled back in London she turned her hand to journalism, writing in a freelance capacity for magazines about travel and food. She is author of the Bradt guide to Montenegro.

Two years ago in Provo I was to make a personal discovery; to come upon the seaside house of my dreams. I should love to share it with you but unfortunately it belongs to someone else, and the owner would hardly thank me for directing you there. But if you're prepared to walk far enough into the breeze along Grace Bay you will know when you find it.

Tricia Hayne is a freelance travel writer and a member of the British Guild of Travel Writers. Formerly editorial director at Bradt Travel Guides, she has travelled throughout North America and to many island destinations worldwide. Swimming, diving and sailing are high on her list of interests, along with walking and generally exploring new places. The author of Bradt's guide to the Cayman Islands, she has also helped to update several other travel guides, and is currently working on a guide to the Cotswold Way national trail. Her articles have been published in a number of national and local magazines and newspapers.

AUTHORS' STORY

For years, the title 'Turks and Caicos Islands' sat on Bradt's editorial wishlist, but for one reason or another it never quite made it to the top. Then, when Annalisa suggested that this was a destination that would interest her, my flippant response was on the lines of 'a great idea, but do you dive?' From that casual remark has emerged a partnership that has seen us sharing out the spoils of these little-known islands, Annalisa to delve deep into their unexpectedly complex past; I to discover their environmental secrets, above and below the waves. On the way we have clinked glasses at Blue Hills, checked out the rock engravings at Sapodilla Hill, and explored seemingly endless beaches of fine white sand. With our husbands, we have travelled on foot, by bike, by boat, by plane, by scooter, jeep and car. While I have dived to watch turtles and rays, Annalisa has experienced the awesome spectacle of the humpback whale migration. Many months later, as I returned home with a bagful of research material, she found herself marooned by bad weather on the tiny island of Salt Cay. Research is rarely all plain sailing! But peeling back the layers of each of these highly individual islands has been tremendously rewarding. We hope that in doing so we have provided an incentive to leave the beach, if only for half a day, and – like the salt traders and the wrackers – to set out in search of rewards that might otherwise be left unclaimed.

PUBLISHER'S FOREWORD   *Adrian Phillips*

The first Bradt travel guide was written in 1974 by George and Hilary Bradt on a river barge floating down a tributary of the Amazon. It was followed by *Backpacker's Africa*, published in 1979. In the 1980s and '90s the focus shifted away from hiking to broader-based guides to new destinations – usually the first to be published on those places. In the 21st century Bradt continues to publish these ground-breaking guides, along with guides to established holiday destinations, incorporating in-depth information on culture and natural history alongside the nuts and bolts of where to stay and what to see.

Bradt authors support responsible travel, with advice not only on minimum impact but also on how to give something back through local charities. Thus a true synergy is achieved between the traveller and local communities.

* * *

If they'll forgive the analogy, Annalisa and Tricia are like sticks of rock – cut them in half and you'll find 'Bradt' running through their middles. Annalisa is the author of our much-acclaimed *Montenegro*, while Tricia not only wrote *Cayman Islands* but served as Bradt's editorial director for over a decade. Now they've joined considerable forces to write Bradt's first guidebook to the Turks and Caicos Islands. They complement each other perfectly. Tricia, a seasoned diver, has gone in search of the most beautiful coral reefs at the very best diving sites, while Annalisa has concentrated her attentions on dry land and explored the islands' surprisingly diverse culture and intriguing history. You truly couldn't be in more passionate or capable hands!

First published October 2008

Bradt Travel Guides Ltd, 23 High Street, Chalfont St Peter, Bucks SL9 9QE, England
www.bradtguides.com
Published in the USA by The Globe Pequot Press Inc, 246 Goose Lane,
PO Box 480, Guilford, Connecticut 06475-0480

Text copyright © 2008 Annalisa Rellie & Tricia Hayne
Maps copyright © 2008 Bradt Travel Guides Ltd
Illustrations copyright © 2008 Individual photographers and artists (see below)

British Library Cataloguing in Publication Data
A catalogue record for this book is available from the British Library
ISBN-13: 978 1 84162 268 2
Photographs Jean-François Chabot (JFC), Bob Hayne (BH), Tricia Hayne (TH), Steve Passmore/Provo Pictures, www.provopictures.com (SP)
Front cover Chalk Sound, Providenciales (SP)
Back cover Turk's head cactus at the Cruise Center, Grand Turk (BH), Pelican *Pelecanus occidentalis* (SP)
Title page Queen conch shell (TH), Hobie Cat, Grace Bay (SP), Purple stovepipe sponge *Aplysina archeri* (JFC)
Illustrations Carole Vincer   **Maps** Malcolm Barnes

Typeset from the authors' disc by Wakewing
Printed and bound in India by Nutech Photolithographers, New Delhi

Acknowledgements

DEDICATION

For Alastair and Bob; what more can we say?

★

This book would never have been written without the support of the Turks and Caicos Islands Tourist Board. To Janet Shankland, Vivienne Williams and Tracy Knight in London, Kayla Lightbourne, Oneika Simons and Director Ralph Higgs in Providenciales, Candesha Swann and Director Lindsey Musgrove on Grand Turk, and all those behind the scenes, thank you.

Countless people and organisations have helped in numerous ways with advice, recommendations and suggestions. More specifically, we are indebted to the following, every one of whom has made a significant contribution to this book:

In Providenciales, Alan Jardine of Dive Provo, whose help and enthusiasm for the project, and for the lure of diving on TCI, was both infectious and invaluable. Brian Riggs at the National Environmental Centre gave freely of his time and expertise, and saved us from many a howler. At the National Trust, Mrs Ethlyn Gibbs-Williams not only took the time to discuss the trust's work on the islands, but also ensured that we could explore the results for ourselves. Thank you, too, to Paul Taylor and Suzanne Hutchings for sharing their pirate secrets; Taylor Drotman of S3 magazine; Tom Lesser and Brenda Zdenek; and Sandra and Ken Macleod.

On South Caicos, Greg Wasik of South Caicos Diver was kind enough to share his knowledge of the island, both on land and below the waves.

On Grand Turk, Neal Hitch, newly arrived in his post at the museum, spared so much of his valuable time to reveal, describe and explain. Dale Barker of Oasis Divers went the extra mile to showcase the underwater attractions of the Turks Islands. Thanks also to wise Robert Hall, Roselyn Malcolm from the philatelic bureau, librarian Janet Williams, Brian Sheedy of *Endymion* fame, and Janet Smith.

On Salt Cay, many thanks to all 70 of them but especially to Constable David Wilson, and to Porter Williams, who knows everything and was willing to tell us quite a lot of it.

In the UK and elsewhere, thank you to Teresa Bennett of Dive Worldwide for opening lots of doors, and to John Moody of Stanley Gibbons for his contribution on philately. In London, thank you to our old friend and sometime colleague Roger Tutt.

For permission to reproduce the quote on page 158, we are grateful to Dr William Keegan and Dr Betsy Carlson. Dr Keegan is curator of Caribbean Archaeology, Florida Museum of Natural History, University of Florida, Gainsville, Florida, and Dr Carlson is an archaeologist with SEARCH Inc, Gainsville.

We have been unable to trace the current ownership of the 16th-century woodcut reproduced on page ix. If notified, we will be pleased to rectify the omission in any future edition.

Of course, a travel guide without maps is no more than half a guide. Bob Hayne deserves a medal for pulling together our various rough sketches and scrawled notes into a coherent form, ready for Malcolm Barnes to work his magic, as always, and turn them into the finished product. Thank you both.

Finally, the end of the research is always just the beginning for the publisher. This, then, is a great opportunity to thank the whole editorial team at Bradt – and in particular Adrian Phillips, Anna Moores and Emma Thomson – for their unfailing support, good humour and professionalism.

FEEDBACK REQUEST

Any book about the Turks and Caicos Islands is necessarily a snapshot in time. New hotels open, restaurants change hands, dive operators come and go. The material in this guide was accurate at the time of research, but by the time you visit there will inevitably have been changes. Do drop us a line, whether it's to pass on details of a new venue, or to tell us about that wonderful meal – or indeed to share any negative experiences. All correspondence will be personally answered, and will help to ensure that the next edition of this guide will reflect the findings of a far wider group of people.

We look forward to hearing from you, either direct to annalisa@rellie.net or tr.hayne@virgin.net, or via Bradt Travel Guides. In the meantime, have a great trip!

Bradt Travel Guides, 23 High Street, Chalfont St Peter, Bucks SL9 9QE, England
☎ +44 (0)1753 893444; f +44 (0)1753 892333
e info@bradtguides.com; www.bradtguides.com

Contents

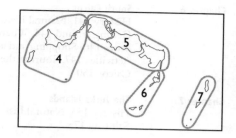

LIST OF MAPS

Introduction

The magic monotony of existence between sky and water

attrib Joseph Conrad

Juan Ponce de León was a Renaissance man, a *'hidalgo* volunteer' among a number of adventurous noblemen to join the second voyage of Christopher Columbus in 1493, in his search for a westward passage to the East Indies. Although the case by no means rests and very likely never will, a proportion of historians argue that it was he, rather than Columbus, who was the first European to step ashore on the island of Grand Turk, not on this but on a subsequent expedition led by Ponce himself and launched from the Greater Antilles. Legend has it that in Hispaniola (comprising the Dominican Republic and Haiti) Ponce – said to be one of the most ruthless conquistadors in his treatment of the Tainos – was beguiled by the native belief in a 'fountain of youth' located on an island due north of there. The name for the place in their unwritten language was Bimini:

> …a spring of running water of such marvellous virtue, that the water thereof being drunk, perhaps with some diet, makes old men young again.

This was the way that Peter Martyr d'Anghiera, an Italian humanist at the Spanish Court, described the island in 1512. One could imagine such a hypothesis would have aroused a fair degree of cynicism but in the context of the times, with tales of dramatic New World discoveries, previously uncharted territory and exotic peoples, who could tell what else might lie out there?

So intrigued was Ponce, that solving the mystery of the rejuvenating fountain was to become his lifelong quest. In pursuit of his quixotic dream he set sail with a fleet of three ships from Hispaniola in March 1513 and it was during this first venture, which would take him ultimately to Florida, that he is said to have checked out Grand Turk. Had he reached Parrot Cay today and been reinvigorated by its pampering spa his search would have been over. 'Ageing is optional' is their dictum.

Looking at the map, travellers might wonder how it was that two discrete banks of islands, the Turks and the Caicos, with a passage the width of the English Channel (22 miles/35km) dividing them, came to be united as a single country. The answer was originally one of historical expediency. Together the groups straddle two major north–south sea lanes, the Turks Island Passage and the Caicos Island Passage, which between them probably accounted for the vast majority of 18th-century Spanish, French, Dutch and other ship-borne freight to and from the Caribbean. Both the Bermudian *wrackers* (salvagers) and a medley of pirates recognised the potential of these deep-water channels with their propinquity to treacherous reefs and submerged outcrops. When in the 18th century the Bermudian saltrakers put down roots they also established stations at points overlooking the passages. The association between the two groups of islands stuck until in 1848 Queen Victoria granted a royal charter that the Turks Islands with the Caicos Islands should together become an independent colony.

Fast forwarding to more recent times, the Turks and Caicos, north of the Antilles therefore not strictly speaking a Caribbean archipelago, had been a secret for decades. Her late-blossoming into the field of tourism only really came after the legal separation from the Bahamas in the 1970s when Grand Turk received her first governor and her own ministerial government. For years previously many a yachtsman cruising downwind toward the Caicos Passage past uninterrupted miles of a deserted Grace Bay would dismiss Providenciales as an apparently barren sandbank. But someone had vision and it took just a handful of American adventurers to start the ball rolling. Soon the property market was growing exponentially but mindfully in tandem with an infrastructure to support it. It was and is a success story but there is of course a caveat, and the trick to recognising it lies in knowing when to stop building – recognising when enough is enough. Part of the difficulty arises from the 'half-full – or half empty' syndrome: because while some parts of the country, Provo a prime example, are becoming crowded, other islands like East Caicos remain untouched; let's hope that that's in perpetuity. *Beautiful by Nature* are the country's own defining words. May that be a pledge, as well as a lovely phrase.

At the time of writing there are no indications of any addition to the once-weekly air connection between London and Provo (with a stop in Nassau). Travellers from the US east coast hubs are much better served and with flying time from JFK only three hours, it is possible to be in Provo for lunch, making a long weekend in TCI (her universal abbreviation) almost as convenient as one in the Hamptons. Tour operator Becky Veith puts her finger on it: 'For a place that still feels remote, it's easy to get to.' She is right; the islands have a faraway quality, and when you factor in an optimum climate it's small wonder that business is booming.

It isn't simply the islands themselves that make the picture so special: it is the whole pattern of sea, sky and land. Chances are that you will be arriving by air, and as you fly into Provo, Grand Turk or Ambergris Cay, marvelling at the variegated palette of blue and green beneath, you can imagine for yourself just which island it was that Columbus and his crew first glimpsed after those long days and nights at sea. And presumed they must at last have come around to Asia.

Airmen call the phenomenon when sea and cloud blend seamlessly into one a 'cheesecake' sky. Kathi Barrington in *Discover Turks and Caicos* describes: 'surreal days when the horizon disappears and the ocean meets the sky in a perfect blend of blues and silvers with no definition at all'. It is a prospect to infinity. Match this to the unimaginable depths of the ocean troughs and we might be contemplating that fourth dimension few (including this author) can comprehend. At sunset in these parts, when the skies are clear and the sea is calm, it is sometimes possible to witness the elusive green flash.

Popular legend places the archipelago neatly within the borders of the so-called Devil's Triangle, often referred to as the Bermuda Triangle, a romantic concept that has grown over the past 50 years from a series of apparently unexplained disappearances of aircraft and sea vessels. Most people take the alarming tales with a pinch of salt and more often than not the riddles do have likely answers, but the shadowy margins between historical fact and myth will continue to attract curiosity.

For many visiting the Turks and Caicos, islands that boast a collection of the most luxurious hotels and resorts in the world, the temptation, a justifiable one, must be to remain within the confines of their chosen property. Aside from some diving perhaps – after all, the extensive coral-reef system has led to the islands being rated one of the top dive destinations anywhere – and maybe an evening taxi to a dinner venue, the temptation must be to stay put and chill out. But it would be a pity not to explore a little further. The delightful National Museum on Grand Turk alone is worth the journey and arguably little Cockburn Town itself is a museum piece. The same could be said for Salt Cay where no one is a stranger. Each of the Caicos Islands is different. North, with its pink flamingoes, claims to owe its tropical vegetation to higher rainfall, but all is relative and a brolly would be a joke. Middle Caicos has the largest cave network in either TCI or the Bahamas and also holds by far the majority of Lucayan sites found to date. East Caicos is the most remote and you will almost certainly have it to yourself; noises off not necessarily Loyalist ghosts jealously guarding ruined sisal patches, more likely the feral donkeys that run the place now. These days South Caicos is all about fish; once upon a time it produced more salt than the two Turks Islands combined.

However you decide to pass your time in these treasure islands, you're bound to have fun. And peace. Those concerned by such matters should note that high-end accommodation on these islands is as paparazzi-proof as you would wish, and resort privacy-protection low key but professional. By the same token don't expect this guide to name a collection of glitterati who already enjoy the non-intrusive quality of TCI. It isn't that kind of book.

If it's stars you're after, ride a boat to a cay, lie back and gaze upon the celestial variety. An out-of-this-world experience.

The Fountain of Youth Woodcut by Hans Sebald Beham, early 16th century

Spotted eagle ray

Part One

GENERAL INFORMATION

Islands Approx 40 islands, of which 8 are permanently inhabited; permanent homes are under construction on a further 2.

Location 21°45'N, 71°35'W. 39 miles (63km) south of the Bahamas in the western Atlantic Ocean, approx 575 miles (925km) southeast of Miami, and 90 miles (145km) north of Hispaniola (the Dominican Republic and Haiti)

Size 166 sq miles (430km²). Grand Turk 6.5 sq miles (17km²); Salt Cay 3 sq miles (7.8km²); Providenciales 38 sq miles (98km²); North Caicos 41 sq miles (106km²); Middle Caicos 48 sq miles (124km²); South Caicos 8 sq miles (21km²)

Climate Tropical, with cooling breeze. Summer ave 81–85°F (27.5–29°C); winter 75–80°F (24–27°C). Rainfall highest in winter.

Status British Overseas Territory

Population 33,202 (2006 estimate). Grand Turk 5,718; Salt Cay 70; Providenciales 24,348; North Caicos 1,537; Middle Caicos 307; South Caicos 1,118

Capital Grand Turk

Economy Major earners tourism, offshore banking, fishing

GDP US$11,160 per capita (2006)

Language English

Religion Christian

Currency US dollar ($)

Rate of exchange £1 = $2, €1 = $1.58 (July 2008)

Time GMT –5 (USA Eastern Standard Time); 1hr daylight saving time Nov–Mar

Electricity 120/240 volts; 60Hz; US-style plugs

Weights and measures Imperial

International telephone code +1 649

Flag Mid blue background; Union flag top left corner; Turks & Caicos coat of arms (Turk's head cactus, conch shell, lobster) on yellow shield

National anthem 'God Save the Queen'

National flower Turks and Caicos heather, Limonium bahamense

National bird Brown pelican, Pelecanus occidentalis

National tree Caicos Caribbean pine, Pinus caribaea

Public holidays 1 January, 12 March, Good Friday, Easter Monday, 28 May, 18 June, 6 August, last Friday in September, 8 October, 24 October, 25 & 26 December (see page 55)

Background Information

HISTORY

The pattern of land and sea and sky that forms this country lies within the West Indies, a region so named from Christopher Columbus's conviction that he would find a westward passage to India and the East. Technically, neither the Turks and Caicos nor its Bahamian neighbours are Caribbean islands, in that none of their shores is bounded by the Caribbean Sea, a basin of the Atlantic encompassed by the Greater Antilles, the Lesser Antilles, Central America and Venezuela.

As to the first inhabitants of this small archipelago it is impossible to give an absolute answer, but research so far has shown no evidence of a human presence before approximately AD700. Excavations on Grand Turk in 1992 led to the uncovering of a settlement now known as the Coralie site (see page 153) dating from between AD800 and AD1200, the oldest to be found so far in the Bahamas and Turks and Caicos chain of islands.

However, in both Cuba only 464 nautical miles (859km) away and – even closer – neighbouring Hispaniola, archaeologists and anthropologists have identified traces of much earlier occupation, dating from as long ago as the second millennium BC. These indigenes have been identified as Ciboney or Guanahatabey (loosely meaning 'cave-dweller' in their language). A branch of the Arawak Indian race, the generic term for all natives of the region, they were forebears of the few still found in isolated settlements in the Greater Antilles at the time of Columbus.

Despite there being nothing to indicate such early occupation in the Turks and Caicos, it's interesting and fun to speculate, when one ventures into the outer limits of the Conch Bar Caves on Middle Caicos, peers into the murky depths of The Hole above Long Bay on Providenciales, or ponders tales of cave systems tunnelling deep beneath Salt Cay, that there might be an awful lot more still to be discovered.

THE LUCAYANS It is really only within the past century that excavations have pinpointed the arrival in these islands of the people who became known as the Tainos, which in their language meant 'noble', the designation distinguishing them from the broader Arawak culture. Those who settled specifically in the Bahamas and the Turks and Caicos were called Lucayans, a name taken from the Spanish *lucayos,* bestowed on them by the first European explorers, or possibly from similar sounding Taino words, meaning 'island men'. These peoples originated from the Orinoco region of South America and had gradually made their way northward, paddling their canoes from island to island through the Lesser Antilles until they reached Hispaniola. From here, they launched exploratory forays further afield, to hunt and fish, before establishing more permanent settlements in the Bahamas and the Turks and Caicos Islands. The Tainos never employed sail-power though it is said their longest canoes (another Taino word), each hollowed from a single log and capable of carrying up to 90 men, could almost match the Spanish caravels for speed.

Over the past 50 years archaeologists have verified some of the anecdotal accounts dating from the rather less than reliable records of the earliest European travellers, and garnered considerably more ethnic information, revealing in astonishing detail just how sophisticated and complex a people the Lucayans were, the manner in which they constructed their villages and the hierarchical arrangement within them. Ordinary villagers lived in conical thatched huts shaped rather like tents, some 15ft (5m) in diameter and clustered round the village square, while their *caciques* or headmen enjoyed intricately decorated mansions three times that size and covered in coloured reeds.

Essentially agriculturalists, the Lucayans achieved notable success in cultivating the shallow, limestone-based soil in spite of an arid climate, and growing dozens of different root vegetables: beans and squash, and several varieties of manioc (*yuca*) for processing into cassava bread, a type that could be stored over long periods. The trick was in the preparation of the land, first cutting down the bush and forest and then burning the wood to release nutrients. The resulting fields could bear crops for several years before being left fallow to allow a period of recovery. They also grew fruit: guava, papaya and pineapple; tobacco to roll into cigars or grind into snuff; as well as sisal and cotton to weave sleeping hammocks (the Arawak word is *hamaca*). It's interesting to compare the Lucayan fortune in this endeavour with that of the Loyalists who arrived several centuries later.

From fossilised fish and mammal remnants that have been found amongst the potsherds of pre-Columbian archaeological sites, it can be assumed that the Tainos were carnivorous, enjoying such reptilian delights as iguana and snake. Indeed, they have been deemed responsible by some naturalists for the extinction of several species. Whatever the case, the Lucayan diet was a healthy one, with a plentiful supply of fish, sea turtle and conch, and by means of salting or smoking – over the barbecue (another word of Taino origin, from *barbicu*, meaning 'sacred firepit') – they would preserve surplus food to trade with neighbouring islands, an enterprise normally conducted between the months of March and August. Expeditions for this purpose were often made in the cool of the night, guided by the North Star and the constellations of the Milky Way. It seems touching that, as we do today, the Lucayans liked to raise small gardens around their individual living quarters, planted with medicinal herbs and seedlings selected for nurture close to hand, while larger-scale production was restricted to allotment-like areas, at some distance from the dwellings.

Their only metal was gold, and that purely for ornamental purposes, but they were skilled carvers of both stone and wood, fashioned animal bones into tools, wove wicker baskets and containers, made jewellery out of shells and made pottery now known as *palmetto* ware from red clay and burned and crushed conch shell. When guano was excavated from caves in the Caicos Islands in the 19th century, many Lucayan artefacts were uncovered. Most of the better pieces were bought cheaply for US museums, notably by Professor Theodoor de Booy, who investigated all the islands except West Caicos in the early 20th century to study Lucayan culture. De Booy deduced – incorrectly as it later emerged – that there had been no Taino habitation on Grand Turk. Yet 75 years later Dr Shaun Sullivan found 40 pre-Columbian sites, all but five of them on Middle Caicos. At least three Taino settlements are now known to have existed on Grand Turk.

And so it was that the Lucayans passed several hundred fruitful and uneventful years, until the coming of the Spanish explorers was fundamentally to change everything, for ever.

THE FIRST EUROPEANS No one knows for sure which European it was who first set foot on Grand Turk. Some are convinced it was Christopher Columbus in 1492; indeed, the spot where it is thought he would have landed is today marmoreally recorded on the western shore of that island. Many others insist the first-footer was Juan Ponce de León, 20 years later. Even, cheekily, two years ago, a Turkish historian laid his country's claim to the honour, his argument based around the origin of the island capital's name, and a possible reference to it on the charts of a 16th-century admiral of the Ottoman Empire.

If such things appeal to you, it is well worth some personal research in preparation for your own visit here (see *Appendix 3, Further Information*, pages 190–1). Bearing in mind the effect that hurricanes and other forces of nature would inevitably have wrought on such low-lying terrain, it is difficult to judge even roughly how these islands would have appeared so long ago. Columbus's own log was lost in a storm, and so was an attempted reproduction commissioned by Queen Isabella on his triumphant return to Spain, with the result that all extant documentation is second hand at best. Early maps are notoriously unreliable – though often charmingly so. One of the oldest is especially puzzling; created by a German monk, Martin Waldseemuller, 15 years after Columbus's first landing, it is extraordinarily accurate in scale and detail, in such a way that should have been impossible at so early a date. The cartographer is said to have based his assumptions on the 1,300-year-old propositions of the Egyptian geographer Ptolemy, combined with contemporary information he gleaned from the papers of the Florentine navigator, Amerigo Vespucci, describing his own turn-of-the-century voyages of exploration in the western Atlantic. This unique map, completed in 1507, which for the first time uses the word 'America', is on permanent display at the Library of Congress in Washington DC.

Christopher Columbus first stepped ashore on an island that was called Guanahani by the Taino, 'a place of encircling walls' – or 'cliffs'; *hani* is synonymous with 'wreath'. Historically and variously it was reputed to contain a wide lagoon, to have a harbour with a narrow entrance, large enough to hold a fleet of ships, and to be encircled by a reef.

Over the centuries in the Bahamas and Turks and Caicos chain there have been a number of contenders for that landfall, of which four are favourites: San Salvador, Samana Cay, Plana Cays and Grand Turk. In *The European Discoveries of America*, Samuel Eliot Morison recounts that on the night of 11 October 1492,

> at 10.00pm an hour before moonrise, Columbus thought he saw [in the distance ahead] a light – like a little wax candle rising and falling.

He later deduced it to have been a bonfire lighted by the Tainos. Later, at 2am, he could make out cliffs, 'white in the moonlight'. Could these perhaps have been the prominent bluffs at Mudjin Harbour on Middle Caicos?

Although no-one can say for certain where Columbus's three ships, the mother ship *Santa Maria* and the two caravels *Pinta* and *Niña*, were pointed on that morning of 12 October 1492, one fact is not contested: that within the following 20 years, the passing of one generation, all the Lucayans had disappeared from the entire archipelago. And by the time Juan Ponce arrived in Grand Turk in March 1512 on his quest for the mythical fountain of youth (see *Introduction*, page vii) legend has it that a single elderly Lucayan was the only man on the island. Hence Ponce called the place Isla del Viejo, a name that remained in use for two centuries. The native people had greeted Christopher Columbus and his companions, their elegant galleons and exotic dress, with a mixture of awe and curiosity. In exchange the Spaniards, assessing these strange, sparsely clad people to present no threat, viewed the Indian population simply as sitting ducks, a bonus supply of labourers; to be taken captive in return for conversion to Christianity was the way the Europeans justified their intentions. In 1509 the Governor of Hispaniola was given formal permission by the King of Spain to abduct native Indians from the Bahamas

Many ships have come to grief on the banks and treacherous reefs encircling the islands, attracting *wrackers* (salvagers from shipwrecks) and bounty hunters for centuries. The lure was not only the artefacts and weaponry that might lie temptingly retrievable in the inky depths; more enticing was the prospect of recovering immeasurable quantities of gold and precious gems from the holds of Spanish vessels that had been homeward bound.

THE MOLASSES REEF SHIPWRECK Some 40 years before the time of writing, a couple of ambitious treasure hunters first located the remains of a 16th-century caravel lodged at a depth of 20ft (6m) on the Caicos Bank to the south of the island of West Caicos and east of French Cay, hideout of the notorious 17th-century pirate Nau l'Ollonois (see page 9). Lighting on ceramic fragments they thought to be Lucayan, they believed they had stumbled on something far more valuable than gold – they figured they had discovered the wreck of Columbus's *Niña*. But when the experts from the Institute of Nautical Archaeology at Texas A&M University stepped in, between 1982 and 1986, the claim was refuted and the provenance of the pottery judged to have been initially mistaken. They did, though, recover over 4,000 artefacts from the wreck, and a fascinating display and description of the finds can be viewed in the National Museum in Grand Turk, which was inaugurated in 1991 to conserve the findings.

Still today the identity of the ship – where she was headed and how she foundered – remains a mystery. It seems highly likely that the watery grave had been previously disturbed, in all probability on more than one occasion, and goodness knows what may have been stolen.

Also in 1991, New Yorker Brian Sheedy, at that time proprietor of the louche and now sadly defunct Mount Pleasant Guesthouse on Salt Cay, re-appraised the *Endymion*

and over the following few years a series of raids resulted in droves of Lucayans being transported to pan for gold in the streams and work in the gold mines of Hispaniola; others were shipped to the pearl fisheries off the Venezuelan coast. All were treated remorselessly and few survived. It is estimated that more than 40,000 Lucayans were forcibly deported from the islands; only the elderly and sick were left behind to die. Unintentionally the slaves were to repay this cruelty in some measure by infecting a number of their new masters with syphilis, a disease endemic amongst the native population but one to which, in its most severe manifestation, they had grown resistant. The Europeans affected, though, were to suffer in all its intensity the sickness for which there was no remedy. In return the Lucayans became exposed to smallpox and other conditions not previously experienced in their environment. Juan Ponce himself died in 1521 from a wound inflicted by an Indian arrow.

Over 60 years passed before, in 1585, Sir Richard Grenville led an expedition of 500 men in five ships from Plymouth to Puerto Rico and Hispaniola. From there they went on to Grand Turk to find salt and stock up with manatee (sea cow) meat. Two years later Captain John White, better known subsequently as governor of Virginia but also a notable water colourist, returned to West Caicos and sketched all the local flora and fauna that he could find. This comprehensive record enabled Great Britain and the continent of Europe to have their first look at some of the apparent oddities of the New World and today they are rightly recognised as unique masterpieces.

THE SALT RAKERS After the disappearance of the Lucayans, the Turks and Caicos Islands remained largely uninhabited, a refuge only for a handful of pirates and

shipwreck (see page 180) and began escorting divers to the site. Since then this has become one of the best known wreck dives in the Islands and is now designated a protected historic site.

THE *NUESTRA SEÑORA DE LA CONCEPCIÓN* The admiral ship of Spain's New World fleet lost north of Puerto Plata on the Silver Shoals between Santo Domingo and Grand Turk, on 31 October 1641, was said to have been transporting an unregistered cargo of gold and other treasure between Havana and Spain. Legend has it that in 1686 William Phipps of Maine recovered 32 tons of silver from the site of the wreck and, in return for one fifth of the total, King James II of England rewarded him with a knighthood and appointed him governor of Massachusetts Bay colony.

Fast forward to the 20th century, and the long-missing log containing compass bearings from Sir William Phipps's salvage was discovered in a private English archive. In 1978 a team of divers led by American treasure hunter Burt Webber located the Half Moon Reef, Silver Shoals site, approximately 40 miles (64km) south of the Turk Islands and 80 miles (128km) north of the Dominican Republic. They were aided in this fresh search by a portable magnetometer Webber had modified for underwater use, allowing readings in hard-to-reach crevices. Amongst the bullion and artefacts recovered in the course of a six-month salvage operation were 60,000 silver coins dated 1639 and earlier, numerous gold chains, and porcelain from the late Ming period. Some of the booty is on permanent display in the museums of Santo Domingo. In 2008 Webber and his team, employing ever more sophisticated equipment, were set to launch a new treasure hunt for other wrecks in this region.

other reprobates (see box pages 8–9) until the mid 17th century. Then the Bermudians began to make seasonal sorties in the driest spring months, steering fore-and-aft rigged sloops notable for their speed and grace across the 700 miles of empty Atlantic Ocean that separated them from their goal: white gold, or salt. Essential for the preservation of fish and meat, it was a commodity whose increasing value they did not underestimate. With the steady trade winds and warm sun combining to create ideal conditions for the evaporation process, the salt lay ready for the taking in the natural *salinas*, or salt pans, found on the flatlands of Grand Turk and Salt Cay.

The Bermudians, merchant seamen rather than agriculturists, were not averse to the spoils that could be earned from a little wracking on the side. That was in their blood, most of them originating from the English southern counties where wracking was a profitable business. The islands were also breeding grounds for sea turtles, making them, too, an easy target for the visitors.

Eventually, as salt grew to be the mainstay of their economy, a number of Bermudians began year-round occupation of the two islands. (A century later they were to extend the enterprise to include the closest island on the other side of the deep trench that forms the Turks Island Passage, South Caicos, which from their wracking activities they already knew to be similarly endowed with ideal conditions for salt harvesting; a similar, later venture, further afield on West Caicos, was abandoned, judged commercially unviable.) At the same time they set about refining the process to increase production which initially had simply required slaves to scrape and rake the salt from around the fringes of the shallow ponds: hard labour, from dawn to dusk under a relentless sun. Now the proprietors devised a method to artificially increase the size of the salt pans, shovelling out new

Piracy in the 17th and 18th centuries was an equal opportunity employer. Nationality didn't matter and the girls were just as tough as, and often more brutal than, the men. The Turks Islands, the Caicos Islands and their satellite cays positioned on the important shipping lanes to and from the Caribbean, provided ideal hideouts from which to launch their raids. At a time when all freight was transported by sea, in much smaller vessels than we have today, it is likely that two or three sailing ships would have used those passages each day.

The word 'pirate' has many romantic synonyms: privateer, corsair, freebooter, picaroon, buccaneer etc. Frequently now used interchangeably, the original definitions differentiated between 'pirates', those who fought only for themselves, and 'privateers' and 'corsairs' who represented a nation and were specifically hired to attack ships of opposing powers. Letters of Marque were issued to privateer ships entitling them to be armed for the purpose of capturing enemy merchant shipping and 'to commit acts which would otherwise have constituted piracy'. The term 'picaroon' was normally applied to a scavenger of wrecks – a wracker; a 'buccaneer', in the true sense of the word, meant a cattle rustler, as it were, a pirate operating on dry-land. The Spanish sailors who came after Columbus brought a cargo of cattle and hogs to breed on the islands. This they did, so successfully that the Turks Islands became a useful source of meat, hides and salt for local privateers, not least the contingent based 80 miles away on Tortuga.

After a papal decree in the 15th century summarily divided the newly discovered territories between Spain and Portugal, the remaining European nations began to look for a way to share the profits Spain was remitting from its new colonies. Encouraged by the success of Giovanni da Verrazano, an Italian sailor in the service of the French crown who had captured a fleet of three ships, two of them filled with Mexican gold and one from Hispaniola laden with sugar, pearls and cattle hides, Britain, France and the Netherlands followed suit and commissioned their own privateers to patrol the Spanish Main (the area of Spanish settlement and trading activity in the Caribbean). This in turn undermined Spanish dominance of the region and subsequently enabled the other countries to establish their own colonies.

Tales of pirate derring-do, pillage and plunder are boundless, over the centuries growing ever more outrageous. History has been embroidered with fictive narrative making it impossible now to determine what was or wasn't fact. But the stories are great and the Turks and Caicos Islands, with their creeks and crannies, feature in a fair share of them. Pirates were never shipbuilders; for them there were much easier ways to acquire a vessel. In their raids they would choose to retain rather than sink craft with a shallow draught, such as the highly regarded Bermuda sloops and their Caicos counterparts, the better to facilitate passage across the low-water banks and through narrow inlets. Speed was the essence for these guys and at least twice yearly under cover of shoreline scrub they would careen (turn on its side) their current vessel to be scrubbed and repaired. A clean hull not only increased the swiftness with which they could overtake their prey but also made it easier to outrun the authorities.

Many pirate ships adhered to quite a strict and democratic code of conduct. The whole crew had a say on policy, they often elected their officers and they shared out their booty on an equal basis. The captain was chosen for his fighting ability and the quartermaster for his administrative skills. The pirate motto was 'no prey, no pay'. Both rules and punishments were unforgiving and the heinous crime of stealing from a shipmate was likely to result in the loss of both ears and sometimes a nose as well. Recidivists were apt to be cast ashore on an isolated island with only a musket and ammunition, some bread and a bottle of fresh water for company.

'CALICO' JACK RACKMAN may well have acquired his nickname and started a serious fashion at the same time, from being the first reprobate to adopt the habit of knotting a piece of fabric around his forehead, an ingenious, multi-purpose kerchief easily whipped-off to wipe away blood or sweat or to form a purse for stowing some small trinket that might take his fancy. Some say he was the first to fly the black ensign depicting a skull and crossed sabres. Pirate flags were designed for their psychological effect as much as anything and when spotted through the lookout's spyglass of an innocent merchant vessel, could strike fear, dread, maybe even instant surrender. A quite different tactic might be employed to close in on the prey by masquerading under the ensign of some un-associated country, the pirates thereby hiding their intentions until the moment of attack.

Before Calico Jack assumed command of his own ship, the *Vanity*, and set up a base in the deserted cays between what is now Providenciales and North Caicos, he had served as quartermaster on the *Neptune* operating out of the Bahamas. While ashore on New Providence he took up with a married woman, Ann Bonney, a wayward girl who by all accounts was more than happy to run away to sea with our hero. Largely because she wished to be fully participant in the high-adrenaline sport of piracy, it was decided she should dress as a man. Everything went swimmingly until Ann's roving eye was attracted by a fellow crew member, who to her initial dismay revealed that she too was a female in disguise. For convoluted reasons Mary Reid, born out of wedlock in London, had actually been raised as a boy and had, according to Herbert Sadler, 'spent most of her early life in Flanders where she served in the Duke of Marlborough's army and acquired marvellous proficiency in the use of weapons'. How the resulting *ménage à trois* shook down is not recorded but the marauding continued apace until, in 1720, in an unguarded moment while the freebooters were anchored off the coast of Jamaica, an armed British sloop drew alongside. The pirates were too full of rum to put up a decent fight and the men, including Captain Jack, retreated below. Only the two women battled on valiantly, the last to be taken into custody.

A trial followed which resulted in every member of the crew being sent to the gallows, except for the women who both pleaded pregnancy, a mitigating condition allowing them to escape with prison sentences. Mary Reid grew sick and died in gaol but after a few months Ann Bonney, resourceful as ever, negotiated her freedom. One account tells that she returned to Charleston, South Carolina, where she had lived as a child and where she was to survive to a ripe old age as the wife of a churchwarden.

FRANÇOIS L'OLLONOIS (aka Jean-David Nau) was a notoriously brutal villain whose reputation for taking no prisoners instilled fear even amongst his fellow pirates (the name derives from his home of Les Sables d'Olonne on the Atlantic coast of France).. It was claimed that on one occasion he beheaded 70 Spaniards with his own sword but not before he had cruelly tortured those he suspected of having information he needed to determine the passage and cargo of other vessels. For some time in the mid 17th century his lair was on French Cay on the southern edge of the Caicos Bank. Ships would pass close by this cay en route for what they presumed to be a safe anchorage while they drew water on the bigger island: a well in the west of Provo was clearly marked on early charts. Today the cay is a peaceful sanctuary for migrating birds. As for the pirate, it was reported he met his just end in 1668 at Darién in Panama where he fell foul of a group of native Indians abetted by some Spaniards and was 'torn from limb to limb'.

areas and dividing these with low stone walls into smaller, more efficient units which could be flooded with sea water via a series of channels with sluices to control the flow. Hand-operated paddles were employed to move the water around the salinas. The harvested salt was bagged for transporting to ports on the east coast of America, Canada and Newfoundland. Some was loaded on to ships already carrying cargo from the Caribbean's sugar-producing islands, other consignments were stowed in dedicated vessels, but often the voyage would involve a convoy of vessels, the better to avoid succumbing to pirate attack en route. The ships would return from the northern waters bearing freight of salted, preserved codfish, food for the slaves whose masters, it was understood, preferred to provide sustenance for their slaves rather than to give them a day off to plant and maintain their own produce.

By the end of the 17th century, a good 60 years before Britain was to claim formal ownership of the Turks and Caicos, the Bermudians considered they had established a proprietary right to the Turks Islands. This assumption had little bearing on those European powers that already had the group within their sights, as much for their strategic position on such an important south–north shipping lane as for the wealth of their salt. Sources vary as to the exact year, but early into the new century, as the effects of the **War of Spanish Succession** began to be felt across the Atlantic, Spain rather easily took possession of Grand Turk. The island was recaptured in 1710 by a Bermudian privateer, Captain Lewis Middleton. For several decades to follow piratic activity was on the increase, and the narrative of the times extravagantly colourful (see box, pages 8–9). On more than one occasion, the French were to attack the islands and in 1762 they defeated a Royal Naval Squadron under Admiral Pocock, with colonial reinforcements from New England, off the Caicos Islands. Two years later, as a result of the **Treaty of Paris** confirming Britain's maritime and colonial supremacy at the expense of France and Spain, the British Parliament declared official ownership of the Turks and Caicos. Thereafter Britain stipulated that William Shirley, the governor of the Bahamas, rather than a Bermudian representative should oversee the islands' administration. Bermuda was far from happy with this outcome, fearing the Bahamian connection would stymie their own monopoly of local salt production, and refused to accept any controls that might be imposed by the neighbouring government.

Two years on, a prominent Bahamian merchant, Andrew Symmer, was appointed resident King's Agent in Grand Turk. His remit was twofold: to support Crown subjects engaged in the salt trade and to provide some political reporting. Although at first Symmer rigorously followed his brief it wasn't long before he began to exceed it and take the law into his own hands, ultimately declaring Grand Turk a free port. The trade that resulted was not just in locally harvested salt but in dozens of other products, which had not originated in these islands and were not necessarily destined for the British colonies. There was even trafficking of slaves. In a matter of years the tiny island port had become the busiest in the region. Meantime the government of the Bahamas remained determined to force Grand Turk to comply with their laws, to levy export duties on salt and to deny the islanders the right to trade in other products. Months of contentious correspondence ensued between Bahamian governor Thomas Shirley (younger brother of predecessor William), Andrew Symmer and the Earl of Hillsborough, Secretary of State for the Colonies. The stalemate persisted until 1776 when more pressing developments intervened and, with the invasion of Nassau, the Bahamas became embroiled in the start of the American War of Independence. Although there is no recorded evidence, it is said that Turks Island salt merchants, ignoring a Royal Navy blockade, even shipped salt to George Washington's army at Valley Forge.

All this underlines how great the profits were to be made in marketing the aptly named 'white gold'. As Cynthia Kennedy elegantly observes in her recent essay on the subject:

> '. . . trade routes were established to transport it, governments taxed it, alliances and empires were built upon it, revolutions were precipitated over it, social classes were partly distinguished by it, and people were enslaved to secure it.'
>
> from *The Historian* of 22 June 2007,
> by kind permission of the author and of Wiley-Blackwell Publishing, Oxford

It was to be almost the end of the 18th century before the Turks islanders, having exhausted every argument to delay acknowledgement of Bahamian legislation, bowed to the inevitable, and in 1791 a customs house was finally established to implement salt export tariffs.

NO VICTORY FOR NELSON Spurred on by reverberations from the American War of Independence, and undeterred by Britain's continuing dominance of the islands in the western Atlantic, France took a further shot at claiming the Turks and Caicos archipelago, seizing Grand Turk in 1783 and appropriating the slaves. The British responded by deploying HMS *Albermarle* with a force of one hundred men, under the command of her 25-year-old captain, Horatio Nelson. Although the mission was a failure, the islands were shortly to be restored to Britain in the aftermath of a second **Treaty of Paris,** sometimes referred to as the **Treaty of Versailles,** that was formally to conclude the American Revolutionary War.

THE LOYALISTS As it became clear that America would succeed in gaining independence, those nationals who sought to remain British were obliged to leave their properties in the 13 Atlantic seaboard colonies poised to form the original United States. In signing the peace treaty (see above) Britain was to retain the Bahamas, the Turks and Caicos and six eastern Caribbean islands while returning Florida to Spain; so in turn the British were in a position to grant compensatory land to these Loyalists, as they became known.

Although in the pursuit of maximum salt production the Turks Islands had long been denuded of their tall cedar trees, the densely forested Caicos Islands had essentially remained uninhabited since the demise of the Lucayans and seemed ripe for cultivation. By 1788, 40 emigrant families, importing well over a thousand slaves, had accepted land allocations on Providenciales, and North and Middle Caicos. Many of the newcomers were experienced planters and at once set their slaves to work clearing the land for the construction of grand stone mansions and the sizeable estates necessary to support them. Their crop of choice was cotton for which there was a steady demand. Short-term omens were optimistic, the plantations soon yielding a decent harvest of sea-island cotton, a fine-quality long-stapled fibre, highly regarded in Europe and in demand for the textile mills of Manchester. But their good fortune was not to hold. Unlike the Lucayan farmers centuries earlier, the Loyalist planters were not adept at avoiding the potential problems inherent in the management of shallow soil on a porous rock base. After only a decade and with production already on the decline, their crops suffered the double blow of infestation from the chenille worm and the red bug. The damage wrought by these pests, alone enough to wipe out a plantation, was exacerbated by falling world commodity prices. A punishing hurricane in 1813 completed the cycle of ill luck, and left almost all of the estates abandoned, their owners having departed the islands in despair.

The despondent planters, most of them sensing the inevitability of emancipation, let their slaves go too, along with the fields. It was the slaves themselves who inherited the fields and were destined to become the true pioneers of the Turks and Caicos Islands.

EMANCIPATION The long-anticipated manumission of all slaves in the British Empire was proclaimed on 1 August 1834. Within the terms of the bill and in theory at least to aid its expedition, liberated slaves were to remain indentured to their former owners under a so-called apprenticeship system. In practice this transitional programme changed little and four years later it was abolished. It was to take many more years for a fairer balance between labour and income to be achieved.

In the Turks Islands it was immediately clear to the proprietors of the salinas that they would now need to develop less labour-intensive methods of production. Windmills were introduced to replace the hand-operated paddles for driving sea water into the pans and donkey carts to transfer the salt to the dock. While streamlining the operation served to reduce the workforce, it meant fewer jobs for the same number of former slaves available to fill them, resulting in lower wages for some and no work at all for others. No longer could the workers be whipped into service, either figuratively or physically, but rising unemployment led to widespread poverty.

Prior to the abolition of slavery, the procurement of African slaves had been outlawed in 1807 but trafficking was to persist for several decades more. Although the Royal Navy grew proficient at identifying ships designated for the transport of slaves it was not always so easy to determine their provenance. A vessel might fly the flag of a country not its own and the crew come from yet another. What has emerged is that at least one of them foundered on the reefs encircling the Caicos Islands. Detail is sketchy but it is recorded that in 1841 a brigantine named the *Trouvadore*, with a 20-strong Spanish crew and carrying 193 slaves, was wrecked on Philips Reef off Breezy Point, East Caicos. All or most of the Africans and crew appear to have made it to the shore where the captain made an unsuccessful effort to arrange purchase of a ship to transport his cargo onward to the lucrative slave market still operating in Cuba. Instead the slaves were taken to Grand Turk and indentured for a year to the salt-pond owners, after which it is believed that many returned to the Caicos Island. Here it is speculated that these freed slaves, or others like them, established the settlement of Bambarra on Middle Caicos. An official exploration team, which in 2004 found an as yet unidentified wooden shipwreck, returned to the site in July 2008. For the latest, see www.slaveshiptrouvatore.com.

FREEDOM FOR ALL Through the early days of the 19th century Bahamian fiscal control remained hugely unpopular amongst the islanders. Only a proportion of the funds raised in salt taxes was actually finding its way back to the Turks Islands, whereas it was now providing a quarter of the total revenue for the Bahamas. Moreover shipping links between the two ends of the chain, even the mail boat travelling the route only quarterly, made it difficult for the islands to be governed from Nassau. The governor of the Bahamas, seeing the problem for himself, supported a petition for devolution. As a result, on Christmas Day 1848, **The Separation Act** established the Turks Islands and the Caicos Islands together, to be henceforward a semi-autonomous colony, with an elected self-governing council under a Crown-appointed president, supervised through Jamaica.

By most accounts Frederick Forth, who in 1849 became the first president, was not a good fit and relations between him and his legislative board were at best uneasy. By 1852 the islanders had launched a request to have him relieved of his duties and although this failed, Forth, whose health was deteriorating, was finally replaced in the spring of 1854 by William Inglis.

During the middle years of the 19th century wracking – or wrecking – became one of the Turks and Caicos Islands' main foreign-exchange earners. From official figures for the years 1851–60, property salvaged from wrecks off Grand Turk amounted to $111,766, $93,186 of it from foreign-flagged ships. The US Consul quite reasonably accused the islanders of acts akin to piracy and the Secretary of State commented, 'The complaints are in a great measure well grounded.' So were the ships.

For the Bahamas as a whole, American insurance underwriters noted that wrecks increased from 30 in 1853 to 52 in 1857 and 89, valued at $3 million, in 1860. The local lighthouse-building industry prospered and there were particular objections about the wanton behaviour of the salvagers of Blue Hills in their treatment of the unfortunate shipwrecked. Things got so bad that the salt trade was threatened by ships' refusal to call at the islands.

The first modern lighthouse in the territory was built on Grand Turk in 1852, but there were still complaints about the frequent invisibility of the light.

Alas the long-awaited self-government was to be short lived. In spite of a prosperous salt trade, the taxes deriving from it were insufficient to sustain the economy and the little country was finding it increasingly hard to support itself. A devastating hurricane in 1866, destroying hundreds of homes, resulting in 63 deaths and paralysing the islands, was the final straw. Unable to maintain an independent government, in 1874 the islands were formally annexed to Jamaica. A board was set up with full legislative and budgetary powers, and the islands remained a dependency of Jamaica until 1959.

In a country that today can pride itself on offering some of the finest reef diving in the world it is interesting to note that the first recorded 'helmet' divers, Irish-American Jeremiah Murphy and some friends, arrived on Grand Turk in 1852. Only Murphy remained on the island. He latterly became a salt merchant, then a partner in Frith and Murphy, who developed the guano and sisal industries. Local lore has it that Murphy's Alley, between the Turks and Caicos Museum and the Arboretum, is named after him. Among his diving trophies was the ship's bell from HMS *Wolfe*, sunk by the French on Silver Shoals Bank in 1762 and rediscovered by Murphy 90 years later. For many years the bell, weighing 367lb (165kg), called the congregation to Grand Turk Methodist Church.

A copy of the Turks and Caicos seal was sent to England in 1889 to be featured in the design of a new flag for the colony. An illustrator apparently mistaking two distinctive piles of salt for huts, chose to improve the picture by inserting a door in one of the heaps. His mistake went unnoticed and the flag unchanged for the following 80 years. Hence the sneaky quiz question: 'Which tropical island used to have an igloo on its flag?'

A submarine cable laid by the forerunner of Cable & Wireless between Jamaica, Grand Turk and Bermuda in 1898 established the first telegraph communication with the rest of the world.

NEW INDUSTRIES, FRESH PLANTATIONS Like the Lucayans before them the islanders of the late 19th century sought to grow crops they hoped would thrive despite the arid conditions. They too recognised a potential in the limestone-based soil for the cultivation of sisal. Late in the century two companies were formed on East Caicos and West Caicos to grow and process the leaves and to export the resulting fibre for the manufacture of rope and matting. Although sisal plants require several years to reach maturity the venture was deemed promising and additional land was leased to set up plantations on Grand Turk and Salt Cay. But by the 1920s, with the advent of synthetic materials, the industry had largely been overtaken and ceased to be economically viable.

In the same period several other initiatives were set up. A fresh attempt was made to grow cotton, this time frustrated by infestation from the boll weevil. Both pineapple and coconut cultivation was introduced on a limited scale but neither withstood the hurricane of 1926.

A limited enterprise to mine guano (bat-droppings) for marketing as commercial fertiliser was initiated in the caves of East Caicos. Guano extracted from locations where the climate is both hot and dry is particularly valued because its intrinsic nitrates remain undiluted and thus retain their effectiveness over time.

Some turtle shell from the hawksbill turtle was exported for use in the manufacture of jewellery and ornamental furniture. Trading continued until a worldwide ban came into effect in the 1970s.

On Salt Cay in 1846 the Turks Island Whaling Company was formed. Employees would endeavour to harpoon and land humpbacks during their annual migration for rendering into whale oil, an important commodity for use as lighting fuel at that time. The company was operational for 37 years; ruins of its headquarter station are still visible on Taylor's Hill.

Since the Lucayan period, conch has been and continues to be a significant asset. Toward the end of the 19th century thousands of sea snails were being dried and sent to Haiti. Twenty-first century exports are on a strictly sustainable scale with the United States and Caribbean islands, many of whom have depleted their own stocks, being the main market.

Early in the 20th century, Caribbean spiny lobster, locally called crawfish, began to be tinned for export but the process was soon suspended due to wartime shortages of canning materials. Fifty years on, with the development of rapid freezing techniques and bulk shipments of lobster tails to the US, profits increased. Local restaurants too were and remain enthusiastic buyers. These days the lobster industry is controlled, with a closed season and a minimum weight regulation. It is based on the Caicos Bank, with some subsistence fishing on the Turks Bank, and the Mouchoir Bank off limits.

The salt industry received a boost during World War I due to absence of competition from the Mediterranean but the 30s' depression brought it almost to a standstill. Forty years later, a final shipment of salt from Salt Cay in 1970 brought the 300-year industry to a close.

WORLD WAR II Over the years of World War II, although the risk of aerial bombardment was slight, an after-sunset blackout was enforced throughout the islands and even the lighthouse on Grand Turk put out of action. A detachment of West Indies Forces was drafted from Jamaica to set up coastal defence patrols and to direct the Home Guard. Then in 1944 the US Armed Forces established an anti-submarine base on South Caicos. Early shivers of the Cold War in 1950 led to the establishment of a US missile-tracking station on Grand Turk, which was finally dismantled in 1981.

POST-WAR TCI As a dependency of Jamaica, in 1958 the islands joined the newly formed West Indies Federation, a ten-member union that was to be plagued by not dissimilar constitutional problems and differences to those experienced by the member countries of the European Union. It was in 1962, after a Jamaican referendum voted to withdraw from the federation and a decision had been taken for them to seek independence, that Dr Eric Williams of Trinidad and Tobago made his famous retort: 'One from ten leaves nought,' and the short-lived West

In early 1942, shortly before the main thrust of German U-boat activity in the Caribbean, a group presenting themselves as American property investors arrived on Grand Turk, purporting to be interested in acquiring a suitable island to develop as a tourist resort. Enthusiastically welcomed, they were given what amounted to an extensive guided tour of the Turks and Caicos and supplied with maps and charts. The photographs they took for themselves. Within a matter of months the authorities in Chicago, Illinois had identified and raided a secret Nazi cell operating under cover of a legitimate financial institution, arrested several of the same so-called 'investors' and recovered a large number of photographs and papers relating to their island sting – but not before the information had been passed on, as subsequent events seemed to prove. An alarming number of merchant vessels travelling through the shipping lanes closest to the islands began to fall victim to German torpedoes, the ultimate object of the exercise being to cut vital commodity supply lines.

Indies Federation was dissolved. The Turks and Caicos, seeing little benefit in remaining under the wing of an independent Jamaica, had already chosen in 1959 to separate from them, though the governor of Jamaica doubled up as governor of the Turks and Caicos. In 1962 the final links were severed. The islands continued as a British Crown Colony and the post of governor was re-christened administrator.

To a large extent the Turks and Caicos islanders continued to run their own affairs through a legislative council consisting partly of elected members with the remainder appointees. In 1965 the governor of the Bahamas was made responsible also for Grand Turk. This arrangement continued until the Bahamas gained independence in 1973, after which Alexander Mitchell was sworn in as first governor of the Turks and Caicos. Under a new constitution introduced in September 1976 the status of Crown Colony was maintained and a provision made for ministerial government.

A decision was taken in 1979 by the islanders in principle to declare full independence for the Turks and Caicos Islands in 1982, but a change of government brought a reversal of the policy. Today the islands are officially designated a United Kingdom Overseas Territory. After a slew of scandals in the mid 1980s momentarily shook the islands, injecting a little colour into an otherwise uneventful decade, ministerial government was suspended in July 1986. Following elections in 1988 the previous constitution was restored.

THE RISE OF TOURISM There were still no footprints in the miles of snow white sand encircling Providenciales on the sunny morning of 25 February 1966, when the Royal Yacht *Britannia* sailed past Boaby Rock Point bringing Queen Elizabeth II to the islands. Decorated cactus plants, flags and bunting lined the streets of Grand Turk to greet her, and in her official speech she observed with regard to the salt industry, then on the verge of collapse: 'This means change, and change is hard, but in this modern world change we must...You have assets here in these islands that you can develop and make into a new source of livelihood. You have a lovely climate and beautiful beaches which many people in [a] northern latitude would be happy to come and pay for the privilege of sharing with you...'

Within a matter of months, in exchange for 4,000 acres, Provident Ltd had begun the development of Providenciales, clearing a landing strip, constructing roads to link the three existing settlements and building the ten-room Third Turtle Inn (see *Chapter 4, Providenciales*, page 81). In the years leading up to this, Hilly

Canadian interest in forming some kind of union with TCI originated in 1917 when Prime Minister Robert Borden came cruising in the Caribbean and thought the two territories might complement each other quite well. The idea simmered quietly on the Canadian back burner until 1974, when a Canadian MP tabled a private member's bill in parliament proposing that Canada should annex the islands. By 1986 there was growing interest in the idea in TCI also, and a survey (how scientifically carried out is unclear) suggested that no less than 90% of islanders favoured a formal association with Canada. Canada recognised that initiating formal talks would be inappropriate without British blessing and was nervous of being accused of neo-colonialism, but did increase its aid programme. Nevertheless by 2003 Canadian PM Paul Martin was ready to discuss the question with Chief Minister Michael Misick and in 2004 another motion was tabled in Ottawa while Nova Scotian politicians voted to invite TCI to join the province if Union happened. There, for the time being, is where the matter rests, dormant but not dead.

Ewing, an early politician and himself from Blue Hills, records that the people of Grand Turk would refer deprecatingly to Providenciales as 'west of the buoy'. Since then, the nascent tourist industry has grown exponentially. The Grand Turk Cruise Center opened in February 2006, with the first ship to dock at the new pier on the 25th of that month, Holland America Lines' *Noordam*, having sailed non-stop from New York to mark the occasion. The adjacent cruise complex is able to accommodate two ocean liners and features an 800ft beach, pool, a variety of dedicated shops and an outpost of Jimmy Buffett's Margaritaville restaurant.

GOVERNMENT AND POLITICS

The Turks and Caicos Islands, one of the last 14 British Overseas Territories, have experienced democratic government since 1962. The head of state is HM Queen Elizabeth II, represented by a governor appointed by her. The present incumbent is Gordon Weatherell, who replaced Richard Tauwhare in August 2008. The governor has overall responsibility for defence, external affairs, international financial services and internal security, including the police. Otherwise he normally acts on the advice of the cabinet, over which he presides and which consists also of the premier, the attorney general and six other ministers. There is also a House of Assembly comprising a speaker, 15 elected members, four appointed members and the attorney general.

The first elected chief minister and founder of the People's Democratic Movement (PDM), 'JAGS' McCartney, was killed in a plane crash in New Jersey in May 1980. In August 2006, a new constitution was approved, under which the title of the head of government was changed to premier. The role is currently held by Dr Michael E Misick of the Progressive National Party (PNP). Born on North Caicos, Dr Misick was elected chief minister of the Turks and Caicos Islands on 15 August 2003. In April 2006 he married American actress LisaRaye McCoy and in August of the same year became the islands' first premier. Dr Misick also holds the roles of minister of tourism, trade, investment and district administration. His party swept to victory in 2007, winning 13 of the 15 seats with 60% of the vote. The next election must be held by May 2011.

LEGAL SYSTEM AND THE POLICE The islands' legal system is based on English common law and is administered by a resident chief justice, chief magistrate and three deputy magistrates. Appeal Court judges visit twice a year and there is a final right of appeal to the Privy Council in London.

The only prison is on Grand Turk.

ECONOMY

Until as recently as the 1970s, the economy of the islands was based on fishing and farming. Today, though, the big earners are tourism (and property development), financial services and fishing. GDP in 2003 was estimated at a total of $297 million, or $13,506 per capita, with an annual growth rate of 6.1% over the previous year.

In 2005 the import/export balance of merchandise (excluding tourism, finance and property) was valued at $301,003 million of imports against $14,723 million of exports.

The islands receive no direct financial aid from Britain, although the Overseas Territories Department supports a number of public service projects. The UK accounted for exports to the islands of £2.24 million in 2006, and in return received around £100,000 worth of imports.

Around a third of the working population is involved in the government and administration sectors. Unemployment is low, at 5.1% in 2005.

TOURISM In just 20 years, tourism has developed to become central to TCI's economy. Visitors are dominated by those from the USA, who numbered 169,662 in 2006, or 68% of the total of 248,343. In the same year, Canadians accounted for a further 29,802 visitors, with Europeans following at 24,834. Also in 2006, the first year in which Grand Turk's Cruise Center was operational, cruise ships brought an additional 295,000 tourists to the island.

FINANCIAL SERVICES The offshore financial services sector represents 7% of the total TCI economy, well behind tourism, but is significant in the field of employment. The regulatory body responsible for this sector is the Financial Services Commission (*Grand Turk: PO Box 173, Harry E Francis Bldg, Pond St;* ℩ *649 946 2550/2791; Providenciales: Caribbean Place Plaza, Leeward Hwy;* ℩ *649 946 5399;* e *fsc@tciway.tc; www.tcifsc.tc*).

FISHING AND AGRICULTURE Outside of tourism and banking, most of the local population are employed in fishing, with the bulk of the industry based on South Caicos.

Despite their protected status (see page 30), major exports are conch and lobster, totalling around 400 tons and 80 tons respectively per year, depending on the year's quota. Their importance to the islands' economy is underlined by their depiction on the country's coat of arms.

Agriculture is seriously hampered by poor soils, due in part to the underlying limestone rock, and accounts for little more than 2% of land use. The few crops grown include corn, cassava, beans and citrus fruits.

GEOGRAPHY AND CLIMATE

Located at the extreme western edge of the Atlantic Ocean, the Turks and Caicos Islands are a widely spread group of some 40 or so islands at the southern end of the Bahamas archipelago. Situated south of the Tropic of Cancer, at 21°45' N, 71°35' W, they lie some 90 miles (145km) north of the Dominican Republic, and approximately 575 miles (925km) southeast of Miami in Florida.

The islands, eight of which are permanently inhabited (with houses being built on a further two), form two distinct groups, separated by the 6,575ft (2,004m) deep Turks Island Passage, also known as the Columbus Passage. To the west lie the Caicos Islands, bordered by the Caicos Passage, and comprising the major islands of West, North, Middle, East and South Caicos, and Providenciales. To the east are the smaller Turks Islands: the inhabited Grand Turk and Salt Cay, and a range of lesser cays that include Gibbs, Long, Pear, East, Penniston, Cotton and – further south – Great Sand Cay. Together they have a total combined land area of 193 square miles (500km²) – or, if the permanent wetlands are included, 366 square miles (948km²). The coastline extends to a total of 242 miles (389km).

GEOLOGY *with thanks to Brian Riggs*

To get some understanding of the structure of the Turks and Caicos Islands, it helps to imagine a mountain range with two separate tall peaks. Now flood the mountains almost to the top, and all that remains visible will be just a few individual islands: that, in essence, is what a model of the Turks and Caicos looks like. Visitors can find a graphic three-dimensional illustration of this structure in the form of bathymetric maps at both the National Museum in Grand Turk and – on a larger scale – the National Environmental Centre on Providenciales. They make fascinating viewing.

Despite considerable information that circulates to the contrary, the islands were not formed from a former coral reef. In part, confusion arises because both the coral reefs and the underlying rock of the islands are comprised of calcium carbonate, and both were formed under the sea. Here, however, it is easy to jump to conclusions, but the geological reality is rather more complex than it might appear. Essentially, the islands – and the platforms on which they are built – are the result of an accumulation of windblown sand that formed in shallow warm water. During the period of the great glaciers, sea levels dropped significantly, and the exposed sand was blown into dunes. Over time, due to the action of vegetative growth and the process of rainfall dissolving and re-cementing the underlying particles, these dunes hardened, or lithified into Aeolian (or wind-borne) limestone, thus creating the islands that we see today.

So what about that sand? While fragments of finely pounded shell and coral do make up a component of several of the sandy beaches, most of them are completely composed of tiny egg-shaped pellets, or oolites (in its purest form known as aragonite). These pellets precipitate directly out of sea water, in a way that is not dissimilar to the formation of salt from the sea. It's an ongoing process and accounts for the chemical manufacture of aragonitic sand to the tune of several tons a day on the Caicos Bank alone.

Back on land, the action of acidic water on the porous limestone bedrock has led to the creation of a significant network of caves, notably on Middle Caicos, which has the largest above-water cave system in the Bahamas archipelago.

CLIMATE The climate is warm throughout the year with an average of 350 days of sunshine, but the heat is tempered by constant trade winds. Between June and October, average temperatures range from 81.5°F to 85°F (27.5–29°C), sometimes hitting the mid 90s towards the end of the summer. The winter months, from November to May, see temperatures fall to an average of 75–80°F (24–27°C), but this is the season when the winds can veer round to the northeast, bringing cloudy skies and cooler temperatures. The prevailing easterly tradewinds ensure that the climate is rarely oppressive.

Rainfall varies, totalling about 40 inches (101cm) a year over Provo and North and Middle Caicos but decreasing to just 21 inches (53cm) over Grand Turk and South

Hurricanes are the revolving tropical storms peculiar to the Caribbean and the Gulf of Mexico. The name 'hurricane' derives from the Taino Indian word, *huracán*, and is, simply, the local name for the tropical cyclones that hit this region in the summer months. In the Pacific, the same weather system is known as a typhoon.

The storms form over warm seas, around 79°F (26°C) or warmer, during periods of high barometric pressure. A central area of calm, known as the 'eye', is characterised by clear skies and light winds, and may grow to as much as 30 miles (48km) across. Around this, violent winds revolve at speeds in excess of 155mph (248km/h), accompanied by torrential rain (sometimes as much as 1 inch/25mm an hour) and thunder and lightning. A typical Atlantic hurricane is some 300 miles (480km) in diameter (Pacific storms may reach a staggering 1,000 miles (1,600km) across) and moves at a speed of between nine and 15mph (15–25km/h) in the lower latitudes.

The National Hurricane Center (NHC) in Miami (*www.nhc.noaa.gov*) tracks weather systems via satellite and reconnaissance aircraft. NHC issues a 72-hour forecast every six hours, at 5 o'clock and 11 o'clock, both morning and evening. Hurricanes are categorised according to the Saffir-Simpson scale of one to five, with category five being the most serious. Between 1950 and 1952, hurricanes were given phonetic names, such as Able, Baker, Charlie, for ease of recognition and communication. Women's names were used exclusively between 1953 and 1979, but since then men's and women's names have been alternated. For the Atlantic, there are six alphabetical lists of 21 names, used on a rotating basis.

In the northern hemisphere, hurricanes move clockwise along a curving track from the mid Atlantic through the West Indies and into the southern USA, often leaving a trail of destruction in their wake. Although worst-affected areas are low-lying coasts, the Turks and Caicos Islands are less susceptible than some of the islands in the eastern Caribbean because the proximity of the large land mass of Hispaniola tends to cause hurricanes to alter course slightly. Further protection comes in the form of the long and continous coral barrier reef which helps to protect exposed shorelines by breaking down the strongest waves. That said, the islands are theoretically at risk from June to November, when the conditions required by a hurricane are prevalent. It was during this period, in 1945, that the islands were hit by the most devastating hurricane in living memory. As winds in excess of 120mph (193km/h) passed over West Caicos, 79 fishermen lost their lives at sea, and another two were killed on land. More recently, in 2004 Hurricane Frances wreaked its own havoc, but fortunately the potentially more deadly Hurricane Isabel of 2003, with winds over 155mph (250km/h), narrowly missed the islands.

EMERGENCY HURRICANE PROCEDURES are in place across the islands, with designated shelters in strategic points such as schools and churches on Providenciales, North, Middle and South Caicos, Grand Turk and Salt Cay. Should there be a hurricane warning, tune to Radio Turks and Caicos (see page 59) or watch the Weather Channel on television for the latest information. Hurricane emergency enquiry numbers are as follows:

Grand Turk ✆ 946 2025, 2061   **Providenciales** ✆ 946 4521, 3897

Caicos. Rain when it comes tends to be in short bursts, usually followed by clearing skies and sunshine, and giving rise to some spectacular sunsets. That said, there are occasionally times when it rains all day, so it's as well to be prepared. The wettest months are normally December and January, and later during March and April.

Background Information GEOGRAPHY AND CLIMATE | 1

Although there is a risk of hurricanes (see box, page 19) from June to November, there has been no significant damage since Hurricane Frances in 2004, which fortunately caused no serious injuries.

NATURAL HISTORY AND CONSERVATION

Essentially, the islands fall into two distinct groups, divided by the Turks Island Passage. Together they boast several distinct habitats, ranging from the leeward reef of western coasts through salt marshes, mangrove swamps and tropical dry forests to the windward shores. Over 30 protected areas have been designated, largely covering uninhabited wetlands and inshore coastal areas.

FORESTS AND SCRUBLAND Tropical dry or deciduous forest once covered much of the Caicos Islands, from West Caicos across Providenciales to North, Middle and East Caicos, and much still remains, especially on Middle and North Caicos. Typically occurring in areas of generally low rainfall and warm temperatures, it is characterised by a low, scrubby bush made up of plants that can tolerate the limestone bedrock and poor soil. Larger, slow-growing trees, including the West Indian mahogany, *Swietenia mahagoni*, and the drought-tolerant lignum vitae, *Guaiacum sanctum*, with its glossy leaves and purple flowers, form part of the forest, although the massive specimens of two hundred years ago have long since been stripped for use in construction and the shipbuilding industry.

Stands of the endemic Caicos Caribbean pine, *Pinus caribaea bahamensis*, that grow on North and Middle Caicos, and on Pine Cay, were also of great value for shipbuilding. In recent years, however, these trees have been devastated by the invasive tortoise-scale insect, a bug that was inadvertently introduced to the islands in imported Christmas trees. The environmental authorities are working with experts at Kew Gardens to devise a recovery plan.

WETLANDS AND SALINAS A large proportion of the Caicos Islands consists of wetlands, or mangrove swamps, the typical vegetation of coasts and estuaries in the tropics, creating a habitat for a range of wildlife. These are the spawning grounds, a nursery for fish, conch, jellyfish, nudibranch and sharks, and a shelter for full-grown stingrays.

The term 'mangrove' is actually a general term for fast-growing, salt-tolerant trees up to 120ft (40m) tall, with roots that are submerged at high tide. Mangroves have glands to exude excess salt – on the under side of their leaves – while specially modified roots provide support for the plant and act as breathing organs.

Mangroves are crucial to land stability, protecting inland areas from high winds and storm surges and helping to maintain areas of fresh water. As they grow, sediment becomes trapped between their roots, eventually creating new land with nutrient-rich soil that is in turn colonised by other species, such as palm trees. Additionally, fallen mangrove leaves decompose to form a complex food web that is vital for the survival of fish and other aquatic creatures. In spite of this, areas of mangrove continue to be threatened with destruction by the pressure on land for development.

Three types of mangrove are found on the Turks and Caicos Islands. The red *Rhizophora mangle*, which makes its home right on the outer fringes of the swamps, has stilt or 'prop' roots, enabling it to grow in relatively deep water. The black *Avicennia germinans* grows inside, in shallower water. It has a dark-coloured bark and finger root projections, or pneumatophores, which work rather like snorkels to bring oxygen to the plants. The third, the white *Laguncularia racemosa*, with its pale trunk, prefers a drier environment.

Also to be found in the wetlands is the gnarled buttonwood, *Concocarpus erectus*, a hardwood tree whose roots can tolerate the brackish water of this environment.

While the salinas offer an inhospitable environment for plant life, they're up there with the best restaurants from the point of view of wading birds, which in turn make these and other wetland areas a significant attraction for visitors.

PLANTS Around 500 plant species have been identified in the Turks and Caicos, of which eight are unique to the islands. These eight endemic species include the creamy-green wild orchid, *Encyclia rufa*, and the Turks & Caicos heather, *Limonium bahamense*, a form of sea lavender that is the national flower.

Widely visible on all the larger islands is the spurred butterfly pea, *Centrosema virginianum*, whose vivid purple or blue flowers grow on trailing vines.

On the coast, look out for the tiny star-shaped pink flowers of the sea purslane, *Sesuvium portulacastrum*, which forms a thick mat and effectively acts as a form of beach defence. The same role is played by the native inkberry, *Scaevola plumieri,* a white-flowering species that is threatened by its Pacific cousin, *Scaevola taccada*.

The shrubby cactus or opuntia prickly pear is common everywhere, but the third emblem on the country's coat of arms, the **Turk's head cactus**, *Melocactus intortus*, is not. This extraordinary plant thrives in a dry habitat, and is to be found growing naturally on any of the islands within the Turks group. The threat comes from a combination of development and plant theft, which also impacts on the islands' orchid population.

Trees While the forest area (see above) supports its own trees, more widely seen by the visitor are the trees that make their home on the coast. The broad leaves of the **sea-grape** tree, *Coccoloba uvifera*, afford welcome shade along many a sandy beach, while its fruits provide nourishment for the native iguanas. Less welcome are the **casuarinas**, *Casuarina equisetifolia*, a fast-growing tree that is a native of Australia. They may look graceful as they wave in the summer's breeze, but they are proving literally deadly to the native flora, because their needles are allelopathic: when falling to the ground, they release chemicals into the soil that prevents anything else from growing in the area, to the detriment of the indigenous flora.

The fragrant **frangipani**, *Plumeria obtuse*, needs little introduction, its showy white flowers displayed all year round, then towards the end of the year, the colourful yellow **elder** or **shamrock**, *Tecoma stans*, brightens up many a dusty hedgerow.

Native **fruit trees** include the wild sapodilla, *Manlikara bahamensis*, soft and very juicy, the wild guava *Psidium longipes* and the seven-year apple, *Casasia clusifolia*. Forming a significant part of the diet of the Turks and Caicos iguana, they are to be found on Little Water Cay, and in other areas where the iguana still holds sway.

Of course, many of the trees have proved useful over the years, not least the sea island cotton, *Gossypium barbadense*, which was used long ago by the Lucayan Indians for making string and nets, then gained fame in the clothing industry. The inagua thatch palm 'silver top', widely known as the **silver thatch**, *Coccothrinax inaguensis arecaceae*, has long been used on the islands to weave mats, hats and baskets. There is also the naturalised locust tree, or wild tamarind, *Tamarindus indica*, which has proved invaluable in the development of medicines and dyes.

Poisonous shrubs Watch out for the less friendly side of nature: the islands have several poisonous native trees and shrubs. The **poisonwood**, *Metopium toxiferum*, is one such; don't touch! Keep out of the way, too, of the **manchineel**, *Hippomane*

Brian Riggs

There was a time when the people of our islands never saw a real medical doctor. And for many, especially in the Caicos Islands, that time was not so long ago.

There has been a medical presence in the nation's capital, Grand Turk, almost since it's founding in the early 1800s. In fact, at the turn of the 20th century, the magnificent Bermudian-style building on Front Street that is now called the Turks Head Mansion was a doctor's office and surgery. But medical doctors were a rare thing in Middle, North and Provident Caicos. The government sent doctors from Grand Turk for a tour of the Caicos Islands once or twice a year, and serious cases were often transported by sea to the Grand Turk facility. But most Caicos folks, of course, never ever saw the inside of clinic or hospital

How did the people of the Caicos Islands deal with the everyday coughs and colds, the cuts and scrapes, the bruises and other ailments that cropped up regularly in their hard fought lives? What was the alternative to being able to stop by the clinic any day of the week and ask for the help of a full-time medical doctor or nurse?

Necessity, as we all know, is the mother of invention. And over a period of many, many decades, and using the cultural knowledge accumulated from generations of agriculturalists and others who became familiar with their 'bush' surroundings, a practice of natural healing and nature-based medications blossomed in the Caicos Islands, and is still going strong.

Bush medicine, as the practice is known, has a long and honoured history in our islands. It is a skill that is passed along and built upon over many generations. In every village, there was at least one resident 'bush doctor', and the rest of the population also knew of scores of natural remedies for everything from headaches to birthing problems.

Many of our common and well-known remedies are actually based upon plants that were brought to the country with the very first colonists, the American Loyalists. *Aloe vera*, a Mediterranean plant, was good, not only topically for burns and scrapes, but also taken internally as a digestive aid and purgative. Periwinkle, a pretty little flowering plant found in every garden, is a treatment for diabetes.

But many native plants were also found, after years of experimentation, to contain healthful and medicinal qualities. Sea oxeye daisy tea is an efficacious treatment for colds, allergies and asthma. Butterfly weed has anti-fungal and anti-viral properties. Blue rat tail can eliminate intestinal worms. And snake stick? Well, if you need it, snake stick can help 'make a man of you'.

While many feel that 'bush medicines' are more fiction or wishful thinking than not, scientific investigation has proven that many of these plants and herbs do contain active compounds that are similar to the synthetic medicines that are prescribed for the same purposes. In fact, a large percentage of prescription drugs are just synthesised versions of natural remedies.

Be careful about ingesting any wild plants, though. While many have health-giving properties, many are also very poisonous.

Brian Riggs is curator of the National Environmental Centre, Providenciales

mancinella; its poisonous sap – which cannot be washed off with water – will cause blisters on contact. You can even be affected indirectly, since rain can wash the corrosive sap on to you if you're walking beneath the tree at the wrong moment. If you intend to wander in the forest, do ensure that you can identify these trees as, although they are rare, both grow wild.

LAND ANIMALS

Mammals Most conspicuous of the islands' mammals are the wild **horses** and **donkeys** that roam free on East and South Caicos and the Turks Islands. Originally employed in the salt industry, these animals were left behind when the traders abandoned the islands. While some were rounded up by the government, others have remained free.

Four species of **bat** are native to the islands, all found in the Conch Bar Caves on Middle Caicos (see page 138).

Birds Some 170 species of bird have been recorded in these islands, many of them migrants en route to warmer or cooler climes.

Pride of place goes to the **seabirds** that have long fished in these fertile waters. The islands' national bird is apt: the brown pelican, *Pelecanus occidentalis*, its acrobatic displays impossible to miss as it swoops low over the sea in search of prey. The rather more graceful royal tern, *Sterna maxima*, with its distinctive bright orange beak and – at the beginning of the breeding season – black cap, is also much in evidence, often standing sentry-like on a jetty or pier, watching for its next meal. Flocks of turnstones scuttle along the beaches, where the occasional oystercatcher, *Haematopus palliatus*, is to be found foraging at the water's edge. And just occasionally you could spot the striking silhouette of the magnificent frigatebird, *Fregata magnificens,* outlined against the sky.

Lording it over sea and land is the **osprey**, *Pandion haliaetus*. Known locally as the fish hawk, it frequents isolated cliffs and crags across the islands, building its nest high up to protect the eggs from predators, and feeding almost entirely on fish. Another predator, the **American kestrel**, *Falco sparverius*, feeds largely on insects, keeping an eye on its surroundings from its vantage point high up on overhead wires. Bedecked in smart blue and russet with a cream chest, this is one bird that stands out from the crowd.

Inland waters bring their own rewards for birders, for this is where the **waders** are in their element. Mangrove swamps and tidal flats, especially on North Caicos, attract flocks of pink West Indian flamingoes, *Phoenicopterus ruber*, in search of shrimp and other crustaceans. Great blue herons and great egrets stand proud and tall over the ponds, along with plenty of their smaller relatives, including the vulnerable reddish egret. Regularly sighted, too, are the black-necked stilts, *Himantopus mexicanus*, with their white chests, long beaks and long red legs, as they wade through the shallow waters searching for food. Look up a little, and you may be lucky enough to spot the **belted kingfisher**, *Ceryle alcyon*, another distinctive bird with its blue 'belt' neatly fastened across its white chest like the strap of a rucksack. Far more difficult to see is the endangered **West Indian whistling duck**, *Dendrocygna arborea*, which breeds on the reserves of North, Middle and East Caicos. Whistling ducks are nocturnal feeders, moving from their daytime home in the mangroves to freshwater ponds in order to feed.

Of the **land birds**, it's relatively easy to make out the attractive and common little bananaquit, *Coeraba flaveola sharpei*, a flower-piercing bird that feeds on nectar, insects and fruits; its black-and-yellow colouring brightens up many a picnic or woodland walk. Keep an eye open, too, for the tiny hummingbird, of which two species occur in the islands. Of these, the most frequently seen is the Bahama woodstar, *Calliphlox evelynae*, its green back and rapid wingbeat drawing the eye of even the least-observant visitor. Rather less attractive is the dark Cuban crow, *Corvus nasicus*, whose extraordinary call has all the subtlety of a set of squeaky brakes.

Further information The National Trust sells two excellent bird-identification cards, one for land birds, the other covering wetland species. They also publish

Richard Ground's *Birds of the Turks and Caicos Islands* (see *Further Information*, page 191).

Reptiles While the seas around the islands are home to several species of marine turtle (see pages 26–7), on land one reptile is hanging on to its life: the **Turks and Caicos iguana**, *Cyclura carinata carinata* (see box, below). An endemic subspecies that was once common on all the islands, it has been forced by loss of habitat and serious predation to retreat to some of the smaller, uninhabited islands, including Little Water Cay off Providenciales, Ambergris Cay, and Long Cay off South Caicos. It is registered on the Red List issued by the International Union for Conservation of Nature (IUCN) as critically endangered, as are all Caribbean iguana species.

Also endemic are a couple of small **lizards**, the endearing Turks and Caicos curly tail lizard, *Leiocephalus psammodromus*, which is easily spotted scuttling through the undergrowth, and the Turks and Caicos anole, *Anolis scriptus scriptus*. Rather less endearing to some, but entirely harmless, are three endemic **snakes**. Of these, there's the rainbow boa constrictor, *Epicrates chrysogaster*, named for its iridescent scales and reaching up to 6ft (2m) in length, and the pygmy or miniature boa, *Tropidophis greenwayi*, which is found only on the Caicos Islands, and is rarely more than 1ft (30cm) long. This little creature can be found at the Cheshire Hall Plantation as well as on North Caicos. Less visible is the blind worm snake, *Typhlops richardi*, which spends its life underground.

TURKS AND CAICOS IGUANA

At just 30in (77cm) long, the Turks and Caicos iguana is one of the smallest rock iguanas, but is still the islands' largest native land animal. It is estimated that just 30,000 of these endangered creatures, which once inhabited all the islands within the group, are still to be found, now confined to just a few of the smaller, less frequented islands covering a total area no larger than 10.8 square miles (28km²).

Iguanas sleep in holes in the ground, emerging during the day both to feed and to soak up the heat of the sun. They shed their skin about once a year, and have the ability to change colour in order to blend in with surroundings. They reach maturity at around six to seven years old, at which time they choose a mate with whom they will continue to share an underground burrow for life. Mating takes place once a year, in the spring. The female, shorter than the male and with a far less prominent crest along the spine, lays about four or five eggs, burying them in the sand, like turtles. When the eggs hatch some two to three months later, the newly born iguanas, just 4in (10cm) long and with huge heads, dig their way out of the sand, then make their way for some form of shelter in an attempt to avoid predation from herons and egrets. They are also at risk from other birds, as well as cats, dogs and indeed humans – this last in part through loss of habitat – which accounts for their retreat to uninhabited islands. Only one in five iguanas is expected to survive to maturity, at around seven years old, with a potential lifespan of 25–30 years.

The iguana eats a predominantly vegetarian diet, with a particular fondness for berries from the sea grape and silver thatch trees, the juicy fruit of the wild sapodilla, and leaves from the wild guava or 'cashia', *Acacia acuifera*. The seven-year apple is another favourite, while seaweed provides essential nutrients, too. All of these grow in the iguana's natural habitat, and on Little Water Cay many are labelled for ease of identification.

Insects and creepy crawlies You'd be unlucky not to spot the enormous **Erebus moth**, *Ascalapha odorata,* with its deep brown colouring and 4in (10cm) wingspan. Almost 50 species of **butterfly** have been identified here, including the endemic Turks & Caicos leafwing butterfly, *Anaea intermedia*, and the bright orange Gulf fritillary, *Agraulis vanillae*. Rather less attractive, but one insect you are unlikely to avoid, is the **mosquito**. While it is to some extent controlled by spraying of the breeding grounds, there are plenty of the little pests out there waiting for unwary visitors, so insect repellent is a must.

MARINE ENVIRONMENT Life below the surface can effectively be divided up into four zones: the reef, down to about 200ft (65m), features fish and coral, and is the limit of the area in which divers can move about. Below this on the wall, between 200 and 600ft (60–182m), are sponges, while deeper still, at 600–1,000ft (182–305m) is the realm of the sharks and starfish. Below 1,000ft (305m) is classified, quite simply, as 'the deep'.

The reef With what has been claimed to be the third-largest barrier reef in the world, after Australia's Great Barrier Reef and Mesoamerican Barrier Reef System from Mexico to Honduras, the Turks and Caicos has an enviable natural attraction that is proving irresistible to divers.

Typically, a barrier reef is an uneven platform of coral separated from the coastline by a deep lagoon, and with a steep slope on the seaward side. In Turks and Caicos waters this 'steep slope' is effectively a wall, an almost vertical drop-off straight down into the abyss. The reef forms a natural protection for the island from the waves that relentlessly roll on to its shores. Home to over a quarter of all marine life, it is among the most fragile and endangered ecosystems in the world.

The reefs around the Turks and Caicos Islands are composed of a combination of hard and soft corals, and algae. **Hard corals** are responsible for the calcium carbonate deposits that over time make up a coral reef. Most hard coral grows at a rate of just half an inch per year (a little over one centimetre), with the living tissue on or very near the surface. Made up of living polyps, it is incredibly fussy, requiring clear, clean water to a maximum depth of 130ft (40m), which is the limit of sunlight penetration. And if that wasn't enough, it needs sea temperatures of 21°C or above in order to thrive, which effectively limits its range to 30° north or south of the Equator. If it is disturbed, or broken, it may never recover. If sand or other sediment is stirred up around it, the polyps can suffocate. Little wonder, then, that divers should treat this living 'rock' with such caution – the coral's life, quite literally, depends on it.

The evocative names of many of the hard corals make them easy to identify, even for the novice. The maze-like structure of the brain coral looks just like a human brain, its swirls and coils creating endless patterns. Similarly tube corals are just that, tall narrow tube-like structures often in vivid colours, while plate coral has all the appearance of a badly stacked set of dishes after a hasty dinner party. And then there are the staghorn and elkhorn corals, clearly named for their resemblance to antlers. Less obvious, perhaps, is the pillar coral, one of the few corals to feed in the daytime. The distinctive 'fuzz' of its long fingers, pointing straight up by some 8ft (2.4m) or so, is actually the polyps extending to ensnare passing plankton.

The craggy, barrel-like structures that perch atop the coral like some gargantuan drinking vessel are actually **sponges**, as are the colourful tubes that protrude from the wall. Sponges grow painstakingly slowly, obtaining nutrients by filtering them out of the water. Unfortunately, their size does not equate with toughness: even an apparently superficial knock to the lip can result in permanent damage.

BLACK CORAL

Even relatively close to the surface, at perhaps 45ft (15m), you may come across the rare black coral, the raw material for much of the jewellery sold in tourist shops across the Caribbean. This fragile and slow-growing creature takes two or three years to grow just an inch (2cm), and is on the Convention on International Trade in Endangered Species (CITES) list.

The best black coral grows at depths of 100ft (30m) or more, with delicate fronds gracing a relatively thick stem. In the wild, it actually looks light brown or even white; it is only after hours of painstaking polishing that the shiny black colour is achieved.

Although black coral has been used in jewellery for thousands of years, world stocks have been seriously depleted by over collection. Harvesting it – and indeed any other coral or sea life – within Turks and Caicos waters is strictly illegal.

Soft corals, lacking the calcium carbonate skeleton of their hard cousins, play no part in reef building, and need rather less light to survive. Typically adorned in bright colours, many of them look more like plants, moving gently in the current. Within this group are the gorgonians, which include the rather rigid purple common sea fan.

Far faster growing than the surrounding organisms, **algae** can gain a hold on damaged coral and if not checked can eventually swamp its host, leading to permanent damage or death. It would be easy to cast algae as the bad guy, yet there is an interdependence between it and the corals that is essential to both. Oxygen, produced by algae through photosynthesis, is essential for the coral, which in its turn produces waste on which the algae feed. It is only when the delicate balance between these two is upset that lasting damage can occur.

MARINE WILDLIFE

Marine mammals One of the major attractions of the Turks and Caicos Islands is their location on the migration route of the humpback whale, *Megaptera novaeangliae*. Every year, between January and April, these huge, gentle creatures find their way to their breeding grounds by way of the Turks and Caicos. Local people remember spotting sperm whales and pilot whales, too, but today it is only the humpback that is seen off these islands.

Many a diveboat will be accompanied out to a dive site by Atlantic bottlenose dolphins, *Tursiops truncatus*, sometimes in groups of half a dozen or more – and one in particular, JoJo, is a regular visitor to Grace Bay (see page 110).

Sea turtles Sea turtles were once abundant in the Turks and Caicos Islands, whose sandy beaches, ideal for nesting, and plentiful supply of sea or turtle grass, *Thallasia testudinum*, are essential to their survival. In recent years, however, their numbers have seen a serious decline, for several reasons. In addition to natural predators such as birds, crabs and sharks, the turtle has suffered significantly at the hand of humans, with illegal or accidental catches still an issue, compounded by loss or degradation of the animal's natural habitat through development and pollution. Dogs, too, have played a part in the decline.

Of the seven species of sea turtle worldwide, the most common around the islands is the green sea turtle, *Chelonia mydas*, so-called because its fat is a greenish colour. Less common, but still regularly seen by divers and snorkellers, is the smaller, critically endangered hawksbill, *Eretmochelys imbricata*, whose exquisite shell is the source of the traditional 'tortoiseshell', long coveted for ornamental purposes, but now outlawed under the Convention on International Trade in Endangered Species (CITES). Other turtles indigenous to these waters are the olive ridley, *Lepidochelys olivacea*, the mostly carnivorous loggerhead, *Caretta caretta*, named for its unusually large head, and the large leatherback, *Dermochelys coriacea*, which may occasionally be found in deeper waters. There has also been the odd unconfirmed sighting of the smallest of the species, Kemp's ridley sea turtle, *Lepidochelys kempi*. All species of sea turtle are on the endangered list, defined as facing probable extinction in the near future, with some – including the hawksbill, leatherback and Kemp's ridley – designated as critically endangered: facing immediate extinction. All are protected under the islands' own marine conservation laws. See also page 28.

Turtles still nest on the islands, although loss of habitat and nesting sites through development of the beaches on Providenciales in particular has seriously affected their numbers. Do take particular care when walking along less-frequented beaches during the turtle-nesting season, between April and September, and don't even consider driving on the beach.

Reef fish Out on the reef, the kaleidoscope of colour created by so many fish is constantly changing. Several species of parrotfish contribute to the effect, the most common being the blue, yellow and green queen parrotfish, *Scarus vetula*. These fish, too, are hermaphrodites, starting as females but eventually ending up as males, each of a different colour. The parrotfish also has an unusual method of feeding,

Background Information NATURAL HISTORY AND CONSERVATION

HUMPBACK WHALES

with thanks to Tony Soper

Every year between January and April, North Atlantic humpback whales make their way in small groups from their Arctic feeding grounds, through the Turks Island Passage, to their tropical home on the Mouchoir and Silver banks, which lie southeast of Grand Turk. This – along with the Cape Verde Islands – is where they come to breed, and to give birth to their young.

During courtship, males may attract the attention of the females in a spectacular display of breaching, when they leap clear out of the water. At other times they may lobtail – bringing their tails down explosively on to the surface, presumably as some form of warning display. The pigmentation of the underside of the tail, clearly seen when the whale is diving, is unique to each animal, in the same way as fingerprints are unique to humans.

The whales are highly vocal, whistling and rumbling musically in songs which are varied and intricate, and clearly designed for long-distance communication. These songs are often heard by divers, long before a whale is sighted.

The humpback grows up to 50ft (15m) in length, and can weigh up to 48 tons (43,000kg). It is named for the hump that lies just in front of the small dorsal fin on the back, with a series of smaller humps, or tubercules, leading to the tail. Its most striking feature is the extraordinarily long white pectoral fins, which can grow to nearly 16ft (5m) – or almost a third of the whale's own body length.

These are baleen whales, feeding primarily on krill which they engulf in great mouthfuls, either on the surface or by rising up from below. They breed every two years, with a single calf born after 12 months, weighing in at a formidable 1.6 tons (1,500kg) and measuring around 13ft (4m). Only then do the animals make their way slowly – at just 4–6 knots – back to the krill-rich waters off Greenland.

Tony Soper is author of 'Wildlife of the North Atlantic', published by Bradt Travel Guides.

SEA TURTLES

Sea turtles live largely in water, coming ashore only to nest. Unlike their landlubber cousins, they are unable to retract either their heads or their flippers into their shell for protection.

The sea turtle has a potential lifespan of up to 100 years, with maturity attained at between 20 and 30, although only about 1% will survive to that age. The female, who has a breeding span of some 20 years, typically nests in the warmer months every three or four years. In each season, she will create several nests deep in the sand, laying around a hundred eggs in each nest, or 300–540 eggs a year.

The eggs take around 60 days to hatch, at which time the hatchlings make their way towards the sea, attracted by the play of moonlight on the waves. This is the moment when the hatchlings are at their most vulnerable to predation from watching birds. In their first year, the hatchlings grow up to 6lb (2.7kg), and can be expected to weigh up to 52lb (24kg) by the time they reach three or four years old.

Turtles are cold-blooded animals, requiring warm water to survive. In fact, water temperature affects the sex of the hatchlings – at 82°F (28°C), a balance between male and female is to be expected; cooler than that and males will dominate; hotter and there will be a predominance of females. The sexes can be differentiated by their tails.

using its nose rather like a blunt chisel against the coral in order to extract the algae that is its food. Having helped to clean up the coral, it continues by excreting sand, thus completing the eco-friendly cycle.

Almost as colourful is the blue-and-yellow queen angelfish, *Holacanthus ciliaris*, although its handsome cousin, the black-and-yellow French angelfish, *Pomacanthus paru*, is far more distinctive – and can be decidedly nosy. Damselfish have something of a reputation for curiosity, as well, and may even be aggressive. At least one member of this family, the little sergeant-major fish, *Abudefduf saxatilis*, with its smart black-and-white bars, is instantly recognisable. Also black and white is the unusual spotted drum, which in the juvenile stage has startlingly long striped wings but no spots at all; these appear only in the intermediate phase. Almost entirely monochrome is the black durgon, *Melichthys niger*. One of several triggerfish to inhabit the reef, it is easily identified by the distinctive pale-blue line that defines the meeting point between its fins and body.

As butterflyfish and bright blue tangs dart in and out, shoals of blue-and-yellow striped French grunt swim lazily around the reef, as do any number of the larger jacks. The erect dorsal fin of the reddish-orange squirrelfish makes it look rather like a ship in full sail. Regularly seen in shallow waters, its large dark eyes are particularly noticeable. By contrast, the expert camouflage of the peacock flounder makes its presence on the sandy seabed very hard to detect.

Pufferfish are curious creatures. When inflated, their almost spherical bodies are unmistakable. The not dissimilar porcupinefish is easily distinguished from the inflated pufferfish by the spines for which it is named. It is particularly important not to touch the porcupinefish – holding it in your hands removes the mucous film which helps to protect it from many of the surrounding corals. If it's curiosity you're after, look out for the almost triangular trunkfish, *Lactophrys sp*, or perhaps the fragile-looking trumpetfish, *Aulostomus maculatus*, its long, thin body almost transparent, and its tail flattened.

Much larger than these are members of the grouper family, including the coral-coloured coney, *Epinephelus fulvus*, the Goliath grouper, *Epinephelus itjajara*, also known as a jewfish, and the smaller Nassau grouper, *Epinephelus striatus*, a slow-growing fish which reaches up to 4ft (1.2m). A lover of shade, this grouper seek out rocks and other outcrops on the reef where its white body patterned with irregularly spaced vertical bands in colours ranging from brown to dark green is well camouflaged. All groupers start their adult lives as females, later becoming males.

At the other end of the scale is a world in miniature, the nooks and crannies in the walls and on the reef inhabited by any number of tiny creatures. Careful observation may be rewarded with the sighting of a balletic banded shrimp, the tiny slender filefish, a flamingo tongue or even the rare fingerprint cyphoma.

Not everything on the reef is friendly. Jellyfish are often seen in these waters, and sea urchins here are much larger than their European cousins, their long black spines decorating many a rocky cove. Don't tread on them of course – the spines are painful and can cause infection. Watch out, too, for the stonefish, well camouflaged against the rocks; its sting is poisonous. And while the venomous lionfish, *Pterois volitans*, may be attractive to divers, its natural habitat is the Pacific, and its presence in Atlantic waters is a significant threat to the indigenous species, which may not perceive it to be dangerous.

Other marine life While several shellfish may be found around the islands, it is the **queen conch**, *Strombus gigas* (see box, page 121) that – along with the lobster – is highly prized by the islanders. A large, edible sea snail that lives in shallow waters, the conch is found throughout the islands, although stocks have been heavily depleted by fishermen. Conch shells, immortalised in *Lord of the Flies* for the trumpet-like noise achieved if you blow through them correctly, are easily found along quieter beaches.

Several species of **shark** may be seen either on the reef or farther out to sea. Most common is the Caribbean reef shark, *Carcharhinus perezi*, which grows up to 10ft (3m) long and is often to be seen cruising in deep waters, but nurse sharks, *Ginglymostoma cirratum*, are also around. Hammerheads (*Sphyrna sp*), too, are occasionally spotted offshore, as are the occasional tiger shark or blacktip, but the smaller lemon shark, *Negaprion brevirostris*, is the one you're more likely to encounter closer to the beach. With a similarly bad reputation, and also an inhabitant of Turks and Caicos waters, is the **barracuda**, *Sphyraena barracuda*. Groups of youngsters are the most common, but there are plenty of full-size adults out there, often seen alone and almost motionless in the water. Divers who come across a barracuda can scare it off by swimming parallel, effectively proving that they're bigger than it is. In reality, though, even the largest of these creatures is normally as wary of divers as they are of it.

Of the **rays**, the southern stingray, *Dasyatis americana*, is the species to be found in shallow sandy waters across the islands, the gentle rise and fall of their 'wings' moving them gracefully through the water. The larger spotted eagle ray, *Aetobatus narinari*, is more likely to be seen just off the wall.

After dark, the underwater world takes on a different feel, as the world of the colourful reef fish is displaced by that of the night feeders. **Moray eels**, lurking in rocky crevices, await the next meal to swim unsuspectingly past. The largest of the species in these waters, the green moray, *Gymnothorax funebris*, can be 6ft (1.8m) or more in length. Stories abound of morays making unprovoked attacks on humans, but contrary to popular myth they are not poisonous, though their bite may easily become infected. The protected **spiny lobster**, *Panulirus argus*, may be seen hiding under rocks or in coral nooks almost anywhere on the islands, even in the daytime, so keep your eyes open for its long antennae. At night, though, this species is on the lookout for food, and much easier to spot. **Octopus** and **squid**, too, are nocturnal, both of them capable of fast movement which enables them to outwit enemies such as the scavenging moray. And so for the most part are the **corals**, which with just one exception, the pillar coral, feed during the hours of darkness.

CONSERVATION A significant area of the islands is protected under a series of marine and land national parks, nature reserves, sanctuaries and areas of historical interest. A total of 34 areas fall within these categories, with a further two under consideration. All are managed by the Department of the Environment and Coastal Resources (DECR; *www.environment.tc*), with considerable help from the National Trust (see pages 61–2).

In 2007, the islands' premier declared that the government intended to keep a 'green' island entirely free from development. Conservation bodies are hoping that this will be East Caicos, currently uninhabited, and with no means off access except by private boat.

One pressing issue is that of rubbish. While tourist areas are generally kept pretty spick and span, elsewhere litter and burnt-out cars are posing quite a problem for the authorities.

Protected areas Many of the areas protected by the ten **national parks** relate to the marine environment. Of these, the largest is the Princess Alexandra Land and Sea National Park, which incorporates the eastern tip of Providenciales and the whole of Grace Bay, effectively protecting much of the area visited by divers and snorkellers; others fall within the Northwest Point, West Caicos and Fort George national parks. To the west of Grand Turk, Columbus Landfall Marine National Park was established with the same goal. Other marine environments which are afforded similar protection include the cays to the south of Grand Turk, and the pristine reefs around South Caicos. National park status has also been conferred on Provo's Chalk Sound, and the Conch Bar Caves on Middle Caicos. Within the protected areas are several small cays which are breeding grounds for birds such as ospreys and terns. It is interesting to note that there are no private beaches in the Turks and Caicos – land up to the high-water mark is Crown property, owned by the Queen.

Despite the protection, conflicting demands can create some serious anomalies. In 2007, for example, treasure hunters seeking 'musket and cannonballs' etc in Caicos Bay were given permission to 'blow sand', which – while outside the national park itself – could not fail to inflict considerable damage to the fragile coral on the surrounding reef. The threat of development is also ever present, with uproar caused early in 2008 when plans were unveiled for the creation of the artificial 'Star Island' in the Leeward Channel to the east of Provo. A group of residents has joined forces to oppose the move, fearing that it could devastate both the coral reef and the fragile balance of the mangroves within the area.

Marine conservation Legislation is in place to prevent activities such as fishing and jet skiing within areas designated as marine parks. There are designated mooring buoys within the parks, and boats may anchor elsewhere only in sandy areas. Dive moorings within the national parks are officially the responsibility of the DECR, although lack of resources means that maintenance is seriously compromised, and many moorings are missing. In reality it is the dive operators who work to maintain the moorings on a day-to-day basis.

Of course, the threat to the islands' coral reefs is by no means limited to divers. Fishing, too, can take its toll, although the industry is regulated by the DECR. And while pollution in these waters may be relatively insignificant, there remain significant issues with development with the interference caused by dredging and infilling having inevitable consequences upon the surrounding ecosystems.

The Caribbean spiny lobster is protected in TCI waters from April to July, while conch cannot be harvested between 15 July and 15 October. Islanders may catch turtles with a carapace at least 20in (50cm) wide or weighing a minimum of 20lb

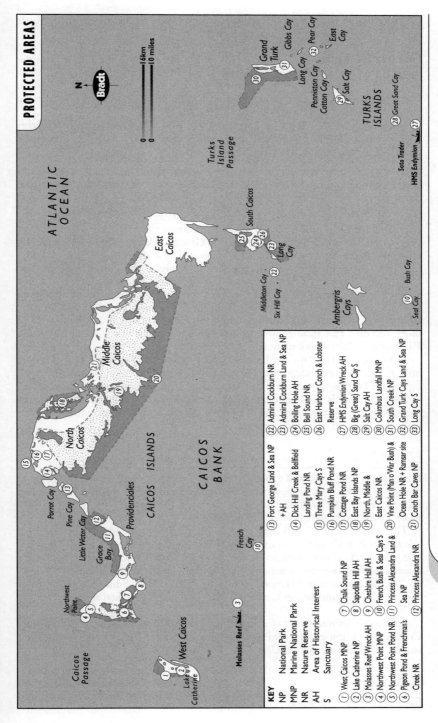

PROTECTED AREAS

ATLANTIC OCEAN

Caicos Passage

West Caicos

① ②

Lake Catherine

Northwest Point

④ ⑤

③ *Molasses Reef*

⑥ ⑨ ⑦ ⑧

Grace Bay

⑪

Little Water Cay

⑫

Providenciales

⑩ *French Cay*

Pine Cay

⑬

Parrot Cay

⑭ ⑯ ⑮ ⑰

North Caicos

⑱ ⑲

Middle Caicos

⑳ ㉑

East Caicos

CAICOS ISLANDS

CAICOS BANK

Middleton Cay · ㉒

Six Hill Cays ·

Ambergris Cays

Seal Cay ⑩ · *Bush Cay*

Turks Island Passage

South Caicos

㉕ ㉔ ㉓ ㉖

Long Cay

Soto Trader ⚓

HMS Endymion ⚓ ㉗

TURKS ISLANDS

㉘ *Great Sand Cay*

Grand Turk

㉚ ㉛ *Gibbs Cay*

Long Cay · ㉜ *Pear Cay*

Penniston Cay · *East Cay*

Cotton Cay ·

㉙ · *Salt Cay*

N

Bradt

| 0 | 16km |
| 0 | 10 miles |

KEY

NP   National Park
MNP Marine National Park
NR   Nature Reserve
AH   Area of Historical Interest
S   Sanctuary

① West Caicos MNP
② Lake Catherine NP
③ Molasses Reef Wreck AH
④ Northwest Point MNP
⑤ Northwest Point Pond NR
⑥ Pigeon Pond & Frenchman's Creek NR
⑦ Chalk Sound NP
⑧ Sapodilla Hill AH
⑨ Cheshire Hall AH
⑩ French, Bush & Seal Cays S
⑪ Princess Alexandra Land & Sea NP
⑫ Princess Alexandra NR

⑬ Fort George Land & Sea NP + AH
⑭ Dick Hill Creek & Bellfield Landing Pond NR
⑮ Three Mary Cays S
⑯ Pumpkin Bluff Pond NR
⑰ Cottage Pond NR
⑱ East Bay Islands NP
⑲ North, Middle & East Caicos NR
⑳ Vine Point (Man o'War Bush) & Ocean Hole NR + Ramsar site
㉑ Conch Bar Caves NP

㉒ Admiral Cockburn NR
㉓ Admiral Cockburn Land & Sea NP
㉔ Boiling Hole AH
㉕ Bell Sound NR
㉖ East Harbour Conch & Lobster Reserve
㉗ HMS Endymion Wreck AH
㉘ Big (Great) Sand Cay S
㉙ Salt Cay AH
㉚ Columbus Landfall MNP
㉛ South Creek NP
㉜ Grand Turk Cays Land & Sea NP
㉝ Long Cay S

(9kg) for home consumption, but international trade in them is banned. Turtle eggs and nursing females are also protected.

Conservation bodies Conservation falls within the remit of the DECR, but the work of the **Turks & Caicos National Trust** (*PO Box 540, Providenciales;* ℡ *649 941 5710;* e *tc.nattrust@tciway.tc; www.nationaltrust.tc*) in this field is not to be underestimated. The trust is involved with long-term projects to preserve the cultural, historical and natural heritage of the islands.

More widely, the Trust is supported by the **UK Overseas Territories Conservation Forum** (*www.ukotcf.org*), which aims to raise awareness about the wealth of biodiversity in the UK Overseas Territories.

PEOPLE

The islands' population in 2006 was estimated at 33,202, an increase of almost 75% since the 2001 census, when the population totalled just 19,886. Whereas the population of most of the islands has remained more or less static over that five-year period, the number of people living on Grand Turk has risen by 44% to 5,718, while the figure for Providenciales has increased by a staggering 87% to 24,348 – just over three quarters of the population, Only a third of the people are indigenous islanders, or Belongers (see box opposite). The remaining two thirds are increasingly diverse. In the last few years, there has been an influx of immigrant workers, with skilled labour coming from the Dominican Republic and Jamaica, labourers from Haiti, and others hailing from Canada, the US and Britain. Even more recently, this immigrant pool has extended to include a small but rising Filipino and Chinese population.

As recently as 1980, the total population of the islands was just 7,413, of whom only 977 lived on Providenciales; the majority of people lived on Grand Turk, with figures for both South Caicos and North Caicos higher than those for Provo. Even by 1990 the islands' total population had risen to only 11,465, but by this stage the changes in Provo were beginning to be felt – and the number of people living there had risen five fold in just ten years.

EDUCATION

Education in the Turks and Caicos Islands is compulsory and free of charge up to the age of 16. The rate of literacy has risen considerably since the mid 1980s, when it averaged 86.7%. In 2006, the figure for over 15s topped 91%, rising to 97% among youngsters aged between 15 and 24.

The government has primary schools on all the inhabited islands, and high schools on Providenciales, Grand Turk, North Caicos and South Caicos. There are also private schools operated across the age range. Pupils at secondary school study towards one of three examinations: the General Certificate of Education 'O' level (GCE), the International General Certificate of Secondary Education (IGCSE) or the Caribbean Examinations Council (CXC) exams. All are taken at around the age of 16.

For those continuing on to further education, the Turks and Caicos Community College has campuses on both Providenciales and Grand Turk. Others pursue their studies at universities in the US.

LANGUAGE

English is spoken right across the islands.

'Belonger' status is a legal classification that confers freedom from immigration restrictions, unlimited residency and voting rights. A Belonger does not require permission to work in any capacity within the islands. While Belongers are entitled to full rights of citizenship, it is important to understand that the status does not equate to nationality.

Those who qualify automatically include persons born in TCI who have at least one parent who is a Belonger, spouses of those who hold the right, and those born outside the country who have both a parent and a grandparent who are Belongers.

In exceptional circumstances Belonger status can be granted by the cabinet under the chairmanship of the governor. In such an instance it constitutes a gift dependent on a combination of criteria; for example, the length of time the individual has resided in the country, the contribution that person has made, as well as the degree of assimilation he or she has achieved within the community.

'Permanent resident' status also provides freedom with regard to length of residence and permission to work without a permit. It may be granted to 'persons of substance who have lived in the Turks and Caicos for several years, or who have made a significant investment in a project approved by the government as being of particular benefit to the islands'.

RELIGION

Belongers are for the most part very religious, and there are Christian churches throughout the islands. Most churches are built in the Bermuda style, with tall spires and stained-glass windows. Congregations are large and gregarious, welcoming visitors with enthusiasm. They sing vigorously, both traditional hymns and gospel music.

CULTURE

CRAFT

Baskets A culture of basket-weaving dates back to the years when they were used to sift corn and even carry water. The basis of these baskets is the local fanner grass, which grows on the salty shores of both North and Middle Caicos. Traditionally, the grass is harvested, dried, then prepared for weaving, with the strands sewn together by a thread made from the split palm top of the raffia plant. When finished, a well-made basket is entirely watertight; if it is turned upside down and tapped, the sound is hollow as though it were made of wood. Women still weave the baskets today, and can sometimes be seen at work near the airport on Middle Caicos. These and other crafts can be bought on Providenciales at the Middle Caicos Co-op (see page 102).

Boatbuilding The traditional boat of the islands is the sloop, a wooden craft of varying proportions which was an intrinsic part of the salt trade between Bermuda and the Turks Islands for over a century. A two-sailed, gaff-rigged boat with a narrow hull and sharply pointed prow, it is based on a Bermudan design and was still used by fishermen well into the 1980s. Then, however, as tourism development took hold and fishing became marginalised, many of the boats fell into disrepair.

Enter the Maritime Heritage Federation (📞 *946 4935,* **m** *243 2093; www.maritimeheritage.tc*), which was founded in 2005 with a view to preserving and passing on the skills inherent in building and sailing the traditional craft. From inauspicious beginnings, with just five registered sloops, today it boasts a total of 14, with a further five in production. Some of the original sailors have been persuaded to put their knowledge back into practice and numerous schoolchildren have been given the opportunity to experience a sloop at first hand. Now allied to other conservation organisations, including the World Ship Trust, the federation is active in promoting sailing events, in which everyone can participate.

MUSIC You might have to search around for the islands' traditional ripsaw music, but it is very much alive. Also known as rake 'n' scrape, it is based around a series of instruments, including a flexible handsaw, bent and shaped to the musician's satisfaction, then scraped with a metallic instrument such as a nail or screwdriver. Alongside this will be played a goatskin-covered drum, an accordion or 'constentina', maracas and an acoustic guitar. One of the best places to hear ripsaw music is on Grand Turk (see page 166).

SPORT Despite the obvious appeal of land-based sports, it's to the sea that the islands may well turn for international recognition. Following an increasing focus on the traditional sloop in recent years, moves are in hand both here and in the Bahamas to make sailing the national sport, and there are several regattas held each year.

For now, though, cricket remains the national sport, and athletics is increasingly popular. This is thanks at least in part to the large new stadium on Providenciales which was built for the CARIFTA Games in 2007. The island hosts a regular triathlon (*www.islandtriathlonseries.com*), combining a 1-mile (1.6km) swim with either a 66-mile (106km) or 33½ mile (54km) bike ride and a 13-mile (21km) or 5½-mile (9km) run. The next event will take place on 29 March 2009.

2

Planning and Preparation

WHEN TO VISIT

There are probably as many 'best' times to visit the Turks and Caicos Islands as there are types of visitors. During the early part of the year, from January to April, visitors congregate to witness the annual whale migration, which is at its peak during February and March. Divers, however, may choose to avoid the winter months when from around December the winds tend to veer to the north, sometimes bringing storms that can stir up the sea bed. At these times, the resultant loss of visibility can be considerable. That said, the opportunity to see whales from the diveboat – or from beneath the waves – is compelling compensation for the occasional rough seas or slightly murky waters.

Those in search of pure R&R often favour the summer months, from around May to October, when temperatures are uniformly in the 80s or higher, but with a cooling breeze. The latter half of the year, however, is also the period of highest rainfall, although typically rain comes in short cloudbursts rather than bringing the grey skies of more northerly latitudes. The fact that June to November is officially the hurricane 'season' in this part of the world means that prices at this time are generally lower than in winter.

When planning a trip in this latitude, it's as well to remember that darkness falls early in the winter months, no later than 5pm towards the end of the year, and that even in the summer it's dark by around 7pm.

Very occasionally, you may be lucky enough to glimpse the all-too-fleeting phenomenon known as a 'green flash', a trick of the light seen at sunset just at the point when the sun dips below the horizon. Caused by a refraction of light through the Earth's atmosphere, it occurs in periods of exceptionally dry weather, and generally forecasts a clear spell during the next 24 hours (see box page 36).

See also *Climate*, pages 18–20. For details of stargazing, see *Chapter 3*, pages 74–7.

CLIMATE STATISTICS

Figures below relate to Grand Turk. Both Providenciales and the other Caicos Islands, except for South Caicos, receive a higher level of rainfall throughout the year.

	Jan	Feb	Mar	Apr	May	Jun	Jul	Aug	Sep	Oct	Nov	Dec
AVERAGE TEMPERATURE												
°F	75.2	75.2	77	78.8	80.6	82.4	82.4	84.2	85	81.5	78.8	77
°C	24	24	25	26	27	28	28	29	28	27.5	26	25
AVERAGE MONTHLY RAINFALL												
Inches	1.41	1.34	0.98	1.41	1.54	1.61	1.69	1.57	2.64	2.95	3.66	2.71
Mm	36	34	25	36	39	41	43	40	67	75	93	69

THE ELUSIVE GREEN FLASH

To entertain any chance of catching the fugitive shot of green that might appear at the precise instant the final glimpse of the sun disappears below the horizon, absolutely clear and calm weather is best. The Turks and Caicos Islands more often than not offer optimum conditions and at the appropriately named Green Flash Café on Salt Cay there are many sightings.

The rarely witnessed sunset occurrence was first briefly acknowledged in 1869 within a paper presented by British physicist James Prescott Joule, recorded in *The Proceedings of the Manchester Literary and Philosophical Society*. Joule, by profession a brewer, was only ever an amateur scientist yet he came to be regarded as one of the finest of the 19th century. He noted 'At the moment of the departure of the sun below the horizon, the last glimpse is coloured bluish-green.'

The peculiarity was taken up a few years later by Jules Verne in his novel *Le Rayon-Vert* ('The Green Ray'), in which he describes an invented Scottish legend said to bestow an extra-sensory perception on anyone who sees the green flash, enabling that person 'to see closely into his own heart and to read the thoughts of others'.

In the 21st century, astronomer Andrew Young of San Diego State University confirms that the green flash is indeed real, a prismatic effect of the sunset more likely to be seen on a low horizon such as a seascape. Theoretically a similar burst of light can be viewed at dawn, though the beam is even less likely to be caught at that hour when it's harder to judge the exact point at which the rim of the sun will appear. Young compounds the issue by declaring the true flash to be yellow, its green colour only an optical illusion. This he says is readily confirmed by photographic imagery of the event.

Whatever the case, those who wish to catch the fleeting green flash are strongly advised not to focus on the setting sun until the final moments before it is to disappear. Even when low in the sky it has the potential to damage eyesight.

i TOURIST INFORMATION

The head office of the Turks and Caicos Tourist Board (*www.turksandcaicostourism.com*) is in Providenciales (*Regent Village, Grace Bay Rd;* ℡ *946 4970, 5746;* e *tci.tourismpls@tciway.tc*). There is also an office in Grand Turk (*Front St;* ℡ *946 2321;* e *tci.tourism@tciway.tc*).

The tourist board has offices overseas in the UK, US and Canada:

UK 42 Westminster Palace Gdns, 1–7 Artillery Row, London SW1P 1RR; ℡ 020 7222 2669; e info@tcilondon.org.uk
US *Florida* 2715 E Oakland Park Bd, Suite 101, Ft Lauderdale, FL 33306; ℡ 954 568 6588, 800 241 0824; *Miami* ℡ 786 290 6199. *New York* Rm 2817,

Lincoln Bldg, 60 East 42nd St, New York, NY10165-0015; ℡ toll free 800 241 0824
Canada 175 Bloor St East, Suite 307, South Tower, PO Box 22, Toronto ON M4W 3R8; ℡ 416 642 9771, toll free ℡ 866 413 8875; m 416 819 4319; e rwilson.tcitourism@allstream.net

Further information about the islands can be obtained from the **Government Information Service** (*Hibiscus Sq; Grand Turk;* ℡ *946 2801 ext. 40916/40917;* e *gis@gov.tc, tcigis@gmail.com; www.turksandcaicosislands.gov.tc*). The website was under construction in 2008.

HIGHLIGHTS

Early visitors to the Turks and Caicos Islands came for the **diving** (pages 63–8), and the islands with their sheer walls remain justifiably popular for those seeking the attractions of the underwater world. Probably the most spectacular of these, the annual migration of **humpback whales**, is best viewed from above the waves, with boat trips arranged by operators on most of the islands but especially South Caicos and the Turks Islands (pages 72–3). The sea is a powerful draw, too, for both **sailors** – whether visiting yachtsmen or those seeking the more immediate thrills offered by craft such as Hobie-Cats or kiteboards (page 74) – and **anglers** (see pages 69–72), while the more hedonistic can bask in the powder-white sands of **Grace Bay** (pages 118–19) or seek out their own secluded beach.

On land, Provo's **golf** course (pages 117–18) provides its own challenges, not least the vagaries of the trade winds, while the less competitive can indulge in a spot of **birdwatching** or **hike** the trails of North and Middle Caicos (pages 73–4). **Horseriders**, too, will find something to suit, with the opportunity to ride along the beaches of Providenciales or Grand Turk (pages 118 and 169).

But the highlights are by no means limited to activity. For all the gloss and sophistication of recent development, island culture remains firmly rooted in history. Ruined **plantations** on the Caicos Islands (pages 119–20, 132 and 137) tell of the infamy of the slave trade as much as the crumbling warehouses and long-disused **salinas** of South Caicos and the Turks Islands (pages 149, 174 and 175). Their dereliction brings rewards for the nature lover as well as for the historian, and their story – along with that of the Lucayan Indians as evidenced in the **caves** of Middle Caicos (pages 137–8) – is told in the excellent **museum** on Grand Turk (pages 172–3).

TURKS AND CAICOS FOR SPECIFIC GROUPS

FAMILIES Providenciales makes an excellent holiday choice for families, not least because it boasts two all-inclusive resorts – Beaches and Club Med – where there's plenty to do for all age groups, and no hidden charges. But even those staying in conventional accommodation will find no shortage of attractions. Hotel rooms that routinely sleep four; a good range of restaurants and ice-cream parlours; and the shallow waters and pristine sands of Grace Bay – what more could a family want? Given about 24 hours' notice, several hotels can help with babysitting, charging from around $10 per child per hour. Some of the resorts have kids' clubs, enabling parents to indulge their own interests while their children are having a whale of a time elsewhere. The range of watersports, from snorkelling and kayaking to parasailing, could keep older children and teenagers occupied from morning to night, while the less water-orientated could always try karting or mini golf, or perhaps head to the sports centre for inline skating.

Families visiting the other islands will find less in the way of organised activities, so will generally need to be more resourceful. For some that's a significant plus; for others it's something of a warning.

DISABLED VISITORS with thanks to Gordon Rattray, www.able-travel.com
The islands are predominantly flat, making them generally excellent venues for those with physical disabilities. On Providenciales and Grand Turk, in particular, good tarred roads and pavements make it relatively straightforward to get around. Note, though, that most of the taxi companies use minibuses rather than saloon cars, which can make access difficult for wheelchair users or 'slow walkers'.

Many of the larger hotels, including the Sands at Grace Bay and Turtle Cove Inn on Provo, have public areas and rooms that are navigable in a wheelchair. Club Med Turkoise on Provo also has one room that has features for those with reduced mobility. Many have boardwalks leading to the beach, although the beaches themselves can pose a problem for those in a wheelchair. The trails on North and Middle Caicos have not been designed with access in mind – the ground is uneven

WEDDINGS FOR OVERSEAS VISITORS

The prospect of a beachside wedding is no longer the preserve of the rich and famous, and many of Turks and Caicos' hotels haven't been slow to cotton on. Several resorts have their own wedding co-ordinators, to ensure that the whole occasion will go smoothly, but there are also specialist wedding organisers who will take care of the event. And if a beach wedding doesn't work for you, there's also the option of tying the knot on a boat, through Providenciales' operators Silver Deep (see page 114), or Sail Provo (see page 116).

No matter where the ceremony is held, it will be conducted by a licensed marriage officer – usually a local minister or a justice of the peace – who is key to the organisation of the ceremony. Couples need to be resident for a minimum of 72 hours before they can apply to the marriage officer for a licence, which costs $50. Once the marriage officer has sent the application to the Registrar General for Special Licenses, it takes two to three days to process, and only when the licence has been granted can the ceremony take place. The minimum age to be married on the islands is 16 (with parental consent if under 21). The authorities are not authorised to conduct gay weddings.

DOCUMENTS Anyone planning a wedding on the islands must provide the following documents in person to the designated marriage officer; documentation cannot be taken in by a third party. All documents must be originals, and should be accompanied by verified photocopies:

- Passport
- Birth certificate
- Proof of status (if single, a sworn affidavit; if divorced, a divorce decree; if widowed, a death certificate)
- Proof of any change of name by deed poll or adoption
- A letter stating for each person their occupation, marital status, age at last birthday, present address and father's full name
- Proof of church membership for church weddings
- Written consent from one or both parents or a guardian for those who are under 21

WEDDING PLANNERS The following specialists will organise everything from the licence, marriage officer and witnesses to the venue, catering, flowers and entertainment:

Nila Destinations m 231 3986; US ☎ 519 512 2009; e nila@niladestinations.com; www.nilavacations.com
Tropical Destination Management Providenciales; ☎ +1 403 668 0739; m 231 4161; e tbrunner@tropicaldmc.com; www.tropicaldmc.com

For further information, and a full list of both marriage officers and companies offering wedding services, see www.turksandcaicos.tc/weddings/index.htm, or contact the Registry of Births, Deaths and Marriages (☎ 926 2800).

and there is no man-made seating – so for the most part they will suit only the most mobile of disabled hikers.

OVERSEAS WORKERS The number of expatriate workers on the Turks and Caicos Islands is lower than you might think, although it is still significant. Most come from Haiti, the Dominican Republic and the British Caribbean islands. Various clubs and societies are run or heavily supported by overseas workers, from charitable foundations such as the animal rescue organisation TCSPCA to amateur dramatics and sports.

Those used to a broader canvas may get the urge to escape from the confines of a small island occasionally, if only to Miami for the shopping. TCI's location on the eastern fringes of the Caribbean makes the Dominican Republic a popular getaway choice, along with the neighbouring Bahamas.

If you are intending to work or take up residence on the islands, see pages 33 and 60–1.

TOUR OPERATORS

While significant numbers of visitors book direct, many tour operators are in a position to negotiate favourable deals, and to offer advice on the best places for your particular circumstances, although few go beyond Provo, and even then tend to have a very limited choice of accommodation. Hotels can also be booked online through the Turks and Caicos Hotel and Tourism Association (*www.turksandcaicoshta.com*).

UK

Abercrombie & Kent ⟍ 0845 618 2200; www.abercrombiekent.co.uk. Upmarket resorts on Providenciales & Parrot Cay.

British Airways Holidays ⟍ 0844 493 0759; www.britishairways.com. Range of resorts on Provo from luxury to mid range.

Caribbean Vacations ⟍ 0800 018 4401; www.caribbean-vacations.co.uk. Good range of 3–5-star hotels on Providenciales.

Caribtours ⟍ 020 7751 0660; www.caribtours.co.uk. Upmarket resorts on Providenciales & Parrot Cay.

Carrier ⟍ 0161 491 7620; www.carrier.co.uk. Providenciales & Parrot Cay.

Elegant Resorts ⟍ 01244 897999; www.elegantresorts.co.uk. Providenciales & Parrot Cay.

Harlequin Worldwide ⟍ 0845 450 6433; www.harlequinholidays.com. Upmarket hotel & dive holidays, covering Providenciales, Parrot Cay & Pine Cay.

Hayes & Jarvis ⟍ 0871 200 4422; www.hayesandjarvis.co.uk. Focuses on Beaches resort.

ITC Classics ⟍ 01244 355300; www.itcclassics.co.uk. Upmarket resorts on Providenciales & Parrot Cay.

Kuoni Travel ⟍ 01306 747002; www.kuoni.co.uk. Tailormade and package holidays using 3- to 5-star hotels on Providenciales.

La Joie de Vivre ⟍ 01483 272379; www.lajoiedevivre.co.uk. Luxury spa holiday specialists featuring Provo & Parrot Cay.

Seasons in Style ⟍ 01244 202 000; www.seasonsinstyle.com. Exclusive operator, covering Providenciales & Parrot Cay.

Scott Dunn ⟍ 020 8682 5020; www.scottdunn.com

Thomas Cook Holidays ⟍ 0870 750 5711; www.thomascook.com

Tradewinds ⟍ 0871 664 7964; www.tradewinds.co.uk

UK dive operators

Barefoot Traveller ⟍ 020 8741 4319; www.barefoot-traveller.com. Covering Providenciales, Grand Turk & Salt Cay, as well as the *Turks & Caicos Aggressor*.

Divequest ⟍ 01254 826322; www.divequest.co.uk. Covers Grand Turk and both liveaboard options.

Dive Worldwide ⟍ 0845 130 6980; e info@diveworldwide.com; www.diveworldwide.com.

Tailormade & package dive holidays to Providenciales, Grand Turk and Salt Cay.

Regal Dive ⟍ 01353 659999; www.regal-diving.co.uk. Providenciales only.

Scuba Safaris ⟍ 01342 823222; www.scuba-safaris.com. Providenciales and both liveaboards.

US Of the numerous tour operators in the US that cover the Turks and Caicos Islands, this is just a small selection; all feature Providenciales only.

Delta Vacations ⟍ 800 654 6559; www.deltavacations.com

Liberty Travel ⟍ 888 271 1584; www.libertytravel.com

TNT Vacations ⟍ 888 468 6846; www.tntvacations.com

2

Travel Impressions www.travimp.com

Vacation Express ☎ 800 309 4717; www.vacationexpress.com

US dive operators

Caradonna Caribbean Tours ☎ 800 328 2288; www.caradonna.com. Diving on both Provo & Grand Turk, as well as the *Turks & Caicos Explorer*.

Caribbean Dive Tours ☎ 800 786 3483; www.cdtusa.com

Scuba Planners ☎ 336 505 1127; toll free ☎ 866 436 6158; www.scubaplanners.com.

US Dive Travel ☎ 952 953 4124; e divetrip@bitstream.net; www.usdivetravel.com. Provo, Grand Turk & both liveaboards.

World Dive Adventures ☎ 800 433 3483; www.worlddive.com. Range of options on Provo & Grand Turk.

CANADA

Air Canada Vacations ☎ 866 529 2079; www.aircanadavacations.com. 3–5-star hotels on Provo only.

Total Vacations ☎ 1 800 769 4147; www.totalvacations.ca

RED TAPE

IMMIGRATION AND CUSTOMS A valid passport is needed by all visitors, but visas are required only by nationals of countries in the former Eastern Bloc.

All visitors must hold an onward or return ticket as a condition of entry, and sufficient funds to last for the duration of their stay. Most visitors are issued with a visa on arrival permitting a stay of up to 30 days, renewable only once. Applications to extend a visa should be made to the Immigration Department, which has its headquarters on Grand Turk (*South Base;* ☎ *946 2939;* e *iam@tciway.tc; www.immigration.tc*), and a second office on Providenciales (*opposite Town Center Mall, Leeward Highway*).

Visitors are issued with a white immigration card on arrival. This should be kept with your passport or other travel document and given up on departure. Those wishing to work on the islands need to apply in advance for a work permit (see *Working in the Turks and Caicos Islands*, page 60). Owners of property worth more than $250,000 are eligible to apply for permanent residency.

Pet owners are free to take their animals to the islands, provided that all vaccinations are up to date and that the animal has the requisite documents, such as a permit or valid animal passport, and an official health certificate issued by the authorities in the country of origin within one month of travel stating that the animal is free of infectious and contagious diseases and has been vaccinated against rabies and distemper. This certificate must be presented to the public health inspector.

DUTY-FREE GOODS Visitors over 18 are permitted to take in 1.136 litres of wine or spirits, up to 200 cigarettes and 50 cigars, and perfume for personal use. The only goods subject to an import restriction are spearguns, Hawaiian slings and – of course – firearms, pornography and controlled drugs. For any queries on the import of goods, contact the Customs Department (☎ *946 4241, 4776*). There are no exchange controls.

When returning home, visitors from the US are permitted to take goods up to a total value of $800, while those from the UK have an allowance of £145.

Ⓔ EMBASSIES There are no embassies or consulates on the Turks and Caicos Islands. American citizens in need of help should contact the US Embassy in Nassau (☎ *242 322 1181, 242 328 2206, http://nassau.usembassy.gov*), which has responsibility for visitors to the islands. All other travellers should get in touch with the local authorities in the event of an emergency.

GETTING THERE

✈ **BY AIR** There are direct flights to the islands from the UK, US and Canada, as well as the neighbouring islands of the Bahamas, the Dominican Republic, Haiti and Jamaica. A departure tax of $35, payable by all visitors over the age of two, is normally incorporated in the price of an airline ticket.

From the UK British Airways has one direct flight a week from London to Providenciales. Flights leave London Heathrow at 09.50 on Sunday morning, with a flight time of 12 hours. The return flight leaves at 19.10 in the evening, arriving in London at 11.05 the next day. Prices in economy, based on booking at least six months in advance, are from around £800 return, with Club World tickets coming out at around £3,850. There is currently no first-class service on this route.

Via the USA Numerous operators, including British Airways, American Airlines and Virgin Atlantic, connect London Heathrow with **Miami**, from where American Airlines operates three flights a day to Providenciales (see below). The trip to Miami takes about eight and a half hours. Fares vary according to the time of year, day of travel and duration of stay, but for guidance a mid-week economy return fare based on a two-week trip in summer 2008 would set you back some £650, rising to an eye-watering £7,000 in first class. It's worth noting that special deals abound on this route, so it's worth keeping an eye out for these if the timing isn't crucial.

Remember to allow a reasonable period of time in Miami to change flights, particularly over public holiday periods. It's a busy – some say chaotic – airport at the best of times, and delays in the immigration hall can be significant.

Via the Bahamas Flying via the Bahamas (see below) will most likely necessitate a lay-over. If this is your preferred route, there is an excellent hotel close to the airport:

Orange Hill Beach Inn West Bay St, Nassau, New Providence; ☎ 242 327 7157; e info@ orangehill.com; www.orangehill.com. A reasonably priced hotel just 1.5 miles (2.4km) or a 5-min taxi ride ($10+ $1 tip) from the airport, this is unlike anything else in Nassau, which is 8 miles (13km) away, or indeed in New Providence. Set above a quiet beach, ideal for a quick swim, it's a Caribbean pastel low-rise building, with a raffish character. Judy & Danny Lowe welcome overnighters: 'some of our guests never leave, but stay on as quasi-staff'. There's a coin-op laundry; AC; in-room coffee-maker; fridge; WiFI, & a pool. The good, brief dinner menu includes delicious johnny cake direct from the oven, & local lobster tail at $26. Would that every short-stop airport had such a hotel close by! $$ (+12% tax); restaurant $$$

From the US and Canada Several North American airlines fly in to Providenciales (PLS), but the only one to connect with Grand Turk (GDT), Spirit Air, currently has no direct flights.

American Airlines operates three flights a day from **Miami**, taking 1¼ hours. American also has daily direct flights from New York (3hrs), and weekly flights from Boston (3¼hrs) and Dallas (4½hrs).

US Airways flies daily from both **Charlotte**, North Carolina (daily) and **Philadelphia**, Pennsylvania (once a week), taking 2¼ hours and 2¾ hours respectively. At weekends, there are additional flights to and from Charlotte.

Delta Airlines connects the island with Atlanta in a two-hour flight which operates from one day a week to daily, depending on the season. The smaller Spirit Airlines has one flight a week from Fort Lauderdale to Providenciales, on a Sunday, taking 75 minutes each way, but its service to Grand Turk has been discontinued.

From Canada, there is currently just one option, with Air Canada, which flies twice a week from **Toronto** (3½hrs).

From the Bahamas Both SkyKing (five flights a week) and Bahamas Air (three flights) connect Nassau with Providenciales, taking just 45 minutes

From the Dominican Republic and Haiti The nearest island to the Turks and Caicos is Hispaniola, comprising the Dominican Republic and Haiti. Flights to Puerta Plata and Santiago in the Dominican Republic, and Cap Haitian and Port au Prince in Haiti, are operated by SkyKing and Air Turks and Caicos.

From Jamaica Both Montego Bay and Kingston are linked to Provo by SkyKing (four flights a week) and Air Turks and Caicos.

Internal flights For details of internal flights, see pages 49–50.

Airlines

Air Canada (AC) US ☎ 888 247 2262 (toll free); 514 393 3333; UK ☎ 0871 220 1111; www.aircanada.com
Air Jamaica (JM) www.airjamaica.com
Air Turks & Caicos (JY) ☎ 946 4999; www.flyairtc.com
American Airlines (AA) US ☎ 800 433 7300; UK ☎ 020 7365 0777; www.aa.com
Bahamas Air (UP) US ☎ 800 222 4262; www.bahamasair.com

British Airways (BA) US ☎ 800 AIRWAYS; UK ☎ 0844 493 0787; www.britishairways.com
Delta Airlines (DL) US ☎ 800 221 1212, 404 765 5000; UK ☎ 0845 600 0950; www.delta.com
SkyKing Airlines (QW) ☎ 941 3136; www.skyking.tc
Spirit Airlines (NK) www.spiritair.com
US Airways (US) US ☎ 800 428 4322; www.usairways.com
Virgin Atlantic (VS) UK ☎ 0870 380 2007; www.virgin-atlantic.com

Private aircraft In addition to the landing facilities on each of the inhabited islands, there is an airstrip on Pine Cay (*www.pine-cay.com*), where visiting pilots are welcome. For detailed information on flying into the islands, see the *Bahamas and Caribbean Pilot's Guide* (*Pilot Publishing, www.pilotpub.com*).

BY SEA

Cruise ships With no natural deep-water harbour, the Turks and Caicos Islands have long been off limits for cruise ships. In 2006, however, the first vessels docked at the southern tip of Grand Turk with the opening of the controversial Cruise Center (*www.grandturkcc.com*). The centre is equipped to take two passenger ships at a time, although further ships can anchor off shore with passengers being ferried ashore by tender. During the peak season, from December to April, there are often at least two a day in harbour, whereas later in the year this can drop to just one or two a week.

Cruise-ship operators featuring Grand Turk in their itineraries include the following:

Carnival ☎ +1 888 CARNIVAL; www.carnival.com
Crystal Cruises ☎ +1 888 722 0021; www.crystalcruises.com
Costa Cruises ☎ +1 877 88 COSTA; www.costacruise.com

Cunard ☎ +44 (0)845 678 0013; www.cunard.co.uk
Fred Olsen ☎ +44 (0)1473 746175; www.fredolsencruises.com
Hebridean International ☎ +44 (0)1756 704704, +1 800 659 2648; www.hebridean.co.uk

Holland America ☎ +1 877 932 4259; www.hollandamerica.com
Oceana Cruise Line ☎ +1 866 765 3630; www.oceaniacruises.com
Regent Seven Seas ☎ +1 877 505 5370; www.rssc.com

Seabourn ☎ +1 800 929 9391; www.seabourn.com
Silversea ☎ +44 (0)870 333 7030, +1 800 722 9955; www.silversea.com

Private yachts With their location on the eastern fringes of the Caribbean, the Turks and Caicos have long been popular with visiting yachtsmen, particularly during the relatively settled first three months of the year. The prevailing easterly trade winds from the Atlantic blow at an average 14mph or 22km/h (force 5), although the islands are at risk of hurricanes between June and November (see page 19), while at the end of the year the wind sometimes veers to the northeast, bringing periods of unsettled weather. Information on tides, based on Sandy Point in North Caicos, can be found at www.tides.info.

Visiting yachts should use one of the designated ports of entry on Providenciales (see *Marinas*, pages 114–15), Grand Turk (*Government wharf*, ☎ 946 2993) or South Caicos (*Government Dock*), having called in advance on VHF 16. There's also North Creek on Grand Turk, which offers the only shelter for yachts en route between Nassau and Puerto Rico. All crew members should have a valid passport.

Charts A good chart is essential in order to navigate through the islands' fringing reefs. Wavey Line Publishing (*www.waveylinepublishing.com*) has a series of detailed waterproof charts covering the Turks and Caicos. The overview chart, number TC001, covers the whole island group, with details of individual ports on the reverse. Two larger-scale charts focus separately on Providenciales and the Turks Islands, again with details of marinas on the reverse. Charts are available from the publisher at $28 each, plus shipping.

Alternatively, there are those published by the British Admiralty (*www.admiraltyshop.co.uk*). Number 3907 features the Caicos Islands, and 1441 the islands of Grand Turk and Salt Cay. A third chart, number 1450, bridges the gap, focusing on South Caicos and the surrounding cays and extending to Grand Turk.

✚ HEALTH

PREPARATIONS There are no immunisation requirements for visitors to the Turks and Caicos Islands, although as a matter of course visitors should be up to date on polio, diphtheria and tetanus inoculations, as they would be at home. It is also worth considering routine vaccination against hepatitis A if you are a lover of seafood. This is a general precaution with seafood anywhere in the world, since shellfish are scavengers. Malaria is not a risk.

All visitors should take – and use – plenty of high-factor suncream, especially during the summer months when the cooling tradewinds can mask the intensity of the sun's rays. If you're planning to spend time snorkelling, consider wearing a T-shirt and perhaps bermuda shorts to protect the backs of your legs.

The incidence of HIV/AIDS on the islands, although low, is on the increase, so if you're tempted to indulge in a holiday fling, be sure that you're properly protected. Be aware, too, that dengue fever is endemic on neighbouring Haiti, and that the number of outbreaks of the disease in the eastern Caribbean is rising. There is no prophylactic that works against dengue fever, which is spread by day-biting mosquitoes, so it's sensible to take precautions against insect bites throughout the year. Use an insect repellent that contains around 50–55% of the chemical DEET and make sure you reapply after swimming.

Dr Jane Wilson-Howarth

Long-haul air travel increases the risk of deep vein thrombosis (DVT). Although recent research has suggested that many of us develop clots when immobilised, most resolve without us ever having been aware of them. In certain susceptible individuals, though, clots form on clots and when large ones break away and lodge in the lungs this is dangerous. Fortunately this happens in a tiny minority of passengers.

Studies have shown that flights of over five and a half hours are significant, and that people who take lots of shorter flights over a short space of time can also form clots. People at highest risk are:

- Those who have had a clot before – unless they are now taking warfarin
- People over 80 years of age
- Anyone who has recently undergone a major operation or surgery for varicose veins
- Someone who has had a hip or knee replacement in the last three months
- Cancer sufferers
- Those who have ever had a stroke
- People with heart disease
- Those with a close blood relative who has had a clot

Those with a slightly increased risk are:

- People over 40
- Women who are pregnant or have had a baby in the last couple of weeks
- People taking female hormones, the combined contraceptive pill or other oestrogen therapy
- Heavy smokers
- Those who have very severe varicose veins
- The very obese
- People who are very tall (over 6ft/1.8m) or short (under 5ft/1.5m)

All visitors should take sufficient prescription medicines to last throughout their trip. Should you run out while you are on TCI, note that pharmacies may only fulfil prescriptions issued on the islands.

INSURANCE There is no free medical provision for visitors, nor any reciprocal agreement with the UK National Health Service, so it is important to take out suitable travel insurance, with significant health cover. This must also cover the cost of emergency air transport should a transfer be necessary, either from one of the smaller islands to Grand Turk or Provo, or – in the case of a serious emergency – to hospital in the USA. If you're planning to dive, do make certain that this is covered by your policy.

LOCAL HEALTH FACILITIES There are small government hospitals on both Providenciales (✆ *941 3000*) and Grand Turk (✆ *946 2333*), both of which have been earmarked for upgrading in the near future. There are also government clinics on both islands, as well as on North, Middle and South Caicos. In addition, there are several private clinics on Provo. For divers, the only decompression chamber is at the private Associated Medical clinic on Provo (*Medical Bldg, Leeward Hwy;* ✆ *946 4242; www.doctor.tc*).

Those with serious conditions that cannot be treated on the islands will be taken by air to hospital in the USA.

A deep vein thrombosis is a blood clot that forms in the deep leg veins. This is very different from irritating but harmless superficial phlebitis. DVT causes swelling and redness of one leg, usually with heat and pain in one calf and sometimes the thigh. A DVT is only dangerous if a clot breaks away and travels to the lungs (pulmonary embolus). Symptoms of a pulmonary embolus (PE) include chest pain that is worse on breathing in deeply, shortness of breath, and sometimes coughing up small amounts of blood. The symptoms commonly start three to ten days after a long flight. Anyone who thinks that they might have a DVT needs to see a doctor immediately who will arrange a scan. Warfarin tablets (to thin the blood) are then taken for at least six months.

PREVENTION OF DVT Several conditions make the problem more likely. Immobility is the key, and factors like reduced oxygen in cabin air and dehydration may also contribute. To reduce the risk of thrombosis on a long journey:

EXERCISE BEFORE AND AFTER THE FLIGHT
- Keep mobile before and during the flight; move around every couple of hours
- Drink plenty of water or juices during the flight
- Avoid taking sleeping pills and excessive tea, coffee and alcohol
- Perform exercises that mimic walking and tense the calf muscles
- Consider wearing flight socks or support stockings (see www.legshealth.com)
- Ideally take a meal each week of oily fish (mackerel, trout, salmon, sardines, etc) ahead of your departure. This reduces the blood's ability to clot and thus DVT risk. It may even be worth just taking a meal of oily fish 24 hours before departure if this is more practical.

If you think you are at increased risk of a clot, ask your doctor if it is safe to travel.

There are several pharmacies in tourist areas on Providenciales, and one on Grand Turk, although their stock is inevitably more limited than that held by pharmacies at home.

WATER The water supply combines rainfall with desalinated water produced by reverse osmosis. It is generally considered safe to drink, if not always particularly pleasant, but outside of the main tourist area on Providenciales it would be wise to stick to bottled water. Bottled water is widely available from shops and supermarkets, as well as in restaurants.

SAFETY

The islands, with their traditional emphasis on the family, are generally considered to be safe, both in terms of property and of personal safety. That said, use the same common sense as you would at home. Don't leave valuables unattended on the beach or in a car. In Providenciales at least, remember to keep doors locked, and don't wander around alone after dark outside of tourist areas. Long empty strips of the beach between hotels are best avoided at night. It also makes sense to avoid unlicensed taxis. Women travellers need take no particular precautions.

If you're heading off the beaten track, do take plenty of water, and be sure you can recognise poisonous plants such as the poisonwood or manchineel.

Ariadne Van Zandbergen

EQUIPMENT Although with some thought and an eye for composition you can take reasonable photos with a 'point-and-shoot' camera, you need an SLR camera if you are at all serious about photography. Modern SLRs tend to be very clever, with automatic programmes for almost every possible situation, but remember that these programmes are limited in the sense that the camera cannot think, but only make calculations. Every starting amateur photographer should read a photographic manual for beginners and get to grips with such basics as the relationship between aperture and shutter speed.

Always buy the best lens you can afford. The lens determines the quality of your photo more than the camera body. Fixed fast lenses are ideal, but very costly. A zoom lens makes it easier to change composition without changing lenses the whole time. If you carry only one lens, a 28–70mm (digital 17–55mm) or similar zoom should be ideal. For a second lens, a lightweight 80–200mm or 70–300mm (digital 55–200mm) or similar will be excellent for candid shots and varying your composition. Wildlife photography will be very frustrating if you don't have at least a 300mm lens. For a small loss of quality, tele-converters are a cheap and compact way to increase magnification: a 300 lens with a 1.4x converter becomes 420mm, and with a 2x it becomes 600mm. Note, however, that 1.4x and 2x tele-converters reduce the speed of your lens by 1.4 and 2 stops respectively.

Modern dedicated flash units are easy to use; aside from the obvious need to flash when you photograph at night, you can improve a lot of photos in difficult 'high contrast' or very dull light with some fill-in flash. It pays to have a proper flash unit as opposed to a built-in camera flash.

DIGITAL/FILM Digital photography is now the preference of most amateur and professional photographers, with the resolution of digital cameras improving all the time. For ordinary prints a 6-megapixel camera is fine. For better results and the possibility to enlarge images and for professional reproduction, higher resolution is available up to 16 megapixels.

Memory space is important. The number of pictures you can fit on a memory card depends on the quality you choose. Calculate in advance how many pictures you can fit on a card and either take enough cards to last for your trip, or take a storage drive onto which you can download the content. A laptop gives the advantage that you can see your

For extended journeys beyond the tarred roads a reliable 4x4 is recommended, as well as a mobile phone – although these may not work in more isolated areas. Should you be unlucky enough to break down after dark it may be difficult to persuade someone to come out and rescue you.

Possession of narcotic drugs is illegal, and penalties for both possession and trafficking are severe.

MARINE SAFETY Safety on and around the sea is an important issue on islands renowned for both diving and sailing. In addition to the precautions you would always take when snorkelling or diving, watch out for currents when swimming near headlands, and for rocks just beneath the surface. Take care, too, where you put your feet – the sea urchins in these waters are huge, and poisonous stonefish can be difficult to see against the camouflage of the rocks. Underwater, divers and snorkellers should avoid cutting themselves on the coral, as such wounds tend to heal slowly. If you remember that you shouldn't touch the coral, then it can't harm you!

pictures properly at the end of each day and edit and delete rejects, but a storage device is lighter and less bulky. These drives come in different capacities up to 80GB.

Bear in mind that digital camera batteries, computers and other storage devices need charging, so make sure you have all the chargers, cables and converters with you; a spare battery is invaluable.

If you are shooting film, 100 to 200 ISO print film and 50 to 100 ISO slide film are ideal. Low ISO film is slow but fine grained and gives the best colour saturation, but will need more light, so support in the form of a tripod or monopod is important. You can also bring a few 'fast' 400 ISO films for low-light situations where a tripod or flash is no option.

DUST AND HEAT Dust and heat are often a problem. Keep your equipment in a sealed bag, stow films in an airtight container (eg: a small cooler bag) and avoid exposing equipment and film to the sun. Digital cameras are prone to collecting dust particles on the sensor which results in spots on the image. The dirt mostly enters the camera when changing lenses, so be careful when doing this. To some extent photos can be 'cleaned' up afterwards in Photoshop, but this is time-consuming. You can have your camera sensor professionally cleaned, or you can do this yourself with special brushes and swabs made for the purpose, but note that touching the sensor might cause damage and should only be done with the greatest care.

LIGHT The most striking outdoor photographs are often taken during the hour or two of 'golden light' after dawn and before sunset. Shooting in low light may enforce the use of very low shutter speeds, in which case a tripod will be required to avoid camera shake.

With careful handling, side lighting and back lighting can produce stunning effects, especially in soft light and at sunrise or sunset. Generally, however, it is best to shoot with the sun behind you. When photographing animals or people in the harsh midday sun, images taken in light but even shade are likely to be more effective than those taken in direct sunlight or patchy shade, since the latter conditions create too much contrast.

For hints on underwater photography, see page 68.

Ariadne Van Zandbergen (www.africaimagelibrary.co.za) is a professional travel and wildlife photographer.

WHAT TO TAKE

Aside from the normal clothes that you would take on holiday to a warm climate, it's worth thinking about the following, although if you do forget something vital, the chances are that a reasonable replacement can be found locally.

- Snorkel, mask and fins
- Dive equipment if you have it – renting is easy but expensive
- Dive certification
- Suncream and sunhat
- Insect repellent
- Prescription medicines
- National or international driving licence
- Camera equipment (remember that so-called 'underwater' disposable cameras cannot be used for diving). See *Photographic tips*, above.
- Binoculars

- Light sweater or similar for air-conditioned restaurants and for evenings during the winter months, as well as for boat trips.
- Light waterproof jacket
- Good walking shoes if you plan to walk on the Caicos Islands' trails

$ MONEY AND BANKING

The unit of currency is the US dollar ($), which is subdivided into 100 cents. There are six banknotes, in denominations of 1, 5, 10, 20, 50 and 100 dollars, and six coins, respectively for 1, 5, 10, 25 and 50 cents and 1 dollar. Non-American visitors used to a greater differentiation between individual notes will need to take particular care not to hand over the wrong denomination by mistake; they're easily confused! Despite the islands' affinity to the UK, the British pound is not generally in circulation.

The **rate of exchange** against the US dollar in July 2008 was: £1 = $2, €1 = $1.58.

CREDIT CARDS As you would expect from a major offshore banking location, Amex, MasterCard, Visa and Diners' Club credit cards are widely accepted in hotels, restaurants, shops and other tourist outlets.

TRAVELLERS' CHEQUES US dollar travellers' cheques may be used like cash in shops etc, provided that you have some form of identification, such as a passport. Alternatively, you can change them for cash at the bank. Some banks will also change sterling, Canadian dollar and euro travellers' cheques and currency; see entries for individual banks. In the event of loss or theft of travellers' cheques, contact the issuer immediately; details will be provided with your cheques.

BANKING Banking hours are normally 8.30am–4.30pm, Monday to Friday, with the new TCI Bank also open on Saturday mornings. It is wise to avoid Fridays when queues can be very long. There are ATMs at several banks and supermarkets on Providenciales and Grand Turk, but you'll need to look for one of the Scotiabank machines; those operated by First Caribbean may be used only by account holders. Even then, don't let your cash supplies run too low, as machines all too frequently run out of money, especially at weekends.

BUDGETING The cost of living on the islands is high, and the tourist dollar doesn't go far, particularly as virtually all food and goods have to be imported, and are subject to a blanket import duty of 30%. That said, with both the pound and the euro riding high against the US dollar in 2008, prices don't seem quite as high for Europeans as they have in the past. As an indication, expect to pay around $1 for a postcard, or $3.40 for a loaf of bread in a supermarket. A small bottle of water in a bar will cost around $2, while the going rate for a bottled beer is about $5. All hotel and restaurant prices are subject to 10% government tax which may be included in the quoted price.

For a two-course meal for two people in a mid-range restaurant with local specialities and a bottle of wine, expect to pay upwards of $120, including tax and gratuity. In a bar, a one-course meal for two, with beer, is more likely to be around $65. And if you fancy a takeaway pizza, you're looking in the region of $8 a head.

It would be possible to spend a small fortune if money were no object, but by being reasonably sensible two people on a mid-range budget would be fine on $400 per day, in low season (mid April to mid December), based on a six-night stay, as follows:

Hotel (with kitchenette & breakfast, inc tax)	$148
Lunch (self catering)	$10
Dinner	$120
Water (large bottle, from supermarket)	$2
Beers x 2	$10
Transport (car hire + fuel)	$90
Sundries (ice-cream, postcards, museum)	$20

These rates exclude activities such as diving and other watersports. On Providenciales, allow about $110 per person per day for a two-tank boat dive, exclusive of equipment, or $75 per person based on a six-night package. Many hotels, dive operators and car-rental companies offer the seventh day free, so do check this out if time allows.

Turks and Caicos on the cheap Those on a tight budget could be in for a shock, but even in Providenciales it's possible to keep costs down, particularly if you're prepared to explore beyond the tourist hotspots. Visit the islands out of season, from mid April to mid December, when it's quieter and prices are lower. Two can stay for the price of one in most places, and four will cost even less per person, so it's cheaper not to travel alone. Accommodation is available at the lower end of the range if you hunt around – try Turtle Cove Inn on Provo, where costs are from $100 per room. Transport on Providenciales using a combination of walking, one of the private bus services and maybe a hired scooter for a day or two is the most realistic.

While eating in is an option, you're not going to experience much of the TCI culture that way. On the other hand, this offers the opportunity to visit one of the islands' chicken shacks, where you'll be vying with the locals for chicken and chips to take home, or perhaps to the beach. Alternatively, prepare a picnic lunch, and buy drinks from one of the supermarkets too – or drink tap water; it's usually safe, though if in doubt ask first. When eating out, remember that lunchtime menus are usually considerably more affordable than those offered in the evening. Alternatively, try one of the more local restaurants and fill up on jerked chicken with rice and peas at a fraction of the price you'd pay on Grace Bay. Happy hours are a great source of budget succour, and as for entertainment, bring your own mask, snorkel and fins or a pair of binoculars and you'll be ready for endless hours of pleasure at absolutely no cost.

TIPPING Tipping is expected in restaurants and other service-orientated establishments. The norm is 15%, which is frequently added to the bill in restaurants and elsewhere, so do check. Many – if not most – hotels will add a gratuity of 10% to the room bill. Should you wish to reward someone for special service, it is wise to give it direct. In many hotels more than one maid may be responsible for cleaning your room and if you leave a departure tip on the side, chances are that the housekeeper will take it for general distribution.

There is no outright requirement to tip a taxi driver, although this is becoming the norm for good service – in which case 10–15% is about right. Other services for which a tip is usually considered appropriate are in the diving, horseriding, tour guiding, and beauty and spa industries.

GETTING AROUND

♣ BY AIR Scheduled flights between the islands are operated by both Air Turks and Caicos and SkyKing, the latter limiting its operations to South Caicos and Grand

Turk. For details, see *Getting there* in the individual island chapters. Both companies can also arrange charter flights, as can Global Airways.

Check-in time for domestic flights is 45 minutes. Note that flights have been known to depart earlier than scheduled, and are also sometimes cancelled without notice. Baggage is limited to two pieces per person, weighing no more than 44lb (20kg).

Air Turks and Caicos | InterIsland Plaza, Old Airport Rd, Providenciales; ✆ 946 4999; e info@airturksandcaicos.com; www.flyairtc.com. Charter flights ✆ 946 4623, 941 5481

Global Airways International Airport, Providenciales; ✆ 941 3222; e global@tciway.tc; www.globalairways.org
SkyKing Airlines International Airport, Providenciales; ✆ 941 3136; e res@skyking.tc; www.skyking.tc

BY ROAD Easily the best means of getting around all the islands is by car. Vehicles are driven on the left, following the British model, and it is compulsory to wear seatbelts. Driving standards are not great, and despite speed limits of just 20mph (32km/h) in the towns, or 40mph (65km/h) elsewhere, accidents on Provo at least are on the increase.

Most of the roads on Providenciales are tarred, with the exception of those leading to the west of the island, and those heading south towards Long Bay Beach. On the other islands, there is an ongoing programme of road improvement, but you could easily find yourself needing a 4x4 vehicle just yards from a wide tarred highway.

Vehicle hire Hire **cars** are available from several outlets on the islands (see pages 86–7, 128–9, 133–4, 144 and 161), costing from around $50–60 a day, plus insurance and tax, currently running at 10%. The minimum age to hire a car is 21, although many companies stipulate 25. Rates quoted in this guide are based on a single day's rental. If you're hiring a car for a week, you'll typically pay for only six days.

Vehicles are for the most part left-hand drive (ie: with the driver seated on the left), so extra care is required by all drivers. This is particularly important when negotiating roundabouts, which may be unfamiliar to American drivers: remember to give way to traffic already on the roundabout. If you feel strongly about which side you sit, it is worth at least requesting a right-hand drive car – although not all car-hire companies will have one available. Unless you are going to be pretty adventurous and explore off the beaten (tarmac) track, you will not need a 4x4.

Residents of the UK, USA, Canada and the British Commonwealth may drive for up to 30 days on their own driving licence; others will need either an international driving permit, valid for the same length of time, or a visitor's permit. These cost $20, and can be obtained from the Road Safety Department (*Old Airport Rd, Providenciales; ✆ 946 4828, or Good St, Grand Turk; ✆ 946 2801*).

Rental vehicles in the Turks and Caicos are easily picked out by the yellow lettering on their number plates; other commercial vehicles have green lettering, while red indicates private ownership, and black is used for government transport.

Vehicle insurance can be something of a minefield. Rates quoted by car-hire companies do not necessarily include even the statutory minimum insurance (liability insurance, usually charged at $4 per day), never mind collision damage waiver (CDW). Even where insurance is included in the basic rate, you can expect to pay $15 or more per day for CDW – bringing the coverage closer (but not equivalent) to the British 'fully comprehensive' policy. Much of the confusion arises because many US car-insurance policies cover their drivers for rental vehicles as well, whereas their British counterparts do not. In addition, some credit-card companies provide vehicle insurance cover, although the level of cover can vary dramatically. It is thus very important to check out all the relevant facts before hiring a car, and to allow sufficient time to find out exactly what is on offer – and what is not.

Most companies will meet you at the airport on arrival and pick up the car when you leave, usually without additional charge. Check carefully for damage to the car when you collect it and see that all dents and scratches are shown on the docket. Similarly, allow plenty of time for a thorough check when dropping off the vehicle.

Scooters may be hired on Providenciales and Grand Turk, but **bikes** – perhaps surprisingly – are less easy to come by. Some hotels have bikes for the use of guests, but there is no bike hire on Provo and availability is scarce on Grand Turk. Bikes, can, though, be rented on South Caicos and through some of the tour companies for use on the cycle trail on Middle Caicos.

Fuel is either unleaded petrol or diesel. It is sold in US gallons, which are slightly smaller than the imperial gallon (six US gallons equal five imperial gallons). Prices on Providenciales in summer 2008 were as follows (but rising fast):

Petrol (unleaded) $5.70 a gallon ($1.50 per litre)
Diesel $6.45 a gallon ($1.70 per litre)

Expect to pay rather more than this on the other islands.

Taxis and buses Licensed taxis are freely available in the Grace Bay area of Providenciales, but less so on the other islands; there are no taxis on Salt Cay. Taxi fares are frequently levied per passenger, so it's sensible to verify this with the driver before setting off. A cheaper private bus system operates in the main tourist and residential areas of Providenciales, but there are no buses elsewhere for the general public. Unlicensed taxis, known locally as *jitneys* (see page 86) also operate on Provo.

Hitchhiking Although hitching is a relatively common means of getting around for local people, it isn't generally recommended for visitors.

MAPS Although there are several maps featured in the various free magazines available to visitors, none of these is particularly suitable for driving beyond the tourist areas of Providenciales, in particular. The sheet map supplied free of charge by the tourist board is reasonably good, too. Sadly, the detailed maps produced by the UK Ordnance Survey are no longer available.

ACCOMMODATION

The range of accommodation in the Turks and Caicos Islands runs from mid-range hotels to opulent resort hotels with everything the visitor could possibly wish for. Those seeking budget options, however, will be disappointed, and good-quality guesthouse accommodation is limited to Salt Cay.

Despite the islands' popularity with divers, there are no dive lodges on Providenciales, although many of the mid-range hotels are popular with the diving community. Grand Turk has one all-inclusive dive resort, Bohio.

HOTELS AND RESORTS There is no shortage of luxury accommodation on Providenciales, with prices to match. There are a few medium-range hotels as well (some with self-catering facilities), but simpler establishments are thin on the ground. On the other islands, you can generally expect a more personal touch, with options ranging from classy boutique-style hotels to family-run establishments. There is no hotel grading system. The only **timeshare** option on the islands is the Alexandra Resort and Spa on Providenciales.

Based on a double room in high season, excluding 10% tax & 10% service, unless otherwise stated.

$$$$$	£250+	$500+
$$$$	£125–250	$250–500
$$$	£75–125	$150–250
$$	£50–75	$100–150
$	up to £50	up to $100

SELF-CATERING Opportunities for self-catering abound, from hotels with basic kitchen facilities to private condominiums and villas. Most have a sofa bed in the living area, so that a one-bedroom suite can usually sleep four people, and a two-bedroom condominium will take six, though extra people may incur an extra charge.

Rental properties can be booked direct, or through one of the islands' agencies, such as Prestigious Properties (*Prestige Place, Grace Bay;* ✆ *946 4379;* e *villarentals@ prestigiousproperties.com; www.prestigiousproperties.com*).

CAMPING There are no designated campsites on the islands, but there is nothing to stop you camping. It wouldn't be terribly prudent on Providenciales, but taking a tent to North or Middle Caicos is perfectly acceptable. It's also possible to camp on uninhabited islands, including East Caicos, provided that these are not protected and that you can arrange your own transport. Just don't forget a strong insect repellent.

PRICES Rates indicated in this guide are walk-in rates per night, and should be seen as a sample of the options available. Almost all establishments offer considerable discounts for advance booking and stays of several nights, with a seemingly infinite range of packages available, including those for divers and anglers.

For the most part, rates are split into those charged in high season, or winter (defined as mid December to mid April), and in low season, or summer (from mid April to mid December). Precise timings may vary from one hotel or resort to another, so do be sure to check before booking. A swingeing supplement may be levied for the two-week Christmas period, particularly by the more upmarket establishments, and this is increasingly the case over Thanksgiving (the fourth Thursday in November). Conversely, special deals abound in the low season, so it pays to shop around. Children sharing their parents' room quite often stay free, though the cut-off age varies.

A 10% government tax is levied on overnight stays at all hotel and self-catering establishments. Some hotels include this in their rates, but many add it to the final bill, so do be aware of this when costing your trip. Gratuities, too, are usually added to the bill, from 10% to 15% depending on the establishment.

Many resorts specify a minimum length of stay, varying from three to seven nights, particularly in high season. Cancellation charges can be hefty, so insurance is advised.

✖ EATING AND DRINKING

FOOD Fresh fish and seafood are the order of the day almost everywhere. Most widely available is conch (pronounced 'conk'), a chewy shellfish which appears on menus almost throughout the year, although the conch 'season' runs from 15 October to 15 July. A staple of the local diet, it boasts a high nutritional value, and is reputed to be a natural aphrodisiac. It comes in various guises, from the established conch salad (spicy but delicious) and cracked conch (tenderised conch which is deep fried in breadcrumbs), to any number of inventive dishes dreamed up by local chefs. Lobster, too, is a local speciality, in season from August to the end of March. Typically it's served grilled in restaurants, but you may also come across it boiled and finished with garlic and lemon butter – which to some tastes may be overcooked. Look out, too, for jerk chicken (or 'jerk' anything else, for that matter) – effectively marinated in a spicy sauce and then grilled.

If you happen to spot dolphin on the menu, don't worry: this is a fish, not to be confused with the mammal of the same name; it is sometimes listed by its Hawaiian name of 'mahi-mahi', or even as 'dorado'. Other popular local fish are yellow-fin tuna and wahoo (a bit like tuna but white), also known as kingfish.

A popular island breakfast consists of fish or pig's tail with peas and grits. In this case, the 'peas' are red beans, while grits – for the uninitiated – consist of corn ground into a fine, rice-like consistency. At other meals, peas put in an appearance with rice as the standard staple of most local dishes. And at weekends, watch out for another breakfast favourite: boiled fish with johnny cake (see box below).

Despite the generally poor agricultural soil, there are pockets of land – on Middle Caicos in particular – where farming is viable. Here, fruits such as guava, sapodilla and sugar apples rub along with cassava, okra and corn, and there are hopes that agricultural initiatives may be expanded to meet the growing need for fresh produce. For now, though, the majority of the fruit and vegetables sold on the islands is imported.

If you've a sweet tooth, do try the heavy but delicious potato bread, a spicy concoction that's both filling and laden with calories. As the name suggests, it's based on (sweet) potatoes, with a texture not dissimilar to bread-and-butter pudding. Light cake, more sponge-like in consistency, is also popular. Rum cake, despite its availability in tourist-type outlets, is not typical island fare.

EATING OUT Any visitor to the Turks and Caicos Islands – especially Providenciales – will be spoilt for choice when it comes to eating out. Even on the other islands – notably Grand Turk and Salt Cay – the standard of cuisine can be exceptionally high. Seafood lovers will be in their element, but there's plenty too for meat eaters, and most restaurants offer at least one vegetarian option.

While standards are generally high, so too are prices, at least compared with their

JOHNNY CAKE

A freshly cooked, local-style bread found throughout the *Caribantic* (Caribbean and Bahamian islands), johnny cake is a possible variant of journey cake, ie: something to take on the road. There are as many versions of this delicious cake/bread as days in the year; some cooks will add a couple of eggs to the mix. Traditionally it would be cooked on top of the stove, over a low heat, turning when browned.

2 cups (500ml) flour	pinch of nutmeg
1tbsp baking powder	1/3 cup (75ml) butter or shortening
1tsp salt	2/3 cup milk
1tbsp sugar	

Mix dry ingredients and rub in butter. Add sufficient milk to form a pliable dough. Knead it a little. Rest for a few minutes, then shape and bake in hot oven at 425°F (220°C, mark 7) for 20 minutes.

counterparts in North America. For European visitors, prices are more or less on a par with those in good restaurants at home. In a reasonable restaurant, lunchtime meals such as salads and sandwiches fall into the $8–12 range. For dinner, expect to pay a minimum of $8 for a starter, with main courses ranging from $18 for a pasta or simple vegetarian dish to $32 or more for seafood and steaks. Prices in restaurants specialising in local food tend to be considerably lower, and with weekend breakfast something of an island tradition, this is the time to head for one of the local establishments and feast on the likes of fish, rice and peas for only $8.50 or so. Even a full-blown lunch or dinner in a venue of this ilk won't set you back more than $15–20, plus drinks. Look out, too, for special lunchtime or evening deals, particularly mid week. And finally, if something on the lunch menu takes your fancy, do ask for it in the evening. In less formal venues, they'll often be happy to oblige.

None of the big fast-food chains has yet put in an appearance: the Turks and Caicos remain a McDonald's-free zone. That said, burgers and the like are relatively easy to come by, especially in shopping malls.

For the most part, individual prices for restaurants listed in this guide have not been specified, but the following should act as a guide. Remember that lunchtime menus tend to be considerably cheaper than those offered in the evening, and that a 15% gratuity is usually added to the bill.

RESTAURANT PRICE CODES

Based on average cost of a main course at dinner

$$$$$	£20+	$40
$$$$	£15–20	$30–40
$$$	£10–15	$20–30
$$	£6.50–10	$13–20
$	up to £6.50	up to $13

DRINKS Turk's Head beer, brewed at Turk's Head Brewery on Providenciales, is available throughout the islands in two types. The darkest, Ambra, is more akin to a British bitter, while the lighter Turk's Head is a lager-style beer. Visitors are welcome to visit the brewery (see page 121). Also widely on sale are several imported beers, including Corona, Heineken and Coors. Restaurant prices for a bottled beer come in at around $5 a head.

No visit to the Caribbean region is complete without trying the rum punch, on offer almost everywhere at upwards of $7. If properly made, it's likely to be a delicious (but sweet) blend of Lucayan rum, coconut rum, orange juice, pineapple juice and grenadine. Several menus feature a wider range of cocktails, so there's plenty of choice.

Wine is all imported, and thus subject to a 30% import duty. In the most modest restaurant prices start at around $25 a bottle, with champagne kicking off at $45. For those who are self catering, a bottle of wine from the supermarket will come in at around $12.50–18.

Soft drinks such as Coca-Cola and Sprite are to be found pretty well everywhere, as are canned fruit juices, with a variety of flavours from orange to mango and apricot and pineapple. The Bluebird range is pretty good, though one or two of them are heavily sweetened. Most readily available is fruit punch, which ranges from a rather synthetic concoction to a very tasty mix of tropical fruit juices: banana, grenadine, pineapple and orange. Iced water is available in jugs in most tourist restaurants on Providenciales, but elsewhere bottled water is more generally served.

The minimum age to drink alcohol is 18 throughout the islands. There are no official licensing hours.

SHOPPING

Although the number of shops on Provo in particular is increasing, the Turks and Caicos Islands are by no means a mecca for shopaholics. Duty-free goods such as jewellery, perfume and cigars are on offer in most upmarket shops geared to tourists, as are designer clothes, but look further and you will find opportunities to purchase the work of local artists and craftspeople. Hand-woven baskets and hats, and wooden model boats, make good souvenirs. Many of the best shops, in terms of selection if not price, are to be found in the grander hotels.

PUBLIC HOLIDAYS

For the most part, shops and banks are closed on public holidays, particularly where they coincide with a religious festival.

January	New Year's Day, marked on many of the islands from midnight to sunrise by junkanoo
12 March	Commonwealth Day
March/April	Good Friday, Easter Monday
28 May	National Heroes Day
11 June	HM Queen Elizabeth II's birthday
6 August	Emancipation Day
September, last Friday	National Youth Day
Monday nearest 10 October	Columbus Day
24 October	International Human Rights Day
25 December	Christmas Day
26 December	Boxing Day

Be aware, too, that **Thanksgiving** is widely celebrated on the fourth Thursday in November, a reflection of the strong American influence on the islands' visitors. Over this week, accommodation and restaurants tend to be booked up several months in advance.

FESTIVALS Festivals in various guises are held throughout the year, many of them incorporating the exuberance of junkanoo, a traditional Bahamian parade with colourful costumes, music and uninhibited dancing. The following are annual events where visitors are welcome. For those relating to sailing, contact the Maritime Heritage Foundation (*www.maritimeheritage.tc*) for details; for information on fishing, see pages 69–72.

February
Kiwanis Klassic Golf tournament, Providenciales
Wahoo Rodeo Fishing tournament, Providenciales

March/April
Kite Flying Competition Easter Monday at the Children's Park, Providenciales
Model Sailboat Regatta Conch Bar, Middle Caicos
Salt Cay Splashdown Days Three-day festival

May
South Caicos Regatta Four-day event held annually since 1967. As well as the sailing regatta, there are speedboat races, parades and junkanoo, donkey races, gospel music and other entertainment. See page 147.

June
Caicos Classic Annual Release Tournament Providenciales
Mariners' Week Grace Bay, Providenciales. Inaugurated in 2007 to bring together the TCI Challenge Cup Regatta, a pan-Caribbean invitation event for traditional workboats, with the annual Fools' Regatta and the Great Raft Race
SummaJam Festival Grand Turk
Heineken Game Fishing Tournament Grand Turk (sometimes as late as August)

July
Rotary Fishing Tournament Providenciales
Turks & Caicos Music & Cultural Festival Providenciales. Developed in conjunction with the tourist board (♦ *946 4970*) from the original Provo Day, this incorporates both music events and beauty contests.

August
Middle Caicos Day

October
Turks & Caicos Film Festival Providenciales
North Caicos Extravaganza Three-day festival

November
Conch Festival Last Saturday of November at Blue Hills, Providenciales. Yes, this does include the opportunity to sample plenty of foody delights – but it also incorporates a race between traditional Caicos conch sloops.
Museum Day (♦ *946 2160,* e *museum@tciway.tc*) Saturday nearest to 21 November, Grand Turk. Celebration of the inauguration of the Turks and Caicos National Museum.

(MEDIA AND COMMUNICATIONS

As you would expect in an important offshore banking location, telecommunications are generally very good.

TELEPHONE AND INTERNET Telephone, telex and fax services are provided by Cable & Wireless (*www.cwcaribbean.com/turkscaicos*). The telephone code for the Turks and Caicos Islands from overseas is +1 649 (from the USA, omit the +1).

For **international calls** from Turks and Caicos, dial 01, followed by the national code, then the number required without the initial 0. The national code for the USA and Canada is 1; for the UK it is 44. The majority of calls overseas from a Turks and Caicos landline cost $0.40 a minute during the day, reducing to $0.35 in the evening, and $0.30 at weekends.

Local calls within the Turks and Caicos are fixed at $0.15 a minute to another landline, or $0.50 to a mobile. Calls from hotel rooms, here as anywhere else in the world, can be exorbitant. Buy a local SIM card, or use your credit card or a phonecard (see below).

Credit cards calls Credit card calls using AMEX, Discover, MasterCard or Visa can be made to any destination, from any phone in the Turks and Caicos Islands, by dialling 1 800 744 7777, followed by your card number. Instructions on how to proceed are given in English. Alternatively, for calls to the USA, dial 1 800 225 5872. Weekend calls to the UK cost from $1.25 a minute, and from $1 a minute to the USA, rising to $2.45 or $1.70 respectively at peak times (6am–7pm Mon–Fri).

Payphones There is a limited number of call boxes across the islands, accepting phonecards and credit cards, but not coins. Phonecards are available from suppliers such as internet outlets.

Mobile phones The islands' three service providers are Digicel, Cable & Wireless (bmobile) and the local island.com. For mobile-phone users spending any time on the islands it's worth investing in a local SIM card for about $5 for your own mobile (preferably a spare one, so you can keep your normal phone for incoming calls), then put in as much credit as you need (top-up cards cost from $5). To do this successfully you will need both the PIN and PUK numbers for your mobile. Alternatively, consider buying a phone; telephone rental is expensive. Cards and top-up cards are widely available throughout the islands. With island.com, international calls to the USA or UK are charged at $0.19 per minute during the day, reducing to $0.15 at weekends.

TCI telephones are much cheaper for calls from the islands to Europe and North America, but calls within the Turks and Caicos can be as high as $0.50 per minute if calling another mobile network. International text messages cost $0.20, but incoming messages are free.

Those with dual-band mobile phones set up for international roaming should be able to receive and send calls in the islands.

Important telephone numbers

Emergency (police, fire, ambulance)	☏ 911	
Emergency clinic	☏ 777	
Police stations:		
Grand Turk	☏ 946 2299	
Middle Caicos	☏ 946 6111	
North Caicos	☏ 946 7116	
Providenciales	☏ 946 4259	
	e police_hq@gov.tc	
South Caicos	☏ 946 3299	

Telephone services

Operator/Directory enquiries	☏ 411
International operator	☏ 010
Credit card calls	☏ 1 800 744 7777

INTERNET Most of the larger hotels offer internet facilities for guests, and numerous restaurants and hotels across the islands offer WiFi access. There are also internet points on Providenciales, Grand Turk and South Caicos. A directory of email addresses is incorporated in the islands' telephone directory.

POST There is no door-to-door delivery service in the islands, so street names do not form part of the address: all addresses feature a PO box number. Letters should be addressed as follows:

PO Box 000000 XX
Providenciales/Grand Turk/etc
Turks and Caicos Islands
British West Indies

Post offices across the islands are normally open Monday to Thursday 8am–4pm, and Friday 8am–3.30pm.

Stamps for a postcard or letter from the Turks and Caicos Islands currently cost as follows:

	Postcards	Letters (½oz)
USA	50c	60c
UK and Canada	60c	80c
Rest of Europe	80c	$1.00
Africa	$1.10	$1.25

Stamps are available at post offices and many shops and hotels, where you can almost always leave cards and letters for posting; postboxes are not much in evidence. In theory, letters take around five to seven working days to reach the UK or USA; in practice this can be considerably longer.

See also *Philately*, below.

PHILATELY

John Moody of Stanley Gibbons, www.stanleygibbons.com

Because of its varied history and bountiful gifts of nature the Turks and Caicos Islands have much to attract both the stamp collector and the holidaymaker choosing postage for their cards.

The islands have been under the control of many different governments: Bermuda (although never officially), Bahamas (1799–1848), Jamaica (as both a protectorate while an independent colony 1848–1873 and as a dependency 1873–1962) and in 1917 Canada even offered to take them over! They are now a British Overseas Territory. All of these changes make for interesting stamps and coins reflecting this varied history. The stamps are generally brightly coloured and also illustrate the islands' natural history.

The first stamps were issued in 1867 but at that time only carried the Turks Island name. During the majority of Queen Victoria's reign only 68 different stamps were issued but from 1900 'Turks and Caicos Islands' was printed on the stamps. Since then, it has been a continuing story with literally thousands of different stamps being issued up to the present time. For a brief period (1981–1985), the Caicos Islands issued their own stamps.

Tucked away in the the North Atlantic Ocean, the Turks and Caicos has largely been passed by (thank goodness), but they did take centre stage in the world news in 1962 when US astronaut John Glenn landed off Grand Turk. Consequently a set of stamps was issued to commemorate the event – albeit ten years later!

Today Turks and Caicos stamps reflect current world political, historical and sporting events, and local natural history, and their links to the British Crown and as a member of the Commonwealth also spark many 'Royal' issues. A visit to the local post office can be something of a surprise to visitors as they have no idea what stamps will be on sale. The country has received some bad philatelic press in recent years because of the numbers of different issues a year that have been produced, far outstripping local use. This, of course, provides valuable revenue for the government from collectors and also provides a plentiful supply of colourful and interesting stamps for visitors to send to friends and relations the world over.

There are dedicated philatelic bureaux (e tciphilatelicbureau@tciway.tc; www.turksandcaicos.tc/postage/index.htm; 8am–4.30pm Mon–Thu; 8am–4pm Fri) on both Grand Turk and Providenciales. For details, see pages 103 and 167.

NEWSPAPERS AND MAGAZINES The *Turks & Caicos Weekly News* (*www.tcweeklynews.com*) is published every Wednesday at $1, with a separate *Weekend* 'magazine' section on Friday, giving details of events across the islands. The *Turks & Caicos Sun* (*www.suntci.com*), also $1, comes out on a Friday, while Thursday sees publication of the *Turks & Caicos Free Press*, a free broadsheet that has details of some of the week's happenings.

The quarterly *Times of the Islands* is widely available free, though where it's offered for sale the price is $4. Without doubt the best of the many magazines that showcase the islands, it's particularly strong on island culture, incorporating both the green pages that feature a regular and informative newsletter from the Department of Environment and Coastal Resources, and 'Astrolabe' – the newsletter of the Turks and Caicos National Museum.

Hotels and other places frequented by tourists are awash with free glossy magazines jostling to outdo each other in the fight to secure advertising from the plethora of developments currently under construction. Perhaps as a result, they tend to be a cut above the norm, featuring good articles on the underwater world, for example. Arguably the best produced and most interesting is S^3 standing for *Sand, Sea, Serenity* (*www.s3magazine.com*). Each issue features a destination and a special activity, and the magazine is also useful for the latest top-of-the-range accommodation, real-estate listings, and spa speak. Others include *Where When How* (*www.wherewhenhow.tc*) and its useful *Providenciales Dining Guide*, which features most restaurant menus and even a range of recipes.

There are also two annual publications, *Discover Turks & Caicos*, and the hardback *Destination Turks and Caicos*, from the Turks and Caicos Hotel and Tourism Association (*www.turksandcaicoshta.com*), the latter published by Times Publications; both are available free of charge in hotels.

International British and American newspapers may be found in the better supermarkets and bookshops, although they're usually weekend editions only and with various sections absent. *The Times* from London arrives in the middle of the following week. If you want to be sure of a copy, it is best to order in advance. You can receive your newspaper on the date of publication through the global digital network Newspaper Direct. Editions of internationally recognised newspapers are available in print and on screen in their original layout. To read on-screen, access the service at www.pressdisplay.com; to receive the printed newspaper contact Newspaper Direct (*Provo Air Center, 1 InterIsland Plaza, Old Airport Rd, Providenciales, Turks and Caicos 191;* ☏ *946 4181;* e *debby@provoaircenter.com*). This service is in place at Amanyara Resort on Provo.

TELEVISION AND RADIO Turks and Caicos **television** broadcasts on WIV cable TV Channels 4 (news) and 5 (the home of TCI-TV – *www.tceyetv.com*. Most hotels on the islands have satellite or cable TV, making a broad range of programmes from the USA available to guests. BBC World Service is also available in most hotels.

The main local **radio** station, Radio Turks & Caicos (*www.rtc107fm.com*), is based in Grand Turk, broadcasting a fairly standard mix of news, music and chat programmes on 101.9FM in Grand Turk, Salt Cay and South Caicos, 103.9FM in North and Middle Caicos and 107.7FM in Providenciales. Other music options on Providenciales are WDDR on 88.7FM and Power on 92.5FM, while KIST gospel radio can be found at 106.3FM on Providenciales, or 95FM on Grand Turk. The BBC World Service, Caribbean, can be heard on shortwave: the morning edition on 6.195MHz or 15.22MHz; the evening edition on 5.975MHz,11.765MHz or 15.39MHz. You may also tune in to BBC programmes on local station Radio Turks and Caicos 94.9/105.9.

BUSINESS

The tax-free status of the Turks and Caicos Islands is central to the establishment of many businesses here. The first point of reference is the Turks & Caicos Islands Investment Agency, TCInvest (*P O Box 105, Hon Headley Durham Bldg, Church Folly, Grand Turk;* ❥ *946 2058, 2852;* f *946 1464;* e *tcinvest@tciway.tc; www.tcinvest.tc*). The agency boasts that benefits of investment include 'long-term crown leases, duty remissions, work permits, zero taxation, and immigration opportunities'. Businesses that propose to offer employment and training opportunities for local workers are generally in particular demand.

WORKING IN THE TURKS AND CAICOS ISLANDS

Overseas nationals seeking to work in the islands need to satisfy the authorities that no-one local is either qualified in or interested in the job.

The cost of a work permit varies between $300 a year for unskilled workers to $7,000 for professionals, with the rate for a dive instructor, for example, being $3,000 a year. Self-employed workers pay the full $7,000 a year. Expatriate workers can in theory stay for only five years on a rolling basis, largely because anyone staying on the islands for ten years can claim the right of abode.

Application forms are available online at www.immigration.tc. Once completed, these must be submitted by the employer rather than the applicant. Self-employed applicants should submit the same form, accompanied by the following:

- Covering letter
- Copy of relevant qualifications and experience
- Recent medical certificate obtained on the islands
- 2 passport-sized photos
- Copy of business licence and financial records
- Bank statement
- Proof of legal status (or of departure)
- Police record
- Administration fee ($100)

In addition, there is an annual $1,000 resident's permit fee.

BUYING A PROPERTY

It's evident to even the most casual observer that property in the Turks and Caicos is a hot commodity. 'For sale' signs line many a road on Providenciales, and they're beginning to put in an appearance on other islands too. Advertisers in glossy magazines spare little expense in extolling the virtues of the newest condominiums – and there's no lack of choice as developers jostle with each other in their quest to pre-sell 30% of each property in order to ensure a profit. Following a change of legislation in 2006, buildings along the beach, which were previously restricted to a maximum of three storeys, may now extend up to seven storeys high – a change of heart that may well prove to be counter productive. Planning and standards of construction fall within the remit of the Government Planning and Development Authority.

The property market is open to all comers, with no restrictions on foreign ownership. At the heart of the system is the Turks & Caicos Real Estate Association (TCREA; *www.tcrea.com*), established in 1999 to coordinate the work of the islands' estate agents and – crucially for potential buyers – to create a centralised 'multiple listing system'. As a result, all property for sale on the islands is in theory to be found on one central database. All property movements are registered on the government Land Registry.

Commission rates, normally paid by the seller rather than the buyer, are set by the TCREA and are relatively high, at least by British standards: 6% of the sales price on developed properties, or 10% on undeveloped land. There are no property taxes, no income taxes for revenue generated by property ownership, and no capital gains taxes for property transfers.

In principle, those investing in a property valued in excess of $250,000 are eligible for a permanent residency certificate, which allows the freedom to come and go without continually renewing a visa.

ELECTRICITY

Electricity is 120/240 volts, 60 Hz. Flat, two-pin US-style plugs are standard, so take an adaptor if you are visiting from the UK or elsewhere. If you forget to bring one, staff at hotel reception desks can generally help out.

CULTURAL ETIQUETTE

While Turks and Caicos islanders are by nature generally hospitable, effusive friendliness and slick service aren't the norm. The traditional pace of life in the islands is slow and relaxed; the need to get things done in a hurry is somewhat alien. So don't try to rush things; it's just not worth it, and you'll lose the opportunity to get beneath the service of the local culture. Remember, too, that island society is very much of the old school, with a high standard of manners born of natural courtesy and an in-bred respect for the older generation in particular. Older women are generally addressed as ma'am, or the more familiar Miss Emily, or Miss Patricia; older men as sir.

For the visitor, the lifestyle is relatively casual, at least during the day, when shorts are acceptable everywhere – although it is normal to cover swimwear away from the beach. In the smarter restaurants, men should expect to wear trousers, not shorts, when dining out in the evening, but others are more relaxed. Ties are rarely worn. Sunbathing nude or even topless is illegal.

On the business front, the norm is for both men and women to wear suits for meetings and formal occasions, with a handshake the usual greeting.

In line with British legislation, gay and lesbian relationships on the Turks and Caicos Islands are legal but they are also generally discreet.

GIVING SOMETHING BACK

The standard of living in the Turks and Caicos is relatively high. Nevertheless, there are significant pressures that local people are struggling to cope with – especially on the environment. Several organisations would benefit from the support of visitors, of which the following are particularly apt:

Turks & Caicos National Trust PO Box 540, Town Center Mall, Providenciales; ℡ 941 5710; e tc.nattrust@tciway.tc; www.nationaltrust.tc. Established in 1994, the trust has responsibility for the cultural, historical & natural heritage of the islands. In common with its British counterpart, it takes a hands-on approach to this role, managing many of the islands' protected sites & developing a series of nature trails, together with associated interpretive booklets, as well as carrying out educational programmes. It also works closely with the **UK Overseas Territories Conservation Forum** (www.ukotcf.org), & other partners from the UK & USA. Membership of the trust is $25 a year, which entitles a discount on entry to the various attractions managed by the trust, as well as a discount on items sold in the National Trust shops on Providenciales (see page 102).

TCI Community Conservation Projects Community Conservation Projects Officer, Dept of Environment & Coastal Resources, Providenciales; ℑ 941 5122; e nationalparksinfo@tciway.tc. The Conservation Fund was established in 1999 to sustain & expand management of protected areas, including reef conservation; beach management; coastal clean-up; cultural and historic preservation; environmental education; protected area support eco-tourism promotion; nature trails; & community orchards.

Turtles in the Caribbean Overseas Territories (TCOT) e info@tcot.seaturtle.org; www.seaturtle.org/mtrg/projects/tcot. Donations are used to support conservation of marine turtles.

TCI Foundation For Persons with Disabilities George Pratt m 343 3562, or Sharvene Rigby m 243 5600; e tci@disabilitiesfoundation.com. Promoting sport for the handicapped & employment for those with disabilities such as visual or hearing impairment; cerebral palsy & Downs' syndrome.

Turks & Caicos National Museum PO Box 188 Grand Turk; ℑ 946 2160; e museum@tciway.tc; www.tcimuseum.org. The museum is working on some exciting new opportunities, including plans to develop the adjacent arboretum as an individual destination; continuation of the oral history initiative; further video & interactive exhibits; & additional work on the *Trouvadore* shipwreck project. Annual membership costs $30 (senior citizen $10; family $50; sponsor $250; patron $750). Benefits include free admission to the museum with accompanying guests; a 10% discount off museum shop purchases; & copies of *Times of the Islands* magazine, which incorporates the museum's quarterly newsletter *Astrolabe*. Make cheques payable to 'Turks & Caicos National Museum' (US residents' support is tax deductible via Friends of the Turks & Caicos National Museum; affiliated institution registered 501(c) (3) in Corpus Christi Texas).

Potcake Foundation ℑ 941 3765; www.potcakefoundation.com, www.potcakeplace.com. Potcakes are island dogs, regardless of size, shape, colour or disposition. The nearest thing to a rule about them is that they are most unlikely to be of a recognisable breed & they won't win a prize at Cruft's. Most of them are wild though they nearly always make loving pets. In the best mongrel tradition, they tend to be tough, loyal & intelligent. The name comes from the old practice of letting the dogs finish the caked remains at the bottom of the family saucepan, but they are definitely not fussy feeders.

The Turks & Caicos Society for the Prevention of Cruelty to Animals (*TCSPCA, www.tcspca.tc*) has since 2000 undertaken a major programme to find good homes for the vast number of potcakes roaming the island. The society tries to spay or neuter feral dogs when it can, but there are too many to keep pace & the population is actually growing.

Foster parents are always in demand, not least for the litters of puppies found on beaches or in the bush. Quite a few potcakes are adopted by TCI residents, but nearly 350 have been taken back to the USA & Canada in the two years to May 2008. (The UK & most European countries have stricter quarantine regulations & do not accept the medical certificates issued by the TCSPCA. This generally means a long stay in kennels in their new home country.) Puppy air tickets to North America are typically $100.

To learn more, & maybe to find a loyal new friend, check out the websites. At the very least you will see photographs to sigh over. And if you cannot take a potcake home with you, give a donation to one of the local canine charities & maybe adopt a needy stray in your own country.

Green sea turtles

3

Diving and Other Activities

DIVING

With their long fringing reefs and almost vertical walls, the Turks and Caicos Islands have rapidly established a reputation for some of the world's best diving. The average water temperature is 84°F (29°C) in summer, falling to around 78°F (25°C) in the winter months. Visibility during the summer is typically around 80–90ft (25–30m), but in winter can be considerably reduced, especially when the winds veer round to the northeast, churning up the seas and signalling a reduction in water temperature. Visibility is also affected by the tides, although except at springs the tidal exchange is usually only 3–4ft (1–1.2m).

Almost all diving on TCI is conducted from a boat; the distance from the beach out to the reef makes shore diving unrealistic in most areas.

SAFETY AND CONSERVATION All dive operators on the islands conform to PADI safety standards, or their equivalent. Thus the maximum depth limit permitted for recreational divers is 100ft (30m). Briefings on dive boats are the norm, with bottom time limited to air availability in conjunction with computer calculations. Always dive with a buddy.

When diving, snorkelling or even swimming from the shore, make sure that you can be seen by any boat that may be in the vicinity by clearly displaying a light or 'diver down' flag. The 'diver down' flag in these waters is normally the American white diagonal stripe on a red background, but could also be the blue-and-white international code 'A' flag. Lights used to indicate diving at night feature a series of three vertical lights in the sequence red, white, red, and should be visible all round.

Preservation of the marine environment is the responsibility of the Department of the Environment and Coastal Resources (DECR). All designated dive sites on the reef have permanent moorings to avoid anchor damage. Boats may anchor in sand away from the reef, provided that there is absolutely no contact with the coral. Moorings should never be left unattended.

Guidelines issued by the DECR remind divers and snorkellers and swimmers never to:

- walk or stand on the coral
- touch, pick up or hold reef life
- remove anything from its habitat (and that includes any artefacts from a wreck site)

It's a sobering thought that poor diving practice is one of the causes of reef destruction. Before you set off, ensure that you can establish and maintain neutral buoyancy and check that trailing consoles are properly secured. Don't wear gloves – you shouldn't be touching anything underwater, so they're unnecessary, and you could inadvertently spread disease too. And watch where you put those fins. Not only can the sediment stirred up choke the surrounding life, but a quick flip against the coral or a sponge can destroy years of fragile growth.

Finally, remember that feeding fish, even with specialist food, may give you pleasure, but it could lead to a dependence on humans that may endanger the fish and other marine life, and eventually upset the delicate balance of nature upon which the whole underwater ecosystem depends.

DIVE SITES The location of individual dive sites impacts significantly on the length of time it can take for a two-tank dive. From Providenciales, for example, you'll need to allow at least six hours for a two-tank dive off West Caicos, whereas the easy accessibility of sites in Grace Bay or off Grand Turk, Salt Cay and South Caicos will halve that time.

The fringing reef that encircles most of the Turks and Caicos Islands provides divers with a constantly changing spectacle of colourful reef fish against some spectacular coral formations. As the reef drops off into the deep, it gives way to almost vertical walls adorned with huge sponges and both soft and hard corals, affording shelter for tiny nudibranchs, cyphomas and graceful shrimps. Those in search of larger creatures will not be disappointed, for the Turks Island Passage between the two island groups forms the link between the cold waters of the Atlantic and the shelter of the Caribbean. Not only is this passage the route taken by the Atlantic humpback whale on its annual migration route; it is also used by countless other marine wildlife, from rays and turtles to dolphins and sharks. There is no 'best' place to dive; although many would put French Cay, Grand Turk and South Caicos at the top of the list, there are others who swear by Grace Bay on a calm day. Remember, though, that there is no such thing as a 'guaranteed sighting' of any creature, no matter how beguiling it may sound.

The only shipwreck on the islands that is visited by divers is that of the *Endymion*, which went down south of Salt Cay over 200 years ago. Alternatively, there's the wreck of a plane off South Caicos which makes a fascinating dive site – and a good story.

Options for shore diving are limited to a couple of sites off Grand Turk, and possibly South Caicos – but even these entail a significant surface swim. Elsewhere, the distance to the reef are simply too great for the average swimmer.

For more on dive sites on individual islands, see pages 000, 000, 000 and 000. And if you have a request for a particular site, do ask – boat captains usually welcome suggestions.

DIVE OPERATORS Diving is well organised on both sides of the Turks Island Passage. To the west, several dive companies operate out of Providenciales, covering an area across to West Caicos and French Cay, while to the east the choice is spread between operators on Grand Turk, Salt Cay and South Caicos. There are no operators based on either North or Middle Caicos at present, although with the relentless march of the developers this is unlikely to remain the case for long. For details of dive operators, see pages 110–11, 148, 170–1 and 180–1.

The style of diving varies according to both the operator and the location of the dive sites. Some will prepare all your kit in advance, and change tanks between dives; others expect divers to manage this themselves. All operators will have a divemaster – usually an instructor – with each group, on an average ratio of 1:6, but he or she will not necessarily lead the group as a whole, although divers may always elect to stay with a guided group. Many of the independent operators assume buddy diving, rather than guided diving, with a full dive briefing and unlimited bottom time – the norm is around 50–60 minutes, but those with sufficient air to continue a dive are often able to stay down longer. Those diving with one of the all-inclusive resorts, however, can expect to be limited to around 35 minutes or so per dive.

Typically operators on the Turks Islands use small, flat-bottomed boats designed for easy access from the beach and for a quick ride out to the sites, whereas those on Provo use more substantial vessels, better equipped for longer trips to the west or south of the island. On the smaller boats, refreshments are usually limited to drinking water, but most of those operating out of Provo offer soft drinks and snacks as well.

Two liveaboards operate in Turks and Caicos waters, both based in Providenciales. For details, see page 111.

COSTS Costs between operators on each island tend to be fairly similar, but a greater difference is to be found between the islands, especially between Provo and Grand Turk, which is largely a reflection of the distances to be travelled to the dive sites. Typically, a two-tank boat dive on Provo will run out at around $125 per person, excluding equipment, while on Grand Turk you're looking more in the region of $85. A single afternoon dive would add a further $50–70 or so, with a night dive coming in at around $60–85. These figures are walk-in rates; most operators offer a variety of dive packages, with or without accommodation, at a significant discount, with further savings to be made for advance booking. So a six-day dive package, based on a two-tank boat dive per day, would cost from approximately $600 if booked on the islands, but pre-booking could reduce this by a further $40 or so. In the event of cancellation, there is unlikely to be any refund where packages have been booked on the islands, while pre-booked packages are normally subject to a minimum cancellation period. Do remember that at a time of rapidly rising fuel charges, prices tend to increase regularly, or – as during 2008 – fuel surcharges may be imposed.

EQUIPMENT Diving fees usually include the use of tanks, weights and weight belts, but all other diving equipment is almost always charged extra, even on all-inclusive dive packages. The average (but not top) rate is $10 to rent each piece of equipment for 24 hours. While many operators limit the rental cost to $25 or so per day, a computer may be a further $10–15, and some will charge for every item individually. Be warned! On the plus side, almost all operators include the hire of equipment in the cost of their training courses.

During the summer, most divers are happy with a skin for protection, or at most a 3mm shorty suit, but in winter the less hardy will find a full wetsuit more comfortable. Most of the dive operators insist on a dive computer per person, not per pair, and in some cases the loan of a computer is included in the rates. If it's not, and you don't want to hire a computer, you'll be restricted to diving within the limits of recreational dive tables, rather than those of a computer – hardly an attractive option when dive times can extend to around an hour. The only other essential is your certification – without which you'll be staying strictly on terra firma.

DIVE ORGANISATIONS

BSAC	British Sub Aqua Club
HSA	Handicapped Scuba Association
IANTD	International Association of Nitrox and Technical Divers
NASDS	National Association Scuba Diving Schools
NAUI	National Association of Underwater Instructors
PADI	Professional Association of Dive Instructors
SSI	Scuba Schools International
TDI	Technical Diving International

Although it's easy enough to obtain masks, snorkels and fins from any of the dive shops on Providenciales and Grand Turk, specialist diving equipment has to be ordered, so if you want your own kit, buy it before you leave home.

COURSES All TCI's dive specialists are PADI affiliated, although most also recognise other qualifications, and some are also licensed to run courses by NAUI, NASDS, SSI, HSA, IANTD, TDI and (occasionally) BSAC. The most popular course on the island is without doubt the resort course, or **Discover Scuba**, which is effectively an introduction to scuba diving. For around $170 per person, including equipment, divers have a two-hour theory session based in a pool, followed by a boat dive to around 40ft (12m). The course may be completed in half a day, but is more usually spread out over a day with a break for lunch.

Costs for the PADI **Open Water** course start at around $580, with Open Water referral or its equivalent (where the classroom element has been completed in advance) at $400. As a rule, both these and other 'entry' courses include equipment; for more advanced courses, equipment is usually – but not always – payable extra. Many of the operators start courses on specified days, so do be sure to check this out in advance.

PADI (*www.padi.com*) has recently introduced PADI eLearning, a new way in which prospective divers can take the Open Water course. Applicants nominate a dive operator, then complete all PADI paperwork online while still at home. They then print out the results, and take them down to their chosen operator, who will conduct the practical part of the course, and pose an 18-question review. While costs are the same as for taking the course in the more traditional way, the benefits are significant in terms of convenience at home, as well as time saved when on the islands.

In addition to the various PADI courses, qualified divers over the age of ten can enrol on the National Geographic **Passport to Adventure**. It's an intensive four-day course but, unlike the PADI courses, is offered on TCI exclusively by Beaches for their own guests, at a cost of $450 per person. The aim is to learn basic scientific techniques, combining navigational instruction and the identification of major underwater plant and animal species.

FURTHER OPTIONS
Night dives The opportunities for night diving are as varied as in the day time, but after dark there's a whole new world to explore. As darkness falls, the seas are the realm of creatures such as the octopus and squid, the lobster and the eel. Most dive operators run night dives, but some keep these to a specific day of the week, so it's worth checking well in advance.

Nitrox Nitrox diving is gaining popularity for the extended bottom time it can give at shallow depths. By adjusting the mix of air in a tank to 32/68 oxygen/nitrogen (the norm is 21/79), divers can dive to a maximum of 100ft (30m) but can stay at that depth for up to 30 minutes on a first dive. On 50/50 oxygen/nitrogen, divers are limited to 30–40 ft (9–12m) but bottom time is increased by up to 50%. Most dive companies can supply nitrox tanks, with tuition usually available on request. Nitrox certification takes two days for an initial course (around $135–225, depending on whether the dives are from the shore or from a boat), but the longer courses are not currently offered on TCI. Nitrox tanks are usually charged at an additional cost to the dive, starting at around $10 per tank.

Snuba diving The technique of snuba diving is designed for those aged eight and over who want to venture further than snorkelling but may be short of time, or not ready for scuba diving. Certainly it offers almost instant results, with no classroom

As you explore the marine environment at the recreational diver's limit of 100ft (30m), spare a thought for the freedivers for whom no such limits exist – but for whom 'bottom time' of 50 minutes or more is an impossible dream.

While freediving is in theory open to all, most ordinary mortals stick to the occasional duck dive while out snorkelling. For Tanya Streeter, however, the ocean's depths offer a challenge every bit as great as Everest for the mountaineer. So when in August 2002 she arrived on Providenciales, her sights were set on conquering the world freediving record. After months of intensive preparation, it took her just short of three-and-a-half minutes to make her record-breaking dive to 525ft (160m), smashing the previous male and female 'no limit' records. Then, having reached that depth, she simply returned to the surface with the aid of an inflated bag. All in rather less time than it takes most of us to get out of bed in the morning – but at the absolute limits of human physiology and endurance.

The support team was pretty impressive too. Pairs of scuba divers were stationed at the surface and at 131ft (40m), with additional safety divers breathing a special air mix positioned at depths of 262ft (80m), 360ft (110m) and 459ft (140m). As Streeter descended, each of the divers banged metal rods together in a predetermined signal so that she would know exactly what depth she had reached.

Streeter returned to Provo the following year when she took the variable weight women's record at 400ft (122m). Madness? Quite possibly – but her two women's records still stand, although the men's no limit record was trounced in 2007 by Austrian freediver Herbert Nitsch, who made it to a mind-blowing 702ft (214m).

tuition, no courses, and very little preamble. Rather than wearing heavy dive equipment, participants are kitted out in standard snorkelling gear (mask, fins, snorkel), but with the addition of a regulator (or breathing apparatus) which is on a simple harness and attached by a long air line to a tank at the surface. This allows for shallow dives to a depth of around 20ft (6m). After just 15–20 minutes' orientation, you'll have the freedom to follow your guide, with your air tank following above on an inflatable raft. Snuba is offered on both Providenciales and Grand Turk (see pages 110 and 170).

Diving for children – and the less confident
Children under ten may not dive with any of the commercial organisations in the open sea, but several PADI initiatives make diving accessible even for young children. Of these, two are available at Beaches Resort on Providenciales, exclusively for their guests.

The Bubblemaker course is designed to introduce children aged eight to nine to scuba diving through various activities in the confines of a swimming pool, at a maximum depth of 6ft (2m). The 1½hr course costs $105 per child. There is also the PADI Seals programme, through which children of eight and up carry out a series of five one-hour scuba-diving 'missions' in depths of up to 12ft (3.7m), both in the pool and in open water. Badges and logbooks are all part of the fun. The programme costs $150 per person and parents who want to participate are welcome to join in too.

UNDERWATER PHOTOGRAPHY
Some of the larger dive operators have their own photographic division, enabling divers to rent equipment or have instruction in underwater photography. Typically, the PADI digital underwater photography course costs around $175. To hire an underwater digital camera without any instruction, you can expect to pay upwards of $50 per day. Some outfits will also

Diving and Other Activities DIVING

3

with Karen Stewart

Many are the snorkellers and divers who have set off with a cheap throwaway camera only to find that the long-awaited results when they get home range from bad to awful. The most important thing to remember here is that these so-called 'underwater' cameras are not intended for divers. Waterproof they may be, but you need to remain on or close to the surface. As with any other camera, you also need to compose your picture carefully, taking care to prevent movement and poor light – both of which are difficult to avoid in the water. If you are stationary, so much the better. As for light, try to keep the sun behind you and avoid reflection on the water. As the contrast right on the surface can confuse the camera (and splashing is a potential problem here too), photographs taken just below may actually be clearer.

For true underwater photography, you'll need to hire or buy a suitable camera; rentals are available from several dive operators. Take a bit of time to familiarise yourself with the equipment – most shops will give you a bit of help here.

One of the most important things to remember is to get close to your subject, then look up to take your shot. Water acts like fog – the farther you are from your subject, the more blurred it will be, so get as close as you can for the lens that you are using. Many underwater cameras that you rent will be fitted with a 35mm lens. That means you need to be about three feet (1m) from the subject (underwater this is about two arm lengths). By staying at this distance you will have sharper and more colourful images. You will also want to make that intriguing fish, or sponge or piece of coral stand out. This can easily be accomplished by shooting upwards, effectively using the deep blue water as background. Underwater shots that are taken shooting down into the sand or coral tend to lose their three-dimensionality and everything blends together.

To really bring out the beauty of the underwater world, your camera should be fitted with some sort of strobe. Remember that, as we descend in water, we quickly lose colour and light. By the time you are at 50ft (16m), everything will appear monochromatic blue or green. If you take pictures at this depth without a strobe, your picture will also appear blue or green. Strobes bring back the vibrant colours and make your subject stand out from its background.

Before you decide to try underwater photography, make sure that you are comfortable in the water with your scuba equipment and also with your buoyancy. Adding a camera when you are not comfortable can significantly increase stress. Having good buoyancy and keeping gauges and hoses tucked away means that you can get closer to subjects without in any way injuring the reef. Watch that your feet don't kick the coral or stir up the sand as you are taking the picture, and never grab on to a live reef to steady yourself.

produce a video of your dive, so do ask (and check the price, too; they can be very high).

FURTHER INFORMATION For a selection of books on diving, see *Further Information*, page 191.

SNORKELLING

Even the most nervous swimmer can have a go at snorkelling: it's inexpensive, simple – and addictive! An ordinary mask and snorkel are all that is needed to open up a world that can otherwise be scarcely imagined; fins just mean you can go that much faster. If you don't have your own kit, you can always hire it for around $10 per day from one of the dive operators, or link up with a dive boat trip from about $30, which will include rental of the equipment and have you on the reef in next to no time. Do try the equipment on first – it's important that the mask should fit snugly to prevent leakage, and the fins shouldn't rub or you'll have blisters in next to no time.

On most islands, the best snorkelling sites are on the fringing reef, accessible only by boat, and on Provo there are only a few good spots within reach of the shore (see pages 111–12). Elsewhere, shore-based options are wider, with some glorious snorkelling just yards off the beach in North Caicos (see page 131), and South Caicos boasting what must rank as one of the world's best-kept snorkelling secrets within swimming distance of the beach (see page 148). Almost all the dive outfits welcome snorkellers as well, as do several of the more general boat operators.

If you are planning to snorkel outside a buoyed swimming area or even a short way offshore, remember that you will be almost invisible to passing boats. Keep a constant watch out for any traffic, and consider using a marker such as a white float or a 'diver down' flag (see page 63), which will be clearly visible from a distance of about 200 yards (180m). Snorkellers, like divers, should never touch the coral, since each time you do so it will affect or damage these living creatures. Remember, too, that you should remove nothing from the water – even an empty shell will become a home for another creature.

FISHING

With several distinct marine environments off the Turks and Caicos, anglers will find plenty to keep them occupied. The summer months, from the end of June through July and August, are the best time for billfish, while later in the season, between November and January, the primary catch is wahoo and small dolphin, or mahi mahi. Further offshore, tuna can be found all year round, while in the shallows there's excellent bonefishing.

Those planning to fish on the islands will need a visitor's sport fishing licence, which is normally arranged by the operator. If not, licences are available for $30 from the Department of Environment & Coastal Resources (*Grand Turk* ❭ 946 2801, South Caicos ❭ 946 3306, Providenciales ❭ 941 5122; e *nationalparksinfo@tciway.tc; www.environment.tc*) and are valid for 30 days. The equivalent licence for residents, valid for a year, costs $60. For details of operators and costs, see individual island chapters, pages 113–14, 131, 136, 148 and 171. Fishing is not permitted within designated reserves, which includes the whole of the Grace Bay area, protected by the Princess Alexandra Land and Sea National Park, and the west coast of Grand Turk.

The islands host several fishing tournaments each year, including the week-long Caicos Classic Release Tournament on Providenciales in June (❭ 941 3781; e *info@caicosclassic.com; www.caicosclassic.com*) and the Heineken Grand Turk Game Fish Tournament (❭ 946 2321; e *tci.tourism@tciway.tc*) between June and August. The smaller one-day Rotary Fishing Tournament (m *231 0341*) takes place on Provo in July.

DEEP-SEA OR SPORT FISHING The deeper waters beyond the reef are home to numerous so-called game-fishing species, as well as large hammerhead and tiger sharks. This is the all-year domain of both yellow-fin and black-fin tuna and the fabled Atlantic blue marlin, while the season for wahoo, mahi-mahi, white marlin and sailfish is limited to the winter months. A catch can sometimes be prepared on board, then transported back for cooking at one of the islands' restaurants.

3

If it [St Elmo's fire] be single, it prognosticates a severe storm, which will be much more severe if the ball does not adhere to the mast, but rolls and dances about. But if there are two of them, and that too when the storm has increased, it is reckoned a good sign. But if there are three of them, the storm will become more fearful.

Francis Bacon (1561–1626) quoting Pliny the Elder (AD23–79)

Stories of ships and aeroplanes vanishing into oblivion in the very region a traveller is set to visit don't necessarily make for comfortable bedtime reading. However, anyone with serious qualms about this enigma, also sometimes referred to as the Bermuda Triangle, can rest assured: the majority of scientists who have examined the evidence, or lack of it, have come to the conclusion that claims of supernatural forces at play are unfounded. Such theories deriving from a series of strange coincidences have been dismissed as fantasy.

Perpetuators of the phenomenon have never been able to agree precisely on the supposed size or boundaries of that segment of the northwestern Atlantic that they believe to be subject to some inexplicable agency which, over the years, has caused the random disappearance of numerous marine vessels and aircraft. From its conception the notion has always involved a triangular area defined with its apex close to the island of Bermuda and the base of the area believed to extend from southern Florida, south of the Bahamas and the Turks and Caicos Islands to a few degrees east of Puerto Rico. But its limits have regularly been adjusted to include yet another inconclusive incident and add support to the case for paranormal powers at work.

Over the years it must be admitted there have been some curious occurrences, in general involving the loss of a single craft at any one time. Perhaps the oddest tale and the one that gave rise to the mass of research and reportage that has since been applied to the history of the conundrum was on 5 December 1945 with 'Flight 19'. An entire flight of five US Navy torpedo bombers failed to return from a routine training exercise over the ocean to the southeast of Fort Lauderdale, Florida, after the flight leader had radioed that the group had become disoriented and were experiencing multiple compass malfunction. A coastguard flying-boat with a crew of 13 was despatched to search for the missing planes but it, too, never returned. Various scenarios have since been offered to explain the chain of events, the most favoured being that Flight 19 simply became lost, ran out of fuel and ditched. As to the fate of the amphibian, PBM Mariners were reputed to have a design fault in the supply tubing from the fuel tank. Indeed it was rumoured that even a small spark had the potential to ignite the whole aircraft. The fact remains that no trace of the accident was ever found, no wreckage or bodies ever recovered from the ocean.

In oral narrative specific to Turks and Caicos Islands, it is related that some years ago local boat captain Joseph Hall found himself, with his passengers and cargo, enveloped by a sudden violent storm. Monster waves made it impossible to pass through the narrow opening in the reef and the captain was unable to prevent the little boat being slammed into the coral. By good fortune all the passengers and stores were rescued but Captain Joe Hall, true to tradition, would not abandon his vessel. All night long he clung to the wreckage until the storm abated. The following morning when he finally made it ashore,

BONEFISHING Typically, bonefishing requires a flat-bottomed boat which does little more than drift through the shallows, allowing the angler to try techniques from fly-fishing to spin-fishing – the latter more suited to beginners. It takes place in waters of no more than 6ft (1.8m) in depth, and is best on a low, outgoing tide. The shallow waters south of Providenciales off Long Bay provide

all his skin had been bleached white by the sea and he was covered in tar. But he survived'. Then on a subsequent occasion with a second boat, in the course of a routine journey ferrying a consignment of kerosene drums across the shallow beds between Middle and South Caicos, he simply vanished. In theory whatever problem he encountered he could simply have waded out, but no trace was ever found, either of him or his cargo.

THE DEVIL'S TRIANGLE

Not every saga ends in disaster. On Saturday, 16 February 2008, en route from the Dominican Republic to the Turks and Caicos, 62-year-old Maurice Kirk, an accident-prone amateur aviator retired Welsh veterinarian and drinking buddy of late actor Oliver Reed, issued a Mayday call as his disabled Piper Cub aircraft, in which Kirk was attempting to fly around the world, crash landed in the ocean 80 miles south of Providenciales. Coastguards responding to signals from his emergency beacon rescued him and delivered him, suffering from head and neck injuries, for treatment on Provo. When informed her husband had discharged himself from hospital, his wife replied, 'He usually does… my husband is indestructible.' Kirk set off forthwith on a salvage mission to retrieve his stricken plane which he reckoned would not sink for another 12 hours. The mission alas was to no avail. Almost at once after Maurice Kirk's helicopter rescue, the Devil's Triangle had claimed another victim and the vintage Piper Cub sank to a watery grave. Undeterred, Kirk purchased a replacement aircraft and set off for Texas with the intention of personally thanking President Bush for the rapid response of the Miami-based coastguards, but when he landed at the Bush ranch he was greeted with handcuffs, removed to a detention centre and, at the time of writing, was due for deportation.

Whatever the exact area of the so-called triangle, it has to encompass some of the most travelled routes in the world. It's therefore hardly a surprise to learn that any number of craft, both air and sea, have perished within its boundaries. Many conflicting currents traverse the Atlantic and with the Gulf Stream alone moving at 4 knots (almost 5mph/8km/h), evidence of a disaster can swiftly be dispersed. Add to that the variations in topography of the ocean floor, from the shallowest waters of the Great Bahama Bank to the deepest part of the Atlantic, close to where it joins the Caribbean Sea. Further and more dramatic explanations for the supposed phenomenon involve magnetic field aberrations to account for mussed up compass and altimeter readings and failed communication systems, some extending the theses to include lightning bolts, St Elmo's fire, or vortexes drawing objects below the surface of the sea. And still more extreme are suggestions of a space-time connection: aliens at work, or gravitational forces from the lost city of Atlantis. The sky – certainly the sea – is the limit.

the ideal conditions, as do the flats that stretch for some 40 miles (64km) off South Caicos. Those based on Provo but with plenty of time could do better to head for the uncrowded waters of Middle or even East Caicos, where there is also the chance of seeing rays and sharks. Guides are available, though keen anglers are advised to bring their own tackle.

BOTTOM AND REEF FISHING Fishing from an anchored boat is popular with novices, including children, who quite often enjoy baiting their own hooks then dropping them over the side. Fish such as grouper or snapper can be caught in this way, and those up to 10lb (4.5kg) may be taken home for the pot (or – for the holidaymaker – to the restaurant of your choice). Use natural bait wherever possible, such as squid or conch.

KAYAKING

What better way to while away a calm afternoon than by kayaking in the shade of the mangroves, or gently paddling up the beach for a sundowner? Operators on all the main islands can turn this into a reality, either through rental of kayaks to individuals, or – as in the case of Big Blue on Providenciales and North Caicos – through a guided trip with an eco-tour guide who will take the time to explain the fragile ecosystem that underpins the islands. Some of the hotels, too, have kayaks available for use by their guests. See pages 116, 131, 148, 171 and 181.

SAILING AND OTHER WATERSPORTS

Sailing is not, of course, simply the preserve of visiting yachtsmen. Those staying on Provo and Grand Turk can rent boats such as Hobie Cats or windsurfers (see pages 114–16 and 117), but renting a traditional sloop is sadly not yet possible. That said, the Maritime Heritage Federation (*www.maritimeheritage.tc*) actively promotes sloop sailing and holds a number of regattas each year between May and November. Visitors are welcome to participate.

In terms of organised activities, most other watersports – including kite boarding, parasailing, waterskiing and jet skiing – are limited to Providenciales. For details, see pages 115–17.

WHALE WATCHING

Between late January and early April humpback whales (see page 27) migrate from the cold waters of the north to mate and to calf in the warm waters of the Mouchoir and Silver banks south of the Turks and Caicos Islands. Observing these majestic creatures as they pass through the deep waters close to the islands can be spellbinding. From some shore positions – notably on the east coast of Ambergris Cay – it is often easy to spot a number of them close by in the course of a single day. Alternatively dedicated boat trips are organised during the season by a few companies on Grand Turk, Salt Cay and South Caicos (see pages 149, 174 and 182–3).

You should of course be aware that as with all events dependent on natural occurrence, an expedition can be something of a hit-and-miss experience; how many of the leviathans you will see or how much surface activity on their part you will witness cannot be guaranteed. But certainly the boat operators know well the optimum spots for close-up viewing. Whale-watching boat excursions are traditionally afternoon activities, accommodating those who may have chosen to dive earlier in the day. Boats depart from Grand Turk or Salt Cay at around 2pm and travel out into the deep waters of the Turks Island Passage. Then it's engines off and expectant waiting. It may be your good fortune to see a mother with her calf, rising and plunging together. Listen carefully: you may even hear the extraordinary echo of whale song; only the males sing but it is a sound once heard, never forgotten. You might catch a glimpse of a head rising above the water, and a whale 'spouting', akin to a human diver clearing his airways as he surfaces. Most fun of all is to see a whale 'breaching': that is, flipping right up out of the ocean and splashing back in. No-one knows why whales do this, whether it is purely *joie de vivre* or some ritual, but it is a spectacular sight.

Whale watching is strictly controlled. Swimming with the whales is not allowed without a special permit, which can be organised through individual operators. Whether or not you feel that such activities, known locally as 'soft-water encounters', are acceptable is up to the individual, but think carefully. These are wild animals on a natural migration route; it is hard to justify the presence of humans swimming alongside them. And if you do go into the water, remember that the whales should never be touched.

Trips can last as long as three hours so be sure to take a good supply of sunscreen, dark glasses and a hat, along with binoculars and of course a camera. Also, and however warm the day, consider bringing a sweater for the brisk motor back to port. Drinking water will probably be provided by your skipper but it's wise to check this in advance.

LAND-BASED ACTIVITIES

Off the water options are generally more limited, but they do exist, though most are restrictedd to Providenciales. The islands' main **golf** course is located on Provo, behind Grace Bay (see pages 117–18). On Grand Turk, there is a nine-hole course in the grounds of the governor's residence (see page 171). Elsewhere, there is talk of constructing a course on South Caicos, to link in with proposed development on that island, and another on Salt Cay.

Other sports available include tennis, gym and skating (see pages 118 and 172), as well as cricket (the national sport), football, hockey, rugby, volleyball, squash, baseball and basketball.

HORSERIDING There's something magical about riding along the beach on horseback, looking down through clear azure waters with the possibility of spotting turtles or rays in the shallows. Conditions permitting, you may even be able to swim your mounts through the surf. There are stables on both Provo and Grand Turk (see pages 118 and 169).

CYCLING The flat terrain and relatively traffic-free roads of most islands mean that cycling is well suited to softies (though on Providenciales, with its wide highways, this is a less attractive option). That said, hiring bikes is something of a challenge, though several resorts on the islands, including North Caicos, have bikes available for guests to use. Commercial rental is at present limited to Middle and South Caicos and Salt Cay (see pages 136 and 176).

There's a designated cycle trail on Middle Caicos (see page 136), but other options are there for the taking. The roads and paths on South Caicos, in particular, offer an excellent circular route (see page 149).

HIKING AND BIRDWATCHING Even the committed beach lizard can thrill to the sight of the brown pelican as it dive-bombs its prey off the beaches of Provo and elsewhere; certainly they're a regular sight both at Blue Hills and near Turtle Cove Marina on Grace Bay, requiring no more effort from the watcher than glancing up from the sands.

For the more active, the possibilities are endless. Chalk Sound on Provo brings many rewards for the patient birdwatcher, while further west, almost untouched vegetation is home to birds that range from the pelican to the tiny hummingbird.

3

There are boardwalks on Little Water Cay (see page 123), affording the opportunity to see plenty of birdlife as well as the iguanas which are the cay's main attraction.

Further afield, the National Trust has been active in creating and waymarking hiking trails along the old 'field-roads' on Middle and East Caicos (see pages 136–7 and 139–40), opening up the otherwise impenetrable vegetation to those in search of the plants and birds that are native to these islands. Ponds and salinas, from North Caicos all the way round to Salt Cay, repay a visit by birders at almost any time of year; you don't have to go far to spot all manner of waders and seabirds. For many, though, the lure of the aristocratic osprey is the greatest. Lord of land and sea, it typically builds its untidy nest of twigs and incongruous strands of coloured twine high up in rocky crags alongside many a lonely beach, but will occasionally select a less likely spot, such as a disused windmill. Try North Caicos and Salt Cay, for starters.

STARGAZING *Thomas A Lesser*

One of the advantages of holidaying in the British West Indies is that you are far away from the bright lights and pollution of cities. Once the beautiful Caribbean sun sets and it grows dark, you will probably see more stars than you ever imagined possible.

At night, all the stars you can see are placed in groups called constellations. The first thing you need to do is to forget trying to see the figures suggested by the constellation names. Most constellations look nothing at all like they should.

THE SUMMER SKY High overhead during the summer you will find that three bright stars are dominating the sky. Since these three form a large triangle which is visible during the summer months up north, they are called the Summer Triangle. Each bright star marks a different star group or constellation.

Brightest and highest in the sky is Vega, in Lyra the Harp. Fainter stars very close to Vega in the shape of a parallelogram form the harp. In mythology this is the harp invented by Hermes, which Mercury gave to Orpheus, the musician who joined Jason and the Argonauts. On another occasion Orpheus went into the infernal regions and charmed Pluto, king of Hades, with the music of his harp to win back his lost bride Eurydice.

To the south of Vega is Altair, in Aquila, the Eagle. Again, fainter stars near Altair form the Eagle and you will need a lot of imagination to find an eagle there. The eagle was the bird of Zeus and is often represented carrying aloft the young boy Ganymede. Aquila was also known as the bird of Jove and the bearer of his thunder. Whatever the legend, it is impossible to take the fainter stars that join with Altair and really make an Eagle out of this part of the heavens.

Deneb is the third bright star and is to the east of Vega and Altair. Deneb marks the tail of Cygnus, the Swan. Perhaps you can see a Swan here. Faint stars form the Swan's body and long neck and others the bird's wings. There are many legends that might account for the presence of a Swan in the heavens. One myth states that the Swan represents Orpheus, who was slain by Bacchus. However Orpheus's music was so wonderful that he was changed into a Swan and placed in the heavens near his beloved harp.

Cygnus is flying south along a hazy band of light. This is the light from billions of stars so far away that you cannot see each one as a point of light. This is the Milky Way, our city of stars in the universe. Follow the band toward the South and you come to Sagittarius, the Archer. You may be able to see an archer here with his arm curved as he pulls back on his bow. Sagittarius really looks like a teapot. You can see a small triangle of stars which forms the lid, the pot itself, Sagittarius's

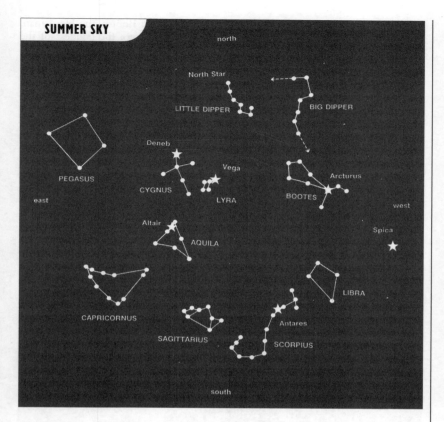

(Figure labels: north, North Star, LITTLE DIPPER, BIG DIPPER, Deneb, Vega, Arcturus, PEGASUS, CYGNUS, LYRA, BOOTES, east, west, Altair, Spica, AQUILA, LIBRA, CAPRICORNUS, SAGITTARIUS, Antares, SCORPIUS, south)

curved arm is the pot's handle and there is even a spout. When you look toward Sagittarius you are looking to the center of the Milky Way.

Sagittarius is firing his arrow at Scorpius, the Scorpion. The Scorpion's heart is marked by the bright red star Antares. Because of its red color, Antares is called the rival of Mars. According to legend, Orion was a mighty hunter. Orion boasted that he could defeat any animal on Earth in battle. Suddenly a scorpion appeared, stung Orion on the foot and Orion died. But Orion was such a great hunter that he was placed in the sky; as was the scorpion. However, you never see Orion and the Scorpion in the sky at the same time.

If the name Scorpius is familiar to you, it is probably because Scorpius is one of the 12 star groups or constellations of the zodiac. West of the Scorpion, in the zodiac, are fainter stars that form Libra, the Scales.

Perhaps one of the easiest signposts to find is the Big Dipper, also known as the Plough. Face north and look for seven fairly bright stars which form a dipper or a cooking pot – three stars mark the handle and four more the bowl. Some people know that if you draw a line through the two stars at the end of the bowl and extend the line away from the bowl, you come to the North Star. Now, remember, the North Star is NOT the brightest star in the sky. In fact, it really isn't bright at all. It just happens to be at a point in the heavens almost directly over the North Pole.

Go back to the Big Dipper once more. This time use the Dipper's handle. Follow the arc of the handle away from the Dipper to the bright star Arcturus and then speed on to Spica. Arcturus is the brightest star in Boötes, the Herdsman. Spica is a grain of wheat being held in the hand of Virgo, the goddess of the Harvest, another constellation of the zodiac.

THE WINTER SKY High in the southern sky in winter you will easily find the seven bright stars that form Orion. Two bright stars mark his shoulders, Betelgeuse and Bellatrix; two more bright stars his knees, Saiph and Rigel; and three mark his belt, Alnitak, Anilam and Mintala. To the south of Orion you will again come to the bright star Sirius, in Canis Major, the Great Hunting Dog. Canis Major is one of Orion's two hunting dogs. North of Sirius and east of Orion is a bright star, of course fainter than Sirius; this is Procyon, marking Canis Minor, the Lesser Hunting Dog.

If you continue north of Procyon, you will come to two bright stars, fairly close together and of about the same brightness. These two are Castor and Pollux and they mark the heads of the Gemini Twins. According to mythology, Castor and Pollux were twin brothers and the sons of Jupiter. The twins accompanied Jason and the Argonauts in the quest for the Golden Fleece. Pollux was famous for his achievements in arms whereas Castor was a superior equestrian. The Twins also were said to have power over the seas and ship builders often paid homage to them by placing effigies of the twins in the prows of vessels.

Turn and face north and you should find the most famous of all star groups, the Big Dipper, also known as the Plough. Seven bright stars form the Big Dipper.

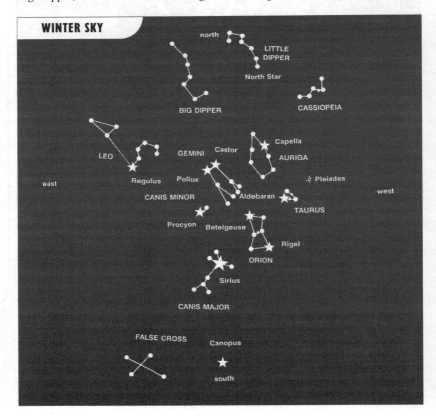

WINTER SKY

north

LITTLE DIPPER

North Star

BIG DIPPER

CASSIOPEIA

LEO

Regulus

east

GEMINI   Castor

Pollux

CANIS MINOR

Procyon   Betelgeuse

Capella

AURIGA

Aldebaran

.⁖ Pleiades

west

TAURUS

Rigel

ORION

Sirius

CANIS MAJOR

FALSE CROSS   Canopus

south

Three stars form the Dipper's handle and four more its bowl. The Big Dipper is one of the few star groups that actually looks like its name. The Big Dipper is not a constellation. Astronomers have divided the entire sky into 88 constellations, each with distinct boundaries, like states on a map. The seven stars of the Big Dipper are part of a much larger constellation, Ursa Major, the Great Bear.

One legend relates that Callisto, the beautiful daughter of King Lycanon, incurred the jealous wrath of Juno. Jupiter fearing that Juno would harm Callisto, transformed her into a bear. When Juno realised this he persuaded Diana to hunt the bear and try to kill her. To protect Callisto, Jupiter placed the bear in the night sky. But the story does not end there. Juno was so upset that Callisto was given this honour that he persuaded Tethys and Oceanus to forbid the Bear to descend like other stars into the sea. Thus, even today, the stars of Ursa Major never set, but circle in the northern sky.

If you draw a line through the two stars at the end of the bowl of the Big Dipper and extend the line onward, you will come to Polaris, the North Star. Polaris is at the end of the handle of the Little Dipper, which is part of Ursa Minor, the Little Bear.

The handle of the Big Dipper forms the long tail of the bear as does the handle of the Little Dipper. The only problem is that bears have short tails! According to another legend, the mighty hunter Orion grabbed the two bears by their tails, swung them around and around and flung the bears into the sky. In doing so he stretched their tails!

If you look toward the northwest you should be able to find some stars in the shape of a 'W'. This is Cassiopeia, the Queen. Of course a W looks nothing like a queen, but do not let that trouble you. According to Greek mythology, Cassiopeia was the wife of Cepheus, king of Ethiopia and the mother of Andromeda.

Looking toward the northeast you will find a bright star. This is Regulus, the heart of Leo, the Lion. Regulus is also the point at the base of a backwards question mark. The top of the question mark is Leo's head and a triangle of fainter stars toward the East marks the Lion's hind quarters and tail. Don't worry if you cannot see a Lion here, most other people can't either, but you should be able to find the backwards question mark.

Leo is one of the 12 star groups or constellations of the zodiac. The zodiac is a band of constellations which encircles the sky and it is to the zodiac that we must look to find the planets.

'Skywriter' articles and maps © 2008 Thomas A Lesser. Dr Lesser is the former senior lecturer at New York's Hayden Planetarium, and author of numerous articles on astronomy. He has lectured on astronomy in the Caribbean.

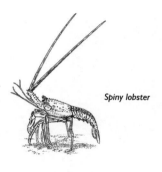

Spiny lobster

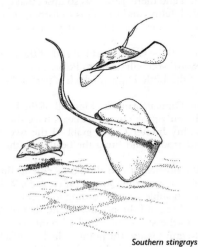

Southern stingrays

Part Two

THE ISLANDS

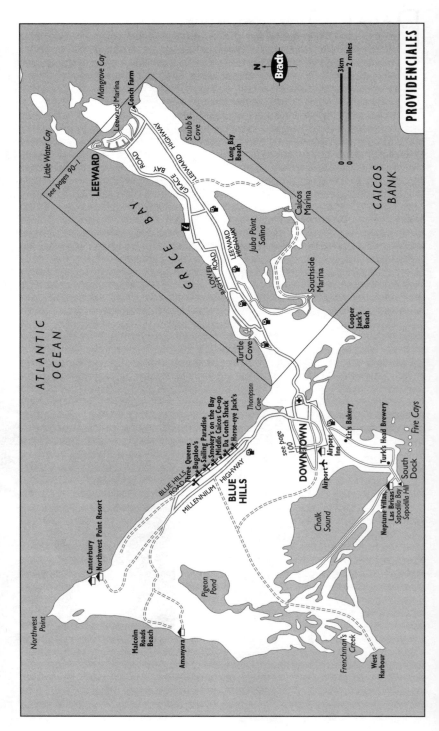

PROVIDENCIALES

4

Providenciales

Until the 1980s, Providenciales was little more than a peaceful island with just a few visitors who came back year on year for the diving. The first hotel, Third Turtle Inn, wasn't built until the late 1960s, and even the arrival of Club Med in 1984 did little to dispel the prevailing atmosphere. Since the 1990s, however, the impact of the condominium culture has been immense, and building in the Grace Bay area in particular has undergone something of an explosion. Whilst oceanfront construction initially was restricted to a maximum of three floors, the level was soon increased to five, and a newcomer has now soared to seven. It would be sad if the utopian nature of this special paradise were to become simply a replica of Miami Beach. Fortunately for residents and visitors alike, regular and clearly marked beach access points have been left between the developments.

With a total land area of 38 square miles (98km²), the island is just 17 miles (27km) long, by a maximum of three miles (4.8km) wide, with a high point at Blue Hills of a mere 160ft (49m); indeed, this is the highest point in the island group as a whole.

HISTORY

It is possible but as yet unproven that the prehistoric Ciboney Indians were far earlier inhabitants of Providenciales, but recent, as yet undocumented evidence suggests there was at least one pre-Columbian settlement on what is today the most populated island in the Turks and Caicos.

A few years ago Brian Riggs, curator of the National Environment Centre, out walking with a colleague in Chalk Sound National Park, came upon an area of ground which he recognised at once was likely to have been the site of a Lucayan fishing village. From his wide understanding of the Caicos Islands, Riggs is well acquainted with the clues that indicate Taino habitation and suspects that when fully investigated this might turn out to be one of the more significant sites in the country. So far all that can be guessed as to the dates of its occupation, is sometime during the period between AD1100 and AD1500.

What is certain is that shortly after the arrival in the region of the first Europeans, Ponce, Columbus and their companions, for whatever reason, the Tainos ceased to have a presence in Providenciales or any of the neighbouring islands (see pages 4–6).

Neither the name the Tainos chose for Provo nor that given it by the first European visitors is clear, but we do know that more recently the island has been referred to variously as Provident Cay, Blue Caicos, or simply Blue Hills – the same appellation as that of the earliest recorded settlement. Interestingly, Nigel Sadler, former director of the National Museum on Grand Turk, has shown that a map drawn by Frenchman Jacques Bellin in 1753 marks a place that could be this as *Habitation de Genes* (presumably this means *housing of people*, rather than *housing of*

Genoa). And it has been suggested elsewhere that survivors from a long ago French shipwreck might have sought refuge on the northwestern shores of this island. Certainly many vessels came to grief on nearby reefs and, as on Grand Turk, there are tales of wrackers (salvagers) beaming lights from the Blue Hills' shores to beguile unwary ships while in truth luring them to their doom. Both the Caicos and Turks Island (Columbus) passages pass through the country's waters and traditionally the majority of ship-borne trade, coming or going between the Caribbean and Europe, would have followed one or other route. Along with Parrot and the adjacent Leeward Cays, Provo provided a notorious lair for buccaneers throughout the 17th and 18th centuries (see pages 8–9). And still today the surrounding ocean guards many secrets. Just one of them lies at a tantalising depth of 20ft (6m) on the Molasses Reef, some 15 miles south of Providenciales. From the style of its armaments and recovered artefacts it can be deduced to be the wreck of a European ship which must have sunk c1515, making it the oldest shipwreck of this provenance to have been discovered in the Americas (see pages 6–7).

For strategic reasons in 1764 Britain assumed governance of the Turks and Caicos and some 20 years later, following the American Declaration of Independence, the islands were to provide a haven for Loyalists (Tories) – those who wished to remain British – escaping from the southern states of South Carolina and Georgia, and bringing with them their slaves. In compensation for their losses the Loyalists were given tracts of Crown land. In Providenciales these grants were used to develop plantations for the production of sea-island cotton, a commodity much valued in Europe. For several reasons, but essentially through a lack of understanding of the climatic conditions, the exercise was doomed to failure within a quarter of a century, and little or nothing is left to show for their efforts at Richmond Hills or the Rice plantation. Of Cheshire Hall estate alone there are significant remains, which since 2003 have been under the protection of Turks and Caicos National Trust (see pages 61–2). While most of the planters gave up and departed, many of their slaves were left behind, and it was they who became the seeds for the Belongers of Providenciales today.

It has been noted that at the end of the 18th century Providenciales was technically not one but two islands, albeit divided only by a narrow waterway, which was subsequently filled in by hurricane activity. In a low-lying area, subject to seasonal tropical upheaval, doesn't this small detail also call into question the validity of historical fact that may be based largely on topography (see page 154)?

When in the mid 1960s a fresh band of adventurers first made landfall in the Turks and Caicos, they were travelling eastward. Unlike the Spanish they had all the maps and navigational aids they needed, and they knew exactly what they were looking for. They were seeking an idyllic retreat, an island in the sun where they could sail and fish and breathe fresh air; a safe anchorage from which they could come and go with ease.

Somewhat oddly they have come to be referred to as the 'seven dwarfs' – perhaps a take on 'gnome' as in financial wizardry. For sure they made up a rum medley and between them were rich enough to enjoy some fun. At the time they sailed into Provo there were just three extant settlements: Blue Hills, The Bight and Five Cays. There was no electricity, no telephone and no amenities. Groceries had to be brought in by boat but mainly the islanders ate conch, fish, lobster and iguana; as did the seven dwarfs. A lobster went for 50 cents and it wasn't long before the visitors were 'lobster'd out and ready to kill for a hotdog'. A lease-purchase deal was struck with the government whereby the travellers were to form a company, Provident Ltd, to construct an airstrip, roads to link the three villages, and to excavate the inlet at Turtle Cove, in exchange for which they would be allowed to lease 4,000 acres of Crown land.

One of the first steps was to build a hotel and in 1968 the ten-room Third Turtle Inn welcomed its first guests. On final approach to the new gravel airstrip, pioneer Earle Perkins recalls looking down from Kip Dupont's nattily tricked out DC3 as they were above the new gravel airstrip and observing 'we can't land there, it looks like someone's driveway'.

'The man with the familiar name, ragged shorts, a belt made of rope and canvas shoes with the toes rolled out, really is famous and is having the time of his life,' Perkins reflects on those halcyon days.

The first manager to be employed by Third Turtle was Suzy Depalma. She had arrived from New York unable to drive, and although one of her duties entailed picking up guests from the airport, that in itself didn't prove too much of a handicap for at that time there were only three vehicles on the island, and one of those a bulldozer. Most of the guests would arrive after dark so it was within Suzy's remit to drive to the strip and position her headlights on to the runway to facilitate touchdown. But on the return journey, with her mind occupied by other concerns, more often than not she would miss the junction from Leeward Highway on to the track running down to Turtle Cove. To remind her of this direction, the dwarfs put up a pole with a rag tied to it but she still managed to miss it, so eventually the rag was replaced by a sign, 'Suzy Turn'. Although Suzy herself lasted only a matter of months, her name had made history

By the beginning of the1970s Providenciales could boast one fuel station and one small grocery/hardware store – 'a good part of the time without groceries,' recalls Perkins. 'In theory a ship came in once a month bringing canned goods and staples. Fresh food was flown in by private plane once a week.' In spite of there being a ready supply of local limestone – roadwork excavations making easy pickings – the logistics required in building a private property were far from simple, with many of the materials needing to be imported. Among the earliest expatriate developments was a set of five houses that still stand today, at the northeastern tip of the island, and a small marina facility adjacent to Leeward-Going-Through. At about this time, too, another group of investors was setting out to fulfil the dream of Ferdinand Czernin, son of the last prime minister of the Austro-Hungarian Empire, and a vision his widow continued to pursue on his behalf, to create a luxuriously rustic retreat at Pine Cay. Later this was to become to become the exclusive Meridian Club (see page 96).

Improvements at the Turtle Club marina were before long able to provide secure berthing for boats up to 120ft (36m) with a 6ft (1.8m) draught, and soon 12-mile (19km) long Grace Bay was to see its first hotel, low-rise and low-budget, and called – in honour of the female conch – Island Princess (later demolished to make way for the up-scale Veranda). Barclays Bank opened a full service branch in 1981 and in 1984, after the extension and paving of the airport runway, Club Med arrived in Turks and Caicos. In 1990 Ocean Club became the first condominium property on the island, starting a trend that has gathered ground ever since.

HISTORY IN THE MAKING At the time of writing, the controversial Star Island project, set to feature a series of $4 million house lots and yacht slips, has been suspended. The artificial island, modelled on Palm Island in Dubai, was being created in Princess Alexandra National Park, north of Leeward Marina which is itself currently being enlarged to accommodate yachts of up to 200ft (60m). On Grace Bay Seven Stars will be in business by July; towards the end of the year Ritz-Carlton are scheduled to open a 125-room hotel on West Caicos, followed in 2009 by Mandarin Oriental on the previously uninhabited Dellis Cay. And a major beach preservation project is about to commence at Babalua Beach on Provo, in preparation for the controversial construction of a 433-room, seven-storey

Rockresort, The Third Turtle Club and Spa, on the site of the original hotel (see above) is scheduled to receive its first guests in 2011. The resort is destined to make a considerable impact on the Turtle Cove area.

On the plus side, a site has been earmarked at Long Bay on Providenciales for a recently conceived Provo branch of the wonderful Turks and Caicos National Museum (headquartered at Grand Turk; see pages 172–3). With work estimated to take between three and five years, dynamic new director Dr Neal Hitch was appointed towards the end of 2007 with a brief that includes the early implementation of these plans.

NATURAL HISTORY

A natural history of Providenciales written even 20 years ago would reflect an island that had remained unchanged for centuries. Along much of the western, southern and eastern shores, mangroves lined the shallow coastline, while elsewhere long, empty beaches were the haunt of numerous seabirds. Inland, scrubby vegetation eked out an existence in the poor, rocky soil, attracting the curlytail lizard, numerous butterflies, and birds such as the tiny blue-gray gnatcatcher. In places, deep sinkholes plunged into the limestone – most effectively at The Hole (see page 120).

So just how much has changed with the tourist explosion? Well the answer is everything, or relatively little, depending on where you're standing. To the west of the island, great tracts of bush still repel all but the most intrepid visitor, with bumpy tracks leading to small, secluded beaches. The improbably turquoise waters of Chalk Sound are protected as a national park, as are the waters around Grace Bay, while a nature reserve covers the mangroves of Frenchman's Creek. And The Hole is still there, albeit not much more than a large hole. Elsewhere, though, it's a different story, at least in part. Tourist development has taken its toll of Grace Bay and the immediate hinterland; luxury houses line the hills around Chalk Sound and the new marina development at Leeward has resulted in the destruction of significant tracts of the mangrove defence system. Mangroves hang on, though, on the protected Mangrove Cay across the Leeward-Going-Through channel, and on Little Water Cay, where the endemic Turks and Caicos iguana has one of its last remaining strongholds.

Arguably the best places to find out about Provo's natural flora and fauna are Little Water Cay itself, and Cheshire Hall (see pages 123 and 119–20), where interpretive leaflets linked to numbered signs indicate various types of vegetation, from orchids and trees to sea-island cotton, which in turn attract many of the island's bird species.

GETTING THERE

BY AIR If you want to get straight into the party mood, time your arrival for a weekend, when live music greets each of the incoming international flights at Provo Airport.

The airport building is modern and light, although when flights are delayed space is at a premium. International departure desks take up most of the main hall, with domestic departures set off to the left. There's a restaurant and bar, Gilbey's (⊕ *6.30am daily until the last flight leaves*), at this point, but once through the immigration gate there's only a bar, with food limited to basic snacks. For those last-minute souvenirs, basic toiletries and confectionery, Nell's Gift Shop has a branch by the international departure desks, and a second in the departures hall.

More upmarket are the duty-free shops in the departures hall, selling everything from perfume to watches and luxury jewellery. But if your departure is very early or very late, don't rely on any of these being invariably open.

Rather more interesting for most travellers is a display of replica inscriptions taken from Sapodilla Hill. If you're just taking an internal flight, and will still have time to see the real thing, they can be found within a short climb of Sapodilla Bay (see pages 121–2).

Local airline offices
Air Turks & Caicos ☎ 946 5481, reservations ☎ 946 4999; www.flyairtc.com
American Airlines ☎ 941 5200; www.aa.com

Global Airways ☎ 941 3222; www.globalairways.org
SkyKing ☎ 941 5464; www.skyking.tc
US Airways ☎ 800 622 1015; www.usairways.com

Getting into town There is no bus service from the airport, but hotels will frequently arrange for someone to meet incoming flights on a complimentary basis. Otherwise a taxi could cost up to $25 per passenger for a one-way trip to Grace Bay, or around $15 to Turtle Cove. A tip for the driver of $2–5 is an appropriate sum, dependent on the amount of baggage heaved. Taxis are usually much in evidence outside the terminal building to mark the arrival of an international flight. At busy times, a despatcher is on hand to allocate a driver to each passenger or group of passengers, but you'll need to confirm a price with your taxi driver.

For those hiring a vehicle, most of the car-hire companies (see page 87) have an office at the airport, or can arrange to have your vehicle ready at a pre-agreed time and place.

YACHT See pages 114–15 for a brief overview of sailing in and around Providenciales' waters.

GETTING AROUND

BY ROAD With the increase in development has come a commensurate improvement in the roads, with most of the major access roads now surfaced. Island tours can be arranged through some of the taxi companies, and a series of tours is run by the Gecko bus (see page 86).

Taxis There are numerous licensed taxis, indicated by red number plates on a turquoise background. Most are effectively minibuses, with a capacity of up to eight passengers.

Taxis are normally metered, though not all drivers are quick to turn them on. There is an official scale of charges – though you'll rarely find this in evidence. Rates are usually revised at the end of each year, with fares based on two people travelling together. Additional passengers will be subject to an extra charge. A fair tip is around 10–15%, with extra for heavy luggage. Although taxis are increasingly expensive, it is worth considering combining them with walking a bit rather than renting a car, at least for part of your visit.

Taxis are often to be found at Ports of Call on Grace Bay Road. Alternatively, try one of the following, many of whom will also quote for an island tour on request. In all cases the fare should be agreed in advance.

🚌 **Capion's Taxis & Tours** m 241 5403, 6206. Island tours £45/hr.
🚌 **George & Sons** m 241 4351
🚌 **Neill's Taxi** m 231 0018

🚌 **Outton** m 241 4098
🚌 **Sonny's** m 231 0658
🚌 **Susan** m 241 8385
🚌 **Uncle Willy** m 231 1945

For that special occasion, why not throw caution to the wind and hire a limousine from:

Island's Choice m 231 0409; e timespub@tciway.tc
VIP Limousine & Tour ℡ 941 5295; m 232 9990; e info@tcilimo.com; www.tcilimo.com. Limos & stretch limos; 3hr sightseeing tour, including complimentary bottle of champagne, $300 for 1–5 persons; $55 each for 6 or more. There is also a 3hr tour at the same price, tailored to the potential investor. Departures 10am & 2.30pm.

Cheaper are the unlicensed taxis, known as *jitneys*, which are frequently saloon cars in varying states of disrepair. Often marked out only because they have too many passengers on board, who share the total fare between them, they'll frequently hoot the horn as they pass. Think carefully before hopping in to one of these, and if you do, ensure that you agree a rate for the journey *before* setting off.

Special mobility service A modified taxi capable of taking a wheelchair is run by E Benjamin (Ben) Williams (m *243 4919; 232 4919;* ℡ *941 7884;* e *b_jamin_1974@ hotmail.com*), offering airport transfers, transport to a dinner location, or indeed an island tour. It is best but not always essential to reserve ahead.

Public transport While public transport is officially non-existent, there are several private operators who are licensed and have stepped in to fill the void. Many of these call themselves 'buses', but unlike public-service vehicles operated in most countries, they don't run to a timetable, and are available on call.

Bus stops are in evidence across all populated areas of Provo, and it's at one of these that you should wait if you want to get from A to B – and are not in a hurry. Alternatively, you could call one of the individual companies direct, and they'll turn up to get you, just like a taxi, but for a flat rate.

Of these, the most widely known and advertised is the bright red Gecko bus, which was aimed at the tourist and operated in and around Grace Bay. Its service was largely suspended in February 2008, but there are several others, albeit with a wider remit.

The Gecko m 232 7433; www.thegecko.tc. Until the service was suspended in February 2008, this tourist shuttle bus operated the length of Grace Bay as far as Turtle Cove and the IGA supermarket; details have been left in case the service is reinstated. Passengers could either wait at one of the red 'gecko' signs by the road, or call ahead to book the bus. Each journey cost a flat rate of $4, or a series of passes cost from $11/5.50 (adult/child 5–12) for a single day, or $30.50 for a family of 4. Tickets had to be purchased in advance at hotel reception desks or similar, not on the bus. In the meantime, the company still runs various organised tours:
Gecko Island Tour – from Leeward Marina to Blue Hills (*Tue & Thu; $30/20 adult/child 5–12*)
Conch Farm/Da Conch Shack Connection (*Fri; $55/40 adult/child 5–12*)
Island Pub Crawl – from Blue Hills to Ports of Call (*every other Fri; $30/20 adult/child 5–12*)
Paintball (*Mon, Wed & Fri; $40 pp, inc 500 paintballs*)
Barbecue Mania (*Mon; $35 pp, inc live music & rum punch*)
Rum Tasting at Da Conch Shack (*Wed; $40 per adult, inc conch dinner*)
Reliable Bus Service m 232 1996. Operated by Keith James. $2 flat rate in Grace Bay area.

Vehicle hire The speed limit on Providenciales is 40mph (65km/h) on the Leeward Highway, where driving can be decidedly erratic, and 20mph (32km/h) on most other roads. Do remember that all car-hire rates are subject to 10% tax, and that the seventh day of hire is frequently free of charge. Most hire companies will accept all major credit cards. For all other information on driving, see pages 50–1.

There are numerous fuel stations, particularly along the Leeward Highway. Most are open from around 6am until 8pm, Monday to Saturday, with shorter hours on a Sunday, but some stay open until midnight during the week.

🚗 **Avis** Dolphin Dr, Grace Bay & airport; ✆ 941 7557/8, US toll free ✆ 1888 897 8448; e reservations@avis.tc; www.avis.com; m 232 1406; ⏲ 8am–4pm Mon–Fri, 8am–3.30pm Sat. Airport office ✆ 946 4705; ⏲ 8am–5pm daily. With an office almost opposite Grace Bay Pharmacy & a 2nd at the airport, Avis is easily accessible. Rates from $48.95/day for a small Charade. CDW $16.95/day; $4/day liability insurance. Additional driver $5/day, or $25/wk. No extra charge for airport drop-off.

🚗 **Budget** Town Centre Mall, Leeward Hwy; & at the airport; ✆ 946 4079; US toll free ✆ 1 800 527 0700; e budget@tciway.tc; www.budget.com. Economy cars $48/288 per day/wk, SUV $75/450. CDW $20.95 a day; $4/day liability insurance. Unlimited mileage. Some right-hand drive vehicles available on request.

🚗 **Grace Bay Car Rentals** Grace Bay Rd, opp Regent Village; ✆ 941 8500; e info@gracebaycarrental.com; www.gracebaycarrentals.com. Cars from $39/239 per day/wk. Toyota 8-passenger van $79/474. Unlimited mileage. Good right-hand drive availability.

🚗 **Island Rent-a-Car** ✆ 946 4993

🚗 **Mystique Car Rental** Ports of Call, Grace Bay Rd; ✆ 941 3910; e mystique@tciway.tc. www.hertz.com; ⏲ 9.30am–4pm daily. The local agent for Hertz. Compact car $59/day plus tax & insurance; 7th day free. Also off Airport Rd.

🚗 **Provo Rent-a-Car** Grace Bay; ✆ 946 4404; m 231 0528; airport office Airport Rd; ✆ 946 4475, 4853.

🚗 **Rent a Buggy** Leeward Hwy; ✆ 946 4158; m 231 6161; e reservations@tciway.tc; www.rentabuggy.tc. Just west of Suzy Turn, with a range of Suzuki and Kia jeeps from $62/day, with unlimited mileage. CDW $11.95.

🚗 **Scooter Bob's** Turtle Cove Marina; ✆ 946 4684; e scooter@provo.net; www.provo.net/scooter; ⏲ 8am–4pm, Mon–Sat, 8am–noon Sun. Cars & jeeps from $60/day, SUV $79; CDW $15; unlimited mileage. Airport drop-off fee $15; credit card fee 5%. Minimum age 25. As the name suggests, this is also the place to go for scooters at $49/day – not to mention children's car seats at $5/day, plus fishing tackle & snorkelling equipment at $15/day.

🚗 **Suzuki Jeep Rental** Leeward Hwy; ✆ 946 4158

🚗 **TC National Car Rental** Airport Plaza, Airport Rd; ✆ 946 4701, 941 3514; e airportinn@tciway.tc. Medium car $70/420 per day/wk; Jeep $98/588; CDW $11.95/day, liability insurance $4. Minimum age 25.

🚗 **Total Rent a Car** Airport Rd; ✆ 941 7751; m 232 3357; e clayewing@tciway.tc, www.totalcars@tciway.tc

🚗 **Tropical Auto Rentals** Tropicana Plaza, Leeward Hwy; ✆ 946 5300; e tropical@provo.net; www.provo.net/tropicalauto; ⏲ 8.30am–5.30pm. Kia Picanto $49.99/299.94 per day/wk; Jeep $86/516. CDW $11.95/day; liability insurance $4.

Excursions Although many of the taxi drivers will organise day excursions on request, there are a few operators who are specifically geared up for day tours:

Catch the Wave See page 113.
Executive Tours ✆ 946 4524; m 231 2358
J&B Tours See page 114.

Majestic Tours ✆ 946 4181; e interisland@tciway.tc
Provo Travel ✆ 946 4035; e provotravel@tciway.tc
Turkoise Excursions ✆ 946 5379

BY SEA For those wishing to visit one of the other islands, there are two options. A new ferry service, introduced in 2007, plies between Leeward Marina at the eastern end of Providenciales and North Caicos (for details, see page 126). Alternatively, contact one of the tour operators specialising in day excursions (see above).

TOURIST INFORMATION

Turks & Caicos Islands Tourist Board Regent Plaza, Grace Bay Rd; ✆ 946 4970; e tci.tourism@tciway.tc; www.turksandcaicostourism.com
Turks & Caicos Hotel & Tourism Association Ports of Call, Grace Bay Rd; ✆ 941 5787;

www.turksandcaicoshta.com. Publishes an annual directory listing most hotels & spas, & offers a reservations service for all major hotels.

Most of Providenciales' tourist hotels and apartments are concentrated around the eastern end of the island, along Grace Bay Beach. For those in search of something a little cheaper and within easy walking distance of a variety of restaurants and bars, it's worth investigating Turtle Cove Marina, but if it's complete seclusion you're after, head for the resorts to the northwest – or for one of the exclusive islands to the northeast of Provo.

With options ranging between the highly private island outpost of the members-only Yellowstone Club, sequestered at Silly Point, an assortment of luxury condominium resorts and only a handful of traditional hotels, David Wickers' description of Mauritius in *The Times* – 'reassuringly expensive and riff-raff free' – could equally be applied to Providenciales. Few real budget choices exist, though prices do drop significantly in the low season, and to a degree in the period in between, and there are often special packages and deals to be snapped up either via the internet, through agencies, or by scanning the travel pages of your own national newspapers. Special rates on soft-opening of a new property is another thing to look out for. Renting a privately owned villa can also sometimes be a more economic solution. But if you're after backpacking and camping beneath the stars, on Provo alas you should forget it, though you might consider one of the uninhabited islands or cays, checking in advance with the Environmental Centre or the tourist information office first, to confirm you will not be choosing a protected area.

LUXURY $$$$–$$$$$

⌂ **Alexandra** (85 studios & 1–4-bedroom suites) Princess Dr, Grace Bay; ⟍ 946 5807; US toll free ⟍ 1 800 284 0699; e info@alexandraresort.com; www.alexandraresort.com. With a less ritzy atmosphere than some of its neighbours, the Alexandra has tennis courts, pool & fitness centre. Orchid Restaurant (see below) for b/fast & dinner; beachfront dining deck for lunch. On Tue, Thu, Sat they do a 'Barefoot on the Beach Romantic Dinner', a gourmet meal for 2 in the dunes with private waiters (max 4 couples) at $250 plus drinks, tax & service charge. There's a Caribbean cookout every Mon eve & Mexican Fiesta on Fri, both with music, at $25pp. Karaoke is Tue. $$$$

⌂ **Coral Gardens** (30 suites) & **Reef Residences** (24 suites) Penns Rd, The Bight, Grace Bay; ⟍ 941 3713; US toll free ⟍ 1 800 532 8536; outside N America ⟍ 1 305 383 1933; e info@coralgardens.com; www.coralgardens.com. Sharing contact details & access to each other's facilities, these are on adjacent sites but Reef Residences, the newer addition, stands 80yds (72m) back from the beach down a small path. Both have 1- & 2-bedroom suites with kitchen, cable TV, AC, fridge & safe. Complimentary American b/fast, de-stress massage, weekly cocktail party, martini evening, internet access & snorkel equipment. Two freshwater pools. **Coral Gardens** has laundry facilities in the building, a dive shop, casual dining at the Beach Café & ocean-view suites. **Reef Residences** has the Ayurveda Spa, fitness centre, a candlelit restaurant & lower-priced garden courtyard suites. Children under 19 sleep free in parents' room. $$$$

⌂ **Grace Bay Club** (21 suites in main hotel, 38 suites at **the Villas**) Grace Bay; ⟍ 946 5050; US toll free ⟍ 1 800 946 5757; e info@gracebayclub.com; www.gracebayclub.com. Built in 1953 & one of the first truly luxury complexes on the island, it shows no signs of age & retains its exceptionally high standards. Until recently it was for adults only, but in 2007 they opened the Villas, with 38 'family suites' at slightly lower rates. Now, beside the infinity poolside bar & restaurant, there is the Grill Rouge for families, while the Anacona remains for adult gourmets only (see below for both). Spa & fitness centre, Kids Town activity centre; beachside pool. Complimentary full b/fast. $$$$$

⌂ **Le Vele** (22 suites) Grace Bay; ⟍ 941 8800; US toll free ⟍ 1 888 272 4406; www.levele.tc. One of the best small hotels on Grace Bay, combining elegant simplicity with very professional staff. Complimentary continental b/fast served in the rooms. Suites are 1, 2 or 3 bedrooms, & include WiFi access, safe, cable TV & *NY Times* Digest. There's also bottled water at the infinity pool, a fitness room, bikes, & airport transfers. $$$$

🏠 **Ocean Club Resort** (86 rooms) & **Ocean Club West** (88 rooms) Grace Bay; ↘ 946 5880; US toll free ↘ 1 800 457 8787; UK toll free ↘ 0 800 917 0694; e reservations@oceanclubresorts.com; www.oceanclubresorts.com. These 2 hotels, a mile apart along the beach, share all facilities & there is a complimentary shuttle between them. They are of very similar design & atmosphere, quite family oriented & not at the top end of Grace Bay accommodation. Both have complimentary internet access in the lobby.

Ocean Club Resort (the original) has a spa, dive shop, fitness centre, 2 pools, gift shop & tennis court, as well as the Gecko Grille & the Cabana Bar & Grill serving Caribbean fusion food (see below for both). $$$

Ocean Club West (marginally the nicer) has the French-Caribbean Seaside Café (self-serve complimentary filter coffee at bar), dive shop, 2 tennis courts & fitness centre. Kids Clubhouse for ages 4–12 (🕐 9.30am–5.30pm, Mon–Wed, & Fri; 1.30pm–5.30pm Thu; 9.30am–1.30pm Sat) $40/70 ½/full day. Babysitting $15/hr plus $2 per extra child. $$$

🏠 **Point Grace Resort** (30 suites) Grace Bay Rd; ↘ 946 5096; US toll free ↘ 1 866 92 GRACE; e reservations@pointgrace.com; www.pointgrace.com. One of the most luxurious resorts on Grace Bay & the winner of several travel trade awards. The Point is named after Grace Hutchings, who honeymooned nearby in 1892 & so charmed the locals that they named the beach after her. The hotel stands in Princess Alexandra National Park, named after a more modern lady of notable charm. There are 1-bed cottages around the pool, oceanfront 2- & 3-bed suites & 2 4-bed penthouses. All have just about every amenity you could dream of. Guests enjoy free transfers, complimentary continental b/fast & evening drinks, tennis & non-motorised watersports. There is a 'Thalassa' Spa. B/fast & lunch are served at Hutchings Restaurant, a coffee shop just inside the gates (see below), the Terrace Restaurant, or on the beach. A Caribbean gourmet dinner is served in Grace's Cottage (see below) $$$$$

🏠 **Regent Palms** (72 rooms) Grace Bay; ↘ 946 8666; US toll free ↘ 1 800 545 5000; e reservationstc@regentexperience.com; www.regenthotels.com/thepalms. Oliver Messel-style mansions set in painstakingly maintained 12-acre gardens on the beach with a 1-acre spa including 8 coral-stone treatment rooms. Public areas are ultra cool & elegant, & staff notably gracious. Lots of

mirrors remind you who you are. Ocean view & oceanfront suites have 1–3 bedrooms & kitchen with fridge & washer/dryer, also a room bar, safe & internet access. Daily butler service available at extra charge. Infinity pool with swim-up bar & restaurant, art gallery, boutique, deli, & one of the best of the hotel boutiques. Conch Kritters Club for kids. International cuisine at Parallel 23 Restaurant (see below). Recommended if you can afford it. $$$$$

🏠 **Royal West Indies Resort** (60 suites & studios) Grace Bay Rd; ↘ 946 5004; US toll free ↘ 1 800 332 4203; e info@royalwestindies.com; www.royalwestindies.com. A tad less grand than some other Grace Bay condo-hotels but offering quite good value for money with garden-view, ocean-view & ocean-front rooms; even studios have useful mini-kitchens & patios, washer-dryers & safes. Several buildings stand in extensive gardens. The Mango Reef Restaurant & Bar (see below) is beside the pool. $$$$

🏠 **The Sands at Grace Bay** (118 suites) Grace Bay Beach; ↘ 946 5199; e reservations@thesands.com; www.thesandsresort.com. 1-, 2- & 3-bedroom suites with kitchen & dining area are arranged in a cluster of 3-storey buildings around a garden courtyard & 3 pools; some have ocean view or are ocean front. Suites have internet access, cable TV, safe, washer dryer & ceiling fans. There is a spa, dive centre, hot tub & fitness centre; also complimentary bikes, tennis & non-motorised watersports. Welcoming & weekly rum swizzles. Hemingways Bar & Restaurant (see below) offers casual dining beside the beach. $$$$

🏠 **Seven Stars** (114 rooms) Grace Bay; ↘ 941 7777; US toll free ↘ 1 866 570 7777; e reservations@sevenstarsresort.com; www.sevenstarsresort.com. This extensive 7-storey complex (the first to break the 3-storey limit on Provo) opened in July 2008 on a 22-acre site with almost ¼ mile (350m) beach frontage. Located across the road from Ports of Call, it has 1- to 5-bedroom suites with galley kitchen, balcony, AC, ceiling fans, safe, flat-screen TV. Underground parking, Seven Stars Boutique, galleries etc in dedicated plaza; tennis courts, pool, fitness centre & spa. Complimentary continental b/fast, WiFi access, transfers. La Pergola Restaurant, Sand Dollar Grill & poolside bar. $$$$–$$$$$

🏠 **The Somerset on Grace Bay** (54 suites & studios) Princess Dr; ↘ 946 5900; US toll free ↘ 1 877 887 5722; www.thesomerset.com. Opened in 2006, this honey-coloured resort has an especially peaceful ambience, with 4½ acres of gardens & fountains

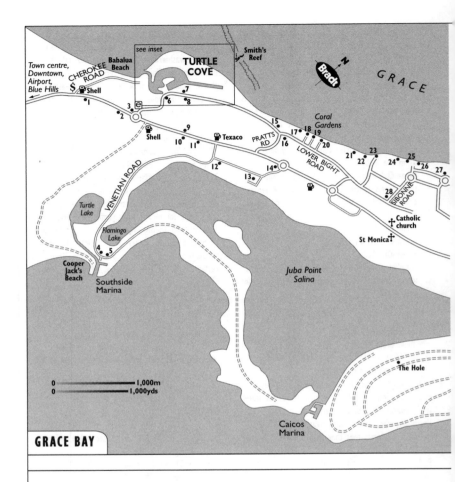

GRACE BAY

KEY (for alphabetical key, see page 92)

1   Associated Medical Practices, Dental Services Ltd
2   Central Square: Goldsmith, Greensleeves, Pennylaine Photo Studio, Provo Travel
3   Suzy Turn, Comptci, Top o' the Cove Deli
4   Flamingo Divers
5   Harbour Club
6   Miramar, Magnolia, Bodies in Motion Gym
7   Turtle Cove Inn, Aqua Restaurant, Terrace Bar
8   The Players' Club
9   Fish market
10 Wine Cellar
11 Provo Plaza: Pizza Pizza
12 National Sports Stadium
13 Graceway Sports Centre, Nautique
14 Graceway Plaza: IGA supermarket, Marco Services, Matsuri Sushi Bar, Serenity Day Spa, Turkcasian Gallery & Gifts, Unicorn Bookstore
15 Aquamarine Beach Houses
16 National Environmental Centre
17 Turks & Caicos Club
18 The Seagate
19 Coral Gardens, Reef Residences
20 Windsong
21 Beaches Resort
22 Flamingo Café
23 Alexandra, Orchid
24 Regent Palms, Parallel 123, The Spa at the Palms
25 The Somerset, O'Soleil
26 Sibonné, Bay Bistro
27 The Sands at Grace Bay, Hemingways
28 Stubbs Diamond Plaza: Police station, Bonnie's
29 Point Grace, Grace's Cottage, Hutchings, Thalasso Spa
30 South Fleetwood
31 Villa Renaissance, Teona Spa
32 Trade Winds
33 Silver Deep
34 Salt Mills Plaza: Anna's Art Gallery, Blue Surf Shop,

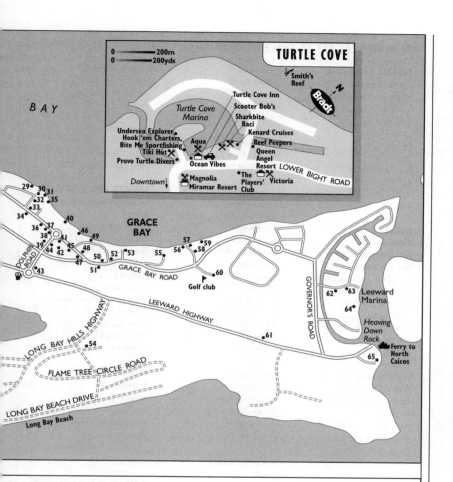

TURTLE COVE

- 0 ——— 200m
- 0 ——— 200yds

Smith's Reef

Beach

Turtle Cove Inn
Scooter Bob's
Sharkbite
Baci
Kenard Cruises
Reef Peepers
Queen
Angel
Resort

Turtle Cove
Marina

Undersea Explorer
Hook 'em Charters,
Bite Me Sportfishing
Tiki Hut
Provo Turtle Divers

Aqua

Ocean Vibes

LOWER BIGHT ROAD

Downtown

Magnolia
Miramar Resort

The
Players'
Club

Victoria

BAY

GRACE
BAY

DOLPHIN ROAD

GRACE BAY ROAD

Golf club

GOVERNOR'S ROAD

LEEWARD HIGHWAY

LONG BAY HILLS HIGHWAY

FLAME TREE CIRCLE ROAD

LONG BAY BEACH DRIVE

Long Bay Beach

Leeward
Marina

Heaving
Down
Rock

Ferry to
North
Caicos

Bambooz, Danny Buoy's, The Iguana, L'Oasis Boutique, Saltmills Café, Treasure S & S Gift Shop, Ventura Boutique, Wine & Spirits, Yoshi Sushi

35 Le Vele

36 Regent Village: Art Provo, Tourist information office

37 Grace Bay Plaza: Island Scoop & Gelato Artigianale, Philatelic Bureau, Pizza Pizza, National Trust

38 Bella Luna

39 Grace Bay Medical Centre, Grace Bay Pharmacy

40 Seven Stars

41 Ports of Call: Big Bamboo, Calico Jack's, Caribbean

Beach'n, Dive Provo, Giggles, Hertz, Island Sportique, Jimmy's Dive Bar, Mama's, Mar Azul Bazaar, Marilyn's Crafts & Apparel, Pizza Port, Spa Tropique, TCI Online

42 Comfort Suites

43 Alverna's Craft Market

44 Avis

45 La Petite Place: Caicos Adventures, Caicos Wear Boutique

46 Ocean Club West

47 Caicos Café

48 Grace Bay Court: Golden Pagoda, Gourmet Goods, Spa Sanay

49 Grace Bay Club, Anacona, Grill

Rouge, Anani Spa

50 Caribbean Paradise Inn, Coyaba

51 Coco Bistro

52 Casablanca Casino

53 Royal West Indies, Mango Reef

54 Provo Ponies

55 Club Med Turkoise

56 Cultural Market Place

57 Ocean Club, Cabana Bar

58 Gecko Grill

59 The Tuscany

60 Provo Golf Club

61 Mini Golf & Go-Karting

62 J&B

63 Big Blue

64 Nikki Beach Resort

65 Conch Farm

ALPHABETICAL KEY TO GRACE BAY MAP (pages 90–1)

SQUARES AND PLAZAS

Central Square 2
Grace Bay Court 48
Grace Bay Plaza 37
Graceway Plaza 14
La Petite Place 45
Ports of Call 41
Provo Plaza 11
Regent Village 36
Salt Mills Plaza 34
Stubbs Diamond Plaza 28
Suzy Turn 3

HOTELS

Alexandra 23
Aquamarine Beach Houses 15
Beaches Resort 21
Caribbean Paradise Inn 50
Club Med Turkoise 55
Comfort Suites 42
Coral Gardens 19
Grace Bay Club 49
Harbour Club 5
Le Vele 35
Miramar 6
Nikki Beach Resort 64
Ocean Club 57
Ocean Club West 46
Point Grace 29
Reef Residences 19
Regent Palms 24
Royal West Indies 53
Seven Stars 40
Sibonné 26
South Fleetwood 30
The Sands at Grace Bay 27
The Seagate 18
The Somerset 25
The Tuscany 59
Trade Winds 32
Turks & Caicos Club 17
Turtle Cove Inn 7
Villa Renaissance 31
Windsong 20

RESTAURANTS, CAFÉS, BARS AND TAKEAWAYS

Anacona 49
Aqua 7
Bambooz 34
Bay Bistro 26
Bella Luna 38
Big Bamboo 41

Bonnie's 28
Cabana Bar 57
Caicos Café 47
Calico Jack's 41
Coco Bistro 51
Coyaba 50
Danny Buoy's 34
Flamingo Café 22
Gecko Grill 58
Giggles 41
Golden Pagoda 48
Grace's Cottage 29
Grill Rouge 49
Hemingways 27
Hutchings 29
Island Scoop & Gelato
 Artigianale 37
Jimmy's Dive Bar 41
Magnolia 6
Mango Reef 53
Matsuri Sushi Bar 14
O'Soleil 25
Orchid 23
Parallel 23 24
Pizza Pizza 11
Pizza Pizza 37
Pizza Port 41
Saltmills Café 34
Terrace Bar 7
The Iguana 34
Yoshi Sushi 34

SHOPS AND MARKETS

Alverna's Craft Market 43
Anna's Art Gallery 34
Art Provo 36
Blue Surf Shop 34
Caicos Adventures 45
Caicos Wear Boutique 45
Caribbean Beach 'n 41
Cultural Market Place 56
Fish market 9
Goldsmith 2
Gourmet Goods 48
Greensleeves 2
IGA Supermarket 14
Island Sportique 41
L'Oasis Boutique 34
Mama's 41
Mar Azul Bazaar 41
Marilyn's Crafts & Apparel 41
National Trust 37
Nautique 13

Philatelic Bureau 37
Spa Tropique 41
Top o' the Cove Deli 3
Treasure S & S Gift Shop 34
Turkcasian Gallery & Gifts 14
Unicorn Bookstore 14
Ventura Boutique 34
Wine & Spirits 34
Wine Cellar 10

AMENITIES AND SERVICES

Associated Medical Practices 1
Avis 44
Comptci 3
Dental Services Ltd 1
Grace Bay Medical Centre 39
Grace Bay Pharmacy 39
Hertz 41
Marco Services 14
Pennylaine Photo Studio 2
Police station 28
Provo Travel 2
TCI Online 41
Tourist information office 36

SPAS AND GYMS

Anani Spa 49
Serenity Day Spa 14
Spa Sanay 48
Teona Spa 31
Thalasso Spa 29
The Spa at the Palms 24
Bodies in Motion Gym 6

PLACES OF INTEREST, ACTIVITIES AND ENTERTAINMENT

Big Blue 63
Casablanca Casino 52
Conch Farm 65
Dive Provo 41
Flamingo Divers 4
Graceway Sports Centre 13
J&B 62
Mini Golf & Go-Karting 61
National Environmental Centre 16
National Sports Stadium 12
National Trust 37
Provo Golf Club 60
Provo Ponies 54
Silver Deep 33
The Players' Club 8

beside the beach. 1- to 4-bedroom suites with plasma TV, WiFi access, zoned AC; fully-equipped Viking kitchens; some balconies with jacuzzi & gas-fired grill. Complimentary continental b/fast, transfers, weekly cocktails, bikes; babysitting; exercise & steam rooms, croquet lawn, infinity freshwater pool with lap currents, 'Lunasea bar' & underwater sound system. Home of the excellent O'Soleil restaurant (see page 97). Recommended. $$$$

⌂ **Trade Winds Condotel** (18 suites) Grace Bay; ✆ 946 5194; e tradewindshotel@tciway.tc; www.tradewindscondotel.com. All suites have kitchen with microwave & washer/dryer, living/dining room, balcony, AC, cable TV, safe, internet port & ceiling fans. Freshwater pool. Free use of bikes. Children under 12 sleep free in parents' room. Extra person in room $30. $$$–$$$$

⌂ **Turks & Caicos Club** (21 suites) Lower Bight Rd; ✆ 946 5800; US toll free ✆ 1 888 4TCLUB; e info@turksandcaicosclub.com; www.turksandcaicosclub.com. 1- & 2-bedroom suites in an elegant atmosphere, with 4-poster beds, separate living rooms, kitchens & balconies. Complimentary American b/fast; also non-motorised watersports. Poolside bar, Simba restaurant featuring Caribbean cuisine (see page 97). $$$$

MID RANGE $$–$$$

⌂ **Sibonné** (30 rooms) Grace Bay; ✆ 946 5547; US toll free ✆ 1 800 528 1905; e info@sibonne.com; www.sibonne.com. Opened in 1989 & previously called The Deck, this was one of Grace Bay's early hotels, & remains among the best value. The British owners also own Turtle Cove Inn. The 2-storey building is set around a pretty garden & there's a small freshwater pool. All rooms have cable TV, fridge, safe, AC & ceiling fan, & coffee maker with complimentary supplies. Complimentary continental b/fast at Bay Bistro (see below) — beside the beach but separately run. Courtyard rooms have only a close up view of bushes & are a bit public; others have a sea view or are beachfront. One sea-view apartment is a steal at $285–395. Recommended. $$$

⌂ **Comfort Suites** (98 rooms) Grace Bay Rd; ✆ 946 8888; e comfort@tciway.tc; www.comfortsuitesci.com. Centrally located within a short walk of Grace Bay Beach & beside Ports of Call Shopping Centre, this is one of Provo's few 'budget' options. Rooms — with garden or pool view — are attractively set in gardens around a 50ft (15m) pool, with open corridors allowing a pleasant through breeze. All have been upgraded recently

⌂ **The Tuscany** (30 villas) Grace Bay; ✆ 941 4667; US toll free ✆ 1 866 359 6466; e info@thetuscanyresort.com; www.thetuscanyresort.com. Set in manicured gardens with lots of palm trees at the eastern end of Grace Bay beach. A consciously top-end resort of 3-bedroom villas, all with 3 baths, kitchen, laundry room, patio, sea view, & all the amenities you could wish for. $1,100–1,325 per villa, but 'bedroom lock-offs' with big reductions are possible. 10% discount from Grace Bay Car Hire. $$$$

⌂ **Villa Renaissance** (44 suites) Grace Bay; ✆ 941 5300; US toll free ✆ 1 877 285 8764; e info@villarenaissance.com; www.villarenaissance.com. All suites have 1 bedroom, bathroom, kitchen & terrace; cable TV, AC, safe, fridge & microwave. Complimentary fitness centre, bikes, tennis. $$$$

⌂ **Windsong Resort** (43 condos) Stubbs Rd, Grace Bay; ✆ 941 7700; US toll free ✆ 1 800 WINDSONG; e windsongresort.com; www.windsongresort.com. Opened in 2008, the resort has 150yds (165m) of beach frontage. 1-, 2- & 3-bedroom & studio apts in 3 well-appointed beachside buildings with underground parking, 2 pools & spas, fitness centre & café. $$$$

with flat-screen TVs, internet access, fridges, ceiling fans & new AC units, but in 2007 there were still problems in some rooms with damp & broken fittings. It's a shame that standards of service don't always come up to scratch. Fitness club, beauty salon, gift shop. Guests receive a complimentary rum punch at the poolside Barefoot Café (⊕ 7am–11pm Sun–Wed, 7am–midnight Thu–Sat), a low-key affair where complimentary self-service b/fast (toast & coffee with disposable plates, mugs & cutlery) is also taken. $$$ & $3 energy surcharge.

⌂ **Caribbean Paradise Inn** (17 rooms) Grace Bay Rd; ✆ 946 5020; US toll free ✆ 1 877 946 5020; e inn@paradise.tc; www.paradise.tc. A charming intimate & less expensive small hotel, whose French owner will sometimes throw a spontaneous supper party for his guests. Set in tropical gardens, just an easy 5-min walk to the beach. Rooms have AC, ceiling fan, TV, small fridge; safe; bathroom with shower only; WiFi & balcony. There's a pool with honour bar; ice machine & the Coyaba Restaurant (see below) featuring Caribbean cuisine. Complimentary continental b/fast buffet (full American $5–10). $$

ALL-INCLUSIVE RESORTS Day and evening passes are available to non-residents for both resorts.

🏠 **Beaches** (453 suites) Lower Bight Rd; ☎ 946 8000; US toll free ☎ 1 888 BEACHES; UK toll free ☎ 0 800 742 742; www.beaches.com; www.beachesresorts.co.uk. The largest property on the islands, Beaches is part of the Sandals empire & is geared to families. Long beach frontage with loungers shaded by casuarina trees. Suites have 1, 2 or 3 bedrooms; a further 162 suites will be opening in the 'Italian Village' in January 2009. Rates include all meals, unlimited drinks, tips & taxes, organised activities, tennis, watersports, large diving facility with dedicated boats (tuition extra); evening entertainment, transfers, nanny service & nursery. The new village will bring the number of restaurants up to 14, with 12 bars, & a nightclub/teen lounge. There are also 5 pools (4 with swim-up bars); a supervised kids' camp; & — part of the new complex — a 'youth' spa & retail area. Beaches is exclusive in offering PADI Bubblemaker & Seals programmes, & the National Geographic Passport to Adventure (see page 66). Fireworks on Fri. $$$$ (all inclusive)

🏠 **Club Med Turkoise** (290 rooms) Grace Bay Rd; ☎ 946 5500; US toll free ☎ 1 888 WEB CLUB; ☎ UK 08453 676767; www.clubmed.com, www.clubmed.co.uk. The company that kickstarted mass tourism on Providenciales opened on Grace Bay in 1984. Each of its rooms has a queen or 2 dbl beds, plus AC, phone, TV, CD player, hairdryer, iron, fridge & safe; 20 of them overlook the sea, & 4 are adapted for wheelchair access. 2 restaurants, 2 bars & a nightclub offer plenty of choice, while amenities include a pool, tennis courts, boutique, spa, internet & weight room — not to mention diving, snorkelling, sailing & a range of live entertainment. In short, it's the full all-inclusive package. $$$$ (all inclusive)

SELF-CATERING VILLAS AND APARTMENTS

🏠 **Aquamarine Beach Houses** (3 houses) Grace Bay; ☎ 941 5690; e info@aquamarinebeachhouses.com; www.aquamarinebeachhouses.com. Three beachfront villas sleeping a total of 36 can be rented separately or together. Tennis court, pool, internet access, cable TV, AC, free transfers. Owner lives on the property. Availability & prices on request.

🏠 **South Fleetwood** (1 cottage, 1 suite) Grace Bay, ☎ 946 5376; e info@southfleetwood.com; www.southfleetwood.com. A few mins' walk from the beach, South Fleetwood has a pool & garden full of palm trees. Cottage has 1 bedroom en suite, kitchen, living room, ceiling fans, AC. Suite has 2 bedrooms, 2 baths, living & dining rooms, kitchen. Rates (on request) include maid service, TV, laundry facilities & transfers.

🏠 **The Seagate** (4 condos) Penns Rd; ☎ 946 4706, US toll free ☎ 877 829 8061; e seagate@tciway.tc; www.theseagate.com. These 1- & 2-bed condos share a freshwater pool. Daily maid service. All major cc. $200–500

TURTLE COVE Turtle Cove is away from the action of Grace Bay, but has its own charm. With several restaurants and bars, a thriving marina and within easy walking distance of the beach, it has plenty to offer, especially for those who find the glitz of Grace Bay not to their taste. The ambience is likely to change with the construction of an extensive new luxury resort on the site of the original Third Turtle Inn.

🏠 **Miramar Resort** (20 rooms) Lower Bight Rd; ☎ 946 4240, e info@themiramarresort.com; www.themiramarresort.com. The Miramar changed its name from the Erebus Inn in 2002, & has since headed considerably upmarket, though its prices remain among the lowest on Provo. Poised 100ft (30m) above Turtle Cove Marina, commanding magnificent sea views, it's a small, family-run hotel, a short walk (uphill) from Turtle Cove marina & restaurants. Serene setting; complimentary shuttle to the beach 5 mins away. Spacious en-suite rooms with ceiling fans, AC, cable TV, internet access, safe, kettle. Good pool with wheelchair access ramp, although there are several wide cement steps to be negotiated between it & the rooms. The Magnolia Restaurant (see below), under separate ownership but sharing the site & the views, offers some of the island's best international cooking at reasonable prices (closed Mon), Recommended. No Amex. $$

🏠 **Queen Angel Resort** (45 suites) Lower Bight Rd; ☎ 941 7907; e queenangel@express.tc; www.queenangelresort.com. In tropical gardens on a 50ft (18m) small hill behind the marina, a short walk from the beach. Suites have living room,

kitchen, fridge, washer/dryer, cable TV. Two pools with waterfall & jacuzzi, spa, fitness centre, sports bar, Victoria Restaurant (see below), nightclub & shopping plaza. $$$$
🏠 **Turtle Cove Inn** (30 rooms) Lower Bight Rd, Turtle Cove Marina; ☎ 946 4203, US toll free ☎ 1 800 887 0477; e info@turtlecoveinn.com; www.turtlecoveinn.com. With a lovely location on the marina, albeit with a 10-min walk to the beach, one of Provo's few budget hotels is well worth

considering. It's an attractive place, set around a tree-shaded pool area, with an on-site bar — albeit with no view — & the waterside Aqua restaurant (see below). Although the cheaper rooms overlook a car park or the swimming pool, the rest have verandas or balconies with a view of the marina. Rooms were refurbished in 2007, & each has twin dbl beds, balcony, AC, fridge, safe & a ceiling fan, as well as space for a sofa or chairs & table. Same British ownership as Sibonné. $$

LEEWARD

🏠 **Nikki Beach Resort** (48 ocean-view suites) Leeward Marina; ☎ 941 3747; e info@ nikkibeachhotels.com; www.nikkibeachhotels.com. This new, rather garishly coloured resort opened in April 2008 at the northeast tip of the island, adjacent to Leeward Marina. European-designed kitchens, TV &

complimentary WiFi, not to mention a personal assistant per guest. There's international cuisine at Café Nikki; a beach club & infinity pool. In the evening, try the late-night club lounge & entertainment, or the casino. Spa & fitness centre opening 2009. VIP airport limo pick-up. $$$$$

CENTRAL PROVO AND BLUE HILLS This largely residential area isn't renowned for tourist accommodation, but there are a couple of options here. Note that the sign for The Travellers Rest on the Leeward Highway should be ignored. It is now a private house.

🏠 **Airport Inn** (12 rooms) Airport Rd, ☎ 941 3514; e airportinn@tciway.tc; www.fortmyers.com/turks/Airlnn.htm. Reopened in Jan 2008 after complete refurbishment, the hotel is 5 mins' drive from the departure lounge (the last building on the left as you approach the airport), with free transfer to airport & beaches. Rooms have cable TV, AC, fridge, minibar & internet access. No restaurant or bar, but there's complimentary coffee/tea, & a National car rental office with 15% discount to hotel guests. $$
🏠 **Harbour Club Villas & Marina** (6 villas) Venetian Way, Turtle Tail; ☎ 941 5748; US toll free ☎ 1 866 456 0210; e harbourclub@tciway.tc; www.harbourclubvillas.com. These Canadian-owned 1-

bedroom villas have Flamingo Lake views but are 5 mins' drive to Cooper Jack's Beach & seldom-visited adjacent coves. Each has a kitchen, patio, AC, ceiling fan, safe, WiFi, cable TV. There's a shared pool. $$$
🏠 **Neptune Villas** (10 villas) Chalk Sound; m 342 0138; e neptunevillas@aol.com; http://neptunevillastci.com. All villas in this quiet location overlooking Chalk Sound & Sapodilla Bay Beach have 2 bedrooms & 2 bathrooms, kitchen/dining area, living room & balcony. There is mid-week maid service, a good pool & Las Brisas restaurant & bar (see below; closed Tue). Kayaks, canoes & paddleboats are available to guests, & a stargazing telescope is planned. Children under 12 sleep free in parents' room. $$$

WESTERN PROVIDENCIALES

🏠 **Amanyara** (40 pavilions) Malcolm's Beach; ☎ 941 8133; US toll free ☎ 1 866 941 8133, e amanyara@amanresorts,com; www.amanresorts.com. Despite the longish drive down a fairly bumpy road, much of it dirt, leading to an entry barrier where you are required to justify your admission, it is difficult to fault this resort, though the prices match the quality. Genuinely beautiful Asian architecture is as good as the scenery, & the mostly Philippine service strikes an ideal balance between courtesy & friendliness. Guests notably keep to themselves. Rooms include WiFi, flat-screen TV,

complimentary private bar (except spirits) & free local & long-distance telephone calls. Asian/Mediterranean restaurant (see below) with an emphasis on seafood. Bar, beach club, watersports, stunning 50m pool, fitness centre, tennis, boutique, spa & complimentary yoga (see below). Minimum stay requirements at peak periods. $$$$$
🏠 **Canterbury** (41 suites, 4 penthouses) Northwest Point; http://canterburytci.com. Sister to Northwest Point Resort, this new development was at the planning stage in 2008.

⌂ **Northwest Point Resort** (49 condos) Northwest Point; ✆ 941 8961; e info@northwestpoint.com; www.northwestpointresort.com. Despite great potential, with a spectacular site right on a lonely beach, adjacent to the national marine park, so far this condo-hotel has not really worked. Now under new management after a financial failure, it needs guests but at the time of writing there were few welcoming staff about. It's a long way from any other tourist establishments, but the bar & snack bar (no restaurant) are open only Nov–Aug & have a very limited menu. A continental b/fast (chargeable) is available. 1-bed suites, a little larger than average, include kitchen & balcony. There is a pool, a hot tub, exercise room, complimentary kayaks & snorkel gear, & free transfers. $$$$

PRIVATE CAYS AND ISLANDS

⌂ **Dellis Cay** ✆ 941 7201; US toll free ✆ 1 800 644 0533; www.delliscay.com. A Mandarin Oriental Hotel extravaganza with associated luxury villas is due to open on this 560-acre (226ha) private cay (beside Pine Cay) in 2009. It should cater to all your whims, at a price. The cay is renowned for its shells.

⌂ **Pine Cay: The Meridian Club** (12 rooms, 1 cottage, 10 s/c houses) ✆ 946 7758, US toll free ✆ 1 866 746 3229; e reservations@ meridianclub.com; www.meridianclub.com. Closed Aug–Oct. A barefoot resort where shorts are quite acceptable at dinner. Some find it too intimate & clubby; others are enchanted by 'delightful informality'. All rooms are beachfront. Activities include sailing dinghies, tennis, bikes & hiking. 4-course dinner nightly. On-site commissary. No children under 12 except Jun, Jul & Christmas. $$$$$

⌂ **Parrot Cay** (42 rooms, 4 suites, 6 houses, 6 villas) ✆ 946 7788, US toll free ✆ 1 877 754 0726; e res@parrotcay.como.bz; www.parrotcay.com. On this 1,000-acre (400ha) very private island with a mile-long beach, 'To come is to hear silence; the point is nature'. A central feature is the Como Shambhala (Sanskrit for 'a sacred place of bliss') holistic spa with yoga & Ayurvedic medicine specially tailored to your requirements. There is also (among others) a Como Shambhala restaurant concentrating on organic nutritious food, much of it raw, without sugar or dairy products. Infinity pool, 2 tennis courts (no resident pro but, by prior arrangement, the hotel manager is happy to fill the gap), gym; quiet library with complimentary internet terminals, boutique, watersports & hiking trails. The Lotus Restaurant serves light Caribbean dishes for lunch & Thai/Japanese for dinner. The Terrace serves Mediterranean food. Rooms have AC & ceiling fans, safe, minibar & veranda. Secluded butlered beach villas, each with a plunge pool or swimming pool, are grander than the garden rooms. There are also 3 private residences available for rent. Discreet service & good security; it's fairly paparazzi-proof. Airport transfers free. 3-night min stay. Children under 12 in parents' rooms free. $$$$$

⌂ **West Caicos: Molasses Reef** (125 suites) US toll free ✆ 1 888 802 3250; www.molassesreef.com. With some 10% of the northern part of the island, the Ritz-Carlton will be the first to bring overnight visitors to West Caicos. Scheduled to open in late 2008, it will have 3 restaurants; a spa; a ½-mile beach. Rooms with garden courtyard & plunge pool. Aside from the resort, the island – a nature reserve with archaeological sites & a lake (see page 124) – will remain 'virtually uninhabited'. $$$$$

✖ WHERE TO EAT

Most of Provo's restaurants request reservations and a few say they are required. It is an unusual establishment that turns away a customer if there is a spare table, but at least in season and at the better places it is safer to book. Quite a few take a holiday and shut for a couple of weeks in September or October, which is another reason for telephoning ahead in those months. Most of these establishments take all major credit cards.

GRACE BAY
Restaurants
Upmarket

✖ **Anacona** Grace Bay Club, Grace Bay Rd; ✆ 946 5050; ⊕ 6.30pm–9pm every night. Open-air gourmet dining beside the sea under large umbrellas. Expect sophisticated elegance: 'proper dress', is required, they say, & no children under 12. International cuisine with exceptional steaks &

seasonal stone-crab claws. An extensive wine list, & a 90ft (27m) bar. Highly recommended. **$$$$**

✗ **Bay Bistro** ❱ 946 5396; e baybistro @ tciway.tc; www.sibonne.com; ⊕ 7am–10pm Tue–Sun, 7am–3pm Mon. The Sibonné's open-sided beachside restaurant is about as near as you'll get to dining right on the soft sands of Grace Bay. Candlelight & cane chairs set the scene, & service is both friendly & professional. The dinner menu majors on fish, sometimes with an oriental twist, but there are plenty of alternatives. Lunch has more salads. They are popular for their $12 Sat & Sun brunch served 7am–2pm. **$$$**

✗ **Bella Luna** The Glass House, Grace Bay Rd, opposite Seven Stars; ❱ 946 5214; e bella @ tciway.tc; ⊕ 11.30am–2pm, 6pm until closing, daily. An elegant, mostly Italian restaurant with some of the best food on Provo — with lots of decent veal at $28.50 — & a welcoming ambience. Good wine list at fairly drinkable prices. No children under 6. Recommended. **$$$**

✗ **Caicos Café Bar & Grill** Caicos Café Plaza, Grace Bay Rd; ❱ 946 5278; e pierrik @ tciway.tc; ⊕ 6–10pm Mon, noon–10pm Tue–Sat. This comfortable restaurant with a tree-shaded veranda is set back from the road opposite just along from Ports of Call. The menu majors on grills, but other dishes include a seafood gumbo: tomatoes & vegetables with shrimp, lobster, fish, scallops & mussels. **$$$**

✗ **Coco Bistro** Grace Bay Rd; ❱ 946 5369; ⊕ from 6pm Tue–Sun until last customer leaves. Attractive open-air dining room under the palms, with a menu described as 'continental Caribbean'. You will eat well. **$$$$**

✗ **Coyaba** Caribbean Paradise Inn, Grace Bay Rd; ❱ 946 5186; ⊕ 6–10pm Wed–Mon. Sit under the stars in the garden or inside with soft music; coyaba is the Taino for 'heavenly'. The English chef's cuisine blends Europe & the Caribbean pretty successfully. Tasting menu; good wine list. **$$$$**

✗ **Gecko Grill** Ocean Club Plaza, Grace Bay Rd; ❱ 946 5880; ⊕ dinner 6–10pm Tue–Sun, & useful late-night appetiser menu 10–11pm, with yummy coconut shrimp. Eat on the garden terrace or indoors with AC & tropical murals. Italian/Caribbean cuisine. Vodka bar with 50 varieties. **$$$**

✗ **Grace's Cottage** Point Grace Resort, Grace Bay Rd; ❱ 946 5096; ⊕ 6pm to late daily. Definitely one of Grace Bay's serious restaurants, the Italian/

Mid range

✗ **Bambooz** Salt Mills Plaza, Grace Bay Rd; ❱ 941 8146; ⊕ 4pm Mon–Fri, 1pm Sat–Sun; food served

Caribbean food, the extensive wine list & the polished service are all of a high standard, & many of the dishes come with a wine recommendation. Tables are both outside & on the terrace set in romantic gardens. Highly recommended. **$$$**

✗ **Hemingways** The Sands; ❱ 941 8408; ⊕ 8am–10pm daily. This large & fairly casual open-air place with direct beach access serves reasonable food at reasonable prices. Tue eve BBQ night with music; Thu eve music; Fri eve live jazz. Takeaway available. **$$**

✗ **Iguana** Salt Mills Plaza, Grace Bay Rd; ❱ 941 8145; ⊕ 5.30–10.30pm daily. Menus feature seafood & steak. Separate Martini Bar. Eat inside or under the palm trees. **$$$**

✗ **Mango Reef Restaurant** Royal West Indies Resort; ❱ 946 8200; www.mangoreef,com; ⊕ 7.30am–10pm daily. Sit inside, on the veranda or outside by the pool. International cuisine with local lobster & conch specialities at $14–32; it won't break the bank. Great lunchtime salads. Separate bar. Takeaway available. **$$$**

✗ **Orchid** Alexandra Resort; ❱ 946 5807, ext 7517; ⊕ 8am–9pm daily, happy hour 3–5pm. Reasonable food but a bit short on atmosphere. Tasty wings at lunchtime only $10. **$$$**

✗ **O'Soleil** The Somerset, Princess Dr; ❱ 946 5900; www.thesomerset.com. Eat inside or out amid elegant white-on-white décor in what is unquestionably one of Provo's most sophisticated restaurants. Excellent Caribbean/international food, a decent wine list & polished service. Recommended. **$$$$**

✗ **Parallel 123** Regent Palms; ❱ 946 8666; ⊕ b/fast 7–10.30am, dinner 6–10.30pm; Green Flamingo Bar ⊕ 11am–midnight, bar snacks from noon. Attractive dining room with large veranda fringed with palm trees. Good international menu & wine list (chef used to cook for Donald Trump); tip-top service &, as you'd expect in this uber-chic resort, good stock of Cuban cigars. There's also a gift shop. Recommended. **$$$$**

✗ **Simba Restaurant & Bar** Turks & Caicos Club, Lower Bight Rd; ❱ 946 5588; ⊕ 8–10.30am, noon–2.30pm, 6–10pm Thu–Tue. Eat under the palm trees or in the air-conditioned dining room. Cooking is international/Caribbean. Delicately sauced fish; try the local grouper or the spicy mahi mahi Casual ambience. Poolside bar. **$$$**

5–10.30pm. This cavernous sports bar with large-screen TV is particularly lively on Thu–Sat, as well as for Caribbean nights on Mon, with a $15 BBQ dinner, a $20 bucket of Corona & a live band from 10pm. Burgers, pizza & Mexican food are the order of the day; it's a popular pit stop for locals. Happy hour 4–7pm; takeaway available. Visa & MCd. $$

✕ **Big Bamboo** Ports of Call, Grace Bay Rd; ☏ 946 5832; ◷ lunch & dinner daily. Upstairs in a small shopping complex close to Grace Bay Beach, this very friendly Jamaican restaurant is not to be confused with Bambooz (above) but shares owners with Pizza Port (below). The décor combines the functionality of individual booths & bench seating with the warmth of yellow & terracotta paintwork. If you don't fancy ackee or oxtail (very good, slightly spicy, & usually ordered only by locals), try the jerk pork or chicken, or a special such as goat curry, finished off with bread pudding. $$

✕ **Cabana Bar & Grille** Ocean Club Resort, Grace Bay Rd, ☏ 946 5880; ◷ 7am–8pm Tue–Sun, 7am–9pm Mon. All day b/fast, or lunch of salads, wraps & burgers from $9.95. Sunset happy hour with complimentary bar snacks. Mon BBQ dinner, $22.95; Sat island food specials, $14.95. Sun brunch 9am–3pm, $13.95–15.95. $$

✕ **Calico Jack's** upstairs at Ports of Call, Grace Bay Rd (above Jimmy's); ☏ 946 5129; ◷ noon till late Mon–Sat, 5pm till late Sun. Relaxed bar offering snacks such as fries & jerk chicken or conch fritters, or more substantial mains, that include daily specials. Slightly cooler atmosphere than Jimmy's, with a fancier menu. Eat indoors or on the large open roof. Takeaway service available. Live music Fri & most Sat. Mon eve all-you-can-eat-pasta at $13.99. $$

✕ **Danny Buoy's** Salt Mills Plaza, Grace Bay Rd; ☏ 946 5921; ◷ from 11am daily. A busy, air-conditioned Irish sports bar with darts & pool, tables & booths. Another locals' local. Takeaway available. Large screen TV. $$

✕ **Golden Pagoda** Grace Bay Court, Grace Bay Rd; ☏ 946 4156; ◷ lunch & dinner daily. Cantonese cuisine. Eat in the garden or in the air-conditioned restaurant. Takeaway available. $$

✕ **Grill Rouge** Grace Bay Club, Grace Bay Rd; ☏ 946 5050; ◷ 7am–9.30pm daily. The beachside family bistro for the hotel, it features a swim-up bar & entry straight from the beach. International cuisine & $10 children's menu served outside under big umbrellas. $$$

✕ **Jimmy's Dive Bar** Ports of Call, Grace Bay Rd; ☏ 946 5282; ◷ restaurant 7am–11pm Mon–Wed, 7am–midnight Thu–Sat, 8am–11pm Sun; bar noon–midnight daily. Happy hr 4–7pm daily. A cheerful bar/grill with both inside & open-air seating, serving up steaks, grills, pasta & burgers in surroundings geared to the diving fraternity. Good place for a bacon & egg b/fast. Note: cappuccinos are $5 with no refill; filter coffee is $2.50 with free top ups. $

✕ **Yoshi Sushi** Salt Mills Plaza, Grace Bay Rd; ☏ 941 3374 ◷ noon–3pm, 6–10pm Mon–Sat. Provo's cuisine goes east with this quite authentic Japanese restaurant which has a second branch called Matsuri in Graceway Plaza. Try the Shinjyuku box, if you like tempura. Takeaway available, of course. Set dinners $27–32. $$–$$$

Cafés, snacks and fast food
Nearly all shopping malls will have one or more reasonably priced eating places, not always open for dinner. Their menus are pretty interchangeable: all-day breakfast, burgers, jerk chicken and grouper, with a $20 bill going quite a long way.

🖵 **Bonnie's** beside Stubbs Diamond Plaza, Grace Bay Rd, ▥ 331 4922; ℮ bonnies@express.tc; www.bonniesrestaurant.com. A friendly & welcoming local bar with food, pool tables & fruit machines. Hamburger $7.50. $

🖵 **Flamingo Café** Grace Bay; ◷ until 11pm in high season. The beach café by the cultural market near Beaches. $

🖵 **Giggles** Ports of Call, Grace Bay Rd; ☏ 946 5394; ◷ 11am–10pm Mon-Sat, noon–10pm Sun. A colourful ice-cream parlour with cones, shakes, ice-cream cakes, sundaes, etc. Children love it. $

🖵 **Hutchings** Point Grace Resort, Grace Bay Rd (just inside the resort gates); ☏ 946 5096; ◷ 7.30am–3pm. Point Grace's upmarket coffee shop serves both continental buffet & full American b/fast, & light lunches featuring salads. All major credit cards. $$

🖵 **Island Scoop & Gelato Artigianale** Grace Bay Plaza, Grace Bay Rd; ▥ 242 8511; ◷ 11am–10pm daily. 24 flavours of ice cream, sundaes, splits & smoothies. Provo is justly proud of its locally made ice cream. $

🖵 **Pizza Pizza** Grace Bay Plaza, Grace Bay Rd; ☏ 941 8010; ◷ 11.30am until late daily. Large pizzas $17–22. Free delivery. $$

🍕 **Pizza Port** Ports of Call, Grace Bay Rd; ☎ 941 7300; ⏰ noon–11pm daily. Pizza, salads & sandwiches. Will deliver in Grace Bay area. Same ownership as Big Bamboo (above). **$$**

🍴 **Saltmills Café** Salt Mills, Grace Bay Rd, ☎ 941 8148; ⏰ 7.30am–3pm Mon–Sat. Eat indoors with AC or on the patio. Big b/fast $10, salads & sandwiches from $9. Friday is pie-day. **$**

TURTLE COVE
Upmarket
✗ **Aqua Bar & Terrace** Turtle Cove Inn, Lower Bight Rd; ☎ 946 4763; ⏰ 7am–10pm daily; bar ⏰ 7am–late. An enviable spot for a meal, shaded by palm & sea-grape trees. The resident birds think it's a great place to raid the crumbs off the tables, though the tiny bananaquit is a rather more welcome guest. An excellent b/fast at around $10 & Sunday brunch until 2pm, with a more classy dinner menu. Indoor & outdoor seating in a fairly casual atmosphere. Takeaway available. Happy hr 5–7pm, with background music in the bar, where snacks are served throughout the day (& a single computer offers erratic internet access by credit card) **$$$**
✗ **Baci** Turtle Cove Marina; ☎ 941 3044; ⏰ noon–2.30pm Mon–Fri; 6–10pm Mon–Sat. By

Mid range
✗ **Sharkbite** Turtle Cove Marina; ☎ 941 5090; www.thesharkbite.com; ⏰ kitchen 11am–9.30pm daily; bar till late. This welcoming sports bar & grill is particularly popular with tourists & expats on Fri nights when drinks are 2 for 1 & when you can get a good view of the fireworks from Beaches. Meals are served indoors or – more attractively – overlooking the dock, where underwater lights catch the occasional nurse shark slipping past. Mains focus on steaks & fish, plus burgers; for something more original try mahi Reuben – a fish sandwich served with sauerkraut. Takeaway available. **$$**
✗ **Tiki Hut** Turtle Cove Marina; ☎ 941 5341; www.tikihuttci.com; restaurant ⏰ 11am–9.30pm

the canal near the marina, with elegant dining either al fresco or inside. Good Italian cuisine & friendly service. Also does takeaways, including pizza. The Canadian owner has been here for 9 years. **$$$**
✗ **Magnolia** Miramar Resort, Lower Bight Rd; ☎ 941 5108; e magnolia@tciway.tc; www.miramarresort.tc/restaurant; ⏰ 6pm–10pm Tue–Sun, closed Mon. Dine under the stars & enjoy sweeping views across Grace Bay, with attentive service. A very decent international menu includes daily specials & a delicious tuna tartare. A good place for a leisurely dinner, especially on Fri night when you can catch a gallery view of the Beaches fireworks. Separate bar. **$$$**

Mon–Fri; 7am–11pm Sat/Sun; bar ⏰ later. A relaxed, buzzing atmosphere pervades this harbourfront restaurant, where local families, boat crews & well-heeled tourists mingle. It features local fish straight off the boat, conch in various guises & a range of burgers & quesadillas, plus daily specials such as West Indian chicken stuffed with curry, peas & rice, & vegetables. Children's menu. Takeaway available. **$$**
✗ **Victoria Restaurant** Queen Angel Resort, above the Players' Club, Lower Bight Rd (opp Turtle Cove Marina); ☎ 941 4195; ⏰ noon–5pm, 6pm–11pm daily. Featuring Caribbean specialities. Try the octopus carpaccio – or choose it crispy fried if you're squeamish. Good spicy chicken dishes. **$$$**

LEEWARD MARINA AND LEEWARD HIGHWAY
✗ **Bangkok Express** Provo Plaza, Leeward Hwy; ☎ 946 4491; ⏰ 11am–3pm, 5pm–10pm Mon–Fri, 4–10pm Sat–Sun. A diner-style Thai restaurant with a traditional menu, well prepared. Just 2 tables seat 4 people each; otherwise it's takeaway. **$$**
✗ **Bernie's Roadside Café** Southwinds Plaza, Leeward Hwy; ☎ 941 4646; ⏰ 7am–5pm for straightforward local food. **$**
🍴 **Chinson Pastries & Jade Garden** Leeward Hwy (opp Do-It Centre); ☎ 941 3533; ⏰ 7am–8pm Mon–Sat, 2–8pm Sun. Delectable home-made pastries & deli items of all sorts, & the Jade Garden Chinese lunch buffet. Takeaway available. **$**

🍴 **Corner Cafe** Graceway Plaza, Leeward Hwy (next to IGA); ☎ 941 8724, ⏰ 7am–8.30pm Mon–Sat, closed off-season. Takeaway available. Pavement café offering mostly soup & sandwiches at $7.95–9.95. **$**
✗ **Gilley's** Leeward Marina; ☎ 946 5094; www.gilleysrestaurant.tc. At the eastern end of the island. Temporarily closed as part of the reorganisation of the marina. American/island cuisine.
✗ **Lutong Pinoy** Queen's Court, Leeward Hwy; m 245 1011; ⏰ 8am–midnight daily. Philippine cuisine. Takeaway available. **$**
✗ **Matsuri Sushi Bar** Graceway Plaza, Leeward Hwy (next to IGA); ☎ 941 3274; ⏰ noon–3pm, 6–10pm

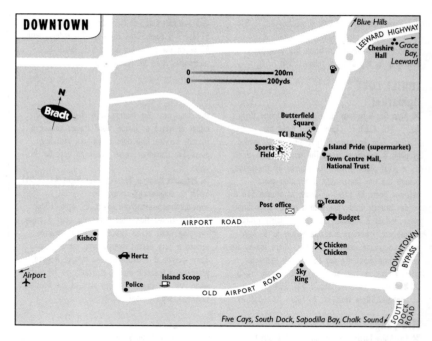

Mon–Sat. The brother of Yoshi's (see above), but as focused on sushi as its name implies. Sushi rolls $9–15. Takeaway available. **$$**

✕ **Pizza Pizza** Provo Plaza, Leeward Hwy; ☎ 941 3577; ⊕ 11.30am–9.30pm Sun–Thu, 11.30am–10pm Fri–Sat. Large pizzas $17–22. Free delivery. **$$**

DOWNTOWN AND SOUTH DOCK ROAD

Chicken Chicken Downtown. Fried chicken & ribs with peas & rice from $3. Some say the best on the island. **$**

Gilley's Providenciales Airport. An unusually good airport café. It's clean with friendly service & perfectly edible fast food at a fair price. There are worse places to kill time before a flight. **$**

Island Scoop Williams Plaza, Old Airport Rd; m 245 5051; ⊕ 11am–10pm daily. 24 flavours of locally made ice cream, sundaes, floats, brownies, shakes etc. An island favourite.

✕ **Las Brisas Restaurant & Bar** Neptune Villas, Chalk Sound; m 243 8398; ⊕ 11am–10pm Wed–Mon. Fri night is Brazilian night & on Sun there is live music 1–5pm. **$$$**

Top o' the Cove Deli Suzy Turn, Leeward Hwy (next to NAPA); ☎ 946 4694; www.provo.net/angelas; ⊕ 6am–6pm Mon–Sat, 7am–2pm Sun. New York-style deli with inside & outside seating. Takeaway available. Well stocked deli shop with ready-to-eat meals. B/fast $5–10.95, sandwiches from $7.95. **$**

Road Side Café Francis Yard, Airport Rd; ⊕ 4am–10pm daily. Miss Helena Green is the friendly owner/cook at this popular, ultra-affordable quick food stop serving b/fast, lunch & dinner. Real home-style cooking, including stew-conch, chicken souse, BBQ ribs, corned beef or tuna & grits. 'She got the place on lock,' they say, meaning Miss Helena is right on top of her job, & the customers love it. **$**

Sweet T's The bright pink kiosk by the airport roundabout is one of the island's best chicken shacks & will sell you one of its cheapest meals. $5 for chicken & fries; corn on the cob $1. Excellent! **$**

BLUE HILLS For a taste of real island culture – and food – on Provo, this is without doubt the place to come. The area is also the venue for the annual Conch Festival, held on the last Saturday in November. If you're driving yourself, watch out for the speed humps all along the coast road.

✗ **Bugaloo** Blue Hills Rd. Bugaloo — 'the conch man' — used to be involved with Da Conch Shack, but his new restaurant was under construction in 2008.

✗ **Da Conch Shack & Rum Bar** Blue Hills Rd; ☎ 946 8877; www.conchshack.tc; ⏰ 11am 'till whenever' every day. Wooden beach chalets painted in blue & white are an unlikely venue for one of the island's most popular restaurants. It's a very laid-back party place, with tables & benches on the beach as well as under cover, & beer at around $4 a bottle. Thu is 'Party, Drink & Music' night. $$

✗ **Horse-eye Jack's** Blue Hills Rd; ☎ 941 4955; ⏰ 11am 'till closing' every day; live music from 4pm. This relaxed beach bar next to Da Conch Shack has evolved over the years, & now has seating both outdoors & under cover — useful when it's wet or windy. Come here for Caribbean specialities such as jerk chicken & pork, with rice & peas, or a range of 'kabobs' with veggies, rather than the more predictable burgers. $$

WESTERN PROVIDENCIALES

✗ **Amanyara** Amanyara Resort, Northwest Point (see above); ☎ 941 8133. For superb food in idyllic surroundings, make the longish drive to Amanyara & arrive in time to have a drink, perhaps a champagne

✗ **Sailing Paradise** Blue Hills Rd; ☎ 941 7485; ⏰ lunch & dinner daily, & b/fast Sat. The exuberantly coloured huts by the beach are home to this local restaurant, as well as a barber's & a sweet shop. A good source of local dishes, including the likes of boiled fish & conch salad, it's a relaxed affair, with seating inside or along the sea-facing veranda. $

✗ **Smokey's on the Bay** Blue Hills Rd, ☎ 941 7852; ⏰ 11.30am 'til late' Mon—Sat. A favourite with locals, Smokey's makes little concession to the tourist, & is well worth the visit. Sit under cover with AC or on the opposite side of the road on the beach. Don't miss the Wed evening fish fry with bread & roast corn & live music at $15. $$

✗ **The Three Queens** Bar & Restaurant, Blue Hills Rd, Wheeland; ☎ 941 5984. Local hangout across from the beach. Atmospheric & often noisy; a good spot to eavesdrop island gossip. Conch & seafood specials at very reasonable prices. Tables outside & in. $

mojito, in the beautiful bar. But first check that they are accepting outside reservations. Meals are expensive, & lunch here is about the same as dinner in most other hotels $$$$–$$$$$

NIGHTLIFE AND ENTERTAINMENT

Many of the restaurants in Grace Bay, Turtle Cove and – especially – Blue Hills have bars that stay open late. Particularly popular with tourists and expats are the bars at the Tiki Hut and the Sharkbite in Turtle Cove, and the likes of Danny Buoy's and Bambooz in Salt Mills Plaza, or Calico Jack's at Ports of Call. If you want to drink in a bit more style and see who has come to Provo this year, all of the hotels have bars, not all of them overpriced and many by the sea.

Despite its aura of sophistication, Providenciales offers little in the way of organised entertainment. Nevertheless, those seeking to try their luck at the tables (or on the slot machines, for that matter) have a handful of options:

☆ **BET Soundstage & Gaming Lounge** Leeward Hwy; ☎ 941 4318. In addition to slot machines, this is the place to head for in search of live music & late-night disco.

☆ **Casablanca Casino** Grace Bay Rd; ☎ 946 3737; www.casablanca.tc; ⏰ 7pm–5am. With 85 slot machines & tables offering American roulette, dice, blackjack, baccarat & Caribbean poker, this is definitely a place for night owls. Admission is free, but the minimum stake is $5. There's a bar on site, of course, & snacks are available, but there's no restaurant.

☆ **Players' Club** Lower Bight Rd; Turtle Cove; ☎ 941 4263 (941 GAME); www.theplayersclub.tc; ⏰ 10am–5am. Live poker tables operate alongside numerous gaming machines offering everything from one-armed bandits to digital blackjack & electronic roulette, as well as live poker. Snacks & sandwiches are available at the bar, which is made out of conch shells, & where there's an electronic trivia system. Minimum age 18. Admission free.

Amateur theatre productions, music festivals and other cultural events are regularly staged at Brayton Hall, the theatre behind the British West Indies

Collegiate on the Venetian Road. For details, contact the Turks & Caicos Friends of the Arts Foundation (✆ *941 4617;* e *info@tcfaf.org; www.tcfaf.com*), ask at Unicorn Bookstore, or check the local press.

SHOPPING

From the visitor perspective, most of the shops on Provo are clustered in the eastern end of the island, close to Grace Bay, particularly in the small purpose-built shopping complexes such as Ports of Call and Salt Mills Plaza and in the better hotels; Palms Boutique is a very good one. More general shops, including the island's major supermarkets, are found on the Leeward Highway heading west towards Downtown. There are also **cultural markets** on the beach at Grace Bay, one of them near Beaches, another by the Ocean Club, with colourful craft and clothing offerings catering primarily for the tourist. These are usually open daily 8am–5pm, depending on the season – and the individual stallholders.

For the most part, tourist shops are open from around 10am to 5pm, Monday to Friday, but hours may vary according to the season; many shops stay open longer in the high season, from December to April. Supermarkets are usually open every day until quite late.

BEACHWEAR, SPORTS, GIFTS AND SOUVENIRS In addition to the following outlets, see also *Diving and snorkelling gear*, opposite.

Alverna's Craft Market off Leeward Hwy. Colourful metal geckos, fish & iguanas hang from every available space in this treasure trove of crafts. It's across from Tropicana Plaza, just after the Leeward roundabout as it leads towards Ports of Call.

Anna's Art Gallery Salt Mills; m 231 3293; local artists' canvases, sculptures, prints & jewellery.

Art Provo The Regent Village, Grace Bay; ✆ 941 4545; www.artprovo.com. Island art, designer jewellery, pottery. Straw work demonstrations on Thu.

Blue Surf Shop Salt Mills Plaza, Grace Bay Rd; ✆ 941 8670; ⏲ 10am–6pm Mon–Sat. Specialises in clothing for the surfing set.

Caicos Wear Boutique La Petite Place, Grace Bay Rd; ✆ 941 3346. Clothing & gifts.

Caribbean Beach'n Ports of Call, Grace Bay Rd; ✆ 946 5769.

Greensleeves Central Sq, Leeward Hwy; ✆ 946 4147; paintings, handcrafts, jewellery, art supplies.

Island Sportique Ports of Call, Grace Bay Rd; ✆ 946 5378; www.provo.net/islandsportique; ⏲ 10am–6pm Mon–Fri, 9am–6pm Sat. Also at 103 Graceway Hse, Leeward Hwy; ✆ 946 8233. Make your way here for tennis racquets — including restringing — as well as general casual wear. (Racquets are also available at the golf club shop; see page 117.)

L'Oasis Boutique Salt Mills, Grace Bay; ✆ 946 5613; ⏲ 9.30am–6pm Mon–Sat. Men's & women's designer clothing, beachwear, hats, sandals & accessories.

Mama's Ports of Call, Grace Bay Rd; ✆ 946 5538; e mamasgift@tciway.tc. T-shirts, dresses, souvenirs & beachwear.

Mar Azul Bazaar Ports of Call, Grace Bay Rd; ✆ 941 3712. Aptly named cornucopia of souvenir-style goodies, as well as boogie boards.

Marilyn's Crafts & Apparel Ports of Call, Grace Bay Rd; ✆ 946 5975. Good source of baskets & hats, as well as beach attire.

Middle Caicos Co-op Blue Hills; ✆ 946 7639; e middlecaicos@tciway.tc; ⏲ 10am–4pm Tue–Sat. This community-owned shop between Da Conch Shack & Sailing Paradise showcases a range of crafts mainly from Middle & North Caicos. The Co-op began as a volunteer project to safeguard island skills in basket weaving, partly by giving the weavers a return nearer the minimum wage of $4 per hour. Prices are not cheap (expect to pay around $50 for a small bread basket made out of fanner grass & the tops of silvertop or whitetop palms) but the standard of workmanship is exceptionally high; some of the baskets can even be used to carry water. For baskets, straw hats, local dolls & even model Caicos sloops, this is *the* place to come.

National Trust Town Centre Mall; ✆ 941 5710; www.nationaltrust.tc; ⏲ 8.30am–4.30pm Mon–Fri. Also has a shop in Grace Bay Plaza on Grace Bay Rd (m 344 6756; ⏲ 8.30am–4.30pm Mon–Sat). A small range of local crafts is on display at both shops, which also sell tickets for National Trust properties.

Nautique Graceway Sports Centre; ✎ 941 5400; www.nautiquesports.com. Sportswear & kit, including in-line skates, skateboards, waterskis, kiteboards & tubes. Tuition is available too.

Nell's Gift Shop 7–11 Bldg, Leeward Hwy; ✎ 941 3228. Something of a tourist bizarre, Nell's is based in a brown building that's widely known as 7–11 — even though there's no sign to that effect! A second branch is at the airport.

Philatelic Bureau Grace Bay Plaza, Grace Bay Rd; ✎ 941 3314; ⏱ 8.30am–4.30pm Mon–Fri; sometimes open Sat. For Turks & Caicos special series stamps; useful too for regular stamps if main post office is closed.

Silver Deep Grace Bay Rd; ✎ 946 5612; m 232 1143; www.silverdeep.com. Opposite Danny Buoy's, & next to the Grace Bay Club, the upmarket fashions in this shop reflect the tone of the tour operator of the same name. Bookings can be made here for all Silver Deep's excursions (see page 114).

Turkcasian Gallery & Gifts Grace Bay Plaza, Grace Bay Rd; m 231 2708. Beside the philatetic bureau.

Treasure S & S Gift Shop Salt Mills Plaza, Grace Bay Rd; ✎ 946 8508. Dresses, bags, hats & souvenirs. Recommended hair braiding by Paulette.

Ventura Boutique Salt Mills, Grace Bay Rd; ✎ 941 7789; ⏱ 10am–6pm Mon–Sat. Beachwear & designer clothing.

BOOKS, MAPS AND GAMES

Unicorn Bookstore Graceway Plaza, Leeward Hwy; ✎ 941 5458; e unicorn @ tciway.tc; ⏱ 9.30am–6pm Mon–Sat. This smart, modern shop has a reasonable selection of books on most subjects, with a good range on Caribbean natural history & the underwater world, including fish identification as well as birds & plants. Some foreign newspapers are available to order. The *Miami*

Herald & the *New York Times* are generally available a day late. Some sections of the London *Sunday Times* & the *Financial Times* weekend edition are both expected to arrive by Wednesday. There are never many copies & they tend to sell out fast. The shop also sells some high-quality children's toys. A smaller branch (no newspapers) is based at Ports of Call.

If you're after **foreign newspapers**, Amanyara will give you the print out of your choice, daily. Some other hotels – Ocean Club West for example – have short digests, generally of the *New York Times*. Only Unicorn sells foreign papers. Almost everyone has satellite TV with US, Canadian and European stations including the BBC World Service. For more details, see page 59.

DIVING AND SNORKELLING GEAR In addition to beach-style clothing, the following stock snorkels, fins and masks – though not more specific scuba gear. This is available to order only, so visitors either need to bring their own, or rent on the island.

Caicos Adventures La Petite Place, Grace Bay Rd; ✎ 941 3346; ⏱ 9am–6pm Mon–Sat, 10am–5pm Sun. Brimful of T-shirts, bags, sandals & other beach 'essentials', rather than serious dive gear.

Dive Provo Ports of Call, Grace Bay Rd; ✎ 946 5029; ⏱ 8am–5pm daily. Plenty of good T-shirts

and beach gear, as well as snorkel equipment and some divewear.

Provo Turtle Divers Turtle Cove Marina, ✎ 946 4232; ⏱ 8am–5pm daily. Also at Ocean Club & Ocean Club West.

DUTY FREE

Goldsmith Caicos Café Plaza, Grace Bay Rd; ✎ 946 5628. All the normal duty-free stock, from jewellery

and perfume to cigars. Also at Central Square, Leeward Hwy; ✎ 946 4100.

FOOD AND DRINK The island's most well-stocked supermarket is **IGA** in Graceway Plaza, but there are several alternatives which are fine for the basics, and some specialist outlets that are worth seeking out. **Island Pride Supermarket** on Town Centre Mall is cheaper than IGA and usually less crowded, but it carries fewer imported brands and doesn't sell alcoholic drinks. You will find many foodstuffs are from elsewhere, particularly from the United States. The reason prices seem high is that one of the few taxes levied in Turks and Caicos is an import duty of 10–30%

Food

Chinson's Pastries Leeward Hwy opposite Do-It Centre; 📞 941 3533; ⏰ 7am–8pm Mon–Sat, 2–8pm Sun. Very good home baked goods & delicatessen.

Fish Market Leeward Hwy; m 241 9567. The place for fish that's as fresh as it gets.

Gourmet Goods Grace Bay Court, Grace Bay Rd; 📞 941 4141; e info@gourmetgoods.tc; www.gourmetgoods.tc; ⏰ 10am–8pm. Takeaway picnics, canapés, lunch & dinner, wine.

IGA Graceway Plaza, Leeward Hwy; 📞 941 5000; ⏰ 7am–10pm daily, inc holidays. Providenciales' best-stocked supermarket has everything from the basics to the luxuries, including champagne, as well as local newspapers, phonecards & a Scotiabank ATM. It also has a selection of prepared foods, such as roast chicken.

Island Pride Leeward Hwy; ⏰ 7am–9.30pm daily. Next to Town Centre Mall, this is a more basic, no-frills food outlet than the larger IGA. Though it stocks slightly fewer imported brands, prices are often a bit lower & it doesn't usually get as crowded. No alcoholic drinks.

Liz's Bakery (and convenience store) off South Dock Rd, Five Cays; 📞 941 3318; f 941 5034 ⏰ 6.30am–9pm Mon–Sat. Deservedly popular with local customers, Liz's sells both excellent bread & local specialities such as potato cake at $1 a slice, all baked on the premises. At b/fast & lunch there's chicken, fish, curry, 'stew beef', peas 'n' rice, not to mention bread pudding & assorted home-baked cakes. To find it, turn left off South Dock Rd, then continue for ½ mile. Her bread is also available from Kathleen's 7–11, Walk-in service station, Island Pride supermarket, & Kewtown.

Quality Supermarket Leeward Hwy; 📞 941 7929. Quite small with a limited choice but useful for the basics.

Top O'the Cove Deli Leeward Hwy (next to NAPA); 📞 946 4694; e angela@tciway.tc; www.provo.net/angelas. New York-style deli combining a restaurant with a good selection of home-made & other deli-style food & some gifts.

Drink
In addition to the supermarkets, there are a few wine merchants (liquor stores) selling beer, wines and spirits.

Carib West Ltd Airport Rd; 📞 946 4215; ⏰ 9am–6pm Mon–Wed, 9am–7pm Thu–Sat.

IDL Liquor Store Leeward Hwy; 📞 941 4781; e liquors@provo.net; www.provo.net/gilleys; ⏰ 8.30am–5.30pm Mon–Sat. They claim to offer discounts on wines & liquors.

Tipsy Turtle Liquor Store Turtle Cove Marina, Lower Bight Rd; 📞 941 5016; ⏰ 9am–9pm Mon–Sat.

Wine & Spirits Salt Mills, Grace Bay; 📞 941 8047; e wineandspirits@tciway.tc. ⏰ 9am–7pm Mon–Sat.

Wine Cellar Leeward Highway; 📞 946 4536; e sales@winecellar.tc; www.winecellar.tc; ⏰ 8.30am–5pm Mon–Sat. Claims to sell discounted wines, spirits & beer.

PHARMACY

Grace Bay Pharmacy Neptune Court, Dolphin Dr, Grace Bay; 📞 946 8242, 941 8243; m 241 6350; e gracebaypharmacy@tciway.tc; www.gracebaypharmacy.com; ⏰ 8am–8pm Mon–Fri, 8am–5pm Sat, 10am–4pm Sun. A comprehensive stock of European & North American brands. Full prescription service. Beauty products. They will deliver. Recommended.

Island Pharmacy Menzies Medical Bldg, Leeward Hwy; 📞 946 4150; e islandpharmacy@tciway.tc. Full prescription service.

Sunset Pharmacy Plus Royal Palms Plaza, Airport Rd; 📞 941 3751; also at Misick Bldg, Leeward Hwy; 📞 941 3564.

PHOTOGRAPHY

Pennylaine Photo Studio Central Square, Leeward Hwy; 📞 941 3549. 1hr developing, digital imaging, portraits & special events.

MUSIC AND VIDEO

Kishco The Music Man Leeward Hwy, Airport Rd & South Dock Rd; ☎ 941 3739. Branches of this music store are a great place to pick up that local CD.

HEALTH AND BEAUTY

SPAS Providenciales is a paradise for those who seek therapeutic beauty treatments, massage, rejuvenation programmes, yoga retreats, pilates and such pleasures. Almost every large hotel offers special facilities and there are any number of independent spas.

Amanyara Northwest Point by Malcolm's Beach; ☎ 941 8133, US toll free ☎ 866 941 8133. The entire resort somewhat resembles a therapeutic spa. Soothing & silent; full team of therapists to provide massages & body treatment in the privacy of guests' pavilions; facials; manicures & pedicures. There's also a fitness centre.

Anani Spa Grace Bay Club, Grace Bay Rd; ☎ 946 5050. Reflexology; Elemis well-being massage; Elemis Aroma stone therapy massage; couples massage.

Como Shambhala Retreat Parrot Cay; reservations ☎ 946 7038; e parrotcay@comoshambhala.bz; www.comoshambhala.bz. Much travelled spa seekers will frequently tell you Parrot Cay has the finest & most beautiful spa to be found anywhere. The name means 'a mythological sacred place of bliss'. The belief of this Asian-style retreat is that under their guidance this bliss comes from within. Their aim is harmony between mind & body. Dozens of programmes are on offer, including Dr Perricore skin care & 3-day special nutritional face-lift menu, & many guests have several treatments each day of their stay. The location, with a beautiful outlook over foliage to the sea, makes for a most tranquil setting. Private sanctuary cottages for couples during treatments with meal service if required (4hrs for $200).

New Waves Hair Designs Provo Mall, Leeward Hwy; ☎ 946 4826. Mickie is recommended.

The Spa at the Palms The Palms; ☎ 946 8666; www.thepalmstc.com. Reflecting pool; massage on special float beds; Zareeba healing treatment with therapeutic Caribbean herbs & ground conch cells to exfoliate; products from the famed Somme Institute, Beverly Hills. Also yoga & pilates. 2 spa suites for couples.

Spa Sanay Grace Bay Court, Grace Bay Rd; ☎ 946 8212; www.spasanay.com; ⏰ 10am–7pm. Day spa; aromatherapy; massage; facials; nails & hair.

Spa Tropique Ports of Call, Grace Bay Rd; ☎ 941 5720, m 231 6938; www.spatropique.com. Also 3 resort locations: Ocean Club; Ocean Club West & The Sands at Grace Bay. Features day-spa & mobile service. 'O La La' special with hot stone massage; full-scalp massage; eye treatments.

Serenity Day Spa Graceway Hse; ☎ 946 5010

Teona Spa Regent House, Villa Renasissance Resort, Ventura Dr; ☎ 941 5051; e teonaspa@tciway.tc

Thalasso Spa Point Grace, Grace Bay Rd; ☎ 946 5096. Experts in marine treatments; Thalgo products & treatments. Special spa menu poolside at Hutchings restaurant: fruit & vegetable shakes with yoghurt & imaginative salads.

Thera Touch ☎ 332 9819; m 243 1327; e theratouch07@yahoo.com. Mobile massage service.

OTHER PRACTICALITIES

BANKS Remember that banks can get very crowded on Friday afternoons and paydays. Be prepared at these times for long queues, and no special windows for foreign exchange. If you are underdressed, eg: wearing a swimsuit, you are likely to be ejected.

$ First Caribbean Leeward Hwy; ☎ 946 5303; ⏰ Mon–Thu 8.30am–2.30pm, Fri 8.30am–4.30pm. Exchanges currency or travellers' cheques in sterling, US or Canadian dollars, & euros, up to the value of $1,000. Currency exchange charged at 1%, minimum

$5; Amex travellers' cheques free, others 1%. Separate Cirrus ATM in Salt Mills Plaza.

$ Scotiabank Leeward Hwy at Cherokee Rd; ☎ 946 4750; www.turksandcaicos.scotiabank.com; ⏰ 9am–3pm Mon–Thu, 9am–4.30pm Fri. Will exchange sterling & Canadian currency but no euros; also dollar & sterling travellers' cheques.without charge. ATMs at Petro Plus on Millennium Hwy, IGA Supermarket & Ports of Call.

$ **TCI Bank** Butterfield Sq, Downtown (next to sports complex); ☎ 941 7500. No fee & (at the time of writing) a better rate than the competition for exchanging US travellers' cheques. Exchanges UK, Canadian & Swiss currency for 5% fee. ATMs accept their own bank cards only.

COMMUNICATIONS

Telephone and internet Telephone rental is expensive at $60 for a fortnight, plus the cost of calls. The best alternative is to buy a $5 SIM card for your own mobile, and put in as much credit as you need (cards cost $5 and up). See also pages 56–7.

🖥 **Comptci** Suzy Turn Plaza; Leeward Hwy; ☎ 941 4266; www.comptci.tc; ⊕ 9am–5.30pm Mon–Fri; 10am–2pm Sat (opening hours on the door are no longer correct). With 8 computer stations & good screens, this is a good (& cool) option for internet browsers. $5 for 20 min, or $10 per hr.

🖥 **TCI Online** Ports of Call, Grace Bay Rd; ☎ 941 4711; www.islandcom.tc; ⊕ 9am–6pm Mon–Sat. TCI's own internet network (island.com) has several computer terminals, with local sites accessible without charge. Island.com & Cable & Wireless SIM cards are available, & international calls can be made. Internet kiosks 35¢ per min, $5 for 15 mins, $10 for 35 mins & pro rata; faxing $5/page; printing (b/w) $1/page; telephone rental $49.95/wk. Staff are helpful & though it's a bit expensive it's recommended.

Post office and couriers The main post office on Provo is located in the Downtown area on Airport Road. The philatelic bureau, however, is in an entirely separate location at Grace Bay Plaza on Grace Bay Road (see page 103).

Courier companies
DHL ☎ 946 4862
Fedex ☎ 946 4352

MEDICAL FACILITIES
The government-run Myrtle Rigby Hospital on Providenciales is on the Leeward Highway (☎ *941 3000*), on the east of the Downtown area. There are also several private clinics. For details of **pharmacies**, see page 104.

✚ **Associated Medical** Medical Bldg, Leeward Hwy; ☎ 946 4242; emergency 📱 231 0000, 231 0642; www.doctor.tc. Has the islands' only decompression chamber.

✚ **Carolina Medical Clinic** Town Centre Mall, Leeward Hwy; ☎ 946 4367; ⊕ 8am–5pm Mon–Sat.

✚ **Grace Bay Medical Centre** Neptune Ct, Dolphin Dr; ☎ 941 5252; emergency 📱 231 0525; ⊕ 8am–5pm Mon–Fri, 8am–1pm Sat. Dr Sam Slattery or his partners are recommended.

✚ **Omnicare Medical Clinic** Town Centre Mall, Leeward Hwy; ☎ 941 5050 (inc after hours & emergencies); 🖥 omnicare@tciway.tc

Dentists
Dental Services Ltd, Medical Bldg, Leeward Hwy; ☎ 946 4321; www.dentist.tc. Dr Johann Pretorius BDS (Rand) or one of his partners is recommended.

International Dental Clinic Ltd, Town Centre Mall, Leeward Hwy; ☎ 941 4700
Dr Ian Macdonald 175 Cheshire Lane; ☎ 941 5063

RELIGIOUS SERVICES
Providenciales boasts numerous churches. The Anglican Church of St Monica is on the Leeward Highway (☎ *946 4046*). Services are held every Sunday at 7am, 9am and 7pm, with a second evening service on Wednesday at 7pm.

On the other side of the road, almost opposite St Monica's, is the Roman Catholic Church (☎ 941 5136), where mass is held on Sundays at 9am, and weekdays at 5pm.

Other Christian churches represented on the island include Methodist (☎ 946 4075), with Sunday services at 7am, 9am, 11am and 7pm; Baptist (☎ 946 2295), Church of Prophecy (☎ 946 2394), Faith Tabernacle (☎ 946 4214), New Testament Church of God (☎ 946 2235) and Seventh-Day Adventist (☎ 946 2065).

TRAVEL AGENTS Expat visitors and locals often take the opportunity to visit the Bahamas or the Dominican Republic for a weekend. These and other trips can be organised through one of the island's travel agents, or of course direct with one of the airlines (see pages 42 and 50).

Marco Services Graceway Hse, Leeward Hwy; ☎ 946 4393; e marcoalan@tciway.tc; www.marcotravel.com. Also offer transfers & local tours.

Provo Travel Central Square, Leeward Hwy; ☎ 946 4035; e provotravel@tciway.tc

ACTIVITIES

As elsewhere in the Turks and Caicos Islands, activities on Providenciales are focused on and below the waters, but there's plenty of choice for everyone. Do be aware that fuel costs on TCI, as elsewhere, are high and rising, so rates are inevitably subject to change.

DIVING A long fringing reef round Provo and its neighbouring islands drops off onto a wall that plunges down into the deep, making this a perfect venue for divers. While novices can train in calm, clear waters, the experienced diver has no shortage of walls, swim throughs and channels to explore.

In all cases, divers are collected from their accommodation within the Grace Bay area, usually from around 8am.

Dive sites In addition to some 40 or so designated dive sites in the water around Providenciales, many of them protected by national park status, there are numerous other sites used by individual operators.

Inevitably, the choice of location will depend in part on the day's conditions, particularly the strength and direction of the wind. There are several sites in Grace Bay itself, within just 10–15 minutes of the beach. These can be excellent, but if the wind is up from east or northeast, then visibility can be seriously compromised. More sheltered are the sites of Northwest Point or the leeward side of West Caicos, with access to these taking around ½–1 hour from Southside Marina, or ¾–1½ hours from Caicos Marina. To the south lies French Cay, a sought-after destination for divers, but accessible only in calm conditions if divers are to avoid both a long and uncomfortable trip out and an unpleasant surface interval between dives.

Most operators leave at around 8.30am, returning sometime between 1.30pm and 3.30pm, depending on the site chosen. Drinks and sandwiches or substantial snacks are provided on board all boats for the surface interval on longer trips.

Grace Bay While most of the island's dive sites involve a boat trip of around an hour, diving in Grace Bay has the huge advantage of easy and quick access, with most operators within just 15 minutes of the sites. The rewards for such a short journey can be significant, especially in summer when calm seas bring excellent visibility. Sharks and rays are frequent visitors, with plenty of colourful reef fish and grouper, and some large shoals in evidence, especially at Aquarium. Here, too, is a good place to spot the day-feeding pillar coral, perhaps at Pinnacles which, like Aquarium, features the characteristic tongue-and-groove formations of the bay. As an added bonus, divers in Grace Bay might see the resident dolphin, JoJo (see box, page 110).

Pine Cay The dive sites around this privately owned island to the east of Provo fall within the Fort George Land and Sea National Park. Characterised by grottos and swim throughs with large hard coral formations, the sites rise to within 50ft (15m) of the surface, and are known for consistently good visibility. Popular sites include Eagle Ray Pass, which needs little explanation, and Football Field, a large patch of sand surrounded by coral where schools (or should that be teams?) of juvenile barracuda, jacks and groupers come out to play. Near the shore lie cannons from a 1790s fort, easily seen by snorkellers.

Northwest Point Protected as a marine park, Northwest Point features steep walls dropping from around 35ft (10m), encrusted with corals and elephant-ear sponges. Deep crevices give rise to names such as The Crack, where each diver emerges individually into the blue, and the Hole in the Wall. It's a dramatic spot, with plenty of large fish including shoals of horse-eye jacks. One of the most popular sites is Amphitheatre, which sits at the foot of an 85ft (26m) wall, and has some beautiful plate corals at the front. Elsewhere, at Shark Hotel, look out for a huge stand of pillar coral – as well as for the reef sharks, of course.

West Caicos The sheltered wall to the west of West Caicos, protected by the West Caicos Marine National Park, offers plenty of variety, showcasing purple tube sponges and black coral, as well as plenty of marine life – not to mention the garden eels that disappear almost instantly when approached. Arches and swim throughs characterise sites such as Highway to Heaven, while at Whiteface, also known as Spanish Anchor – a narrow crack in the reef runs beneath a large (but not Spanish!) 17th-century anchor embedded in the rock.

Falling outside the boundary of the West Caicos National Park, about 10–15-minutes' boat ride to the north, is **Sandbore Channel**, where stingrays bury themselves in the sandy sea bed. The channel can be dived only an hour each side of high tide but is well worth the wait. At Land of the Giants, frequented by rays and reef sharks, oversized tube sponges face the ocean like so many open mouths waiting to be fed. But even in giant land, there are tiny surprises; this is a good place to look for the rare fingerprint cyphoma.

Southwest Reef Confusingly located southeast of West Caicos, Southwest Reef can be hit by strong currents. Its vertical wall nurtures some huge barrel sponges and deep-water gorgonians, and it's a great place to see sharks and eagle rays.

Molasses Reef An isolated spot on the Caicos Banks, roughly equidistant between West Caicos and French Cay, Molasses Reef is renowned for its wall, which attracts regular visits from sharks, eagle rays and turtles. It is also the location of several wrecks, although most of their remains have been removed to the museum in Grand Turk.

French Cay A wealth of healthy sponge and coral tops the wall at French Cay, where one of the greatest draws for divers is the nurse sharks that congregate here towards the end of the summer to mate. There are six designated dive sites around the island, all accessible only in calm weather. Spur-and-groove formations in around 45ft (15m) of water lead to a sheer drop off, where frequent sightings of the larger

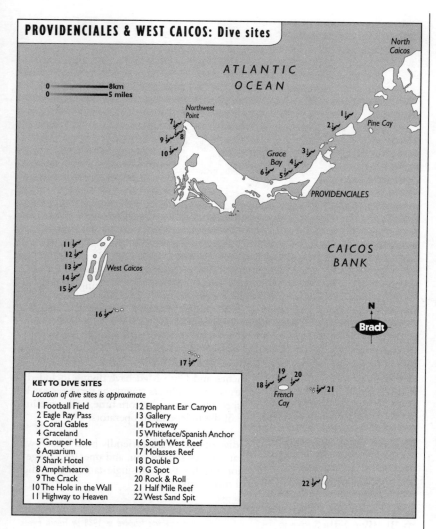

PROVIDENCIALES & WEST CAICOS: Dive sites

ATLANTIC
OCEAN

0 ⎯⎯⎯⎯ 8km
0 ⎯⎯⎯⎯ 5 miles

North
Caicos

Northwest
Point

Pine Cay

Grace
Bay

PROVIDENCIALES

West Caicos

CAICOS
BANK

N

Bradt

French
Cay

KEY TO DIVE SITES

Location of dive sites is approximate

1 Football Field	12 Elephant Ear Canyon
2 Eagle Ray Pass	13 Gallery
3 Coral Gables	14 Driveway
4 Graceland	15 Whiteface/Spanish Anchor
5 Grouper Hole	16 South West Reef
6 Aquarium	17 Molasses Reef
7 Shark Hotel	18 Double D
8 Amphitheatre	19 G Spot
9 The Crack	20 Rock & Roll
10 The Hole in the Wall	21 Half Mile Reef
11 Highway to Heaven	22 West Sand Spit

creatures – manta rays, hammerhead sharks and, during the migration, humpback whales – make this a firm favourite with divers. The island itself is part of the French, Bush and Seal Cays Sanctuary, and is home to the rock iguana, as well as a breeding ground for ospreys and terns.

Half Mile Reef East of French Cay, and as long as the name suggests, this reef is frequented by large schools of barracuda and mahogany snappers. Although the reef as a whole tends to take the full force of the currents, the central section is sheltered, and it is here that two large elephant-ear sponges can be seen.

West Sand Spit Like French Cay to the north, West Sand Spit is swept by the currents and can be dived only in good weather. Low tide exposes a sandy cay which slopes away to a wall that drops off vertically from about 60ft (18m). Some 120 species of fish have been identified on the site, including a large school of

JOJO THE DOLPHIN

Regularly seen in Caicos waters since the early 1980s, JoJo is an Atlantic bottlenose dolphin who voluntarily interacts with humans, making him a firm favourite with tourists. Yet it is his very friendliness that almost caused problems for JoJo, for when unthinking visitors tried to get too close and touch him, he reacted aggressively. Fortunately the forward-thinking concern of a local environmentalist, Dean Bernal, saved him from captivity, and at the end of the decade, he was designated a 'national treasure' with his own warden.

It's been some time since JoJo has been spotted. Anyone fortunate enough to catch sight of him should remember that he remains a wild animal, and is entirely independent of humans for all his needs, including food.

goatfish, three Goliath groupers and four stingrays with a span of over 5ft (1.5m), not to mention a range of pelagics.

Rates Most of the independent operators on the island charge a similar rate, although some – notably Big Blue and Ocean Vibes – are geared to a slightly more upmarket clientele, and charge accordingly. For a two-tank dive, visitors can expect to pay a walk-in rate from about $125, although pre-booking will secure considerably lower prices, from around $325 for three days' diving. Typically, the PADI Open Water course will cost in the region of $580 from scratch, or $400 for a referral course, to include equipment. Other divers who need to hire their equipment can expect to pay $25 a day, with use of a dive computer sometimes included, and sometimes an additional $10. Note that rising fuel costs are likely to lead to higher seasonal price rises than usual.

Residents at the all-inclusive Beaches and Club Med have diving included in their rates, although courses are charged extra. Divers staying at these resorts but seeking a greater level of freedom, especially a longer bottom time, will sometimes elect to spend a day or two with one of the independent operators.

Dive and snuba operators Provo's dive operators are a friendly bunch, each with its own slightly different niche. All are professionally run, and operate a range of dives, from the standard two-tank morning dive through single-tank dives to night dives. Some also offer the occasional three-tank dive.

Big Blue Unlimited Leeward Marina; ✆ 946 5034; m 231 6455; e bigblue@tciway.tc; www.bigblue.tc. Based at the eastern point of the island, with easy access to both sides of the island, Big Blue operates a range of courses up to instructor. Morning 2-tank dives for up to 9 divers are usually in their 40ft (12m) catamaran. They are also the only operator on the islands currently to offer rebreathers. This is a fairly exclusive outfit, with rates to match – the Open Water certificate, for example, is usually on a 1:1 basis, and is thus considerably more expensive than those offered by other operators. All rates include the use of a dive computer.
Caicos Adventures La Petite Place, Grace Bay Rd; ✆ 941 3346; e divucrzy@tciway.tc;

www.caicosadventures.tc. This PADI- & NAUI-affiliated dive centre was founded in 1988 by French owner Philippe Kunz, & offers tuition & materials in both French & Spanish, as well as English. Of its 3 catamarans, from 28ft (8.5m) to 54ft (16.5m), 2 are based at Southside Marina, with a smaller boat at Turtle Cove. These take up to 20 divers, with a ratio of 6:1 per instructor, & a staggered group entry. Snorkellers can also be accommodated, & packages arranged.
Dive Provo Ports of Call, Grace Bay Rd; ✆ 946 5029; US toll free ✆ 1 800 234 7768; US ✆ 1 945 351 9771; e diving@diveprovo.com; www.diveprovo.com. British owned by Alan & Clare Jardine since the mid 1990s, Dive Provo is the largest dive company on Providenciales, & a PADI

5-star Gold Palm resort. Professional, efficient & friendly, it offers excellent safety & dive briefings, with equipment set up for each diver. Its 3 comfortable, custom-designed diveboats are based at Turtle Cove & Caicos marinas, the latter involving a trip of around 1½hrs to the sites to the west. Numbers are kept small (usually 10–12 per boat, & never more than 14–16). Although the prime focus is on diving, they will also take snorkellers on a dive trip ($30–55 pp), & in addition offer regular snorkel trips to Grace Bay (2hrs) or West Caicos & French Cay (4hrs each). Dive Provo can organise both accommodation packages & most excursions across the islands.

Flamingo Divers Southside Marina, Venetian Rd; ☎ 946 4193, US toll free ☎ 1 800 204 9282; e greatdiving@flamingodivers.com; www.flamingodivers.com. The smallest of Provo's dive operators has 2 28ft (8.5m) boats, each taking no more than 8 divers per trip. Owned & run by Micky & Jane, they visit Northwest Point, West Caicos & French Cay, & offer a range of courses, including the Junior Open Water certificate.

Ocean Vibes Turtle Cove Marina; m 231 6636; e info@oceanvibes.com; www.oceanvibes.com. Ocean Vibes prides itself on valet-style service, offering on-board drinks & a full lunch, & working closely with resorts such as Amanyara. Up to 12 divers are taken on each of its two 43ft (13m) boats (back roll entry) with 4–6 per divemaster, who will lead the whole group unless divers are known to the company. PADI & NAUI courses, & universal referrals. Boats may also be chartered for ½ or full-day, taking up to 12 divers, or 20 snorkellers, for $800–$3,000.

Provo Turtle Divers Turtle Cove Marina; ☎ 946 4232; US toll free ☎ 1 800 833 1341; e info@provoturtledivers.com; www.provoturtledivers.com. The first dive operator on Providenciales was established by Art Pickering in 1970. Now a PADI 5-star Gold Palm resort & instructor training centre, it operates out of Turtle Cove & Southside marinas. Numbers on their 42ft (12.8m) & 36ft (11m) Newton diveboats, which are limited to 21 & 14 divers respectively, with up to 7 guests per divemaster. After a 2-tank morning dive, the boat returns to the marina no later than 2pm each day. Operates dive packages with several hotels, including Ocean Club & Ocean Club West, & acts as a booking agency for excursions.

Snuba Turks & Caicos Windsong Resort, Stubbs Rd; m 241 7010; e info@snubaturksandcaicos.com; http://snubaturksandcaicos.com. Jodi Taylor offers the technique of snuba (see pages 66–7) for small groups of 4 people. Trips depart from the beach in front of the Windsong Resort at 9am, 11am & 1pm daily, with an average of 45 mins underwater on the colourful Bight Reef. On-site shop selling T-shirts etc, & with digital cameras for rent. A boat tour is in hand. $70/60 adult/child 8–12, inc equipt & underwater photo. Video on request.

Liveaboards Two liveaboard dive boats operate in Turks and Caicos, limiting their range to the waters around Providenciales. Each can take a maximum of 20 divers.

Visitors can expect a similar package from each company, with divers arriving for a week-long trip on a Saturday, ready for departure the following day, with six days spent at sea. Typically up to five dives are offered each day, with a range of courses available (at extra cost), as well as nitrox. For full board, accommodation, transfers and all diving (including tanks, weights and weight belts), expect to pay $1,695–2,595 per person sharing, depending on the time of year and the standard of accommodation, plus 10% government tax and any fuel surcharge. Other extras include air fares, insurance, certificated courses, and any equipment rental. Gratuities are at the discretion of the diver, with 10% considered reasonable.

Turks & Caicos Aggressor II US toll free ☎ 1 800 348 2628, 1 985 385 2628; e info@aggressor.com; www.aggressor.com. Based at Turtle Cove Marina, to the west of Grace Bay.

Turks & Caicos Explorer II US toll free ☎ 1 800 322 3577, 1 307 235 0683; www.explorerventures.com. Operating out of Caicos Marina, the *Explorer* takes up to 20 divers in 10 rooms.

SNORKELLING, FISHING AND BOAT EXCURSIONS With a significant part of Providenciales accessible only by boat, there's a wide range of options on offer, and even then most of the boat operators are prepared to customise trips for their clients on request. For details of sailing, kayaking and speedboats, see pages 114 and 116–17.

Reef patches in the shallow waters along Grace Bay are all too easily damaged by careless swimmers, for these are fragile eco-systems. Their loss in turn results in a loss of habitat for the creatures that depend on them for survival. Fortunately, technology in the form of Reef Balls has stepped in to give a helping hand. Deployed at various locations off Provo for several years, each Reef Ball is shaped like a hollow igloo, and constructed of a specially formulated concrete that is harmless to the surrounding environment. Holes through the structures offer a refuge to passing creatures and, within just a few years, a healthy new reef is formed. For more information, see www.reefball.org.

Snorkelling Although there's some excellent snorkelling to be had on the reef, this entails a boat trip with one of the island's dive or boat operators. For those wishing to gain an understanding of what they're seeing beneath the waves, it's worth considering a half-day snorkelling trip with Big Blue *($120 pp, inc equipt & wetsuit)*, whose marine guides take the time both to explain what you're seeing, and to interpret this in the context of the overall environment. Trips depart three times a week, with times depending on the tides to ensure maximum visibility.

With the distance to the reef too far to swim, snorkelling from the beach is effectively limited to just a few small sites. On Grace Bay, the most accessible snorkel area is **Coral Gardens**, which lies in shallow water just in front of the resort of the same name. All but destroyed by inconsiderate swimmers who took to standing on the coral, it has recently been buoyed off, ensuring that snorkellers can see the newly resurgent reef without creating further damage. In addition to a range of colourful reef fish, many of them juveniles, keep an eye out for the occasional pufferfish and – on the surface – the slightly ghostly presence of the slender needlefish. A family of turtles has taken up residence, too, affording one of the few opportunities for visitors to see these creatures without taking a boat trip. Please do respect the ropes; just a casual flip of a fin will fatally damage the coral.

Further west, but still within the bay, the relatively large **Smith's Reef** lies a short swim offshore, between the two beach access points from Turtle Cove, but closer – just a five-minute walk – to the eastern side. It's marked at the back of the beach by a low stone cairn and a couple of red and green buoys, while underwater a string tied with pink ribbons leads to the reef itself. As with Coral Gardens, this acts as a nursery for many of the reef fish species, but adults are in evidence too; look out for grouper, parrotfish and angelfish, or perhaps a shoal of horse-eye jacks.

Fishing Anglers in search of excitement come from far afield to try their hand in the deep waters beyond the reef surrounding Grace Bay, where large specimens of mahi mahi and wahoo are to be found. For the most part, boats operating in this area take just 15 minutes or so to get to the fishing grounds, so little time is wasted en route. Shallow-water angling, such as bonefishing and bottom fishing, largely takes place to the south of the island. Expect to pay an additional $10 per person per day to cover the cost of a fishing permit.

If you plan to set out on your own, fishing tackle and bait can be purchased from Scooter Bob's at Turtle Cove (see page 87).

Glow-worming and other boat cruises Glow-worming outings take place at dusk during the two or three days immediately after a full moon, in search of the marine worm as it performs its elaborate mating ritual (see box opposite). Some of the sailing companies also run excursions (see page 116).

More regularly, there are numerous options that include visiting Little Water Cay (see page 123), **Pine Cay** – where you can beachcomb for shells and sand dollars – or **Fort George**, with its submerged 18th-century cannons. Beach barbecues, and the opportunity to free dive for your own conch – which is then prepared as a traditional conch salad – also feature high on the agenda. Or for a day away from the crowds, those with a romantic bent can arrange to be ferried to their own secluded stretch of beach, complete with chairs, umbrella and a picnic.

Snorkelling, fishing and boat charters In addition to the following, see *Glass-bottomed boats*, page 114, some of which offer snorkelling trips, as do most of the dive operators (see pages 110–11).

After 5 Concierge ℡ 946 4585; m 242 6506, 231 2078; e after5tci@yahoo.com; www.after5.tc. A one-stop shop catering for everything from boat charters & diving tuition to dining reservations & airport shuttles.

Big Blue Unlimited Leeward Marina; ℡ 946 5034; m 231 6455; e bigblue@tciway.tc; www.bigblue.tc. Providenciales' eco-conscience is firmly established at Big Blue, which has a specialist ecotour division. Marine guides accompany their kayaking & snorkelling trips, putting them in a different class from the run-of-the-mill outings offered by other operators. Additional trips cover kayaking & sightseeing on North Caicos ($235 pp), & cycling on Middle Caicos ($275 pp) — see pages 131 & 136. Private charters can also be arranged combining any of their activities, while - for the serious enthusiast — there are courses in marine life identification & reef ecology. Kayaking from $95 per ½ day; snorkelling $120 per ½ day (max 8 people). Kayak rental $15/20 sgl/dbl per hr.

Bite Me Sport Fishing Turtle Cove Marina; ℡ 946 4918, 946 4398; m 231 0366; e biteme@tciway.tc; www.fishingtci.com, www.tciworldtravel.com. Captain Chris Stubbs — locally known as Fineline — takes up to 4 anglers in search of mahi mahi & wahoo in the 28ft (8.5m) *Hallelujah*. ½ day $750.

Bottom Fishing ℡ 946 4874; m 231 0133; e bonefishprovo@tciway.tc; www.provo.net/bonefish. Owner Barr Gardiner specialises in bonefishing, although he also offers island trips. Expect to pay upwards from $500 per ½ day (2 people), plus $50 pp extra, inc bait, tackle, fuel, soft drinks & water.

Caicos Dream Tours Alexandra Resort & Spa; m 231 7274; www.caicosdreamtours.com. Both ½- & full-day trips, including their 'dream day get away' with snorkelling, diving for conch & lobster, Little Water Cay, beach BBQ & full bar, ($199/89.50 adult/child up to 10).

Caribbean Cruisin' ℡ 946 5406; m 231 4191; www.caribbeancruisin.com. The operators of the ferry service between Provo & North Caicos do full- & ½-day charters in their fleet of boats, as well as watersports.

Catch the Wave ℡ 941 3047; m 231 3875; e catchthewave@tciway.tc; www.tcimall.tc/catchthewave/default.htm. With its fleet of 4 boats, Catch the Wave can organise most excursions. It's known for its fishing trips & full-day beach BBQ ($1,600 for up to 4 people), while for those on a ½-day trip ($800 for 4–6 people), a fresh conch salad is prepared. Other options include a day for romance on a secluded beach, visits to Little Water Cay, & trips to Middle Caicos.

GLOW-WORM ROMANCE

The lowly marine worm, *Odontosyllis enolpa*, may not seem terribly exciting, but once a month, a half-hour or so after sunset, and up to five nights after the full moon, its mating ritual produces a scintillating light display that is the focus of glow-worming outings to the Caicos Banks, south of Provo.

When the time comes for the female to spawn, she swims towards the surface, releasing her eggs as she goes in a luminescent pale-green ball. Meanwhile the male performs a dance as he waits for the eggs, emitting a glow as he moves, which brightens as he darts around the eggs. Once the two meet at the surface, they continue to rotate around each other, with the whole ritual lasting just a few minutes.

Gwendolyn Fishing Charters Turtle Cove Marina; ↘ 946 5321, US ↘ 1 866 990 3474; m 232 4430; e ramslt@tciway.tc, captain.geoff@hotmail.com; www.fishtci.com. The on-board chair should fulfil every angler's film-fuelled dreams of the big catch. Up to 10 people $1,200 ½ day or $2,000/day plus permit.

Hook'em Fishing Adventures Turtle Cove Marina; ↘ 941 7536; m 231 3586, 2220; e fish@hookem.tc; www.hookem.tc. Capt Wing Dean offers a range of options, including deep-sea fishing, bottom fishing, bonefishing & light tackle trolling, as well as boat & snorkel trips & even conch & night fishing. If you're not sure, he can suggest a mix of fishing styles & snorkelling to suit everyone. Also handles trips to Little Water Cay & Middle Caicos. Around $550 ½ day bonefishing, or $750 deep-sea fishing.

J&B Tours ↘ 946 5047; e jill@jbtours.com; www.jbtours.com. Guided trips cover bone & bottom fishing ($650), deep-sea fishing ($225 pp), glow-worm excursions ($68 pp), & visits to Middle Caicos ($195 pp), as well as a full-day boat trip with BBQ around Providenciales ($149 pp) or a day on a secluded beach ($225 per couple). There are also 2 ½-day trips at $68 pp: the beach cruise, with a

visit to Little Water Cay, & the native cruise, to include freshly prepared conch salad.

Kenard Cruises Turtle Cove Marina; m 232 3866, 231 2414; e kenardcruises@tciway.tc; www.kenardcruises.com. Full & ½-day & sunset cruises on a 42ft (12.8m) 'luxury' motor catamaran *Dream Aweigh* — kitted out with AC & plasma TV. Costs from $1,850 ½ day for up to 8 people, inc light lunch & drinks. Cruises start from Turtle Cove Marina.

Ocean Outback ↘ 941 5810; m 231 0824. Regular 'outback adventure cruises' in a 38ft (11.5m) catamaran start from Sapodilla Bay & head west, with time for snorkelling, exploring a cave & a beach BBQ. $69 pp; glow-worm trips $49 pp (children ½ price).

Silver Deep Leeward Marina; ↘ 946 5612; m 232 1143; e info@silverdeep.com; www.silverdeep.com. With its large fleet of boats, this upmarket operator can organise most water-based excursions: beach cruises, glow-worm cruises, island getaways, BBQs & snorkel trips; fishing trips (bone, bottom, deep-sea, fly, night-shark), diving, excursions to Middle Caicos caves & private charters. They can even organise weddings on one of their boats. Prices start at $78 for a half-day beach cruise, or $50 for children aged 3–11.

GLASS-BOTTOMED BOATS For those yearning for a glimpse of the underwater world without getting wet, rescue is at hand in the shape of the *Undersea Explorer* (m 231 0006; e caicostours@tciway.tc; www.caicostours.com; *several trips daily exc Sun; $49/39 adult/child*), otherwise known as a semi-submersible. The concept is simple: up to 16 visitors climb aboard an ordinary-looking boat, but go below deck and you'll find a series of windows on both sides of the boat looking at the world that's 5ft (1.5m) below the surface. Individual window seats on each side ensure that everyone gets a good view, and an explanation of the life seen from the boat comes from a trip-specific commentary. All ages are welcome, from children as young as four, but the steps down into the cabin make it inappropriate for those with walking difficulties, and there is no shade on deck. Each trip takes an hour, with departures from Turtle Cove Marina; passengers are collected within the Grace Bay area.

More conventional glass-bottomed boats are run by a couple of companies, including Silver Deep (see above) and:

Reef Peepers Turtle Cove Marina; ↘ 941 8605; e info@reefpeepers.com; www.reefpeepers.com. 3hr cruises in a 40ft (12.2m) catamaran depart at 9.30am & 1.30pm daily, stopping at Little Water Cay to see the iguanas (additional $5 pp). Snorkelling

equipment is provided for those who want to see below the waves at first hand. In the evenings, there are sunset & karaoke trips. Adult $70; child 3–12 $50/40 day/evening, inc drinks & snacks.

SAILING

Marinas Yachtsmen approaching Providenciales currently have the choice of three marinas, one to the north in Grace Bay, and two others in the south. A fourth, Leeward Marina, was being rebuilt during 2008, and was scheduled to reopen in 2009. As an alternative, many sailors opt for the sheltered anchorage of Sapodilla Bay (see page 121), while larger vessels can be accommodated at the freight terminal at South Dock (☎ *946 4476, 4241*). Visiting yachtsmen should call ahead on VHF 16, and can arrange for guided assistance into harbour if required. For advance clearance of customs and immigration, contact the marina direct, or call Al Services (☎ *941 3267*).

Caicos Marina (☎ *946 5600*; e *caicosmarinashp@tciway.tc; www.caicosmarina.com;* ⏰ *7.30am–5pm Mon–Sat, 7am–noon Sun*) Primarily a shipyard, equipped with a 75-ton lift, Caicos Marina has a maximum draught of 7.5ft (2.4m) at high tide. Its berths cost $1 per foot per day, with an additional charge for water and electricity. Harbour facilities include showers and toilets, a coin-operated washing machine, and free WiFi internet.

Leeward Marina (☎ *946 5553*) This once quiet area at the eastern tip of Provo was undergoing a revolution during 2008. Whole sections of mangrove have fallen at the hands of developers as a smart new marina prepares to emerge from its lowlier predecessor. Billed as the 'world's first eco-marina', it will have its own customs house and hotel (see page 95), the latter decked out in a rather gaudy red and yellow. Although the marina is scheduled to open in 2009, work is likely to continue until at least 2011.

Southside Marina (*Venetian Rd;* ☎ *946 4747*) The smallest of Provo's marinas is based in Cooper Jack Bay. Offering relatively quick access to the dive sites to the west of the island, it is popular with several of the dive companies.

Turtle Cove Marina (☎ *941 3781*; e *tcmarina@provo.net; www.turtlecovemarina.com*) The sheltered natural harbour of Turtle Cove at the western end of Grace Bay Beach has been extended into a full-blown marina, its lines softened by coconut palms. Several restaurants and a hotel are set around the small harbour, giving it the best facilities of the local marinas.

Turtle Cove has 100 berths, capable of taking boats to a maximum draught of 7½ft (2.3m) at high tide, with facilities that include fuel docks, drinking water and ice, electricity points and cable television. Rates are $0.95 per foot per day, with electricity, water and TV charged extra (minimum $20 per day). It's also possible to hire cars or scooters, and to purchase a fishing licence.

Dinghies and catamarans Many of the hotels and condos along Grace Bay, as well as Club Med and Beaches, have their own dinghies and catamarans for use by guests, but a couple of operators, Sail Provo and Windsurfing Provo, specialise in sailing boats.

WINDSURFING AND KITEBOARDING For those dedicated to chasing the wind, there's a choice of Grace Bay or – for stronger winds – Long Bay Beach, to the south of the island, opposite Grace Bay.

At Windsurfing Provo (see page 116), Mike Rosati specialises in **windsurfing**, with equipment suitable for everyone from beginners to advanced. To check the wind forecast for the islands, use the link on his website.

Kiteboarding or **kitesurfing** is the domain of Mike Haas at Kite Provo (see page 116). Complete novices must first learn the principles of power kiting. It's a far greater challenge than might be imagined, and is in itself enormous fun. A two-hour course costs $150 per person. From here, the skills are applied in the water – a second course lasting three hours and costing $225 per person – while a third option is to learn board skills while being pulled from a waterski boat ($300/hr, for up to four people). There's also the option of private instruction.

The more experienced can join one of the local riders on a Tuesday, visiting areas of their choice around the island. Advance reservation is essential.

Operators

Beluga ➚ 946 4396; m 231 0732; e sailbeluga@tciway.tc; www.sailbeluga.com. Captain Tim Ainley takes small charter groups of up to 6 people sailing for a ½ or full-day in his 36ft (11m) Polynesian catamaran. With 20 years' experience of sailing in these waters, he can accommodate most requests, wind and weather permitting. Prices on application.

Kite Provo US ➚ 727 490 4258; m 242 2927; e kite@tciway.tc; www.kiteprovo.com

Sail Provo Grace Bay Plaza, Grace Bay Rd; ➚ 946 4783; e sailprovo@tciway.tc; www.sailprovo.com. Cruise the waters of Provo on a 48ft (14.6m) or 52ft (15.8m) sailing catamaran, each with a large central trampoline, a hard top deck & simple beach access. Options, at $63–124 pp, range from 3hr cruises in the daytime or at sunset, visiting Little Water Cay & snorkelling along the reef, to a full-day which takes in lunch, & stops at some of the uninhabited cays. Also run glow-worming trips ($65 pp).

Sun Charters m 231 0624; e suntours@tciway.tc; www.suncharters.tc. Aboard the *Atabeyra*, a traditionally rigged 77ft (23.4m) schooner that once plied between Hispaniola & TCI, hands-on sailing is there for the taking – or just chill & let others do the work. Full & ½-day trips or charters include snorkelling & Little Water Cay. There's also a twice-weekly 3hr 'pirate' cruise (yes, you can walk the plank!) at $59/49 adult/child, a glow-worm cruise ($49 pp), & on Fri in summer a happy-hour sunset cruise ($39 pp, including 'bottomless' rum punch).

Windsurfing Provo Ocean Club or Ocean Club West Resort; m 241 1687; e mike@ windsurfingprovo.tc, windpro@tciway.tc; www.windsurfingprovo.tc. Not content with just windsurfing, Mike Rosati also handles sailing, kayaking, kiting & even motorboat rentals. Windsurfing rates start at $25 for 1st hr, or $100/day; private lessons $90 pp (up to 2 people).

KAYAKING Kayaking through the island's mangroves reveals a world rich in underwater life, for these are the nurseries for all manner of fish, conch and nudibranchs, and their shade provides shelter for the likes of stingrays and sharks.

Big Blue (see page 113) leads tours to some of the best places for kayaking on Provo, each with a guide who will explain about the wildlife in the context of its coastal habitat. The mangroves around Little Water Cay, off Leeward Marina, feature on a popular half-day trip ($95) in usually calm waters that includes a stop on the island itself to see the iguanas. During the trip, participants will be given an introduction to tropical coastal ecology and island geography, as well as to the wildlife of the area. Guided trips also go to Frenchman's Creek (see pages 122–3), as well as further afield to North Caicos (see page 116). On a practical note, dry bags are provided on each of the kayaks, so that cameras and other kit can be taken without fear of it becoming wet.

For those wanting to strike out independently, both single and double kayaks can be hired from Big Blue for $15 and $20 per hour respectively, with half- and full-day rates available too. Kayaks can be either collected from the office near Leeward Marina, where maps of the immediate area are available, or – for those paying the daily rate – delivered to your accommodation. They are also available through Windsurfing Provo (see above) on Grace Bay, on a similar basis.

OTHER WATERSPORTS AND BOAT HIRE **Parasailing** along Grace Bay gives a great bird's-eye view of the beach from 500ft (150m) up. Participants can fly solo, tandem or even triple, although the minimum weight to fly solo is 90lb (40kg). Before the off, you can expect a briefing to include detailed instructions, hand signals and emergency procedures – then the sky is yours.

If speed is more in your line, Sun & Fun Seasports charters **speedboats**, as well as organising guided **jetskiing** along the chain of cays to the east of Providenciales. Jetskis – or waverunners – can also be hired from their base at Caicos Marina for use on unprotected beaches such as Long Bay Beach. Note, though, that such craft may not be used within any national park area, which includes Grace Bay.

The rather more sedate Carolina **skiffs**, taking up to four adults, can be hired through Windsurfing Provo. Fully equipped with radio, coolbox and lifejackets, they cost from $90 for two hours, plus fuel.

Closer to the beach, **banana-boat** rides, taking up to ten people, are operated by Caribbean Cruisin'.

Specialist operators also cater for enthusiasts of **waterskiing**, **wakeboarding** and related activities. For details, contact Doug at Nautique Sports or JP (m *231 3440*).

Operators

Captain Marvin's Watersports ☎ 946 4956; m 231 0643; e info@captainmarvinsparasail.com; www.captainmarvinsparasail.com. Offers parasailing, waterskiing, wakeboarding & banana boat rides.
Caribbean Cruisin' ☎ 946 5406; m 231 4191; www.caribbeancruisin.com. Waterskiing & wakeboarding cost $200/hr (max 5 people), or take a banana-boat ride at $20 pp.
Eagle Parasail m 243 4226; www.oceanvibes.com. Run by the dive operator Ocean Vibes, whose 28ft (8.5m) boat was custom built for parasailing.
Nautique Sports m 231 6890, 4330; e nautiquesports@tciway.tc; www.nautiquesports.com. Specialists in charters

offering waterskiing, wakeboarding & similar activities, from $300/hr for up to 4 people. Private tuition is available (m *231 7543*). For more information and any appropriate kit, take a look in their shop at the Graceway Sports Centre.
Parasailing Turtle Cove Marina; m 231 7245
Sun & Fun Seasports Caicos Marina; ☎ 946 5724; e sunandfun@tciway.tc; www.tcimail.tc/sunandfun. Daily 1hr & 2hr guided jetski trips at $175/275, or hire one of the craft without a guide from $125/hr. There are speedboats, too, with prices (exc fuel & captain) from $175/hr in the 15ft (4.5m) *Challenger*, up to $775 per day in the 22ft (6.7m) *Islandia*.

SPORTS FACILITIES
Provo's sports might focus on the water, but there are options for landlubbers, too, not least an 18-hole golf course.

Golf
The 18-hole Provo Golf Club (☎ *946 5991*; e *provogolf@tciway.tc*; *www.provogolfclub.com*) is the island's only golf course. Flanked by a series of condominiums, it lies behind Grace Bay and was originally opened in 1992. It's a smart, somewhat formal environment with a traditional dress code; men are expected to wear long trousers or tailored shorts, and collared shirts. The use of golf carts is mandatory.

The course is dotted with tall palms, limestone outcrops and numerous lakes, which attract a range of waterbirds, including flamingoes and herons. In fact, water is something of a theme, since ten of the 18 holes have water features, and the course is under the same ownership as the islands' water company.

The two-storey clubhouse was fully refitted during 2007, with a new-look shop and, upstairs, the revamped Fairways Bar & Grill (☎ *946 5833*), which overlooks the course. The club also has a driving range (*$6 per bag of balls*) and floodlit tennis courts (see below).

Green fees (inc cart): 9/18 holes $90/160; 3 rounds $375; 5 rounds $550; 'twilight' rate from $110. Club rental $25–55 per day. Lessons $90.

Mini golf and go-karting
If mini golf (*Leeward Hwy*; ☎ *941 4653*; *http://funworldtci.com*; ⊕ *11am–10pm Mon–Fri; 10am–late Sat/Sun; $15/10 adult/child*) is more up your street, don't despair. Provo has an 18-hole course that is even floodlit to allow play through the evening. Take the Leeward Highway east and shortly before the Conch Farm, you'll find mini golf & go-karting on the north side of the road. The on-site restaurant/bar (m *231 4653*; ⊕ *10am–late daily*) has a jolly atmosphere with karaoke evenings; it serves hot dogs, salads and other fast food.

Tennis Many of the hotels and several villas have their own courts, but open to all comers are the two floodlit tennis courts at Provo Golf Club (✆ *946 5991*). These may be rented by non members during the day until 5pm, at $10 per hour for adults, or $7 for juniors. Racquets and balls can be purchased in the shop at the golf club, or rented at $5 per hour.

Skating Graceway Sports Centre (✆ *941 8321*) behind the IGA supermarket offers in-line skating. A day pass costs $5, with skate rental a further $5. Session times change daily, so call ahead for details.

GYMS

Bodies in Motion Gym Miramar Resort, Turtle Cove; ✆ 941 8321; m 231 2950; e bimgym@tciway.tc; www.bodiesinmotiontci.com; ⏰ 5.30am–8pm Mon–Thu; 5.30am–7pm Fri; 8am–noon Sat; 9am–noon Sun. Fully equipped gym with regular aerobics classes. Gym $15/day; aerobics $10/class. New for 2008 is a range of spa treatments.

Devon's Gym Town Centre Mall, Downtown; ✆ 941 8014, 8018.
The Studio Ports of Call, Grace Bay Rd; ✆ 946 5802. Pilates, yoga & other fitness classes.
Pulse Salt Mills, Grace Bay Rd; ✆ 941 8686; ⏰ 6am–1pm, 4–8pm Mon–Thu; 6am–1pm, 4–7pm Fri; 9am–noon weekends & some holidays.

HORSERIDING Provo has two riding stables, one based to the south of the island; the second to the north. Although their styles are very different, both offer the opportunity to ride along the sands.

Caicos Corral m 331 3939; e info@ caicoscorral.com; www.caicoscorral.com. Fred Neehuis looks every inch the western rider as he leads groups along the beach at Grace Bay. Riding is on Western saddles; only 1 hat is available. Participants, including complete beginners, are collected from accommodation in the bay area at around 3.45pm. Riding lessons on request. 1½hr $75; moonlit rides $125/hr.
Provo Ponies Dolphin Lane, Long Bay Hills; ✆ 946 5252; m 241 6350; e provoponies@provo.net, camille@tciway.tc; www.provo.net/ProvoPonies. The leading stables on Provo organises 2 rides a day along Long Bay Beach, at 9.30am & around 4pm, depending on the time of year. The 20 or so ponies, many of which came from Grand Turk, wear

English saddles & are not shod, instead wearing rubber 'boots' if protection is required. Following a short session in the ring to determine ability, each group (11 riders max) sets off with 2 guides & a motley selection of dogs for the beach, where stingrays, turtles & even the occasional nurse shark may be spotted in the shallows. The horses sometimes swim, but at others will walk, depending on the tide. Either way, this is not nose-to-tail riding, although beginners can be accommodated (there's a $30 leading fee), & lessons are available. Weight limit 200lb (90kg). Hard hats are supplied, & must be worn by under 16s. Reservations essential. 1–1½hr $80–90 pp. Private ride (min 2 people) additional $30 pp. No children under 6.

WHAT TO SEE

GRACE BAY AND THE EAST The beach that put Providenciales on the map, Grace Bay offers 12 miles (19km) of unbroken soft white sand, slipping like the finest talcum powder between the toes. While today it is backed by ever-taller hotels and condominiums, the beach itself remains broadly unsullied, except of course for the ranks of sun loungers spread out in front of buoyed swimming areas, punctuated here and there with clusters of small sailing craft hauled up on the sands. Even in the most built-up areas behind the beach, blue-and-white signs indicate beach access points at regular intervals.

Grace Bay is largely sheltered from the northeast trade winds, but if the wind is up, the eastern end of the beach is likely to be the calmest. The bay falls within the Princess Alexandra Marine Park, affording it protection from jet skis and the like. In the absence of beach hawkers touting their wares, any break in the prevailing air

above **Junkanoo** (SP) page 55

below **Children on beach, Grand Turk** (TH) page 172

top	**American kestrel** *Falco sparverius* (SP) page 23
above	**Osprey** *Pandion haliaetus* (SP) page 23
left	**Great blue heron** *Ardea herodias* (BH) page 23
bottom	**Bananaquit** *Coeraba flaveola sharpei* (SP) page 23

top	**Black-necked stilts** *Himantopus mexicanus* (SP) page 23
above	**Royal tern** *Sterna maxima* (SP) page 23
right	**Yellow elder** *Tecoma stans* (TH) page 21
below	**Bahama woodstar** *Calliphlox evelynae* (SP) page 23

top   **Old commissioner's house, South Caicos**
(TH) page 23

above left   **Entrance to Blue Hills, Providenciales**
(TH) page 122

above right   **Donkeys, Salt Cay**
(SP) page 23

left   **Town Salina, Salt Cay**
(BH) page 182

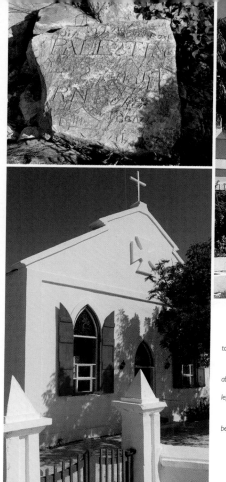

top left	**Rock engraving, Sapodilla Hill, Providenciales** (TH) page 121
above	**Court House, Grand Turk** (BH) page 172
left	**Anglican Pro-Cathedral, Grand Turk** (SP) page 167
below	**Cheshire Hall, Providenciales** (TH) page 119

above **Harbour, South Caicos**
(TH) page 149

right **Fishing boat, South Caicos**
(BH) page 149

below **Fishermen, Grand Turk**
(TH) page 171

above **Sailing Paradise, Blue Hills, Providenciales**
(TH) page 101

above right **Boys on jetty, Salt Cay** (SP) page 175

right **Turks and Caicos iguana** *Cyclura carinata carinata*
(TH) page 24

below **Little Water Cay** (TH) page 123

above   **Mudjin Harbour, Middle Caicos** (SP) page 137

below   **Sunset over Sapodilla Bay, Providenciales** (SP) page 121

of peace is more likely to come from the occasional police officer patrolling on a dune buggy – or perhaps a local with a ghetto-blaster..

Caicos Conch Farm (✆ 946.5643; e info@caicosconchfarm.com; www.caicosconchfarm.com; ⏰ 9am–4pm Mon–Fri, 9am–2pm Sat, closed Sun & holidays; admission $6/3 adult/child)

The world's only operating conch farm grows 5,000 or so queen conches, mostly for the export market – although they also supply a small number of local restaurants. Displays depict the life cycle of the conch and give a full explanation of sustainable farming. There's also a gift shop and café. Note that opening hours can be erratic, especially out of season, so do call ahead if you're visiting independently. There's another facility on Grand Turk under the same management.

Villa del Raye (last turn off Governor's Rd before Leeward Hwy, nr Leeward Marina)

The Premier's residence is an impressive large white house with big wrought-iron gates and three large flagpoles. The tallest sports the national flag, the other two have the Union Jack and the Stars and Stripes. The house is not open to the public.

National Environmental Centre (Lower Bight Rd; ✆ 941 5122; www.environment.tc; ⏰ 8am–4.30pm Mon–Fri; 8am–1pm Sat. Admission free, but donations welcome).

Curator Brian Riggs took up the challenge to set up the National Environmental Centre, having previously worked at the National Museum on Grand Turk. The result, opened in April 2007, is one of the island's unsung attractions, well worth a visit for adults and children alike.

From the outside the centre looks rather like the base of a disused windmill, set on a low rise with its walls of cut native limestone already weathering to a creamy tan. Inside, displays are well laid out, with a large bathymetric map at the centre showing the islands in the context of their marine surroundings, complete with trenches and shallow reefs. Well-illustrated panels are arranged by habitat, taking the visitor through the extensive biodiversity of the islands. There are also several individual exhibits, as well as hands-on terminals and a children's quiz, so there's little chance of being bored.

Around the centre, there are plans to establish a garden, with short trails running alongside areas planted with 70 or so native plants, and further planting on the land opposite, known locally as 'the children's park'.

DOWNTOWN In addition to housing the offices of various government departments, this area is predominantly the preserve of Dominican shops and restaurants.

Cheshire Hall (Leeward Hwy, close to Downtown; National Trust; admission $8, or $10 with guide; ⏰ 8.30am–4.30pm Mon–Fri; visits outside these hours possible with advance notice)

These are the wonderfully evocative ruins of one of the island's first Loyalist cotton plantations. If they do not have ghosts, they should have.

Under the 1783 Treaty of Paris, Great Britain returned Florida to Spain in return for undisputed possession of the Bahamas (which at that time included the Turks and Caicos Islands) and some other Caribbean islands. Many of the Loyalist settlers who did not want to stay in America or remain in Spanish Florida were granted compensatory land in the Turks and Caicos. Others, encouraged by the stories they were told, decided to settle here anyway and among those was Thomas Stubbs of Gawsworth in Cheshire, whose brother Wade had already settled in North Caicos on a plantation he called Bellefield (later to be known as Wade's Green; see page 132).

At first Thomas and his slaves prospered in the Cheshire Hall plantation, set on a hill to catch the breeze and enjoy the view. The newly cleared land initially produced good crops of sea-island cotton, much in demand for the mills of Lancashire, but the soil was thin and the plants were attacked first by the chenille worm and then by the red bug. In the absence of fertilisers and pesticides, production dropped drastically and a fall in world cotton prices led Thomas to sell Cheshire Hall to brother Wade in 1810. A cornerstone inscribed 'W Stubbs 1810' commemorates the deal, which was not a good one for Wade. Although he built up his holdings in North Caicos to 3,000 acres and at Cheshire Hall to 5,000 acres, not to mention a total of 384 slaves, the great hurricane of 1812 pretty much finished off cotton cultivation. Thomas left the island but Wade stayed on until his death in 1822 and is buried at St Thomas's Church in Grand Turk.

When the planters departed the islands, their former slaves often took over where they had left off and became the real pioneers of the territory, but the buildings of Cheshire Hall fell into disuse. They were suffering seriously from vandalism and neglect until the National Trust took over the site in 2000, re-opening it to the public in April 2003. It is now well signed, and partially restored with the aid of a British government grant, although much more remains to be done. The trust has produced an excellent brochure on the plantation, its flora and fauna, which leads you on an informative half-hour walk around the old plantation. Add a modicum of imagination, keep your eyes open (but close them for a few moments every now and then), and you will be captivated. You will also see birds, butterflies and plants indigenous to Provo, all described in the brochure, as well as the setting for plantation life 200 years ago – living quarters, cotton machinery buildings and even a defensive cannon. The brochure is available from the admissions kiosk or the National Trust office (see page 102).

SOUTHERN PROVIDENCIALES

Long Bay Beach Three miles of often deserted sandy beach can be somewhat windswept, making this the ideal spot for windsurfers and kiteboarders. The rest of the time you could be sharing it with just the odd jogger or beachcomber.

The Hole Prominently marked on most local maps, The Hole is aptly named, if something of a disappointment. To find it, take the untarred and potholed Long Bay Hills Highway from the Venetian Road, then turn right and then left, following the signposts. The Hole is on the left.

A natural, 80ft-deep (24.4m) sinkhole, backed by a large cave, it was created when the roof of an underground cavern collapsed, leaving a 40ft (12.2m) void. Viewing is from the top, and the drop is sheer, so this is no place for children or the vertiginous. In theory a path leads down to the bottom, but it's very overgrown, and not worth the effort unless you're fascinated by the geological structure. The shallow water lining the sinkhole used to be an attractive spot to cool off but is currently both stagnant and dirty.

Cooper Jack's Beach This secluded beach is one among several along this coast and to the west that are crying out to be explored by the more adventurous.

Five Cays Named for the five small islands just offshore, the Five Cays area lies to the east of the South Dock Road, and is the base of the fishing trade on Provo. It is also home to a largely Haitian community. On most days, local fishermen bring in the night's catch early in the morning, and it's well worth popping down for a look (or to buy something for dinner). Be aware, though, that trade is inevitably weather dependent. If you're hungry after an early-morning start, drop in to Liz's Bakery (see page 104) on the way home.

Perhaps the word 'queen' summarises the importance of the conch in the Turks and Caicos, for this queen of the seas not only provides part of the staple diet of the islanders, it is also a significant export commodity, valued at almost $2 million each year. According to CITES, TCI is one of the largest exporters of queen conch meat and shells in the world, along with Jamaica and the Bahamas.

Until the 20th century, the waters of the Caicos Bank were filled with conch in their thousands. In the days before cold storage, this nutritious shellfish represented the ideal food, both for the islanders and as a trading commodity. After a drying time of around three weeks, it can be kept without refrigeration for up to six months. It's not surprising, then, that as shipping routes became more established, trade with the neighbouring Haiti was brisk.

The industry continued to expand unchecked until the 1930s, but by the late 1970s was being regularly monitored. Today it is listed by CITES as 'commercially endangered', and export quotas are capped in relation to the estimated population in the wild. The industry is heavily regulated, too, to prevent overfishing: all conch fishermen require a licence from the DECR, the use of any aids such as scuba gear or chemicals is banned, and strict quotas are imposed. Fishing within a national park area is strictly off limits, as are the breeding grounds to the south of Providenciales, where thousands of conch reared at the Conch Farm are released each year – albeit with mixed success rates. In addition, conch are protected by a closed season, which varies each year depending on the level of exports but is usually between 15 July and 15 October.

The female queen conch, *Strombus gigas*, lays egg masses comprising up to half a million embryos, each of which takes five days to hatch into veligers. The snails are mature at three years, when they weigh around 2lb (0.9g), with the shell measuring approximately eight inches (20cm) in length. While most of those taken for the table are around five or six years old, the minimum size at which they can be harvested under TCI regulations is seven inches (18cm). The thickness of their shell depends on their environment: those inhabiting rougher seas develop a thicker shell than their cousins in calm water. The snails live in water from ten to 65ft (3–20m) in depth, so that fishermen, who take the conch by free diving, sometimes have to dive to considerable depths for their catch. The bulk of the industry is today based on South Caicos.

Turks Head Brewery (*Provo Industrial Park;* \ *941 3637;* ⊕ *1–4pm Wed*) Close to the South Dock, TCI's only brewery offers tours on Wednesday afternoons only, and has a small souvenir shop.

Sapodilla Bay Shallow, sheltered and usually calm, Sapodilla Bay is a favoured anchorage for yachtsmen. With its crescent of sand it's also a pleasant place to while away a few hours for a picnic and a cooling dip, or to watch the sunset over the waters. There are no facilities here, only a few private houses, so bring everything you need.

A short but steep rocky path leads up from the gravelled parking area behind the bay, bringing you after five minutes or so to the top of **Sapodilla Hill**. (There's also a slightly easier path from the dock gate.) Uninterrupted views look on the one side over the bay, and on the other to South Dock, the lifeblood of the island where all goods are brought in by sea. Look around at your feet to find a series of rocks engraved with the graffiti of their era, dating back to 1760. A display in the international departures hall at Provo airport gives some explanation of the individual inscriptions, which range from simple sketches of ships, to family names and initials in neatly chiselled lettering, to the elaborately carved name of the SS *Palestine*, which appears to have called at the island twice in the mid 1800s before being wrecked in the 1866 hurricane.

Chalk Sound National Park Just a short drive from the industrial South Dock, the shallow expanse of Chalk Sound is protected as a national park. Overlooked by some of the island's most expensive properties, the sound itself lies tranquil and calm, its turquoise waters dotted with seemingly unreal green islands.

Motorised vehicles are not permitted in the national park, but it's a magical place for kayaking if all you want is to explore – although with such shallow waters and a sandy bottom, the underwater life isn't up to much. There's no commercial kayaking here, but kayaks can be hired from Big Blue (see page 113) from $15–20 per hour.

BLUE HILLS AND THE WEST

Blue Hills The oldest settlement on the island, Blue Hills is home to numerous extended families, and its beach restaurants have made it a popular stop on the tourist agenda. Behind the beach, though, the area's schools, churches and family graveyards speak of a community that remains firmly rooted in tradition.

The beach at Blue Hills is effectively an extension of Grace Bay, but is less sheltered than the eastern end of the island. Backed by casuarinas and sea-grape trees, the sands here are relatively narrow, but with little of the commercialism that characterises their glitzier neighbour. Royal terns line up like sentries along the wooden jetty, keeping watch on the traditional Caicos sloops that bob around on their moorings. Brown pelicans cruise in search of lunch, their somewhat ungainly appearance belying some stunning acrobatic displays as they swoop on unsuspecting prey. For a relaxed drink or a meal, it adds up to a fitting backdrop.

Western Providenciales The western side of the island can come as something of a surprise to visitors for whom Grace Bay is 'home'. Just a few tracks break up the densely vegetated low hills that stretch to the horizon in every direction, giving a sense of isolation that is hard to fathom on such a small island. It's not likely to last, but for now this is one part of Provo that is entirely unspoiled.

Highlights of this area are Northwest Point and Malcolm Roads (or simply Malcolm's) Beach, as well as Frenchman's Creek.

Northwest Point and Malcolm Roads Beach In the far west of Providenciales, backed by low-lying hills thick with vegetation and wild flowers, Malcolm's Beach lies alongside the Amanyara Resort within the Northwest Point National Park. Purple morning glory winds through the undergrowth and red-and-yellow-flowered opuntia cacti line the narrow track to the beach. Keep your eyes open and you may be lucky enough to spot a hummingbird among the wild fruit trees.

The secluded, sandy beach is broken by flattened rocks, with shallow water entry into the sea. Naturally sheltered from the prevailing northeasterly winds, the water can get fairly rough on those occasions when the wind veers round.

Access to Malcolm's Beach is along an unpaved road off the Millennium Highway, and is fairly flat until the last mile or so. Drive *very* slowly down this last section; it deteriorates badly into a steep and very rocky track that could easily cause significant damage to the under side of a normal saloon car.

Frenchman's Creek and West Harbour A rough, potholed track leads from the Millennium Highway towards an isolated part of Providenciales known as West

Harbour, which lies at the southern tip of the Pigeon Pond and Frenchman's Creek Nature Reserve. (Coming from Blue Hills, it is the first road to the left; if you reach the turning to the 'solid waste dump' you've already passed it.) The road runs south for about six miles (9.6km) along the narrow stretch of land between Chalk Sound and Frenchman's Creek. It's an isolated spot, so do make sure that you have plenty of time to get back before dusk, and ideally go in a 4x4.

Frenchman's Creek itself is an attractive place for kayaking through the network of mangrove channels. There are also early 19th-century engravings on the rocks here, similar to those found on Sapodilla Hill. Big Blue (see page 113) leads three-quarter-day guided kayaking tours *($145 pp)*, which finish on a secluded beach to the west and include lunch at Blue Hills.

Continuing to the end of the road brings you out at the so-called **West Harbour**, a narrow beach with low rocks that's likely to be shared only with the occasional group of local youngsters at weekends. Not far away is an osprey's nest, a pirate cave and some rock engravings. To find these, turn left along the beach, and follow it south on foot for around ¼ mile (0.4km) to a scrub-covered bluff. From here, if you're reasonably fit, you can either wade or swim around the base of the cliff (variously marked West Harbour Bluff or South Bluff on local maps, and sometimes even Osprey Rock) until you come to a sizeable cave (said to have been the lair of some nameless 17th-century pirate). From here you can either scramble up the bluff or climb a rope ladder through a chimney to emerge at a point with a great view, and not too far from the bird's nest, wisely located on an adjacent egg-shaped rock. (Please view in silence, without disturbing the occupants of the nest.) You can now descend back to the beach, checking out some mysterious rock carvings en route. This is a remote corner of Providenciales and many locals are unaware of the cave.

ISLANDS AROUND PROVIDENCIALES

LITTLE WATER CAY (*National Trust;* ☉ *8.30am–5.30pm daily. Admission & guided tour $10 for short trail, $15 for extended trail, inc copy of field guide*)

Managed by the National Trust, Little Water Cay is a nature reserve set up to protect one of the last strongholds of the endangered Turks and Caicos iguana (see page 24). Covering an area of 116 acres (47ha), of which 7.2 acres (3ha) are made up of ponds, the island is home to some two to three thousand of these small creatures. It also features many native trees, as well as creatures such as the curly-tail, and numerous birds, including ospreys, several herons and the tiny bananaquit. National Trust wardens are on hand to guide visitors along a series of boardwalks near the entrance, explaining aspects of the iguanas' lifestyle and their relationship with their habitat. The iguanas here are occasionally hand fed, so it's a great place for photographs. For those wishing to explore further at their own pace, a nature trail continues along boardwalks – which in places form a cover for burrows created by the iguanas – across to the north shore of the island, where a large, partially insect-proofed shelter affords the opportunity to watch birds among the mangroves. Allow about half an hour for the guided tour, or at least two if you want to take in the whole walk and return to the start. Alternatively, arrange for a tour operator to collect you at the other end of the island.

Several companies, most notably Catch the Wave and J&B Tours (see pages 113 and 114), run tours to the island as part of a half-day excursion, costing around $70 a head. Big Blue (see page 113) also escorts a kayaking trip that takes in the island. Alternatively individuals with access to a boat can purchase tickets direct from the National Trust in Grace Bay or Town Centre Mall (see page 102). A laminated interpretive leaflet is available from the trust, or on the island itself, costing $10.

MODEL SAILING BOATS

Sloop sailing is intricately entwined with the culture of the Turks and Caicos – but it's not limited just to full-size boats. Model sailboats in this part of the world are taken seriously: lovingly carved, rigged, painted – and then raced. To call them 'toys' is to do them an injustice.

The Middle Caicos Sailing Association incorporates the Model Sailboat Club, which organises regular races at Blue Hills every Friday and Saturday afternoon between 11am and 4pm, except in inclement weather when the seas are up. Before the off, the 'helmsman' of each craft carefully checks the set of the sail to ensure that it gets off to the best start. It's a colourful race, sailing in miniature, but with all the tension of a full-sized regatta. For details, including the chance to learn how to make or sail one of the boats, contact Herbert (**m** *242 1233*; **e** *middlecaicos@tciway.tc*). And if you want to see the full-size boats at play, hang around on a Saturday near Sailing Paradise, and you should be in luck.

WEST CAICOS Normally approached by boat from Providenciales across the vivid turquoise waters of Caicos Bay, in the company of the occasional bottlenose dolphin, West Caicos is a low-lying strip of land some 11 square miles (28.5km) to the west of Providenciales. Its Taino name, Makobusa, means 'beautiful island'. The island's western waters are protected by the West Caicos Marine National Park, but at its northern tip, the apparent fortification rising up from the sea is the Ritz-Carlton's new tourist development (see page 96), scheduled to open in 2008. The company has bought 10% of the island, but the rest of the island will remain uninhabited.

At one time the island was a base for the Drugs Enforcement Agency, used to intercept drug smugglers, and further back Dulain's Cove on the north shore was once a pirate hang-out. Inevitably this means there are stories of treasure either on land or under the sea. More recently, Generalissimo Rafael Trujillo, dictator of the Dominican Republic, wanted to buy West Caicos as a hideaway shortly before his assassination in 1961. Then, in 1972, there were plans to build an oil refinery but construction got no further than an airstrip. It has taken many years and a luxury tourist development to bring any form of habitation back to the island.

For most visitors in recent years, the island has been known almost exclusively for the excellent diving off its leeward shore rather than for any land-based attractions. That said, although there are no regular trips run to the island itself, it is possible to organise an excursion to go on land. Among the attractions is the inland Lake Catherine, a nature reserve which is connected to the sea by a maze of subterranean caves. Yankee Town, near the lake, was built when the island had salt and sisal industries, but abandoned when the industries folded. Now a ghost town, it still has a sisal press, the remains of railway tracks and engines, and a stone wall. For details, contact Big Blue (see page 113).

Pufferfish

5

North, Middle and East Caicos

Despite the meteoric population rise on Providenciales in recent years, the number of people inhabiting the other Caicos Islands has remained almost static for over two centuries. In 1788 the Caicos Islands – North, Middle and East combined – are recorded to have had in total a population of 40 white families and 1,200 slaves. By 1960, the population of North and Middle Caicos had risen to just 1,628, with only an additional 20 souls by 2001. Life on the islands remains as it has done for years, reflecting a deep-rooted conservatism. It is against this background that development of these hitherto quiet backwaters of tourism will inevitably be measured. Let us hope that tourism's gain will not be at the expense of the islands and of the people who call them home.

NATURAL HISTORY

The wetlands of North, Middle and East Caicos combine to form one of the most natural of those protected as a Ramsar site (so named after the town in Iran where, in 1971, a convention met to discuss wetlands of international importance). The nature reserve incorporating these wetlands covers 243 square miles (629km²), and features a broad diversity of habitat, from coral reef through to mangroves, saltmarsh, Caribbean pine and great stands of tropical dry forest. Protection also extends to many of the cays off the coast.

Large numbers of wetland birds are drawn to the islands, from the West Indian whistling duck to flocks of pink flamingoes, with egrets and herons readily spotted by even the most casual observer, and the belted kingfisher darting through the mangroves. Look up to spot the American kestrel perched on many a telegraph wire, or the nest of an osprey in the craggy cliffs to the north, while off the coast of Middle Caicos, Man O'War Bush is a rare stronghold of the magnificent frigatebird.

Inland, lizards, iguanas, snakes and geckos thrive in the undergrowth. Bats, too, inhabit this area, frequenting the limestone caves which have formed deep within the rock – some protected in their own right by the Conch Bar Caves National Park (see pages 137–8).

Development will inevitably impact on this natural biodiversity. Indeed, it already has, with the construction of the causeway between North and Middle Caicos destroying significant tracts of mangrove. Let's hope that the authorities will ensure that any future development is sensitively handled, so that the natural beauty of these islands will remain their primary attraction.

GETTING THERE

Until 2007, visitors to North and Middle Caicos from Providenciales had the choice of taking a flight or hiring a private boat. Now, however, a ferry from

Providenciales and the opening of a causeway between North and Middle Caicos has made access considerably easier. In order to get to East Caicos, however, it is still essential to go with an organised tour, or to have your own boat.

BY SEA A ferry service runs between the eastern tip of Providenciales and North Caicos. The crossing, in a cheerful yellow waterbus, takes around half an hour. It's an interesting trip in itself, passing close to the cays that line the outer edge of the shallow channel.

The ferry service is run by Caribbean Cruisin' (*946 5406;* m *231 4191*) from their office at Leeward Marina on Providenciales. Tickets cost $40 return, or $25 one way. Ferries run daily as follows:

Depart Provo	Arr N Caicos	Dep N Caicos	Arr Provo
Monday to Saturday			
6.30am	7am	7am	7.30am
10.30am	11am	1pm	1.30pm
3.55pm	4.25pm	4.30pm	5pm
5.45pm	6.15pm	6.30pm	7pm
Sunday and public holidays			
7.25am	7.55am	8am	8.30am
10.30am	11am	1pm	1.30pm
5.45pm	6.15pm	6.30pm	7pm

Day trips Excursions to North and Middle Caicos are run by several of the tour operators on Providenciales, notably:

Big Blue (see page 113)
Catch the Wave (see page 113)
J&B Tours (see page 114)

BY AIR Regular flights ply daily between Providenciales and both North and Middle Caicos, operated by Air Turks and Caicos (see below). Between Provo and North Caicos the flight time is between ten and 15 minutes, and to Middle Caicos is 20 minutes. Note that flights between North and Middle Caicos are operated on request only, with a minimum of four passengers required. The cost of tickets is as follows:

	Single	Return
Providenciales to North Caicos	$40	$75
Providenciales to Middle Caicos	$50	$95
North Caicos to Middle Caicos	$40	$75

Charter flights can also be organised with one of the scheduled airlines, or through Global Airways.

Local airline offices
Air Turks & Caicos North Caicos *946 7036;* Middle Caicos *946 6199*

Global Airways North Caicos *947 7093*

For those arriving by sea, first impressions of North Caicos are dominated by the brand new marina with its fledgling palm trees lining the stark new concrete docks. By air, however, a truer picture emerges, of a thickly vegetated landscape interspersed with numerous ponds and considerable areas of swamp land. The island's greatest appeal has until recently been its relative isolation from the ravages of development, with a long stretch of unspoilt sandy beach to the north, and the ruins of a 19th-century cotton plantation to add a spot of culture.

Significant changes are in hand, at least on the western point of the island, where the new North Caicos Yacht Club and Marina is the focus for over a hundred residential and commercial buildings, with beach or canal frontage, while to the east a new causeway means that Middle Caicos is now accessible overland rather than just by sea or air.

The island's population stands at just over 1,500, supporting two primary schools and a single high school.

HISTORY The earliest known inhabitants of North Caicos were the Lucayans. As long ago as the final decade of the 19th century a Taino stone chisel was found in the caves at Sandy Point in the west of the island. While the Lucayans are understood not to have been cave dwellers as such but to have used the underground chambers as sanctuaries for ritual purposes, they may also have taken advantage of the shelter offered by the caves from hurricanes and violent storms. It was their belief that their own ancestors alone had originated from a sacred cave of great spiritual importance whereas all other Indians derived from a cave of no significance. Blue holes were similarly respected and the Lucayans would have greatly valued nearby Cottage Pond, an inland example, 165ft (50m) in diameter with a 30ft (9m) layer of fresh water floating above its saline base.

After the arrival of the first Europeans in the archipelago and the subsequent annihilation of the Tainos, the Caicos Islands remained largely uninhabited until the coming of the Loyalists who, having declined to swear allegiance to a newly independent America, were rewarded with land grants in the recently declared British territory. A number of them received tracts of land in North Caicos. Whitby formed part of the Moore Hall Estate where Joseph Moore established a cotton plantation in 1790. Scanty remains of the great house can still be seen, as can the ruined house of the St James Plantation at Sandy Point. One can't help wondering how the owners rubbed along together; whether one or other of them was in fact the cruel master reputed to have ordered miscreant slaves to be tossed brutally into a watery grave at Cottage Pond. If true, a shameful tale.

Outside the settlement of Kew stand the ruins of one of the more successful cotton plantations of that era. Wade's Green Plantation, established in 1789–80 by Florida Loyalist, Wade Stubbs, is now under the care of the Turks and Caicos National Trust. In its heyday the property covered 3,000 acres (1,214ha). Today all that can be seen are the ruins of the manor house, as well as those of a few of its outbuildings and surrounding walls.

Despite the problems with infestation and hurricane damage that wiped out the plantations within a few decades, it is rather surprising that the immigrants were not able somehow to subsist. North Caicos, with a higher level of rainfall than its neighbours, has always been described as the lushest of the islands and by careful farming, the descendants of those plantation slaves (freed for ever in 1834) were able to cultivate, albeit on a smaller scale, yam, cassava, sweet potato, pumpkin and sugarcane, as well as fruit trees such as tamarind, papaya, pineapple and mango. Indeed in the 20th century North Caicos became known as the proverbial

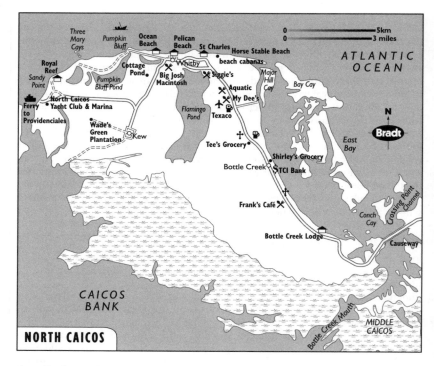

NORTH CAICOS

'breadbasket' of the islands. It has to be said that this productivity was not maintained either on the thin soil and these days the island produces, other than fruit and vegetables grown for private consumption, only a small quantity of tomatoes and cucumbers.

In September 1960 the main force of Hurricane Donna was directed against the Caicos Islands and it was estimated that almost half the residents were left homeless. Tidal waves submerged large sections of land, the coastline at Bottle Creek became entirely reshaped and the settlement of Whitby was cut off by a new channel of seawater.

The island's original hotel was The Prospect of Whitby. Opened in 1974 it took its name from the famous Thames-side pub in London. It closed a couple of years ago. It may surprise some to learn that the first condominium to be opened on North Caicos predated any on Providenciales. In 1982 a ten-unit complex, Ocean Beach Condos, opened at Whitby. Strangely this corner of the island was the last to receive its own electricity and for a time in the early days of the Ocean Beach a cable had to be run from the Prospect of Whitby's private generator. At that time there was only an infrequent government barge connection with Providenciales and Turks Air flew in once a week. The road was 'atrocious' and it took one hour to travel the few miles between Whitby and the airport.

GETTING AROUND Many visitors to North Caicos come as part of an organised trip with one of the tour operators such as Big Blue, J&B or Catch the Wave (see pages 113–14).

Nevertheless, it is possible to hire a **car** through Al's Rent a Car (*Major Hill;* \f *946 7232;* m *241 1355*). Roads across the island have recently been upgraded, with a whole new infrastructure emerging around the marina area, and access across a new tarred causeway to Middle Caicos. There are a couple of fuel stations on the island, one in Bottle Creek, and the second, Texaco (⊕ *6am–10pm Mon–Sat, 8am–5pm Sun*), a little further north. Petrol prices in summer 2008 were $5.50 a gallon ($1.45 a litre).

For a more leisurely way of getting around, guests at several of the hotels, condos and villas have free use of **bicycles**.

Taxis

🚗 **Charlie's Taxi** 🕽 946 7167; m 231 6966
🚗 **M&Ms** m 231 6285
🚗 **Pelican Car Rental** m 241 8275

🚗 **Tiger Taxi** m 231 4859
🚗 **Safe Car Rental** 🕽 946 7770

➤ **WHERE TO STAY** Until as recently as 2006, accommodation on North Caicos was broadly limited to a couple of well-established options, Pelican Beach Hotel and Bottle Creek Lodge, and a handful of small, self-catering villas and apartments. Suddenly, though, North Caicos is the developers' buzzword. Significant investment is being showered onto the island, with heavy construction particularly in the west as part of the new marina complex. In addition to the following, a further two developments are planned along Horse Stable Beach, and the Fairmont Three Cays near Three Marys Cays is targeting an opening date of 2009.

⌂ **Blue Rondo** (2 rooms) no tel; e tciguy@ comcast.net. Self-catering place on the beach with 2 dbl rooms, 2 baths, kitchen, family room, laundry room, 45ft (14m) patio with sea view; TV & internet connection. No children. *$1,800-2,400 pw (Sat–Sat).* $$$$

⌂ **Bottle Creek Lodge** (3 villas) Bottle Creek, Belmont; 🕽 946 7080; US 🕽 1 703 297 8224; e bottlecreekldg@aol.com; www.bottlecreeklodge.com. A family-run lodge that emphasises fishing & kayaking. Two 1- and 2-bedroom villas with kitchenettes, baths & sitting areas; AC costs $10/day. Complimentary kayaks, bikes, windsurfers & snorkel equipment. Free internet access & phone calls to Canada & the US. *Dbl £155–215; quad $180–240; children under 12 sleep free in parents' room.* $$$

⌂ **Creek Mouth Guest House** (2 rooms) Horse Stable Beach; 🕽 946 7141; e gardinersauto@tciway.tc. Four acres of palms and gardens & no neighbours; bliss! The house has 2 dbl rooms, 1 bath & a kitchen, taking 4 people max. There's also AC, fans, a TV, & a washing machine. Complimentary airport pickup. Maid service available. Visa & MCd. *$160/day inc tax & use of a jeep .* $$$

⌂ **Datai Villa** (2 suites) 🕽 946 7755; www.datai-villa.com. On the beach, & sleeping up to 8 people, with maid service available. 2 kayaks & 2 bikes free. *$3,200–3,600/wk; $2,300 for 2 people low season.* $$$$

⌂ **Hollywood Beach Suites** (4 suites) Whitby; 🕽 973 6659; US toll free 🕽 1 800 551 2256;

e vacations@hollywoodbeachsuites.com; www.hollywoodbeachsuites.com. Beachfront suites on a 7-mile (11km) stretch of sand lined with casuarina trees. Suites have 1 bedroom, bathroom, kitchen with fridge, washer/dryer, AC, fan, internet port, DVD but no TV; cellphones but no landline. Complimentary watersports, bikes, internet access. Grocery shop ½ mile (800m) away. *Dbl $253.* $$$

⌂ **Jamilton's Nest** (2 apts) m 331 7056; e donna@hibiscuspropertymanagement.com. On a small hill 2 mins from beach each of these apartments has AC, fans, TV, washer & dryer, with maid service available. *2-bedroom apt $1,800/wk, 1-bedroom $1,200/wk, both apts $2,500/wk, all plus 15% service.* $$$

⌂ **La Casita** (1 apt) Whitby Heaven Beach, m 243 7032; e info@northcaicoslacasita.com; www.northcaicoslacasita.com. 2 dbl rooms, 1 bath, kitchen, living room, terrace, TV, DVD, 2 bikes. Grocery & babysitting services available. *$1,400–1,600/wk. AC extra.* $$$

⌂ **La Villa Rose** (1 villa) no tel; e nicky7141@ yahoo.com. On a 7-mile (11km) beach for 6 people max. As well as 3 dbl rooms, 2 with sea view, there are 2 baths, AC, fans, DVD, CD, internet connection & 2 kayaks. *2 people $2,000–2,200; 4 people $2,400–2,600; 6 people $2,700–3,000. 10% discount for 2wks, 15% for 3wks.* $$$

⌂ **Ocean Beach Hotel & Restaurant** (10 suites) Whitby; 🕽 946 7113; US toll free 🕽 1 800 710 5204; e oceanbeachhotel@aol.com. Each of the

1- or 2-bedroom suites has a kitchen, living room & ocean view; AC costs $25/day. Freshwater pool. Bikes $12/day. Meal plan (b/fast & dinner) $50/day. Silver Palm Restaurant & Bar. Nightclub. 14th night & children under 12 in parents' room free. MCd & Visa. $$

🏠 **Ocean Front Villas** (2 rooms, 2 suites) ✆ 946 6101; e oceanfrontvilla@yahoo.com; www.oceanvilla.net. Set back a short walk from the beach. Dbl $150/day, suite $250/day, whole villa $2,500/wk. $$

🏠 **Pax Villa** (1 villa) Whitby; US ✆ 215 297 1073; e paxvilla@comcast.net. 150yds (140m) from beach with 2 rooms, kitchen, metered AC, fans, DVD, TV, VCR & the usual appliances, Pax Villa sleeps up to 6. Free rafts & bikes. $180 pp, min 2 nights. $$$

🏠 **Pelican Beach Hotel** (16 rooms) Whitby; ✆ 946 7112; e pelicanbeach@tciway.tc; www.pelicanbeach.tc. This family-owned & run beachside hotel was built by Susan & Clifford Gardiner in the early 1980s. It's an ideal spot for those seeking to escape, but not if you're looking for non-stop entertainment. Good-sized en-suite rooms are built in a neat row, sheltered by trees but facing the beach. Susan herself does all the cooking, making this a very homely place to stay, with an excellent b/fast, & dinner cooked to order. Lunch or a picnic can be prepared on request from $5 pp. On the activities front, the beach in front of the hotel is ideal for swimming, bikes are available free to guests, and snorkelling or fishing trips can be arranged. Dbl $265 DBB. $$$

🏠 **Royal Reef Resort** (45 suites, 160 condos) Sandy Point; ✆ 941 8120; US toll free ✆ 1 800 728 REEF; e info@royalreefresort.com; www.royalreefresort.com. This vast new resort on an 18-acre site is scheduled to open in 2008. When complete, the project will combine a hotel with 6 condominium blocks & is aiming at the top of the market. Facilities anticipated include 3 restaurants, a bar, 4 pools, a spa & fitness centre, tennis courts & shops. $$$$$.

🏠 **St Charles** (90 condos) Horse Stable Beach; ✆ 946 7042; UK ✆ 0208 812 4734; e info@stcharlesnc.com; www.stcharlesnc.com. In an 8½-acre garden beside an isolated beach on the secluded north shore, this development first opened in 2006, albeit with only a proportion of its 90 condos. The 1- to 3-bedroom furnished units, with their terracotta tiles, marble work surfaces & Bose sound systems, form a horseshoe around the large pool, with a swim-up bar & outdoor restaurant. There's also a dive shop, fitness centre & tennis courts. $$$$$

🏠 **Whitby Beach Villa** (1 villa) no tel; e emeraldshorestci@aol.com. Each of the 3 rooms is en suite with a sea view, fan & room safe; there's also a kitchen & living room. $2,500–3,000/wk + 10% tax. $$$

✖ WHERE TO EAT AND DRINK

✖ **Big Josh McIntosh** Blueberry Hill, Whitby; ✆ 946 7022. The order of the day here is chicken & beer. $

✖ **Frank's Café** Richmond Hill, Bottle Creek; m 243 5256, 249 9124; ⏱ 9am–10.30pm Mon–Thu, 9am–midnight Fri–Sat, closed Sun. American & Italian dishes, as well as native seafood. All major credit cards. $$

✖ **My Dee's Restaurant** ✆ 946 7059; m 231 4005. Another restaurant with a menu focusing on local, American & Italian dishes. $$

✖ **Papa Grunt's Seafood Restaurant** Whitby Plaza; ✆ 946 7301; ⏱ daily. The name says it all. $$

✖ **Royal Reef Resort** (see above) $$$$

✖ **St Charles** (see above) $$$$

✖ **Silver Palm** Ocean Beach Hotel (see above). 2-course menu $31, 3-course $38, plus tax & service. $$$

🍺 **Siggie's Café** m 244 7788, 243 7031; ⏱ daily. Local dishes. $

🍺 **Titters Club** Airport; ✆ 946 7316. Local dishes served for b/fast, lunch & dinner. $

SHOPPING For the most part, shops on North Caicos are general stores, catering for the basics, but with no frills.

KJ Foods Whitby; m 231 1117. All the basics, from burger buns to fruit juice & frozen meat, as well as torches & batteries — useful for those visiting the caves on Middle Caicos.

My Dee's Airport Rd; m 241 8121. A complex of small shops near the airport that includes a general store and a separate sports shop. ⏱ 9am–4.30pm Mon–Sat, specialising in fishing & camping gear. Also on sale are fins, masks & snorkels, and tennis balls.

Robinson's Variety Store Kew; m 232 0085

Shirley's Grocery Bottle Creek; ✆ 946 7708

Tee's Grocery's ✆ 946 7338

OTHER PRACTICALITIES

Banks A small branch of the TCI Bank is located in Bottle Creek, just to the west of the government buildings.

Communications

Telephone, fax and internet Top-up cards for both Digicel and Cable & Wireless are easy to come by in most of the small shops on North Caicos.

Post office There are post offices in both Kew (which also has a communications centre) and Bottle Creek.

Medical facilities North Caicos has two health clinics, one at Kew (✆ 946 7397), and a second at Bottle Creek (✆ 946 7194). There is also a dental clinic (✆ 946 7319). For all other health needs, including anything but the most basic of medication, you will need to go to Providenciales.

Religious services There are several churches in Bottle Creek, including a Baptist ministry and the Lighthouse Church.

ACTIVITIES

Snorkelling The best snorkelling on North Caicos is without doubt around Three Mary Cays, a protected area west of Whitby where you could find yourself competing for fish with just a pair of nesting ospreys.

It's a glorious, natural spot, with an easy and in part very shallow swim out to the first of the rocks. Coral heads in the shallows afford protection for the spiny lobster, and reef fish dart between sea fans as they move gently in the current. There's the occasional barracuda here, too, but more important is to be aware that speedboats thread their way between the cays, usually first thing in the morning on their way out to the fishing grounds.

Fishing Would-be fishermen have plenty of choice of fishing grounds across the island, with grouper and snapper the main catch. Both tackle and bait are available from My Dee's (see opposite), where you can organise for Mr Henfield to take you fishing.

Alternatively, both snorkelling and fishing can be organised with Bottle Creek Lodge Charters (see Bottle Creek Lodge, page 129), who have a 19ft (5.8m) flat boat, and a 30ft (9m) fishing boat.

Kayaking and mountain biking Big Blue Unlimited (see page 113) has a base at Major Hill, near the airport alongside Bottle Creek, where both kayaks and mountain bikes can be hired, and from where they run their eco-tours. Both single and double kayaks are available, costing $45/60 for a half or full day single, or $60/80 double. Bikes can be rented by the day ($60) or by the week ($300). Delivery of both bikes and kayaks can be arranged for $40.

The mangroves around Bottle Creek make a good spot for kayaking. A full-day trip, which can be arranged with Big Blue ($235 pp), combines exploration of this area with a local lunch at Kew, and a tour by car of the local sights: Wade's Green Plantation, Flamingo Pond and Cottage Pond.

Hiking trails Although Middle Caicos takes most of the accolades for hiking, there are a couple of designated walking trails – or 'field-roads' – on North Caicos, too. One passes through Wade's Green Plantation (see below), while a second, the Silver Buttonwood Field-road, takes in stands of the island's tropical dry forest and the silver buttonwood forests inside the Ramsar reserve. For details and to organise a guide, contact the National Trust (see page 102).

A TOUR OF THE ISLAND Most visitors nowadays arrive by ferry, so a tour of the island starts at the marina in the west. It takes no time at all to leave behind the new development, heading east towards the 'real' North Caicos. To the west and north, extensive beaches of white sand sparkle where shiny conch shells catch the sunlight. While Sandy Point and Horse Stable Beach have their following, and there are beach cabanas at the community centre near St Charles resort, this is a place to find 'your' beach rather than to follow the herd.

Inland, it's the island's ponds that vie for attention with its historical past: the choice is that of natural world or ruined plantations. **Flamingo Pond, Pumpkin Bluff Pond** and the 250ft (76m) sinkhole at **Cottage Pond** are all designated nature reserves, and merit a detour – although as with the beaches, there is no shortage of competition, and you could find yourself birdwatching along many a lonely creek or pond of your choice.

Wade's Green Plantation (✆ *941 5710*; m *231 2277*; ⊕ *8:30am–4:30pm daily; admission $10 inc field-road guide from National Trust office in Provo – see page 102*) Originally called Bellefield by founder Wade Stubbs, Wade's Green lies near the village of Kew, and once covered an area of 3,000 acres. Today, the former plantation buildings lie in ruins. Guided tours can be arranged through the National Trust, which now looks after the buildings. Alternatively, follow the Wade's Green Plantation Field-Road from the car park. This is actually two separate but connected paths extending over 1,000yds (1km) and 800yds (800m) respectively, but with one steep descent and ascent to a well. You may see pygmy and rainbow boas, both snakes perfectly harmless to humans, as well as swallowtail butterflies and a variety of birds.

This short trail along even ground is a round trip of less than a mile (1km), and takes in the main buildings.

MIDDLE CAICOS

If ever an island deserved the Turks and Caicos slogan 'beautiful by nature', it is Middle Caicos. Defined by an impressive cave system, it is also blessed with numerous freshwater ponds, mangrove-fringed coastal waters and, at Mudjin Harbour, possibly the most perfect of beaches.

Today, where once children would wade across the shallows to attend school, a new paved causeway links the island with North Caicos. Yet so far traffic remains conspicuous by its absence; it is perfectly possible to drive to the eastern end of the island and meet no other vehicle – or indeed pedestrian – at all.

HISTORY The largest cave system in the Bahamian and Turks and Caicos chain is to be found on the north shore of Middle Caicos, sometimes known as Grand Caicos. Besides Lucayan artefacts so far uncovered from within these most sacred places, more pre-Columbian above-ground sites have been identified on this 48-square-mile (124km²) island than anywhere else in the Turks and Caicos. For students of the fascinating culture of these sophisticated native Indians it is an assembly of the greatest interest and research continues.

In the Caicos Islands the earliest archaeological finds within caves were made accidentally during a 19th-century commercial excavation for bat guano to be used as fertiliser. This was followed in 1912 by Theodoor de Booy working on behalf of various American institutions. Many artefacts were discovered in the caves,

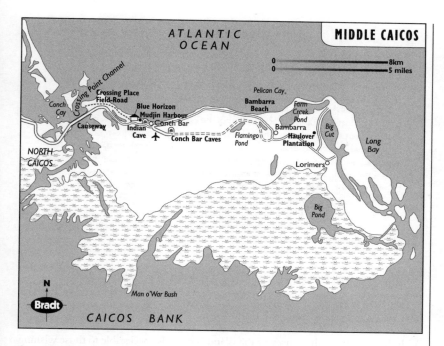

ATLANTIC OCEAN

MIDDLE CAICOS

Crossing Point Channel

Crossing Place
Field-Road

Conch
Cay

Pelican Cay

Bambarra
Beach

Farm
Creek
Pond

Blue Horizon
Mudjin Harbour
Conch Bar

Causeway

Indian
Cave

Conch Bar Caves

Bambarra

Haulover
Plantation

Big
Cut

NORTH
CAICOS

Flamingo
Pond

Lorimers

Long
Bay

Big
Pond

N

Bradt

Man o'War Bush

CAICOS BANK

including pottery, wooden objects and impressive *duhos* (ceremonial seats), of which there's an example in the Turks and Caicos National Museum on Grand Turk (see pages 172–3).

Researching above ground 75 years later, Dr Shaun Sullivan discovered no less than 35 Lucayan sites on Middle Caicos alone. In 1978, close to Armstrong Pond, Sullivan excavated a settlement of houses laid out around an apparent plaza with a much larger building at the eastern extremity. At first this arrangement was believed to represent a Lucayan ball court but when the archaeologist completed a topographical diagram of the site he realised that the perimeter walls were not parallel and he further deduced that the lines of sight crossing the court referred to the rising and setting of the stars at the time of the summer solstice, which would have provided vital information for the native American agricultural calendar.

As was the case in North Caicos, a number of Loyalists at the time of American independence were granted land rights on Middle Caicos. Among them was John Lorimer, who established Haulover Estate and has earned the historical reputation, true or untrue, of having treated his slaves more fairly than did some of his fellow proprietors. A few ruins can still be seen on the property, with evidence of chimneys and a well with steps descending into it.

'Bambarra' is an unfamiliar word to Turcasians. The area on Middle Caicos bearing that name is now believed to have been settled by slaves being transported on the brigantine *Trouvadore* which was wrecked on Philips Reef off the coast of East Caicos in 1842. It is said the slaves had been taken from the Bambarra tribe on the Niger River. The Middle Caicos settlement was to develop a fine reputation for shipbuilding.

GETTING AROUND As on North Caicos, most visitors to Middle Caicos come as part of an organised tour. If you'd like to hire a car or a taxi, try one of the following:

During Christopher Columbus's second voyage to the New World, from 1493 to 1496, he commissioned Friar Ramón Pané to record such information as he could deduce from close observation of the Tainos. Most of what is known today derives from that study. It seemed the native Indians believed that all beings originated from two caves.(Pané in fact understood these two to be in Haiti, where his research was chiefly conducted, but the exact location of the caverns is perhaps less certain). The Tainos apparently felt assured that while they themselves came from one particular sacred cave, everyone else came from another of little significance. Indeed there appeared to have been a theory of duality threading throughout their beliefs, frequently divided along male and female lines. The male god Yocahu was seen to be the 'giver of manioc' – a root from which vital flour could be processed – while the female god Attabeira was associated with water and fertility. This sense of duality they saw expressed in the good and bad qualities of natural forces. For example the right amount of rain was a gift but too much of it, brought by a storm, could result in flooding. Twins were popular symbols in Taino design.

🚗 **Cardinal Arthur** Conch Bar ➘ 946 6107; m 241 0730
🚗 **Ernest Forbes Sr** Bambarra ➘ 946 6140. Mr Forbes will also do sightseeing tours & cave tours.

🚗 **Headley Forbes** Bambarra ➘ 946 6109
🚗 **Hormel Harvey's Taxis** Conch Bar; ➘ 946 6101. Air-conditioned van.

With the opening of the causeway the island is now also accessible to those wishing to hire a car or even a taxi in North Caicos. There's a fuel station at Conch Bar.

For a more leisurely appreciation of the island, travelling by bike could be the answer, with hire bikes available from the Sports Shack in Conch Bar (➘ *946 6174*) or Big Blue in North Caicos (see page 113). Alternatively, take a day and explore one of the field-roads on foot.

🏠 WHERE TO STAY

🏠 **Blue Horizon** (2 villas & 5 cottages) Mudjin Harbour ➘ 946 6141; e bhresort@tciway.tc; http://bhresort.com. Set in 50 utterly beautiful and isolated acres (20ha) of tranquil beaches & rolling hillside, with a mini-isthmus leading across to the tiny Dragon Cay, the resort (a most misleading title) has 2 villas, 3 studio cottages & 2 2-bedroom cottages, all with rather necessary kitchens. Safe, sandy swimming & a large cave to explore on the 2,200ft (700m) beach. The newish manager is Ernest Forbes, also pastor of the Lighthouse Church in Conch Bar. You will definitely be making your own entertainment here, but if you send them a grocery list 2wks in advance it will be sourced in Provo & delivered to your door + 15% handling charge. The only accessible eating place is the rudimentary Shanique's Café at the airport, but some local cooks will prepare food to take away, or sometimes to eat at their house. Bikes & kayaks can be rented in the village, I car is available for rental at the resort. Maid service available. No Amex; other ccs +5%. Min stay 3 days. *Dbl studio $225/day or $1,400/wk, villa $325/day or $2,100/wk for up to 5 people.* $$$
🏠 **Dreamscape Villa** (1 villa) Bambarra Beach; owners' ➘ (Vermont) 1 802 295 2652; e mmilne2652@aol.com; www.middlecaicos.com/pages/actvit.html. Just yards from the beach, this private villa with a large veranda has 3 bedrooms (2 with ocean view), 2 bathrooms, living room with ceiling fans, fully equipped kitchen, outside shower, satellite TV & AC. There's snorkelling from the beach, & 2 17ft (5m) kayaks for rent. *$2,000/wk for 4 or less, then $300/day; extra people $300/wk.* $$$
Eagle's Rest Villas (2 villas) ➘ 775 7200; US toll free ➘ 1 800 645 1179; e eaglemindspring.com; www.caicosproperties.tc These duplex villas with kitchens are beside a very isolated beach & set in tropical gardens. It's a good spot for fishing or snorkelling but you are very cut off. *4 people $875–1,200/wk in winter, $650–850 in summer, extra people $150 pp/wk. Cook or maid $35/day.* $$

Oceanfront Villa (1 villa) Conch Bar ☎ 946 6101 (also Hormel Harvey's Taxis); e oceanfrontvilla@yahoo.com. Beside the beach, with quite local décor. Whole villa $4,500/wk, 1 suite $2,500/wk, 1 room $1,200/wk. $$$$

Sundial Villa (1 villa) Bambarra; owners' ☎ (in Canada) 1 604 576 9369; e caicos@sundialvillas.com. 2 bedrooms, bathroom, family room, kitchen, 2 covered verandas; CD, DVD & usual appliances. $945–1,050pw, or $135–150/day. $$

✗ WHERE TO EAT AND DRINK

✗ **Daniel's Café** Conch Bar; ☎ 946 6132, 941 7034; ⏰ 11am–7pm Tue/Wed, 11am–3pm & 7–9pm Fri, 7am–7pm Sat. Housed in the same premises as the Middle Caicos Co-op, Daniel's is *the* place to go for local specials – as well as the usual b/fast & lunch standards. Tue is conch day, or come on Fri for fried chicken, fresh biscuits (like scones to British readers!) & salads. Then on Sat, there's the full works: boiled fish

& grits, souse & Johnny cake, & fried bonefish. Reservations strongly recommended. $–$$
✗ **Passion Sweets** Bambarra; m 241 5536
✗ **Sapodilley's Café** (also known as Shanique's Café) at the airport; ☎ 946 6128; m 232 3727; ⏰ around flight time. Serves drinks & a very limited menu. Meals must be ordered in advance. $

SHOPPING AND OTHER PRACTICALITIES

Annie Taylor's Grocery ☎ 946 6117. Basic foods & some fresh produce
Arthur's Variety ☎ 946 6122. Canned & household goods
Dotti's Shop Groceries & toiletries
Middle Caicos Co-op Conch Bar; ☎ 946 6132, 941 7034; e middlecaicos@tciway.tc; ⏰ Tue, Wed, Fri, Sat. All manner of handcrafted goods are on sale at the Co-op, which also stocks basic groceries, supplies & souvenirs, & phonecards. It's really as much of a

community centre as a shop, with an on-site restaurant (Daniel's – see above), & craft demonstrations (every Wed 1–3pm): a must to see just how those solid straw baskets are woven. Regular boat trips (every Mon), & outings to Bambarra Beach (every Thu) are a further incentive to make contact. And stop here, too, for general information & to use the internet or a public phone. See also page 102 for the Provo branch.

Medical facilities The island has its own medical clinic (☎ 946 6145), based at Conch Bar, next to the district commissioner's office. Nurse Sheila Bobb is in attendance here, but anything more serious is referred to one of the clinics on Providenciales. In an **emergency**, here as elsewhere on the islands, dial 911.

Police
Constable Harvey ☎ 946 6111

Religious services The following all have Sunday services and are delighted to welcome visitors:

Bethlehem Baptist Church Bambarra
Mt Hermon Baptist Church Lorimers
Mt Moriah Baptist Church Conch Bar

God of Prophecy Church Conch Bar
Lighthouse Mission Church Conch Bar

FESTIVALS Every April the **Model Sailboat Regatta** is held at Conch Bar with boats locally handcrafted from branches of the gum-elemi tree. Boats are sailed in shallow water with owners running alongside to adjust the tiller and trim the sails. You can order your boat with a four-week delivery from Middle Caicos Co-op (☎ 946 6132, e middlecaicos@tciway.tc).

ACTIVITIES For those seeking a taste of the island's activities, tours are organised by both Big Blue on Provo (see page 113) and the Middle Caicos Co-op (☎ 941 7034; e middlecaicos@tciway.tc). Every Thursday, the Co-op runs a beach party at Bambarra Beach, with opportunities for kayaking, sailing, volleyball and –

somewhat unexpectedly – dominoes. Other excursions include trips to East Caicos, picnics at Mudjin Harbour, tours of Haulover Plantation or the Conch Bar Caves, and a guided walk.

Hiking trails Middle Caicos is dissected by a series of walking trails, or 'field-roads' as they are designated by the National Trust (traditionally a trail cut through the vegetation to reach crops, a well, or some important site). Numbered waymarks along each trail link into leaflets published by the National Trust, giving details of the surrounding vegetation and historical notes. These are available in advance from the Trust's offices in Providenciales (see page 102), where you can also obtain cards depicting land animals, birds and butterflies and moths, and organise local guides.

The most significant of the trails, the **Crossing Place Field-road** runs the whole length of the island, starting in the east at Lorimers. It takes in Bambarra Beach, the Indian Cave, Conch Bar, the 'blowing hole', Mudjin Harbour and Norbelis Cove, ending to the west at the point where local people have long crossed the sandbar on foot at low tide. It's a trail steeped in history, for it follows the old slave route across the island; their owners rode in carriages along the main King's Road. If you're driving across the causeway, there's an entrance to the trail at station 25, shortly after you've arrived on the island, on the left-hand side. Most people don't have time to attempt more than a small part of the trail, in which case one option is to cover the section between Conch Bar and Indian Cave, a distance of about a mile (1.6km), either returning along the road, or retracing your steps.

Cacti rising to 6ft (2m) or more and low palms dominate the shrubby vegetation but the land is relatively flat, with just the occasional low hill. Underfoot is karst limestone, unkind to the feet, so good shoes are strongly recommended; you'll also need a hat, insect repellent and plenty of water. Walking – or cycling – affords a great opportunity to spot some of the Caicos Islands' flora and fauna, from scuttling curly tails underfoot to sweet-smelling orchids, the great Erebus moth, and the noisy Cuban crow.

Garden Pond Field-road is only a mile (1.5km) there and back, but it leads through dense brush where it is extremely easy to get lost. A local guide is very strongly advised. The start of the walk is on the north side of Lorimers at Bambarra Road.

Other trails focus on Haulover Plantation (see below), Lorimers, Big Pond and Bambarra Village.

Cycling The dedicated 12-mile (19km) **Middle Caicos Cycle Trail** is regularly used for mountain biking. It runs from Conch Bar to Bambarra, through pine forests and along the north coast, linking the coastal Crossing Place Trail with the old King's Road further south. Trips are run every Saturday from Provo by Big Blue (*$275 pp*; see page 136), who supply participants with American-built Mongoose bikes, with 21-speed Shimano gears. Departure is by ferry from the Leeward Marina, with transfers to the start of the trail made by taxi. From here, it's a three-hour ride, with time along the way to visit the Conch Bar Caves and the beach at Mudjin Harbour, as well as for lunch at Bambarra Beach. The trip can also be organised by those staying on North or Middle Caicos.

Snorkelling Pelican Cay off Bambarra Beach makes a good spot for snorkelling (and offers an enjoyable walk, too; you can wade across at low tide). Other options include the coral gardens off the same beach, and Samuel's Landing near Conch Bar. For trips further afield, you'll need to go with one of the fishing operators below.

Fishing Bone-fishing in the shallows or deep-sea fishing out beyond the reef are a major attraction for visitors to Middle Caicos. Trips can be organised with various guides, including Dolphus Arthur (✆ *946 6122*), Cardinal Arthur (✆ *946 6107*), Brodie Forbes (✆ *946 6144*) and Hormel Harvey (✆ *946 6101*). The best option is to ask around locally.

A TOUR OF THE ISLAND
The new tarred causeway leading across from North Caicos soon gives way to gravel as it wends it way southeast across the island, parallel to the northern coastline.

Mudjin Harbour Imagine the clearest of clear turquoise waters and the finest of deep soft sand. Add a stretch of rock to create a natural harbour – and a low, natural waterfall – and create a huge cave behind for shade. With only an osprey overhead for company, Mudjin Harbour is the kind of place that deserves to be a jealously guarded secret. While it is visited by various tour groups, you might still have the place to yourselves, especially mid week.

Access is from the Blue Horizon Resort (see page 134). The signpost isn't terribly clear, but it's in a small parking layby near the top. From here, just follow the path down the cliff to the beach.

Haulover Estate (*National Trust, see page 102*) Covering 504 acres (204ha), Haulover was originally established by John Lorimer on 23 February 1791. Lorimer was a Loyalist plantation owner who left the USA because he opposed independence and wanted to remain British. He enjoys a largely undeserved reputation for taking a liberal approach to his slaves and freeing them on his death. He probably did treat his slaves a bit better than most of his peers but all things are relative and the only one he actually freed appears to have been 'my negro woman, Rose'. On Lorimer's death the estate was bought by Wade Stubbs, whose name lives on in the Wade's Green plantation on North Caicos; Lorimer had to be content with Lorimer's Creek.

A narrow **field-road** leads west from the road running between Lorimers and Half Creek to the ruins of the plantations. At the start of the trail, a wooden viewing platform makes a good spot for birdwatching, with a second closer to the plantation itself. Watch out for the tiny blue-gray gnatcatcher and the thick-billed vireo, with its yellow chest; both can be seen here. And keep well clear of the poisonwood tree at number 4a.

The trail is just a few hundred yards long, and heads straight towards the ruins of the plantation buildings, set on a low hill. An interpretive leaflet is available from the National Trust, linked to numbers along the trail. To get the most out of the walk, allow at least an hour.

Indian Cave Really a cave in name only, this is more of a high arch set into a hill, with an opening at the top. Trees form a natural arch of their own as you approach the cave. It's an interesting place to explore, though do be careful; the rocks are uneven and it would be easy to fall.

In 1998, archaeologists uncovered evidence of the Lucayan Indians here, with fragments of pottery and the bones of birds, lizards and tortoises. Today, the cave supports a range of flora, from the short-leaved fig, *Ficus citrifolia* and the pitch apple, *Clusia rosea*, to various vines that twine up and around the rocks. Bats come here to feed, and barn owls, *Tyto alba*, to roost, while at ground level crabs provide sustenance for the yellow-crowned night heron, *Nyctanassa violaea*.

Conch Bar Caves (*National Trust, see page 102; admission $10 pp in advance from NT shops*) The road to Conch Bar Caves National Park is a turning off the main road by the airport. The surface is poor and overgrown with tall grasses, but it is at least flat initially, making the caves accessible in a two-wheel drive vehicle. Beyond the caves, however, the road deteriorates significantly, and is firmly off limits for those without a 4x4.

Visitors must have a guide to visit the caves, organised either through an excursion company (or direct with the National Trust. Local guides are Ernest Forbes Sr (✆ 946 6140) and Cardinal Arthur (✆ 946 6107). A torch is essential; you can buy one locally, including at KJ's on North Caicos. And please do not touch any formations within the caves. Not only do they break easily, but oils from your skin can bond to the stone and prevent any further deposits forming.

The network of caves comprises the largest above-water cave system in the Bahamas archipelago, formed by the steady drip of acidic rainwater on the porous limestone. The main chamber is well lit by natural sunlight, spotlighting stalactites and stalagmites in a variety of shapes and sizes – and some deep fissures in the rock floor.

Of the five species of **bat** that live in or around the caves, the most easily seen by visitors is the buffy flower bat, *Erophylla sezekorni*, an omnivore that will eat both fruit and insects. More specialist, but also found throughout the cave system, is Waterhouse's big-eared bat, *Macrotus waterhousii*, whose diet of insects includes the Erebus moth, which itself roosts on the roof of the caves – albeit at its peril. Another insect eater is the much less common red bat, *Lasiurus borealis*, which while not a cave dweller (it roosts in the trees), has occasionally been spotted feeding within the caves. The largest inhabitant of the caves, the Cuban fruit bat, lives in just one chamber, which – because of the limited presence of this animal – is strictly off limits to visitors. And then there's the tiny and very shy Redman's long-tongued bat, *Monophyllus redmani*.

The water system in the caves is linked to that of Buttonwood and Village **ponds**, which fall within the national park area. The latter is clearly visible from the road near Conch Bar, and makes a great place for birdwatching. Black-necked stilts, the great and snowy egret, and little blue herons are often seen here, while less common are birds such as the Bahama pintail and the West Indian whistling duck. In the summer months, juvenile flamingoes may pause here to rest. Along the roadside, the clusters of rounded pink flowers are marsh fleabane, which attracts butterflies, moths and bees.

EAST CAICOS

Now entirely uninhabited, East Caicos was nevertheless a centre of the sisal industry for about 50 years until early in the 20th century. All that remains today is a disused railroad track, some of which has subsided into the water, and the wild donkeys, descendants of those used a century ago to pull the railway trucks.

The island as a whole is not protected against development, although a significant area falls within the North, Middle and East Caicos Nature Reserve. This incorporates a turtle-nesting beach along the north coast. It's a great place to explore if you're prepared to carry everything with you, not forgetting a good mosquito repellent.

HISTORY The Lucayans, believing themselves originally to have emerged into the sunlight from the darkness of a cave, had a high regard for owls, bats and other creatures which inhabit such places. Yet petroglyphs – prehistoric rock carvings – have so far been found in only one cave in Turks and Caicos, thought to be close to Jacksonville Harbour on East Caicos. Theodoor de Booy claimed to have discovered it during his busy and widespread excavations in 1912. At that time the

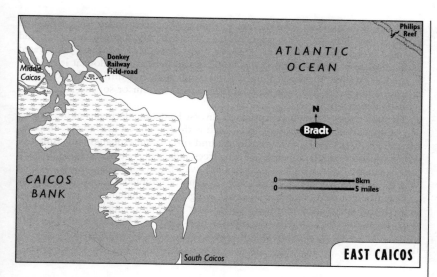

ATLANTIC OCEAN

Philips Reef

Middle Caicos

Donkey Railway Field-road

N

Bradt

CAICOS BANK

0   8km
0   5 miles

South Caicos

EAST CAICOS

East Caicos Sisal Company was still functioning, and bat guano was being widely harvested for fertiliser. Efforts since to relocate the cave have always proved unsuccessful and no other petroglyphs have ever been found in the entire Bahamian archipelago. Maybe the American was dreaming.

East Caicos is, however, thought to have contained one of the largest Taino settlements, prior to the arrival of the Europeans. It is believed that its scrubby shores served well as a hiding place for a variety of 17th-century pirates, its eastern, Turks Island Passage shores fringed by the treacherous Philips Reef that secured the fate of many a vessel. When the authorities came in search of them the pirates were adept at careening their caravel, sloop or whatever ship they had most recently purloined, and camouflaging it with branches and undergrowth.

In 1842 the *Trouvadore* slave ship was wrecked on Philips Reef but, it is reported, surprisingly the slaves and Spanish crew all made it to the shore, 'where one slave was shot dead and 15 escaped into the bush'.

It seems that East Caicos did not receive a similar post-American war influx of Loyalist settlers as did its neighbours, perhaps because of the dry nature of the island. Not until the middle of the 19th century was a significant estate constructed, and here the crop was to be sisal and the workers imported from Middle Caicos. A large cattle-rearing station was established at this time too and some of the animals' feral descendants remain today. For the last decade of that century the caves were mined for guano until it ran out. The sisal estate was wound up during the depression of the 1930s. Since then there has been no serious settlement.

GETTING THERE Visitors to the island currently have to make their own arrangements to get to the island, usually with one of the fishermen from either Middle or South Caicos.

EAST CAICOS DONKEY-RAILWAY FIELD-ROAD For the most part, visitors to East Caicos are left entirely to their own resources. There is, though, a trail which repays exploration.

The 2.5 mile (3.5km) East Caicos Donkey-Railway Field-road runs along the old railroad track, some of which has now subsided into the water. Designated an 'adventure walk' by the National Trust, it is overgrown in places, with hidden sinkholes underfoot and areas that are very slippery or even underwater. A guide is essential (see National Trust, page 102), as are a hat, insect repellent, water, and strong – preferably waterproof – shoes or boots. A copy of the Trust's illustrated leaflet, linked to numbers along the route, is also invaluable. Allow at least three hours to complete the walk; longer if you want to spend time birdwatching or taking photographs. The boat trip will take a further hour or so, and is of course weather dependent.

The trail passes through a surprisingly diverse landscape. Remains of the railway can be spotted near the jetty, an area which is thick with red mangroves. In parts, the railway was raised above marshy ground on a stone embankment, much of which was later engulfed by fast-growing trees and cacti. A diversion leads through Stubbs Guano Cave, which in the late 1900s was mined for guano, and is home to Waterhouse's big-eared bat. At number 12, don't be tempted to continue along the railway; the detour is designed to avoid a highly toxic manchineel tree. Beyond here, the mud flats are sometimes flooded after heavy rain, which could curtail the walk. Assuming they are not, the trail continues across a slippery causeway then uphill past a deep sinkhole to end at a large cave. From here, retrace your steps to the jetty.

6

South Caicos

If Middle Caicos epitomises the islands' motto 'Beautiful by Nature', South Caicos on first acquaintance seems to have drawn the short straw. The centre of the Turks and Caicos fishing industry, it has something of a wild-west feel, with a predominantly young male population and considerably more drinking dens than is decent in the small capital of Cockburn Harbour. But head away from the town and you'll begin to get more of a feel for the island's natural attractions, from the unspoilt bush that surrounds the salinas to the beauty of Bell Sound.

Slowly, the tourist potential of South Caicos is being recognised, focusing on a combination of excellent diving and the potential for exclusivity. Roads across the south of the island were tarred during 2007, street signs were put in place, and signs of construction are around every corner. It is interesting to note that the first visitors came to the island in the 1970s, with the construction of the Admiral's Arms Inn. While its prosperity was relatively short lived (the hotel is now home to Boston University's School for Field Studies), the current plans look set to tackle tourism on a far grander scale. If sensitively handled, the development could bring much-needed jobs to an island where, at present, those not involved in the fishing industry head out at the first opportunity, their places filled by an influx of unskilled workers from nearby Hispaniola. At stake is the very environment – both on land and at sea – that will attract visitors in the first place.

South Caicos, at just eight square miles (21.2km²), is the smallest of the Caicos Islands, and had an estimated population in 2006 of just 1,118 people, most of whom live in the capital. The island forms part of the South Caicos and East Caicos District, which encompasses most of the cays in the Caicos Bank, except French Cay.

HISTORY

Although South Caicos falls geographically within the Caicos Islands, it has far more in common historically with the Turks Islands, which lie just 22 miles (35km) across the Turks Island Passage to the east. With significantly lower rainfall than the other Caicos Islands, and extensive salt ponds, the island became a centre for the salt industry, rather than the cotton plantations that took hold further west.

Long before the arrival of the salt traders, though, the island was the preserve of Lucayan Indians, presumably drawn by the abundance of fish. Evidence of their small, probably temporary settlements, dating from around AD1100, has been found on both South Caicos and the surrounding cays. With the arrival of the first Europeans early in the 16th century, however, the Lucayan population was wiped out, leaving the land clear for the advent of the salt traders a century or so later.

To the casual observer, it is the relics of the island's salt industry that are immediately apparent. It isn't difficult to picture the large ships laden with salt ferrying their cargo out of the shelter of Cockburn Harbour. The central salinas, created by the original traders, dominate the south of the island; the crumbling

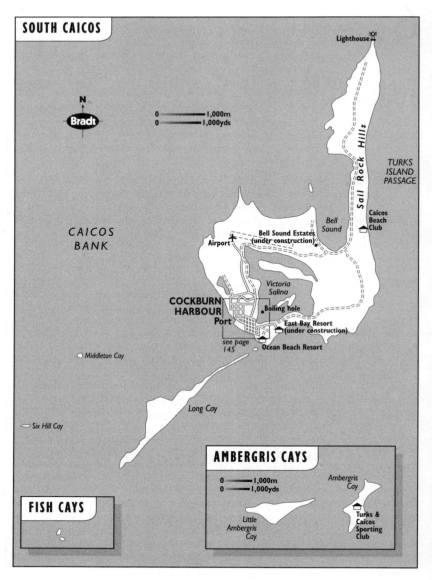

SOUTH CAICOS

Lighthouse

Sail Rock Hills

TURKS
ISLAND
PASSAGE

N

Bradt

0 ———— 1,000m
0 ———— 1,000yds

Bell
Sound

Caicos
Beach
Club

CAICOS
BANK

Bell Sound Estates
(under construction)

Airport

Victoria
Salina

COCKBURN
HARBOUR
Port

Boiling hole

East Bay Resort
(under construction)

see page
145

Ocean Beach Resort

Middleton Cay

Long Cay

Six Hill Cay

AMBERGRIS CAYS

0 ———— 1,000m
0 ———— 1,000yds

Ambergris
Cay

Turks &
Caicos
Sporting
Club

Little
Ambergris
Cay

FISH CAYS

ruins of a salt warehouse still stand near the harbour; and the old commissioner's house with its commanding view over the Caicos Bank to the south still stands on Tucker's Hill.

While industries based on both sisal and sponges enjoyed brief success in the late 19th century, it was to the sea that the population turned as the salt industry declined in the 1960s. Lobster and conch, which had always been the mainstay of the local diet, remained plentiful, and demand from overseas was beginning to pick up. Today, the island is home to the entire Turks and Caicos' fishing industry, which – despite a decline in natural resources – continues to make a significant contribution to the islands' economy.

Some three-quarters of the population of South Caicos are employed in the fishing industry, either as fishermen, or in one of the processing plants. It is tempting to assume that the young men hanging around the streets of Cockburn Town are out of a job, but the reality is usually the opposite. For the most part, fishermen on the island are self-employed, paid piecemeal for their catch at the end of each day. If they've had a good day, then the pay is good – and for some that's as good a reason as any to head for the nearest bar and spend the day's earnings. It's a hand-to-mouth existence, fostering a culture of drunkenness that may be halted only when the money runs out, and the sea beckons once more.

Both lobster and conch are still primarily fished by free divers using a mask and fins; no artificial breathing apparatus is permitted, nor the use of spearguns or harpoons. Conch are taken by hand, while lobster are drawn out of their hiding places using a pole with a hook at the end. As stocks of lobster and conch decline, so the men have to travel further offshore, and dive deeper, to bring home a catch. The most experienced divers can go down to some 40–50ft (12–15m), returning with three or even four lobsters from one dive. Even for them, it's a tough way to make a living.

From around mid afternoon, the catch is landed at the harbour, where there are two processing plants. Now it's the turn of the women, who from 3pm to 10pm work in the plants processing the lobster and conch brought in by their menfolk.

NATURAL HISTORY

The island's large central salt pond is the focus of both its history and its natural history. Industry may have turned its back on the salt pans and surrounding bush, but there are still plenty of takers – albeit 21st-century style, in the form of birds and butterflies.

Poor soil and low rainfall mean that vegetation is sparse. Drought-tolerant species such as acacia and cacti dominate the rough bush, while mangroves fringe both the salinas and the improbably blue Bell Sound, which is protected as a nature reserve in its own right. Similar in extent is the Admiral Cockburn Land and Sea National Park, which covers a total of 2,094 acres (847ha), incorporating much of the reef that runs along the eastern side of the island, and south round to Long Cay. Both offer ample rewards for birdwatchers, especially in terms of wading birds.

A conspicuous legacy of the salt years is the herds of wild horses and donkeys. When the salt traders abandoned the island, they left behind the animals that worked in their industry. While many of the horses were rounded up on Grand Turk, the South Caicos population was left to run wild, and today their descendants roam across the open flats surrounding the central pan, cropping the rough grass.

GETTING THERE

South Caicos (XSC) is a stop on the flight between Providenciales and Grand Turk operated by Sky King. Three flights a day are operated in each direction every day except Sunday, when there are just two outward journeys. The flying time from Provo is 20 minutes, and that from Grand Turk just ten. In spring 2008, a return flight to South Caicos from Provo cost $126, plus any fuel surcharge, or $73 single, with flights from Grand Turk costing $96 return, or $53 single.

The small, wooden airport building that was in use in early 2008 has all the atmosphere of a warehouse, overlaid with a faint whiff of fish and chips. Next door, however, a brand-new airport was under construction in 2008, the first indication that change is afoot on this, the least-developed island in the group.

A taxi from the airport to what is currently the island's only hotel should cost around $5.

LOCAL AIRLINE OFFICE

Sky King ☎ 941 5464, ext 700

GETTING AROUND

Options for exploring the island are surprisingly comprehensive – albeit with a very limited choice of operators. All the basic amenities – shops, restaurants, bars and the hotel – are currently in one small area of the town, and can be easily covered on foot. New developments, however, will be slightly further away, which will make some other form of transport useful, although those who have arranged diving or another activity with South Caicos Diver will be collected from their resort.

BY TAXI There is just one regular taxi driver on the island:

Lightbourne Taxis m 242 7716. Born and raised on South Caicos, Mr Lightbourne will not only provide transport, but is full of stories and information about life on the island. Island tours can be arranged on request.

Alternatively you could try either Niles Francis (m *242 3019*) or Ossie Wilson (m *242 1051, 241 1352*). There's also a Spanish-speaking service, **Latin Taxis**, an indication of the high proportion of Dominicans and Haitians working on the island.

CAR HIRE Vehicles can be hired from Sea View Marina (*Stubbs Rd;* ☎ *946 3219*), costing $100 per day.

There's a new fuel station half way to the airport from the resort, on the right by the school. Fuel can also be found at Sea View Marina, by the port (⏲ 8am–9pm). In 2008, petrol was priced at $5.70 per gallon ($1.50 a litre).

BY BICYCLE Mountain bikes are available for hire at $10 per day, including a proper bike helmet, from the restaurant (not the reception) at Ocean Beach Resort. Although they were new in 2007, they're not the most comfortable or well-constructed of models, so it would be wise to take that into account when planning a day out. That said, a circuit encompassing the salinas and taking in the edge of Bell Sound, provides a very enjoyable way to see the island at its best – and the route is almost entirely traffic free.

WHERE TO STAY

Despite a considerable level of on-going construction, during 2008 there was still only one hotel open for business on South Caicos. However, work on two further developments has been in hand for many years, with completion of one at least now imminent.

Rather less tenuous is a relatively large-scale project being undertaken by the American developers CMK (*www.bellsoundestates.com*). In addition to a series of individual properties along Bell Sound, and various 'canal' homes, they are

COCKBURN HARBOUR

working towards construction of a large new resort on the northeast coast, complete with golf course, as well as a fishing lodge, a new marina and various smaller hotels. Assuming that all goes according to plan, it looks as though South Caicos is going to be firmly on the tourist map rather sooner than many had expected.

🏠 **Caicos Beach Club** (800 condos) ☎ 946 6606; e info-request@caicosbeach.com; www.caicosbeach.com. Known locally as High Point development, this is finally set to open in November 2008. The 100-acre (40ha) site ranges from sea level to the top of the ridge, with a mile (1.6km) of sandy beach to the east. Amenities will include a couple of restaurants, a pool, a health club & spa, & a casino, while tennis, parasailing, sailing, fishing & diving will be among the activities offered.

🏠 **East Bay Resort** (200 condos) Another long-awaited development, in the south of the island, is also scheduled for completion in late 2008, although late 2009 is more realistic.

🏠 **Ocean Beach Resort** (24 rooms, 6 condominiums) m 331 1800; e info@ southcaicosoceanbeachresort.com; www.southcaicosoceanbeachresort.com. Opened in May 2007, this is at present the only viable hotel on the island. Rooms are spacious, light & airy, each with AC, 1 or 2 dbl beds, en-suite modern bathroom with shower/bath & hairdryer, & a curious mix of modern & rather ornate furniture. Screened sliding doors lead to a small balcony, some with views over the sea & the islands to the south. In the cavernous restaurant & bar, coffee & tea are free to hotel guests. A full b/fast is on offer for $12, with an à-la-carte menu for lunch & dinner (see Dolphin Grill, below). Outside, a large freshwater pool is set in front of the restaurant & bar, overlooking the sea. There's a dive operator on site, & steps lead down to a small beach, from where there's superb snorkelling. It's early days, & the hotel is still slightly soulless, but the staff are certainly friendly & helpful. $$$

✖ WHERE TO EAT AND DRINK

In addition to the Dolphin Grill at the Ocean Beach Resort, there are a few local venues with considerably more character. Of these, Muriel's is reckoned to be one of the best. Note that none of these local establishments accepts credit cards.

✖ **Dolphin Grill** Ocean Beach Resort. The only restaurant on the island that serves b/fast, lunch & dinner is in the capable hands of a professional chef from the Dominican Republic. Aside from a full b/fast at $12, the menu is à la carte, ranging from lobster, fish or conch prepared any way you like to pizzas, burgers, salads & various Latin dishes. $$

✖ **Dora's Restaurant** Airport; ✆ 946 3247. If you're after a lobster sandwich, this is the place to go. And yes, it really is at the airport. $

♀ **Eastern Inn** Hilgrove St; ✆ 946 3301; m 232 5705. Also known as the Chicken Bar — the name says it all. $

✖ **Love's Restaurant** New Airport Rd. Rosie Love continues to serve great food & memorable pineapple rum drinks. $

✖ **Muriel's** Graham St; ✆ 946 3535; ⊕ b/fast, lunch & dinner daily. It's easy to dismiss this white house with a red roof as a private house, but it *is* a restaurant, serving good local dishes based on locally caught conch, lobster & fish, as well as chicken. $

✖ **Myrna Lisa** Cnr Hilgrove & North sts. A notice on the door states that prayers are said at noon on Mon–Sat. $

✖ **Pond View Restaurant** New Airport Rd; ✆ 946 3276; ⊕ 10.30am–3.30pm, & evenings daily. On the main road from the airport, south of the police station, this simple bar & restaurant caters mostly to the Hispanic population. Chicken & fish are served with rice or chips. $

SHOPPING AND AMENITIES

Any ideas of shopping as an expedition should be put firmly to one side. South Caicos has a few supermarkets, of which only two (Cham B's and Sea View Market) are properly stocked – but even then don't go expecting anything but the essentials. Fish, lobster and conch can be bought from the local fish market at the harbour – the fishermen usually return at around 3pm. For anything more elaborate, you'll be waiting until you return to either Grand Turk or Providenciales.

SUPERMARKETS

Cham B's Stubbs Rd; ⊕ 8am–9pm Mon–Sat; 8–10am, 6–9pm Sun. From its premises up the hill from the harbour, Cham B's stocks all the basics.
Sea View Market Jn Hilgrove St & Stubbs Rd; ✆ 946 3219; m 232 4554; ⊕ from 8am Mon–Sat. Bedecked in the green & blue Cable & Wireless livery, this general store is highly conspicuous. It stocks a decent range of foodstuffs – & yes, it also sells phonecards!

Super Value Supermarket Hilgrove St; ⊕ 8am–1pm, 2–8pm Mon–Sat. Despite the name, food supplies in this shop are seriously limited.

BANKS There's an agency for the **First Caribbean Bank** on North Street (✆ 946 3268; ⊕ noon–2pm Wed only).

COMMUNICATIONS Public **internet** access is available at two locations. At the comfortably air-conditioned library on Front Street (⊕ 8am–4.30pm Mon–Thu, 8am–4pm Fri, 9am–1pm Sat), costs are $3 for half an hour, or $5 per hour. A second option is at the Western Union office, located to the left of Sea View market (*junction Hilgrove St & Stubbs Rd*), where you can expect to pay $15 per hour. They also have computers for rent.

The **post office** (✆ *946 3211*) is located in the Customs and Treasury building on Front Street, across from the library.

MEDICAL FACILITIES There's a brand-new **medical clinic** (✆ *946 3216, 3800, 3799;* ⊕ *8–12.30pm, 2–4pm Mon–Fri*), complete with a neatly marked out tarmac car park, on the eastern edge of Cockburn Harbour. It is permanently staffed by a doctor and nurses, and there is also a visiting dentist. There are no pharmacies on the island.

POLICE The police station (✆ *946 3299*).is on the New Airport Road, heading north out of Cockburn Harbour.

RELIGIOUS SERVICES Services at the 18th-century Anglican Church of St George the Martyr (see page 149) on North Street are held every Sunday. Other denominations represented on the island include Methodist and Baptist, but there is no Catholic church.

FESTIVALS

SOUTH CAICOS REGATTA (*http://bigsouthregatta.tc*) The highlight of the island's social calendar is held every year at the end of May, attracting participants from across the islands, as well as visitors from overseas. It was founded in 1967 following the visit of Queen Elizabeth II and Prince Philip, and involves the whole island in a succession of events from beauty pageants, concerts and fireworks displays to dancing and junkanoo. There are traditional pastimes such as maypole plaiting and hula-hooping, too, not to mention an afternoon of cricket. Special Sunday church services culminate in a gospel concert in the evening. And then there are the races themselves, incorporating boats that range from traditional sloops through fishing vessels to speedboats.

ACTIVITIES

DIVING Although the tourist infrastructure on South Caicos is only in its infancy, the island's diving – reported by the tourist board to be the best in the islands – is potentially a considerable draw. The fact that these waters are used as a research base by the University of Boston Marine Biology School for Field Studies (*www.fieldstudies.org*) indicates just how considerable that draw is, with students able to study steep walls, pristine coral reefs and sea-grass beds within minutes of the shore.

Visibility is typically at least 65ft (20m), highlighting the sharks and schools of eagle rays that frequent these waters, as well as plenty of turtles and some serious-looking barracuda. There are awesome coral formations too, attracting an abundance of fish life.

Dive sites A total of 16 sites are regularly visited by divers off South Caicos. Most of these are concentrated to the south of the island, just behind Long Cay, mirroring the wall that runs around the south. The wall here, as elsewhere on the islands, is sheer, with enough life to keep even the most frequent diver demanding to go back.

Names such as Eagles' Nest. Shark Alley and The Arch speak for themselves. From one dive, a tunnel leads up from the wall into the Grotto where, like all good Santa's grottos, everything seems larger than life. Enormous plate corals, tubes and barrels furnish this cave-like domain, inhabited by squadrons of spotted eagle rays, large sharks, hawksbill turtles and reef fish in the hundreds. At Airplane, dodging brightly coloured fish as you swim through the wrecked fuselage of a 1980s drug-running plane makes for a slightly surreal experience. The story goes that the pilot was coming in to land his Convair 29A at South Caicos when he was tipped off that the authorities were waiting for him. Aborting his landing, he continued south, only to run out of fuel and come down in the sea. The pilot was rescued, the plane wrecked; but what happened to the cargo remains a mystery. The wreck lies in 60ft (18m) of water, giving ample time for investigation after a leisurely dive along the wall.

Round to the east, a further four dive sites feature a series of caves, which make ideal spots for the more experienced diver to explore.

Dive operator

South Caicos Diver m 331 1800; US ☎ 1 239 281 0768; e info@southcaicosdiver.com; www.southcaicosdiver.com. Experienced American diver Greg Wasik has established his PADI- and NAUI-affiliated dive company at the Ocean Beach Resort, with easy access to the small harbour by the old salt warehouse. His 26ft (8m) boats are comfortable, taking up to 10 people, but with most of the dive sites just 5mins offshore, there's no hanging around. Further afield, the wreck of the *Endymion* (see page 180) is accessible in calm weather, with trips costing $120 pp. Courses up to divemaster. 2-tank dive $95, Resort course (inc 2 dives) $200, Open Water $400, equipment $25 (no wetsuits available). Accommodation & dive packages on request.

SNORKELLING Snorkelling on South Caicos is arguably the best in Turks and Caicos waters. To the south of the island, close to the hotel, steps lead down to the water where there's a narrow stretch of beach at low tide. Opposite is a cluster of rocks and a small island, with the larger Long Cay beyond. A swim of just 200m or so takes you across a shallow, sandy channel where eagle rays and southern stingrays are regular visitors. On the rocks, huge elkhorn and plate coral and purple sea fans attract all manner of reef fish, while spotted morays lurk in unexpected crevices, and mean-looking great barracuda hang motionless above.

For those seeking to explore further afield, snorkelling trips can be arranged out to the wall with South Caicos Diver at $50 per person for half a day.

With such attractions come responsibilities. The island has to date seen very few tourists, which accounts in part for the pristine condition of the reefs. The area around Long Cay and the dive sites is protected within the Admiral Cockburn Land and Sea National Park, but if tourism takes off the impact on this superb coral could be significant, unless everyone – both visitors and locals – takes considerable care.

FISHING Both bonefishing and deep-sea fishing can be organised throughout the year through Bibo Jayne at Beyond the Blue (m *231 1703; US ☎ 1 321 795 3136; e bonefishbtb@aol.com; www.beyondthe blue.com*). Their little black airboats, similar to those used in the Florida Everglades, are 24ft (7.3m) long. Rather aptly dubbed 'mosquito' boats, they zip through the shallow 6in (15cm) flats of the Caicos Bank in search of bonefish. When fish are spotted, anglers wade into the water to try their hand, always on a catch-and-release basis.

Typically, the boat leaves at around 8am, returning to shore at around 4pm. A four-night package comes out at approximately $2,070 per person, including full board at the hotel. Alternatively, it's possible to charter a boat for the day at around $500–600. Bonefishing is also practised in Bell Sound.

The Ocean & Beach Resort also arranges daily bonefishing charters, from $500 per day including a packed lunch.

KAYAKING Both single and double kayaks can be hired from South Caicos Divers for $40 per day. An ideal excursion is to take a picnic and paddle across to the uninhabited Long Cay (see page 150).

WHALE WATCHING South Caicos is on the whale migration route, with the whales clearly visible from the shore during the first three months of the year. Watching from a boat generally gets you closer, though, and trips are offered by South Caicos Diver for $60 per person. Typically these go out in the afternoon between January and March, lasting from three to four hours. For general details on whale watching, see pages 72–3.

TOURING THE ISLAND

COCKBURN HARBOUR Despite the rather seedy initial impression, Cockburn Harbour is well worth an hour or so's exploration. The focus of the town, its small harbour, is at its most interesting early in the morning, when from shortly after daybreak fishermen come to prepare their boats, returning during mid afternoon with the day's catch. At these times it's a bustling but friendly place, with plenty to watch; at others, it's low key, with just a few small boats bobbing at their moorings.

In the area around the harbour are the town's few shops: general stores that stock a surprising range of necessities. Recently tarred streets, their houses lined up behind low, white-painted stone walls, hint at a hoped-for prosperity, courtesy of the developers. Following the road to the east, along the coast, you'll pass an abandoned salt warehouse and small jetty, before working your way to the somewhat grandly named Regatta Village. Rather more realistically described as a wooden pavilion overlooking the sea, and backed by a large parade ground, it was built for the visit of Queen Elizabeth II and Prince Philip in February 1966.

Head inland from here along North Street and you'll pass the red-roofed Anglican Church of St George the Martyr, built in 1795 and still in regular use. Inside, it is light and airy, with dark pews, simple stained-glass panels and a steeply vaulted ceiling offset by whitewashed walls. It's interesting to note that in the secondary belltower hangs the ship's bell from the Royal Mail Ship *Rhone*, the tolling of which was the last sound heard by the 124 passengers (out of 147) who drowned in the great hurricane of 1867 in the Virgin Islands. The bell was recovered by the legendary diver Jeremiah Murphy (see page 13) and brought by him to South Caicos.

But of the various buildings in this area that hark back to colonial times, none recalls those times so much as the old white commissioner's house. Overlooking the bay from a low hill near the hotel, it stands amid the tangle of a once well-tended garden, crying out to be restored to its former glory. When – or if – the long-mooted visitor centre on South Caicos materialises, tourists will be able to trace the history of the island. For now, though, it's up to buildings such as these to give free rein to the imagination.

BEYOND COCKBURN HARBOUR Exploring beyond the confines of the hotel and Cockburn Harbour is a must if you're to get any feel for the natural attractions of South Caicos above the waves. The ideal way to do this is by bike (see *By bicycle*, page 144), but walking is certainly possible, as is hiring a car.

Perhaps the perfect circuit by bike is to spend a couple of hours and head anti-clockwise around the salinas that dominate the centre of the island. Although long disused, the pans remain divided into sections as they were when the salt industry was at its peak, but now pelicans, ospreys and flocks of flamingoes and other wading birds have replaced the great heaps of salt that sparkled in the sun. The **boiling hole** near here was important during the years of salt production, when it effectively acted as a pump to bring water between the salinas and the sea. The area around it has recently been improved through cooperation between the National Trust and the School for Field Studies, with a view to encouraging people to visit the area and discover more about its wildlife.

Once off the tarmac, the track is for the most part hard-baked sand, with little to disturb the silence bar the occasional small herd of horses or the rustle of wings as a heron takes flight. Initially, the track winds alongside the pond, lined with patches of mangroves. Further on, it branches off to continue through natural vegetation until you reach the bottom of Bell Sound. To your right rises a high ridge, sometimes known as Sail Rock Hills, that runs right up the eastern side of the island as far as the lighthouse at its northern tip. At 160ft (48m), this ridge is almost the highest point in the Turks and Caicos, fractionally lower than Blue Hills on Provo.

Continuing further north, beyond the High Point development (Caicos Beach Club Resort and Marina), you'll come to the former **Coastguard Station**; just look for the 150ft (45m) radar tower. The station dates back to World War II, when it was a US base, and some old barracks remain. Now it is mostly deserted, but there is a caretaker on site every day.

It's worth cycling parallel to the ridge for a short while as the road runs along Bell Sound, just to take in the sheer beauty of the scenery. If you're feeling energetic, clamber up to the top, to be rewarded by great views on both sides.

Returning back towards the salinas, take the road to the right, initially around Bell Sound then bearing to the south, away from the new development, then follow this back to join up with the airport road.

ISLANDS OFF SOUTH CAICOS

LONG CAY As the name suggests, Long Cay is long and thin, covering an area of just 0.4 square miles (1km²). Its southwestern shoreline is defined by a craggy cliff that rises up to 50ft (15m) high, making an ideal breeding site for both the osprey and the white-tailed tropicbird. Down below, look out for the Turks and Caicos rock iguana, which has recently been reintroduced. Lucayan archaeological sites dating to around AD1100 have been found on the island, as they have on neighbouring Dove Cay and – more significantly – on Middleton Cay. The island is protected within the Admiral Cockburn Nature Reserve.

Getting to Long Cay takes around half an hour by kayak from the harbour. Alternatively, ask one of the local fishermen to take you across, either to here or perhaps to Six Hill Cays a little further offshore. Be sure to have plenty of water to last the day, as well as food, a hat and sunscreen. If you're feeling adventurous, you could even camp overnight under the stars – though do remember that this is wild camping: there are absolutely no facilities, and everything taken in must be removed when you leave.

'GREAT' AMBERGRIS CAY One can only wonder what Loyalist Colonel Thomas Brown would have made of an African safari encampment set today on the shore below his property. Little remains of the sisal plantation he created on compensatory land granted him in the late 18th century when along with other British patriots he was obliged to leave his home in Atlanta, Georgia. Ambergris Cay is one of the more distant outposts of the Turks and Caicos Islands and he with his family and slaves once settled must have lived a pretty solitary existence. Swapping an *ante bellum* southern American lifestyle for a lonely Atlantic island with few familiar comforts would have felt quite a wrench.

A hundred-and-thirty years on, all that is left are a few broken walls, the structures they represent unknown but the stones, probably brought to the island as ship's ballast, are thick and beautifully set. Reflect on the artistry of those slaves erecting them in the unremitting sun; think too of the all-too-likely fractured relationships amongst the Brown family in that isolated place. The site, located in the south, is indicated by a plaque and is close to the planned Spa and Wellness centre, a facility to be offered by the **Turks and Caicos Sporting Club** (↘ *US toll free 1 877 815 1300;* e *info@tc-sportingclub.com; www.tc-sportingclub.com; Providenciales office: The Salt Mills, Grace Bay;* ↘ *941 4392*).

The South-African made safari tents already in place at Whale Watcher's Point comprise four sleeping tents, a luxuriously appointed dining area and a bonfire pit, an extra novelty for the members of this special club (see below). From late January to early April the east and south coasts of the island offer grandstand views of migrating humpbacks making their way to and from the warm waters of the Silver and Mouchoir banks for two purposes, courting and calving (whale gestation is 12 months).

As with all the other Loyalist ventures on the Caicos Islands, the sisal plantation prospered only briefly and the Brown proprietorship was short-lived. After reverting to government ownership, Ambergris again changed hands several times. In 1826, we are told, Horatio Stubbs of South Caicos traded '6,000 bushels of salt for the island, its dwelling house and one female slave'. Most recently, following decades of being uninhabited, in 1995 'Great' Ambergris Cay was acquired for a rather higher price by a group of investors with a view to developing a members-only club, a private Shangri-La for those prepared to pay for it.

The island is 3.3 miles (5.3km) long and 1.5 miles (2.4km) wide with its highest point at 92ft (28m) commanding a superb 360° panorama. No hotel is featured in the plans and privately owned homes will be arranged mainly along the eight miles of coastal bluff, white sand and translucent ocean. The attractively named Ambergris relates to a rather less pretty substance secreted in the gut of the whales but of considerable value in the cosmetic industry. Seasonally washing up on the island shores, it was once harvested here, possibly a more profitable exercise than sisal cultivation. Colonel Brown would certainly have appreciated the airstrip; at 5,700ft (1,737m) it is the longest private runway in the Caribbean with a flying time from Providenciales of only 18 minutes. One of the objectives of the club, whose excellent bar and restaurant Calico Jack is already up and running, will be to provide ease of access to any number of recreational activities, so as well as a deep-water harbour, an equestrian centre, squash and tennis courts, a swimming pool, a bowling alley and a movie theatre, residents will be able to summon up an air taxi service to transport them to the golf course of their choice in the Bahamas or the Caribbean. Paradise for some.

But the previously remote nature of this eastern extremity of the Caicos Bank can't be forgotten and the Ambergis Cays, along with neighbouring Bush, Seal and Pear islets, remain equally the property of some delightful wildlife. Of particular concern is the large colony of rock iguana. To their credit, The Turks and Caicos Sporting Club have pledged 450 acres of their 1,100-acre domain to be retained and maintained as a nature preserve. It is their intention to employ a full-time staff naturalist.

On-island transport will continue to be by bike or motorised golf buggy. The management have decreed very firmly that driving on their island will be on the right. Unlike Salt Cay, where driving is happily in the middle.

LITTLE AMBERGRIS CAY To the west of its greater neighbour, this is a nature reserve. Heaps of conch shells long ago discarded by fishermen now form a series of natural groynes on the eastern shore. A creek to the southwest of the islet, its banks thick with mangrove, is teeming with marine life, and from the western tip a sandbar, extending at low tide for an astonishing seven nautical miles, is claimed to be one of the longest sandspits in the world.

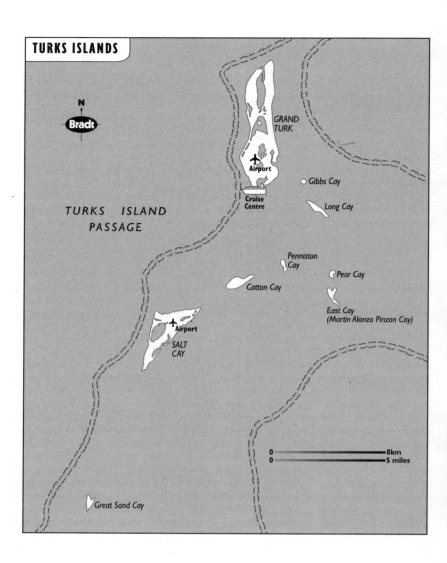

TURKS ISLANDS

N

Bradt

GRAND
TURK

Airport

Gibbs Cay

Cruise
Centre

Long Cay

TURKS ISLAND
PASSAGE

Penniston
Cay

Pear Cay

Cotton Cay

East Cay
(Martin Alonzo Pinzon Cay)

Airport

SALT
CAY

0 ━━━━━━━━━ 8km
0 ━━━━━━━━━ 5 miles

Great Sand Cay

7

The Turks Islands

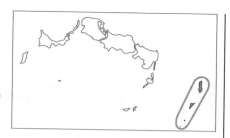

Once known as the Salt Islands, Grand Turk and Salt Cay represent the largest of the Turks Islands, which together cover an area of 10.3 square miles (26.7km²). Lined up on the eastern side of the Turks Island Passage, they are characterised by a very different climate from that of the Caicos Islands. It is this climatic difference, which created broad expanses of salt pans, that during the 19th century led the Turks Islands on their own unique course, and thus created the framework for the islands that are visited today.

Until as recently as 1998, two-fifths of the Turks and Caicos Islands' 14,000 population lived on Grand Turk and Salt Cay. Today, though, their estimated population of 5,832 accounts for just 15% of the total.

HISTORY

A tantalising archaeological discovery in 1992 posed more questions for the experts than it answered. Excavation for a housing project on the northwestern shores of Grand Turk's North Creek uncovered potsherds, all proving to be Ostionan in origin, a style never before found north of Hispaniola. The significance was that this type of pottery was quartz-sand tempered, whereas utensils fired in the limestone-based islands of the Turks and Caicos were always shell tempered Palmetto-ware, indicating that the pottery must have been brought from elsewhere. Now known as the Coralie site, it is likely to have been occupied over several centuries from AD900 and almost certainly earlier, confirming it to be the oldest pre-Columbian site to date in either the Turks and Caicos Islands or the entire Bahamas chain.

It can be assumed that before human occupation the islands were host to a complex eco-system. Bones retrieved from the Coralie site indicate the existence of a number of faunal species long extinct and perhaps give a clue as to why the Tainos might have chosen to colonise these islands. With sea turtles weighing 300lb (136kg), any number of iguana and giant tortoises as well as an extensive choice of birds and fish, and a plentiful supply of salt for preservation, their larder would have been the least of the Lucayans' worries.

In February 1997 a Lucayan canoe paddle was fished from North Creek itself, close to the Coralie site. Carbon dated to around AD1100, it now has pride of place in the National Museum.

At least two other early settlements have been noted on Grand Turk, one producing a large number of Lucayan shell beads, and there is some evidence of a Taino presence on both Gibb's and Cotton cays. Villages on these smaller islets are curious. Why was one chosen, not another? Perhaps they were less permanent habitations occupied as staging posts for fishing excursions further afield.

It is known that by 1512, when Juan Ponce de León came to the islands, the Lucayans had all but disappeared. As the story is told, rather improbably, he found just one elderly Taino resident on Grand Turk and thus named the island Isla del

Viego in his honour. Without a doubt the early Spanish explorers had seized the opportunity of shipping the unfortunate Lucayans into slavery and within a very short time the Tainos had been eradicated from all of the Bahamian islands and the Turks and Caicos.

The biggest mystery is one that may never be solved. Was Grand Turk – called by its then inhabitants Guanahani – on 12 October 1492 the first landfall of Christopher Columbus in the New World? Many people on the island itself and some historians are convinced that it was; so strong is their conviction, a stone monument has been erected within a small designated park on Front Street, in commemoration of that momentous day. Other scholars are less sure and there are a number of locations in the Bahamas that contest the claim, notably San Salvador.

Columbus's log recording the event was inconveniently lost, as were later copies, and depictions of that first island's physiography are at best ambiguous. Those that remain are mainly interpretations from the 16th-century journal of Bartolome de las Casas, whose father was an officer on the original voyage and who himself accompanied Columbus on his third westward venture in 1498. It appears indisputable that Guanahani was a 'large island – with a lagoon'. But such a vague description could be applied to any one of dozens of islands in the region.

As the 400th anniversary of the first landfall approached arguments grew particularly heated:

> . . . No two investigators agree as to the first landfall without disagreeing as to the
> second; and if they happen to coincide on the first, it is only to fall out on the fourth. . .
> Frederick A Ober, *In The Wake Of Columbus*, 1893

Debate grew contentious again as the quincentenary drew near, with a rash of new theories aired. Although several early maps name Guanahani, it is shown in a variety of locations. The late H E Sadler in his entertaining and detailed chronicle, *Turks and Caicos Landfall: A History of the Turks and Caicos Islands* (see *Further Information*, page 190) puts forward a strong case for Grand Turk.

WRACKING, THE SLAVE TRADE AND THE BATTLE FOR SUPREMACY Grand Turk's
role in the Lucayan tragedy was only the beginning of its slave history. Toward the middle of the 17th century Bermudian chancers, recognising the potential of the salt pans, began sailing south to take up residence in the Turks Islands between the months of March and November. It was their practice to import their own African slaves who would be put to work from dawn till dusk under the unremitting sun, first raking and then shifting the salt for onward transport. Little documentation has survived but one oral history from a century later, attributed to a Bermudian slave called Mary Prince, provides a startling record of appalling conditions and inhuman treatment. It is not known how much of the content of the narrative, published in England in 1831 by abolitionist Thomas Pringle, might have been edited by him to underline the urgency for emancipation, but nor is it certain that Prince herself was not withholding the full extent of her suffering.

In tandem with their entrepreneurial salt gathering, the Bermudians were also accomplished wrackers and the busiest season for the passage of ship-borne cargo through the major sea lanes out of the Caribbean tied in nicely with their primary enterprise. The northerners would post lookouts at points with a view over the Turks Island Passage and close to hazardous stretches of reef. By the beginning of the 18th century the Spanish, growing increasingly riled by their losses, saw it as appropriate to establish title to the islands their navigators had reached two centuries earlier. Four years after they successfully captured Grand Turk, the island was regained on behalf of the Bermudians by the privateer Lewis Middleton. The French too were sniffing around the islands with a view to increasing their territory and by the middle of the century were making reconnaissance voyages from their base in Hispaniola, purportedly to chart the waters. In 1764 they took the liberty of erecting two massive stone pillories, towering 90ft (27m), one on Grand Turk – where the name has stuck – and another on Great Sand Cay. Whilst denying that these monsters constituted an assertion of French sovereignty and maintaining that they were purely a navigational aid, they demanded that the Bermudian salt rakers swear allegiance to France, naming Grand Turk and Salt Cay respectively Grande Saline and Petite Saline. Later that year Britain, on the defensive, officially declared ownership of the Turks and Caicos, with governance to be administered through Nassau. Accordingly the governor of the Bahamas appointed an agent, Andrew Symmer, to represent him on Grand Turk. The Bermudians, by now well established in year round occupation, were never going to be happy with a subsidiary role as part of a greater colony and rejected forthwith any suggestion that they should further be taxed for the privilege. Symmer optimistically laid out plans for improvements he perceived would increase production in an already successful salt industry but as the Bermudians continued to protest, and as time went by, little by little he grew more partisan to their cause. Within a matter of years under his auspices Grand Turk had to all intents become a free port with no export taxes levied, let alone finding their way to Nassau. Over the duration of the American War of Independence Grand Turk was even notoriously rumoured to have run the Royal Navy blockade and supplied salt to George Washington's troops at Valley Forge. The long-disputed tax issue was ultimately resolved to the disadvantage of the island in 1799 when the Turks and Caicos became formally part of the Bahamas.

The French who had supported the American revolution, riding on the ensuing threat to Britain's mastery of the seas, took Grand Turk by storm in the aftermath and a recovery attempt by young Captain Horatio Nelson in command of HMS *Albermarle* was a failure. The island was eventually restored to Britain as an outcome of the 1783 Treaty of Paris.

THE 19TH CENTURY Herbert Sadler in his history of the islands describes the hurricane of 22 August 1813 as having destroyed 120 houses on Grand Turk and a similar number on Salt Cay, but whatever damage was done to the capital, the storm created equal havoc amongst the doomed plantations of Providenciales and the Caicos Islands. Of the few Loyalist refugees who did not pack up and leave the archipelago for good, a small number brought their slaves to Grand Turk and sought a new career in the salinas.

Grand Turk was at this time frequently referred to as Grand Cay (in Mary Prince's words it is spelt 'Grand Quay' maybe simply because the name was unfamiliar to the person in England transcribing them). The name 'Turk' is usually understood to derive from the indigenous Turk's head cactus, itself so-called because the mature fuchsia-coloured head resembles a fez. But it has also been suggested the name could reflect the term 'turk' used in describing a pirate or invader of the Ottoman Empire, Grand Turk and its neighbouring islands having provided a lair for so many swashbucklers.

Original plans for Cockburn Town – named after a Bahamian governor – were drawn up at the beginning of the 19th century and they show the area of the Old Prison as public ground. It is likely the prison would have been built towards the end of the 1830s. Before the 1834 Emancipation Act, punishment was not regulated and criminality insufficiently defined. Nigel Sadler, museum director 2000–2006, points out: 'It appeared slave owners were a law unto themselves.' We do know the gaol was operational by 1841 when the slaves and crew of the *Trouvadore,* wrecked on Philips Reef off East Caicos, were temporarily lodged there, for want of anywhere else to place them. The oldest vernacular architecture was constructed in an attractive medley of Bermudian and traditional Caribbean styles, many of the houses incorporating verandas and balconied upper storeys with wide eaves to provide protection from the sun. Waterloo, today the governor's residence, was built in 1815 and named for Wellington's famous European victory over Napoleon. Guinep House, now home to the Turks and Caicos National Museum, is – like many of the early buildings – partly supported by timber salvaged from shipwrecks. By 1850 the hated pillory had been dismantled, along with its twin on Great Sand Cay, and its stone redeployed in more modest constructions. Schooners arriving on the island to take up salt would often carry stone as ballast and this too was used to build houses.

The long-awaited Emancipation Proclamation was announced on 1 August 1834. Locals say the monumental statement was made from Oddfellows Lodge, one of the oldest buildings on Front Street. In practice little was to change for the manumitted slaves in the following years. Despite an apprenticeship system introduced to ease the transition, with specially appointed magistrates to monitor its application, the scheme continued to be abused and was officially concluded four years later. 'It was not until the years of World economic slump in the 1920s and 1930s that descendants of the slaves could gain employment on ships and get free passage off the Islands,' observes Nigel Sadler.

On both Grand Turk and Salt Cay the Bermudian-founded salt industry was augmented for a short period in the mid 19th century by a whaling enterprise, though how successful the venture was is unclear. One whale could provide sustenance for a large number of people over a long period and the meat could of course be preserved in salt. Like dolphins, whales are highly intelligent creatures, their behaviour still not fully understood, and there has always been a mystique associated with them. It's said children born on the island after a whale had been slaughtered were bathed in its blood in the belief they would be infused with its strength.

To the north of Grand Turk, the reef shielding the island from the full wrath of the Atlantic Ocean became over the centuries the graveyard for dozens of ships. Frequent petitioning by those who regularly used the Turks Island Passage had fallen on deaf ears until at last a 60ft (18m) lighthouse, its lamps fuelled by whale oil, was installed in 1852. Folklore has it that local wreckers, unwilling to be deprived of their livelihood, were not averse to extinguishing the light during promising periods of intemperate weather. Whatever the truth it proved inadequate and ships continued to come to their grief. When the light was upgraded in 1943 and the fuel replaced with kerosene, the resulting beam was visible for 15 miles (24km).

The 19th century brought many innovations to the capital including the 1845 launch of its first newspaper, *Turks Island Gazette & Commercial Reporter*. Postage stamps, introduced in Britain in 1840, went on sale on Grand Turk with the opening of its first post office in 1854 but 13 years were to pass before they would bear their own 'Turks Islands' imprint, the beginning of a long tradition for the production of beautifully designed limited issue stamps, sought by collectors worldwide. The completion in 1898 of a submarine cable linking Jamaica, Grand Turk and Bermuda must have been an extraordinary landmark for the, until that moment, remote treasure island.

THE 20TH CENTURY In some ways Grand Turk was moving with the times but economically the island and her satellite, Salt Cay, found the first half of the 20th century a struggle. The inhabitants depended on the salt industry for survival but the market was becoming increasingly competitive. While modernisation on

Grand Turk meant the introduction of rudimentary windmills to replace hand-operated paddles in the movement of water, and donkey carts rather than slaves to carry the loaded bags, rival producers were developing more technically sophisticated methods. Two world wars didn't make matters any easier. Since 1874 the country had been annexed to Jamaica whose domestic concerns naturally took priority and many islanders began to consider emigrating to the Bahamas where plenty of employment was available. So when in 1950 the United States installed a state-of-the-art missile-tracking station on Colonel Murray's Hill (Colonel Alexander Murray having served as king's agent for a decade in the late 18th century) it did more than raise hopes of a few much-needed jobs: it lifted spirits. And when in 1962 Grand Turk was to play a minor role in the space race, with John Glenn and later Scott Carpenter taking their first steps back on earth to be debriefed and for medical checks at the same American facility, the island's 15 minutes of fame was enjoyed by all. Further celebrations followed four years later when the Queen made a royal visit to Grand Turk and she too was escorted to the American Missile Tracking Base, though as far as we know not to have her heart-rate monitored.

More than 300 years after the first wave of Bermudians had begun the laborious task of raking salt beneath a torrid tropical sun, the failing industry nationalised in 1951 as The Turks Island Salt Company finally ground to a close with the last sacks heaved on to a lighter at Salt Cay dock in 1970.

The enormous interest generating from the 1980s' discovery of the Molasses Reef shipwreck (see pages 6–7) enforced the Turcasian desire to create their own museum. Such a facility would both give the islanders ready access to a display of items and events that had shaped their history, and provide a safe depository for valuable artefacts, all too many of which to that date had tended to disappear into private collections or be taken for safekeeping in other museums. It would also be a wonderful asset for the budding tourist industry. In 1991 the dream came to fruition and the Turks and Caicos National Museum received its first visitors. Today it is acknowledged as one of the finest small museums in the region (see pages 172–3) and historic Guinep House as a most attractive setting. In 1996 the Donald Keith Research Building, named in recognition of the leader of the Molasses excavation team, was opened at the rear of the building with laboratories enabling on-the-spot investigation and conservation. A timely addition for that was the year Bob Gascoine recovered a Lucayan paddle from North Creek (see above).

NATURAL HISTORY

With limited rainfall, extremely poor soil and a high incidence of saline ponds, the Turks Islands present a hostile environment for any form of vegetation. What little there is consists of drought-tolerant shrubs such as acacia, or the extraordinary Turk's head cactus, whose red seeds are a delicacy for humans (albeit an acquired taste) as well as for birds. Feral donkeys meander along the roads, stooping to graze on the tough grass; most of the horses that once shared this rough pasture have long since been rounded up.

For the birdwatcher, though, it's those saline ponds that are the chief draw. Several species of egret and heron stalk these shallow waters, alongside flocks of flamingoes – especially to the south. Royal terns and gulls, too, are frequent visitors, with ospreys, oystercatchers and pelicans also to be seen here and on the beaches. If the birdlife off the water seems rather less interesting, keep an eye open for the tiny hummingbird.

Much of the islands have been afforded government protection in the form of national parks and the like. For the visitor, the most significant of these is

Columbus Landfall National Park, an area of 1,280 acres (518ha) which covers the entire western coastline of Grand Turk, encompassing the area from the barrier reef to the water's edge. In common with other marine national parks, this means that no motorised sport is permitted within these areas, and the speed of fishing and dive boats leaving the beach is strictly regulated. To the east, South Creek National Park incorporates the mangroves of this estuary, which with its natural salina attracts numerous wading birds.

Other protected areas encompass Gibb's Cay and other cays to the southeast of Grand Turk, and Big Sand Cay to the south, which are nesting sites for birds that include sooty and noddy terns, brown boobies and frigatebirds.

There are no venomous snakes or scorpions. Just don't get bitten by a donkey.

GRAND TURK

There are very few places in the world – and Grand Turk is among the best – where you can watch the full moon rise at dusk from the sea on one side of the island and then travel to the other side to see it at dawn back into the ocean. This is an exceedingly rare and rewarding (not to mention romantic) experience.

So wrote Bill Keegan & Betsy Carlson in 'Talking Taino: Starry, Starry Night' published in the *Times of the Islands*, and reproduced with permission

In part, Grand Turk retains much of the character of an archetypal small English village. The road from the airport towards the small Cockburn Town winds past a village pond lined with neat picket fences surrounding small bungalows, then continues into Duke Street and Front Street. Here, wooden architectural gems, lovingly restored and maintained, sit cosily side by side, the history of each briefly documented in a plaque erected by the developers of the cruise terminal for the edification of their passengers. Perhaps this is why the area away from the beach just to the north of the town, with its run-down houses and unkempt air of poverty, comes as such a shock: manicured 1950s England meets rubbish-strewn 21st-century shanty town. Fortunately, this situation is being addressed with the construction of five new community parkland areas ranged across the island, incorporating recreational areas and public lavatories. This development is in part a result of increased revenue deriving from the new cruise facility.

Grand Turk is six miles (9.6km) long and just over a mile (1.7km) wide, its sheltered western shores fringed by long sandy beaches and protected by an offshore reef.

HISTORY IN THE MAKING It's early days yet but it seems likely that travel guides of tomorrow will describe the most significant introduction of the new millennium on Grand Turk to be the Carnival Cruise Center, which received its first visiting liner in February 2006. In its first full year of operation, 136 visiting ships brought in 295,000 passengers.

Some years ago, when plans were instigated for the eventual construction of a series of causeways linking the Caicos Islands, similar to the system in the Florida Keys, the idea to create a cruise-liner terminal on East Caicos was under consideration. When the final decision was made to site the port on the capital, Grand Turk Belongers, seasonal residents, and regular diving vistors alike voiced some concern as to the negative effect it might have on the environment and on the community. In the event assurances were given that great care would be exercised with regard to the reef system in the dredging and pier construction, and two years on the economic benefits are clear to see: employment is up, and importantly the unique charms of Cockburn Town have not been lost in the process. By all accounts the port has rapidly become one of the most popular on cruise itineraries.

It's interesting to remember that barely three decades ago in the Turks and Caicos Islands only Grand Turk had an airstrip long enough to handle freight planes. At that time also it was the sole banking centre for the islands, and – in the days before street lamps – it was easy to find your way home along the white sandy roads by the bright light of the stars.

GETTING THERE

By air Until recently, there was one international flight a week between Fort Lauderdale and Grand Turk's JAGS McCartney International Airport, run by Spirit Air. At the time of research, that service had been suspended, but in the words of one local, 'Spirit Air doesn't operate like other airlines' – and the future of the service remains uncertain.

Regular internal flights operated by both SkyKing and Air Turks and Caicos link Grand Turk (GDT) to Providenciales daily. The 20-minute journey, typically in a 19-seater Beechcraft, twin-engine turbo-prop plane, affords spectacular views of Providenciales, and North, Middle and South Caicos islands before it traverses the Turks Island Passage to land on Grand Turk. Don't be tempted to arrive late for one of these flights; this must be the only place in the world where a scheduled aircraft sometimes departs early! A return trip with SkyKing from Providenciales runs out at $161, or $88 one way, or $135/85 with Air Turks and Caicos. SkyKing also connects Grand Turk with South Caicos, while flights to and from Middle and North Caicos, and Salt Cay, are operated by Air Turks and Caicos.

Up to three SkyKing flights a day stop off at South Caicos, taking just ten minutes from Grand Turk. For details, see page 143.

Facilities at the airport are limited to a small duty-free shop, and the Cockpit Lounge (⊕ *6am–9pm Mon–Sat, 6am–8.30pm Sun*). The building has WiFi internet access, with payment made at a machine.

A taxi from the airport into the centre of the island will cost from around $7 per person.

You cannot fail to notice the space capsule displayed at the entrance to the airport, a reminder of the occasion in 1962 when astronaut John Glenn touched down in the sea to the east of Grand Turk (see box, page 161).

Airline offices
Air Turks & Caicos ↘ 946 1667
SkyKing ↘ 941 5464, ext 800/801

By sea

Cruise ship The purpose-built Cruise Center (*http://grandturkcc.com*) at the southwestern end of the island was opened in February 2006, opening up the islands for the first time to cruise ships. Although it was built to take two ships at a time, it is possible for additional vessels to anchor offshore and for passengers to be ferried ashore by tender. Between December and February, during the height of the season, there are indeed two ships in harbour each day, but this eases off to around four or five a week, with sometimes just one a week in the summer months. Ships usually stay in port for between four and six hours, giving passengers a reasonable time to explore the whole island should they wish to do so.

GETTING AROUND Aside from a hop-on, hop-off bus that operates out of the Cruise Center for cruise passengers, there's no public transport on Grand Turk. That said, tours of the island can be organised with the taxi companies, or in a 4x4 vehicle with

7

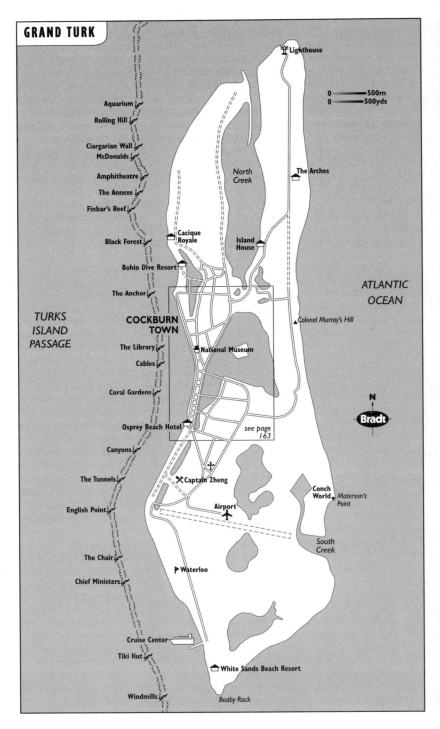

GRAND TURK

Lighthouse

Aquarium

Rolling Hill

Ciargarian Wall
McDonalds

Amphitheatre

The Annexe

Finbar's Reef

Black Forest

Bohio Dive Resort

The Anchor

COCKBURN
TOWN

The Library

Cables

Coral Gardens

Osprey Beach Hotel

Canyons

The Tunnels

English Point

The Chair

Chief Ministers

Cruise Center

Tiki Hut

Windmills

North Creek

The Arches

Island House

Cacique Royale

ATLANTIC OCEAN

Colonel Murray's Hill

TURKS ISLAND PASSAGE

National Museum

see page 163

N

Bradt

Captain Zheng

Airport

Conch World

Materson's Point

South Creek

Waterloo

White Sands Beach Resort

Boaby Rock

0 — 500m
0 — 500yds

Picture the excitement in Grand Turk when, on 20 February 1962, news spread that the space capsule navigated by astronaut John Glenn, *Friendship 7*, was about to splash down in the sea just 166 miles (267km) to the east of Grand Turk. Glenn's flight was part of the US Project Mercury Space Program, inaugurated in October 1958.

The first American to orbit the earth, Glenn was airborne for just under five hours in his capsule, *Friendship 7*. During that time, he completed three circumnavigations of the Earth, covering a total distance of 80,778 miles (130,000km). To the excitement of countless people tuned in around the world, he radioed back:

Zero-G and I feel fine. Capsule is turning around. The view is tremendous, it is beautiful, a beautiful sight.

At the time, both the United States Navy and the Air Force operated bases on Grand Turk, the latter incorporating a tracking station. It was here that Glenn was taken for a medical check up and debriefing after his landing. Three days later, Vice-President Lyndon Johnson arrived on the island, posing with Glenn for photographs before escorting him back to a triumphant reception in the United States.

The bell-shaped space capsule itself was recovered and brought ashore the day after it landed, before being shipped out to Florida. A replica of the capsule is displayed near the entrance to JAGS McCartney International Airport. It seems ironic, 46 years on, that one of the mission support team interviewed at the time regretted there was so little reference in the press to 'the charms of unknown Grand Turk'.

Chukka Adventures (see page 168). The company also operates horse-drawn buggies are operated out of the Cruise Center when ships are in port, bringing their passengers north through the narrow streets of Cockburn Town.

On a practical note, do be aware that the road running parallel to the shore in Cockburn Town changes its name from Duke Street to Queen Street to Front Street as it heads north. On the ground, though, Front Street tends to be used for anywhere north of Duke Street – and this is the practice that we have followed in this guide.

By taxi It should be noted that taxi drivers in Grand Turk charge per passenger, rather than per trip.

🚕 **Cool Ride Taxi** m 241 5327, 6243
🚕 **Coney's Taxi** m 231 6640
🚕 **GT Taxi** m 241 6243
🚕 **Salt Cay** m 242 2804

🚕 **Val's Taxi**, Duke St, m 231 6442
🚕 **White Man Super Shuttle** Old Airport Rd; m 231 1684, 242 2810. Dennis Williams also makes a good tour guide.

Car and scooter hire

🚕 **Dutchie's Car Rental** Airport Rd; ✆ 946 2244
🚕 **Island Auto Rentals**, Airport Rd; ✆ 946 2042; e islandautorentals@hotmail.com. Cars have AC; daily/weekly rental.
🚕 **Porky's Garage** Lighthouse Rd; ✆ 946 2743
🚕 **Tony's Car Rental** Grand Turk Airport; ✆ 946 1879; after hrs: 946 2934; m 231 1806;

e thriller@tciway.tc; www.tonyscarrental.com. Cars from $70 per day, exc taxes; scooters $60 per day, inc taxes. Also hire out snorkelling equipment at $30 per day, and organise scooter tours.
Val's Scooter Rental, Triangle Sq; ✆ 946 1022. Scooter $55/day, inc tax.

The **speed limit** in Grand Turk is 25mph (40km/h).

Fuel is available from one of three service stations. The Triangle Service Station lies in the centre of the island, close to the supermarket. Beyond here are Fulford's Gas Station (*Pond St N;* ℡ *945 1231*) and Missick's Gas Station (*Church Folly;* ℡ *946 2595*). In summer 2008, unleaded was priced at $6.10 a gallon ($1.61/litre).

By bicycle Bikes are available free to guests at Bohio Dive Resort (see page 164) and for rent to guests at Grand Turk Inn (see below), but are not currently available for hire elsewhere.

TOURIST INFORMATION The tourist board office is on Front Street (℡ *946 2321; www.turksandcaicostourism.com;* ⊕ *8am–5pm Mon–Fri*). There is also a supplementary tourist office booth operating at the Cruise Center when any ship is docked.

WHERE TO STAY Despite the status of the island as the capital of the Turks and Caicos, there are relatively few places to stay. Rates on the island are generally quoted per person sharing, with a single supplement that will vary according to the season. As elsewhere, all rates are subject to 10% government tax, and – usually – 10% service.

Hotels

Grand Turk Inn (5 suites) Front St; m 231 7023; www.grandturkinn.com. A converted 150-year-old Methodist manse, this boutique hotel faces the sea & is run by 2 widely travelled Australian sisters. A decent continental b/fast is served in the rooms but no other meals are on offer; their key lime pie does not count: miss this at your peril. The suites are decorated to an exceptionally high standard, with appropriate furniture & linen. Each has a kitchen, living room & bath, with cable TV, room safe, internet access, AC & ceiling fans. There is a large communal sundeck. Bikes are available for hire to guests. The hotel is deservedly winning awards & sets the standard for Grand Turk, but they like their guests to be over 16. In-hotel boutique with hand made jewellery items. $$$$

Manta House (2 bungalows, 3 suites) Duke St; ℡ 946 1111; e info@grandturk-mantahouse.com; www.grandturk-mantahouse.com This Canadian-owned place next to Salt Raker Inn has a fairly communal atmosphere. There's AC throughout, but while one bungalow is en suite & with a kitchen, the rest of the accommodation has shared bathrooms & fridge. MCd & Visa. $

Osprey Beach Hotel (39 rooms) 1 Duke St; ℡ 946 2666; e ospreybeach@tciway.tc; www.ospreybeachhotel.com. Centrally located on a narrow road (though traffic isn't an issue), this is the island's largest hotel. 27 rooms look directly over the beach, 15 with patios & direct beach access & 12 on the 1st floor with balconies. There are also 12 cheaper rooms in the Atrium across the street, without

sea views. The entrance is arresting: a good-size swimming pool, backed by the dining area, frames a view straight out to sea. Rooms are well proportioned & nicely fitted out, some with antique island furniture. All are en suite with AC, ceiling fan & fridge; beachfront rooms also have a TV & phone, & some have a kitchen with microwave. Service is both professional & helpful. B/fast (not included) is available at Michael's Atrium Restaurant across the street, but a b/fast service is planned for 2009. In principle, min 3-night stay in high season, though it is always worth asking for a daily rack rate. $$–$$$ inc tax.

Salt Raker Inn (13 rooms) Duke St; ℡ 946 2260; e saltraker@tciway.tc, erikafaller@bluewin.tc; www.hotelsaltraker.com. Oozing character, this ramshackle inn opposite the beach dates back to the mid 19th century & is one of Grand Turk's oldest buildings. Now in the capable hands of German owner Erika Faller, it retains every inch of its character, but is slowly being introduced to the 21st century. Rickety wooden steps lead up to 2 large rooms & a balcony with a hammock swinging in the breeze, with other, smaller rooms set out below. If the fabric of the building is in some disarray, & electricity decidedly erratic, this is offset by en-suite showers, fridges, comfy beds, modern AC & ceiling fans, & WiFi access throughout the premises. At the back is the aptly named Secret Garden restaurant. B/fast $12; full board $50. $$

Turk's Head Mansion (8 rooms) Duke St, ℡ 946 2066; e info@turksheadmansion.com; www.turksheadmansion.com. This fine old house built

Bohio Dive Resort

A Taste of the Island

0 ——— 100m
0 ——— 100yds

HOSPITAL ROAD

LIGHTHOUSE ROAD

Island House, Lighthouse

FRONT STREET

Town Salina

R&R Supersaver, Cool Beans

Police station

Turks & Caicos National Museum

Al's

TCI, Scotia Bank

PRISON ST

Clocktower

Old Prison

Library

CHURCH FOLLY

Cee's supermarket

FRONT STREET

HALL'S ALLEY

St Mary

Canal Bridge

Post office

1st Caribbean

BARRACK ST

QUEEN STREET

MISSION FOLLY

GOOD STREET

Red Salina

St Thomas

Grand Quay Salt Company

POND ST

Cable & Wireless

CHANCERY LANE

Grand Turk Inn
Columbus Landing

BREEZY BRAY RD

MOXIE FOLLY

Turk's Head Mansion

Court House

DUKE STREET

Oasis Divers

OSBOURNE ROAD

Sandbar
Manta House

Salt Raker

Blue Water Divers

Michael's Atrium

N

Osprey Beach
Grand Turk Diving

JAMES ST

Bradt

Airport
Cruise Center

COCKBURN TOWN

7

in 1823 was subsequently the governor's guesthouse & the US Consulate. Recently re-opened as a hotel it's still settling down in its newish role. All rooms — upstairs, garden rooms & in the coachmen's quarters — are en suite with AC, satellite TV & WiFi access. Calico Jack's restaurant & bar (see below). Children under 12 sleep free in parents' room. $$$

Dive lodge

🏠 **Bohio Dive Resort** (16 rooms, 4 suites) Pillory Beach; ☎ 946 2135; e Kelly@bohioresort.com; www.bohioresort.com. With its beachfront location about 20 mins' walk north of the centre of 'town', Bohio (the name means 'home' in the Taino language) is fully geared to divers. Rooms are modern, large & airy, all with a sea view, & cooking facilities. A good-sized swimming pool is useful for dive training in rough weather. The restaurant (see below) & 2 bars are open to all-comers. Bohio's boat typically goes out at 9am, taking only their own guests unless there's space for others. They also have kayaks (free to guests; non residents $20 pp), Hobie Cats ($45 ½ day), & snorkel equipment. Bikes are available free to guests. Whale-watching excursions in season $70 pp. Excursions to other islands — including Gibb's Cay & diving off Salt Cay. Yoga classes available. $$$ + $70 pp for 2-tank morning dive.

Self-catering

🏠 **The Arches** (4 villas) North Ridge; ☎ 946 2941; e archesgrandturk@tciway.tc; www.grandturkarches.com. Set at the top of the ridge, this is another Canadian-owned place. Each 2-bedroom villa sleeps 6, with 4 balconies, AC, ceiling fans, kitchen with washer/dryer & cable TV. There's a decent shared pool & good sea views. Housekeeping services & dive packages available. Children under 6 half price. $$

🏠 **Cacique Royale** (116 condos) Pirates' Bay; ☎ 946 1000; e info@caciqueroyale.com; www.caciqueroyale.com. Eighteen buildings beside the beach house 1-, 2- & 3-bedroom condos. Facilities include 3 pools, a spa, gym & watersports. Due to open in 2008.

🏠 **Columbus Landing** (60 condominiums) Duke St; ☎ 946 4600; e info@columbuslanding.com; www.columbuslanding.com. Another large condotel that is scheduled to open at the end of 2008, this is aimed at the luxury end of the market. Sea views, a landscaped courtyard, an infinity swimming pool & jacuzzis are just some of the features incorporated in the design. There will also be a spa & fitness centre, 2 restaurants, a small shop, a business centre & underground parking.

🏠 **Island House** (8 suites) Lighthouse Rd; ☎ 946 1519; e ishouse@tciway.tc; www.islandhouse-tci.com. Set on a ridge in an attractive inland location to the north of the island, Island House overlooks one of the salinas, & beyond to the sea. It is run by a well-established English owner & his wife, who hails from Grand Turk. Self-catering suites each have a fully equipped kitchen, as well as AC, phone, TV & free WiFi access. Outside there's a freshwater pool & plenty of space to relax. Staying here includes the use of a vehicle, making it ideal for those who want to explore or to reach the central area easily. Free transfers. Children under 12 stay free in parents' room. $$$ inc tax.

🏠 **White Sands Beach Resort** (16 condos) Just north of Cruise Center; ☎ 946 1065; US toll free ☎ 1 866 548 1065; e info@whitesandsbeachresorttci.com, gascon@tciway.tc; www.whitesandsbeachresorttci.com. Newly built, & convenient for the Cruise Center shops & bars when ships are in, this is terrific if you are a liner-spotter, but lacks the old-world flavour of much of the island. Identical 1-bedroom condos have a kitchen, TV & ocean view. There's also a freshwater pool, & a beachfront restaurant & bar: Big Daddy's Beach Shack (see below). Up to 2 extra people $30 each. Dive package available. $$$ inc tax.

✖ WHERE TO EAT AND DRINK
Restaurants

✖ **Big Daddy's Beach Shack** White Sands Beach Resort; ☎ 946 1065. Features bar menu & covered outdoor eating area, with an imaginative & reasonably priced range of salads, sandwiches & burgers. $

✖ **Calico Jack's** Turk's Head Mansion, Front St; ☎ 946 2066; ⏱ 7am–11pm. Slightly limited international menu & the rather amateurish ambience that can go with a newish establishment. $$$

✖ **Captain Zheng** Salina Houses, Close-Haul Rd; 📱 242 2436; ⏱ noon–3pm Mon–Fri; 6–10pm Tue–Sat. Pretty authentic Chinese food even if the chef is called Joan. Takeaway service available. $$$

GRAND TURK KEY LIME PIE

Before they moved to the islands the owners of Grand Turk Inn lived on Key West in Florida. If you are fortunate, some mornings' continental breakfast might include a slice of their delectable, home-made, key lime pie. They have agreed to share the recipe with us.

Filling
1 8oz pkt Philadelphia cream cheese
1 tin condensed milk
1 egg yolk
½ cup fresh squeezed lime juice (more or less to taste)

Base
1¼ cups digestive biscuits (Graham crackers)
3 tbsp brown sugar
⅓ cup melted butter

In a small bowl, mix biscuits, brown sugar and butter. Press firmly into pie dish. Beat cream cheese until smooth; add condensed milk and egg yolk. Mix well and pour in lime juice. Pour into base and bake for 20 minutes at 350°F (180°C, mark 4).

Cool Beans Lighthouse Rd. Coffee & ice-cream.
Guanahani Bohio Dive Resort, Pillory Beach; 946 2135; restaurant 7.30–10am, noon–2.30pm, 6.30–9.30pm daily; bar till late. The restaurant at Bohio is open for b/fast, lunch & dinner — averaging $13 at b/fast & lunch; dinner $19 pizza, $39 steak/lobster; also local dishes. There's a BBQ a couple of times a week at $20–29 for steak, fish, etc. **$$$**
Michael's Atrium Restaurant Duke St, 946 2878. Across the street from Osprey Beach Hotel (in the location of the previous Courtyard Café), this is where they send people for b/fast but it also does lunch & dinner. Mostly local or Jamaican food, or decent salads & omelettes. **$$**
Poolside Restaurant & Birdcage Bar Osprey Beach Hotel, 1 Duke St; 946 2666. Cheerful service, good sea views & sea breezes combine with some of the better food on the island. The varied menu features island specialities. There are regular themed nights, inc BBQs & live music from Mitch Rolling & his High Tide band on Wed & Sun nights: an island highlight. **$$$**
Sandbar Duke St; food: noon–3pm, 6–8pm Sun–Fri; bar: noon–late. This popular beachfront bar

Cruise Center

Margaritaville 946 1880; www.margaritaville.com; when cruise ships are in harbour. Mass-produced rum cocktails & snacky food with technicolour décor

on a jetty opposite the Salt Raker Inn is a great place for sundowners. It also serves good bar food — think cracked conch with chips & salad, or burgers & quesadillas. Don't bank on them taking credit cards. **$–$$**
Secret Garden Salt Raker Inn, Duke St; 946 2260; restaurant 7.30–10.30am, noon–2.30pm, 7–9.30pm Thu–Tue, bar 7.30am–late daily. At weekends, the Salt Raker's covered courtyard restaurant is a magnet for hungry islanders in search of b/fast. Tall tales fuelled by last night's drink create a lively atmosphere that doesn't dissipate until the last of the fish with peas & grits ($8.50) has been polished off, & it's time for bed. Ordinary mortals can stick to any combination of bacon & eggs, while surfing the net courtesy of the restaurant's WiFi connection. At lunch, or in the evening, choose from fish & seafood, or the likes of a veggie platter or stewed beef. **$$**
A Taste of the Island Restaurant & Beach Club Ocean Drive at West Rd Beach; 946 2112; m 231 6268; e atasteoftheisland@tciway.tc. Specalises in local dishes & seafood. You can swim & shower, then eat & drink (or vice versa). **$**

& a vast pool with swim-up bar. Young & crowded with 500 seats & 52 varieties of Margarita. Need one say more?

ENTERTAINMENT There's live music at the Salt Raker Inn on Friday evening played by Mitch Rolling's band, High Tide, featuring ripsaw or rake 'n' scrape music and soca. The band plays at the Osprey Hotel every Wednesday and Sunday evening.

SHOPPING Grand Turk may not be geared to shopaholics, but it's possible to get a surprising range of goods from the individual shops. Many of these are along the streets that line the shore to the west, but for supermarkets you'll need to head slightly inland, close to the salinas – and don't be too choosy about brands.

Books and stationery
Al's Front St. The bookshop next to the bakery, just south of the museum, also stocks stationery & a good range of batteries.

Clothes, gifts and snorkelling supplies
Blue Water Divers ℡ 946 2432. A range of T-shirts, plus camera batteries & the like, as well as snorkelling gear.

Cin & Bon's Boutique Pond St, by Fulford's Gas Station; ℡ 946 1231

Oasis Divers Duke St; ℡ 946 1128; ⊕ 8am–5pm daily. Some decent snorkelling equipment, plus a good range of beachwear.

X's Place Duke St; ℡ 946 1299. Arts & crafts & a boutique.

Duty free For those in search of goods such as spirits or jewellery at duty-free prices, there's a branch of Goldsmith at the airport. Duty free shops in the Cruise Center are strictly for cruise passengers only and boarding cards must be shown before purchase.

Food and drink Those in search of fresh fish should head for the fish market on Front Street, which also sells fresh fruit, vegetables and eggs, all imported from the Dominican Republic. Imported food comes in at the harbour next to the Cruise Center every Tuesday. Alcohol may not be sold on Sundays.

Cee's Church Folly at Pond Rd; ℡ 946 2030; e cwilliams@ceesenterprisesltd.com; ⊕ 8am–7pm Mon–Sat. Grand Turk's best supermarket. They sell household goods & tools as well as food & drink, most of which are imported from the USA. Internet café.

City Market Moxy Folly; ℡ 946 2560

Dot's Food Hospital Rd; ℡ 946 2324

Dot's Liquor Moxy Folly; ℡ 946 2324

Durham's Lighthouse Rd; ℡ 946 2929

Missick's Bakery Church Folly; ℡ 946 2891.

Palm Cove Variety Store Palm Cove; ℡ 946 1555

R&R Supersaver Wynns St; ℡ 946 2238; ⊕ 8.30am–1pm, 4–9pm Mon–Sat

Sarah's Shopping Centre Frith St, Back Salina; m 231 0843; ⊕ 7.30am–6.30pm Mon–Sat. Food & drink.

Timco Front St; ℡ 946 2480. Drinks.

OTHER PRACTICALITIES
Banks
$ **Barclays Bank** Barclays Bank Bldg, Front St; ℡ 946 2831

$ **First Caribbean** Front St, beside Grand Turk Inn; ℡ 946 2831. Will exchange currency & travellers' cheques in sterling, euros, US & Canadian dollars for a 3.125% fee. Visa ATM.

$ **Scotiabank** Harbour Hse, Front St, ℡ 946 2507; ⊕ 9am–3pm Mon–Thu, 9am–4.30pm Fri. Will

convert Canadian currency but, at the time of writing, no sterling as 'there has been a security problem'.

$ **TCI Bank** Front St, cnr Prison St; ℡ 946 2368; e tcib@tciway.tc; ⊕ 8am–3pm Mon–Thu, 8am–4.30pm Fri; 9am–noon Sat. Will exchange US travellers' cheques free of charge, & sterling, Canadian dollars, Swiss francs & euros for $5 fee.

Communications
Internet Internet access is available at **Victoria Public Library** (*Front St;* ⊕ *8am–5pm Mon–Thu, 8am–4pm Fri, 9am–5pm Sat; see also page 173*). To avoid

having to wait, it's best to come during school hours. Expect to pay $3 per ½hr, or $5 per hr.

There's also an internet café at **Cee's** supermarket on Pond Street (see above; ⊕ *8am–7pm Mon–Sat*). Costs are $2.50 for 15 minutes. International phone calls can be made from here, costing from $2.50 to the US and Canada.

Post office Grand Turk's post office (☎ *946 1334*; ⊕ *8am–4.30pm Mon–Thu, 8am–4pm Fri*) is on Front Street. Avid stamp collectors should note that there's a **philatelic bureau** (☎ *946 1534*) upstairs, with the same opening hours and very helpful staff. Note that the Church Folly bureau has recently closed.

Medical facilities The island's **hospital** is on Hospital Rd (☎ *946 2333*). There is also a health clinic (☎ *946 2328*), and a pharmacy, **K's Drugs** (☎ *946 2799*). **Public lavatories** are behind the library and behind the tourist office. They are officially open only on cruise-ship days, but in practice you will generally be lucky in daylight hours at least. They are free and are cleaned every half hour and are generally spotless.

Religious services Visitors will be made extremely welcome at any of these churches, all of which hold services every Sunday:

Grand Turk Methodist Church Good St, beyond the salinas; ☎ 946 2351. Built in 1930 to replace the original wooden structure destroyed in the 1926 hurricane.

Holy Cross Catholic Church Osbourne Rd; ☎ 946 1374; www.catholic.tc. Sunday masses at 9am (English), 10.30am (Creole) & noon (Spanish).

St Mary the Virgin Anglican Pro-Cathedral Front St; ☎ 946 2289. Built in 1899, this is a popular & busy church that receives lots of visitors. The organ plays from 11am–2pm whenever cruise ships are in port.

St Thomas' Anglican Church Church Folly. Sunday services 6.30 & 9am, & 7pm. They are collecting $60,000 for new windows & roof.

Travel agent
T & C Travel Ltd Duke St; ☎ 946 2592

ACTIVITIES

Cruise Center The construction of the Cruise Center (*www.grandturkcc.com*; ⊕ *when cruise ships in harbour*) was highly controversial, involving the destruction of at least one dive site, and with an environmental impact that can as yet only be estimated. On the other hand, the arrival of regular day visitors to the island has brought numerous benefits, not least an increase in the range of activities available to tourists, an improvement in the general cleanliness of beaches and streets and a significant increase in employment and revenue. At least some of those given a taste of Grand Turk will come back for a longer stay in TCI. More than 200 cruise vessels were expected in 2008, accounting for 400,000 passengers.

Short-stay visitors have a diverse list of activities to choose from, the opportunity to tour the island in dedicated vehicles or simply the option to pass their time within the extensive and well-equipped entertainment and shopping facility at the dock itself. Here, in addition to local craft and souvenir vendors, they will find a wide selection of retail outlets featuring watches, jewellery and clothing; Little Switzerland; Ron Jon Surf Shop; Bruno fine art; Goodman's gems; and an extensive Dufry duty-free outlet, as well as an authentic rendition of Jimmy Buffett's Margaritaville, a high energy tropical-themed bar and thatched-roofed restaurant alongside a spacious freshwater pool with a 25-seat swim-up bar offering cocktails, beer, wine and light food. Even when two liners are berthed together, the little island never feels overcrowded, precisely because of the variety of pursuits and entertainment on offer. Although many of the cruise companies offer customised activities and packages specially priced for their own passengers, options can be summarised as follows:

Land based Beach, spa, horseback and swimming with horses, cycling, 4x4 adventures, horse-drawn carriage tours, dune buggies, visits to outer cays, lighthouse, Conch World, museum, salt exhibit, lunch in Bermudian-style home and beach with floats etc, 'desert-island escape' (2hrs on your own 'private' beach).

Marine Snorkelling, scuba-diving, snuba, self-drive boating, deep-sea and bone fishing, helmet diving, semi-submersible tours, power-snorkelling, kayaking, sea-trekking, surfing, sightseeing yacht trip.

Activities on offer to cruise-ship passengers are either based at the centre itself, or handled from there, but there's no reason why those staying on the island shouldn't visit the centre and participate in the activities. It's worth noting that some operators go to considerable lengths to keep 'island' visitors and day visitors separate, in order to conserve the sense of individuality that is one of the primary appeals of Grand Turk. Similarly, rates for many activities enjoyed by cruise passengers will differ from those undertaken by independent visitors to the island, because they are fixed by the cruise-ship companies rather than by individual tour operators.

Beaches At the Cruise Center, a large, buoyed swimming area has been created off the 800ft (244m) beach, with an ample supply of loungers. On the water, jet skis can be hired for use further up the beach, or there's a 70ft (21m) catamaran for sailing enthusiasts. A dive boat, catering for about 20 divers, is dedicated to visitors from the cruise ships, and shore-based snorkelling trips, complete with equipment, are also offered. There are changing rooms with showers and lockers on site. The casuarina-fringed Governor's Beach (in front of the governor's residence, Waterloo) is only a short taxi ride away (*$4 pp*) and offers an attractive option with ample shade available. Every 20 minutes a trolley bus also shuttles between the centre and this beach (*$2 pp*). Walking between the two is another possibility but it can be hot work. (On foot, exit the Cruise Center in a northerly direction, with the sea on your left and passing the White Sands Beach resort.) Chair rental at Governor's Beach is $5.

Exploring the island For those preferring to spend shore time on land, there are taxis and horse-drawn buggies ready to take visitors around the island, or you could opt for a 4x4 safari. During the time any ship is in port *Iguana* 'hop-on, hop-off' buses travel in a continuous loop from the centre throughout the island. Tours are fully narrated and the price of a ticket or wristband (*from $39.95 pp*) can include a variety of visits to historical and other sites.

The more adventurous can drive their own dune buggy, or explore the east coast on horseback. The Jamaican-run **Chukka Adventure**s (m *341 6963, 244 9010;* e *info@chukkacaribbean.com; www.chukkacaribbean.com*), which handles trips from horseriding to 4x4 safaris and dune buggies, limits them to a maximum of 20 participants. Women who are pregnant may not take part in their activities.

4x4 safaris In a trip lasting two hours, up to ten passengers per 4x4 vehicle are driven north on Grand Turk, taking in a 15-minute walk in Cockburn Town before continuing off road to North Wells and North Creek. The return journey is down the eastern side of the island. Minimum age six, minimum four people.

Dune buggies If your idea of fun is to drive what looks like a Meccano kit car, then you've come to the right place. Designed to travel over sand dunes, these slightly space-age vehicles with a tubular frame travel in convoy right round the island, passing the airport, the salinas and Cockburn Town, then on to the northern tip of the island, before returning along the east coast. The whole journey takes just over two hours, and is suitable only for the over 18s, who must have a valid driving licence. Each vehicle takes two people, and safety helmets are included.

Other options
Horseriding Riding along Grand Turk's northeastern shore offers some unexpected opportunities. A drive along the western side of the island, through Cockburn Town and past the salinas, leads to the stables. Initially the horses are saddled up for a walk along the beach, with time to learn something of the island's past, but for many people it's all about riding bareback as the horses take to the water for a swim. On the practical side, go prepared with swimwear and a towel, as well as long trousers and waterproof shoes; showers are provided. Each trip lasts a total of 2 hours 40 minutes, including transport. The maximum weight per rider is 250lb (113kg); the minimum age is six. No hats are provided. *$65/46 adult/child.*

Lunch in a typical Bermudian house includes all soft drinks, sun-loungers, floats for swimming and half-day use of shower facilities etc. The house faces the beach. *$44 pp.*

Semi-submersible Take in a narrated tour of colourful marine life, in completely dry comfort aboard a semi-submersible craft.

Sea-trekking An underwater walking tour that enables guests to 'wander through coral beds' while holding a steady hand-rail.

Flowrider New at the Cruise Center in summer 2008, this artificial surfing wave caters for both body boards (*$24/½hr*) and stand-up boards (*$34/hr*). Tickets are sold on the ships, but should soon be available on line.

Diving and snorkelling
Diving Typically, all the operators offer two-tank morning dives, single-tank afternoon dives, and night dives, with options of diving off Salt Cay in calm weather. All are PADI affiliated, but will take divers certified by other organisations.

Costs tend to be much the same wherever you go, so expect to pay around $85 for a 2-tank morning dive, although those booked on a package will pay considerably less. For equipment, charges are typically $25 per day for the whole kit, or – for those needing just one item – $10 for a BCD or regulator, $15 for a computer, or from $5 for a mask and fins.

Dive sites Locally, divers compare the sites of Grand Turk with those of French Cay (off Providenciales), and they're considered to be up there with the best. The island's dive sites are situated on the sheltered western side, along the fringing reef. It's never more than a 10–15 minute boat ride, so a two-tank morning dive normally leaves at around 9am, returning in time for lunch. All the island's operators use flat-bottomed Carolina skiffs of around 26ft (8m) for most dives; dive entry is a backward roll. With soft sand beaches and few obstructions, the boats are brought right up to the beach at the beginning and end of each dive, making access simplicity itself.

Some 90% of the dive sites are permanently moored; at others, boats are anchored in the sand.

Typically divers are dropped off on the reef in about 35ft (10m) of water, although this varies according to the site; at one, Annexe, it's just 18ft (5.5m). From the top of the reef, it's a short swim to a steep drop off on to the wall lining the 6,575ft (2,004m) Turks Island Passage. Turtles, barracuda, rays and plenty of large fish are much in evidence, with sightings of the humpback whale a regular occurrence early in the year.

Dive sites are surprisingly varied, given what appears to be a single location. The northerly Rolling Hills is characterised by lots of soft corals including beautiful tall purple sea flumes, whip carol and large barrels, inhabited by a whole range of reef fish, including such curiosities as the boxlike trunkfish. At the other end of the island, English Point – so named because the beach here was popular with English visitors – is predominantly sandy beneath the boat, moving on to the reef at 45ft (13.7m). With numerous turtles and southern stingrays, and shoals of fish such as horse-eye jack, there's plenty to see. Then in the middle is the Library, named prosaically for its location opposite the library rather than for the nooks and crannies which make it a particularly good night dive. There are also sites with swim-throughs and arches, as indicated by names such as Amphitheatre and – somewhat cringingly – McDonalds.

All the operators offer night dives, with plenty of time to explore and close enough to shore to avoid getting cold after the dive. This is the chance to spot octopus, some enormous crabs and nurse sharks, as well as macro creatures such as the tiny banded shrimp, its startling colours caught in the bright light of a torch.

Shore diving is limited to just two potential sites: English Point and The Chair. Even these involve a surface swim of around 200yds (200m), though, not to mention some means of transporting gear to the south of the island, so access by boat is infinitely preferable.

Snuba This relatively new concept permits even the least confident of swimmers to see the underwater world for themselves. It's designed for snorkellers who want to venture further but aren't ready for scuba diving and is an ideal option for families. For details, contact Broadreach (❲ 946 1695 or ❲ 244 6977, 244 6976), and see pages 66–7.

Snorkelling Snorkelling from the beach is an option in several places to the west, particularly in front of Bohio Dive Resort and off the beach near Oasis Divers. There's also a sunken barge in front of the library, attracting some juvenile life. To explore the reef, you'll need to go by boat; any of the dive operators below can organise a snorkelling excursion, costing around £30 per person. You could also go further afield to Gibb's Cay (see page 175), where a resident population of southern stingrays has become habituated to snorkellers.

Some of the best snorkel sites are to the east of the island, but since most of the accommodation is to the west, these sites are also the least accessible, and a calm day is essential.

Snorkelling equipment can be hired from most of the dive outfits for around $10 per person.

Dive operators

Blue Water Divers ❲ 946 2432; ❲ info@ grandturkscuba.com; www.grandturkscuba.com. Mitch Rolling set up in business in 1983, having been bewitched by the islands on an earlier dive trip. A well-known character on the island, he's originally from Iowa, & leads a popular local band. A PADI 5-star Gold Palm operator, the company offers courses up to instructor – at least in theory. Their 3 Carolina skiffs, of 24ft & 28ft, each take 10 divers max, but average 6–8. Typically they dive Grand Turk on first dive, then on to Salt Cay, with the 40min trip between the islands forming the surface interval. Those wishing to snorkel can either go out with divers ($30 pp), or take a dedicated snorkel trip (min 4 people). Blue Water can also organise accommodation packages & inter-island flights.

Grand Turk Diving James St; ☎ 946 1559; e info@ gtdiving.com; www.gtdiving.com. Owned & run by the personable Smitty – who hails from Grand Turk – this small operation covers all the sites visited by the other companies, using a Carolina skiff. PADI courses up to advanced can be arranged, and they can also organise accommodation packages.

Oasis Divers ☎ 946 1128, US reservations ☎ 1 800 892 3995; e oasisdiv@tciway.tc; www.oasisdivers.com. Highly professional & organised, & the largest operator on the island, Oasis handles the full package for divers, including inter-island flights & accommodation, & acts as an agent for other activities. They also handle all cruise-ship diving & snorkelling on Grand Turk – but for cruise-ship clients there's an entirely separate fleet of boats from those for 'island' guests, operating at different sites; the two are never mixed, and Oasis maintains a separate office & shop at the cruise-ship terminal. At their main office & shop, there are 4 boats, of which 3 are skiffs (up to 8 divers); the 4th is used only for groups (18–22 people). Their morning two-tank dive is usually off Grand Turk, returning to land for the surface interval, although a full day off Salt Cay is a great alternative, with time on land to explore. Other facilities include camera rentals & tuition, & the option of a video of your dive, as well as snorkel & kayak trips, & sailing.

See also *Bohio Dive Resort*, above.

Other watersports

Kayaking and sailing Kayaking parallel with the shore makes a pleasant way to pass a few hours, pulling the craft up on the sand for a swim then perhaps stopping later for lunch or a sundowner at the Sandbar. Kayaks are available to rent from Oasis Divers (*$25 pp*) or Bohio Dive Resort (*$20 pp, or free to guests*). Alternatively, join a guided tour with Oasis Divers, who offer kayaking in the mangroves of South Creek at $50 per person.

With relatively predictable easterly winds, these are great waters for sailing, too. Hobie Cats can be rented from Bohio Dive Resort (*$45 ½ day*).

Fishing Options for fishing off both Grand Turk and Salt Cay fall into two categories – flats fishing for bonefish, tarpon, jack and snapper, and deep-sea fishing in search of species such as tuna, marlin and shark. Finding a suitable guide with the right tackle is best arranged through your hotel or resort; the guide will sort out fishing permits as required.

Each July, Grand Turk hosts the Heineken Game-Fishing Tournament: competitive anglers take note!

Other activities

Walking There are a couple of short walking trails up by the lighthouse, leading around the headland and giving a clear view of the reef on which numerous ships have been wrecked over the years.

Golf The nine-hole Waterloo Golf Club (☎ 946 2308; f 946 2903; green fees: resident non member $15; junior $5; visitors $25) is rather strangely in the grounds of the governor's office and residence. Designed by Governor John Kelly, it was laid out in 1998 by himself and a number of volunteers, with the assistance of inmates from the island prison. The club is somewhat idiosyncratic, but popular with locals.

Spas and beauty salons

Fabulous North Back Salina; no tel
Hanchell's Beauty Salon off Osbourne Rd; ☎ 946 1884
Ruth's Beauty Salon Old Airport Rd; m 232 1460

Spa Anani m 232 1503; www.spaanani.com; ⊕ 9am–1pm Tue–Sat. The island's only spa is owned by the Osprey Beach Hotel. In a modern building opposite the hotel, this is the place to come for facials, massages & other relaxing therapies. There is also a branch at the Cruise Center.

Gyms

No Limits Fitness Gym Saunders Pond East; m 231 6204; e tci.sports@tciway.tc

True Fitness Gym Palm Grove; ☎ 946 1555

WHERE TO GO AND WHAT TO SEE

Beaches To the west of the island, beaches are protected from the prevailing easterly winds and, with little current to speak of, these are the most popular for the majority of visitors. The small tree-shaded beach in the centre of the island, on either side of the Sandbar, offers easy access for those staying at Osprey Beach or other hotels in the vicinity.

Beaches on the eastern side can take the full brunt of the weather, but also offer some great snorkelling.

Cockburn Town The tourist board publishes a leaflet featuring a heritage walk around Cockburn Town. This starts at the National Museum on Front Street, and continues south past the arboretum as far as the Victoria Library. From here, a detour takes you left down Pond Street towards the large Town Salina, passing the Old Prison en route, to give a view across the salina towards the red-roofed Methodist church. Just down the street from here, the pink building on the opposite side of the road is the Court House, which was partly destroyed by fire a couple of years ago.

Returning to Front Street, the walk continues past St Mary's Anglican Pro-Cathedral, over the canal and on towards Duke Street, home to the Turks Head and Salt Raker inns. Several roadside plaques indicate the historical significance of the buildings along this route.

Turks & Caicos Islands National Museum (*Guinep House, Front St beside Murphy's Alley North;* ☎ *946 2160;* e *museum@tciway.tc; www.tcimuseum.org.* ⊕ *9am–4pm Mon–Fri; 9am–1pm Sat; closed Sun & holidays; admission $5, Belongers free*) One of the oldest houses in TCI, Guinep House (called after the large guinep tree outside) was built in the mid 19th century of limestone and old ships' timbers and contains a truly splendid small museum which opened for business on 23 November 1991. Each year, on the Saturday closest to that date, Museum Day celebrates the anniversary of the inauguration with a range of special activities, presentations and an entertainment created by local children.

Serious consideration of the founding of the museum was prompted by the excavation of the Molasses Reef shipwreck between 1982 and 1988. In those days nearly all major archaeological discoveries in the islands were taken to the USA for conservation, some eventually finding their way back home to the TCI for inadequate storage and display but most staying in America. The Molasses Reef team understandably believed that it was unacceptable for so much of the islands' heritage to end up in US museums and private collections; after considerable struggle they managed to raise sufficient funds to acquire Guinep House and to set up environmentally stable research and display space. Since then the TCI National Museum has gone from strength to strength and the present display is admirable.

One of the main gaps in the collection was until recently the absence of a *duho*, two of which had been stolen from the Victoria Library in 1978. *Duhos* are Lucayan carved wooden ceremonial seats used by chiefs during religious ceremonies or tribal meetings. They are generally found in caves, so far nine of them in TCI. After extended negotiations, and with the positive help of the family who had inherited it, one of the seats was restored to the museum in October 2003.

Do come to see it and do allow yourself enough time to do it justice. Think in hours, not minutes.

The new director, appointed in September 2007, is Dr Neal Hicks. By training he is an architect and historian who has been working for the Ohio Historical Society, teaching Colonial American History at Capital University and directing camping programmes for the Baptist Churches of Ohio.

The National Arboretum is run by the museum on the next door plot, formerly occupied by another old house which burnt down except for its chimney stack in 1986. The arboretum will not rival the museum for most visitors, but it includes many of the plants which feature in the latter's collections and in their useful botanical pamphlet. There is also a peaceful shaded bench on which to rest and commune with nature in tune with *Revelations 22, v2*: '…and the leaves of the tree were for the healing of the Nations'.

Old Prison (*Prison and Pond sts,* ✆ *946 2130;* ☉ *cruise days or on request by telephone. Alternatively, walk past and see if the gate is open; admission $7, under 12s $3.50*). An interesting place to spend an hour or so, the former HM Prison is well preserved and well labelled. It was built in the 1830s and finally closed in 1994. The crime rate in the TCI used to be among the lowest in the world – occasional drunkenness and the odd scuffle being the main offences – until the 1970s brought the start of serious drug smuggling. The average prison population rose abruptly from four to forty.

Inmates got 12 hours rest each night, locked in their cells with a candle in the corridor for minimal light. They also got three meals a day. Townspeople threw cigarettes and tit-bits over the wall and exchanged news the same way.

There used to be extremely infrequent executions by a hangman visiting from Jamaica. As the gallows was higher than the prison wall, children were kept away from the area when events demanded it.

The Turks Islands Yearbook, 1935, said the police force 'consists of five men stationed at Grand Turk. The Police also perform the duties of Prison Warders and they operate the telephone exchange. The Magistrate acts as Inspector of Police.' The force was renamed the Royal T & C I Police in 1966, following the visit of Queen Elizabeth (the first reigning monarch to visit the territory) and Prince Philip.

Victoria Public Library Front St, at corner of Victoria Alley (see page 166). The library was built on the old militia parade ground to commemorate Queen Victoria's Golden Jubilee. Janet Williams, the charming and helpful librarian, will sell you good coloured prints for $1 or black-and-white ones for 50¢. She would be delighted to receive second-hand books, especially those for children, and DVDs (NTSC only). Donations are also welcome.

Stamp Museum This is to be created in conjunction with the philatelic bureau (see page 167). It will be housed in the Old Legislative Council building on Pond Street, and will operate in conjunction with the Turks & Caicos National Museum, with a joint admissions ticket available.

Canal bridge A small bridge over the canal that crosses under Front Street has a metal sign reading:

Welcome to Grand Turk
White Cliffs of Dover
28 July 1978

We have not been able to establish its provenance or significance. If you can, please tell us for the next edition.

Around the island In the centre of the **Town Salina**, close to Cockburn Town, is an island which is today an excellent location for birdwatching. In the 1800s, though, it was used as an isolation hospital for residents and ships' passengers exhibiting the symptoms of contagious diseases such as cholera or typhoid. Numerous graves in the vicinity testify to the poor recovery rate at the time. These graves, and the island as a whole, are protected by the government.

Broadly in the centre Grand Turk, the **Grand Quay Salt Company** (⊕ *subject to cruise-ship timetables*) opened at Town Ponds – also known as Town Salina – in November 2007. Displays connected with Mary Prince's slave history (see page 154) are set alongside details of the salt-raking tradition on the Turks Islands. A retail outlet sells every conceivable salt product.

North Creek drives an extensive wedge through the north of the island, its sheltered waters a haven for juvenile fish and lobster. Birds are a major attraction here, too, with flamingoes often seen towards the southern end of the creek.

At the northern tip of the island is the **lighthouse** (⊕ *when cruise ship in port; admission $7/$3.50 adult/child*), built in London in 1852 and shipped from there to Grand Turk. Standing 60ft (20m) high, it was installed following numerous wrecks on the island's treacherous northeasterly reef, which can be clearly seen from footpaths that lead around the headland. Indeed, the introduction of the lighthouse put paid on Grand Turk to the often lucrative business of 'wrecking' – when islanders across the region would salvage the cargo carried by the boats and trade it for a significant profit.

There are toilets on site, and a tree-shaded restaurant, the Beacon bar and grill, selling the likes of smoothies and hot dogs, but these are open only when a cruise ship is in harbour. The same restrictions are placed on climbing the lighthouse itself, although the small landscaped gardens surrounding the lighthouse are supposed to be accessible every day.

Conch World (✆/f *946 1228;* e *sales@cvfltd.com; http://conchworld.com;* ⊕ *11am–7.30pm Sun–Thu; Fri–Sat 11am–9pm daily depending on season & cruise-ship timetables; tour price: $15/7.50 adult/child 12 & under*) Conch World at Materson's Point on the east coast features the life cycle of the native Turks and Caicos conch. A short film stars the queen conch and her historic role in the islands' economy, and there's a guided tour of the farming pavilion with live shellfish displayed through their various stages of development and illustrating the Providenciales Leeward Conch Farm, still the only one of its kind in the world. Rather bizarrely, 'tame' male and female conches demonstrate emerging from their shells on command.

There's an on-site café, the **Bare Naked Conch**, whose outdoor covered dining area has views over the east coast of Grand Turk and to Gibb's Cay. There are hammocks, a range of beers, wines and cocktails, and WiFi throughout. Dishes include battered conch salad, cracked conch and conch crêpes, as well as chicken, burgers and vegetarian dishes.

The **Pink Pearl Gift Shop** offers local art, polished conch shells, conch-shell bowls and lamps, silk sarongs, T-shirts and hats, soaps ad beauty products, beach towels, books and maps, as well as sauces from the café.

BOAT TRIPS

Whale watching Although theoretically you could see whales any time between January and April, reliable operators such as Bohio and Oasis Divers offer excursions only between February and March, when sightings are more certain.

The cost of a three-hour trip comes out at around $70 per person. For details of whale-watching trips generally, see pages 72–3.

Gibb's Cay and further afield Afternoon trips to Gibb's Cay are run by various operators including Oasis Divers and Grand Turk Diving, at a cost of around $60 per person, with a minimum of four people. These incorporate a picnic lunch on the beach, and may allow for free diving for fresh conch. The afternoon is the opportunity to swim with the graceful southern stingrays that congregate near the island, lured by food handouts from fishermen. Oasis also goes as far as Great (or Big) Sand Cay (see page 183), with a day trip coming in at $150 per person, including lunch.

SALT CAY

Writers are fond of describing Salt Cay as an island that time forgot. And so it appears to be. As soon as you set foot in the place, either clambering down from the ridiculously titchy barrel of an aircraft or guided ashore at Deane's Dock from the twice-weekly Grand Turk tub, on the steady arm of gentle pirate and Salt Cay Divers' proprietor Ollie Been, the wide empty salinas assail you. For more than three hundred years these fields of brine one way or another constituted the livelihood of every person on the island. Only a closer look reveals that now ospreys have colonised the wooden windmills and they no longer turn creakily in the prevailing breeze. But spume still rises from the silvery residue, whipped like ghostly snowflakes every which way, and somehow the salt rakers seem even more conspicuous by their absence.

Diane Grey Page succeeds only irregularly in escaping the United States to her seaside cottage here. She tells of forgetting her flip flops on the beach and returning a year later to find them exactly where she left them.

Salt Cay is that kind of place. A century ago there were over a thousand inhabitants; today there are barely 70: a population far outnumbered by feral donkeys, cattle and chicken. To be exact, it's 69 souls and one police officer; his duties are not usually too stressful. At one time, the single police cell doubled as the town archive until the inevitable happened and a prisoner set fire to the lot.

Neatly triangular in shape, Salt Cay is just 2.5 miles (4km) long. Traditional whitewashed houses with wooden shutters are dotted along the island's gravel roads. The school has just nine children aged between seven and ten, with two teachers; that's 'almost more grades than pupils,' someone remarked.

The island's own website, www.saltcay.org, is a mine of useful – and occasionally trivial – information. Visitors seeking to engage with this tiny community should be aware everyone is warmly welcomed as new old-friends, and might bear in mind the words of Michele Belanger-McNair: 'Everyone has a recollection . . . part of the history and fabric of this small place in the sun.'

A highlight on the Salt Cay calendar is in December, when the Turks and Caicos Police band comes to the island to play a Christmas concert – carols to a Caribbean beat – and everybody, islanders and visitors alike, joins in the fun. 'The children learn to dance with the older ladies who [themselves] cannot sit still and dance with each other as well' enthuses Miss Netty, Belonger and local shopkeeper. Other events are a costume party to celebrate Mardi Gras, and a pot-luck pirate party at the end of March. To quote Island Thyme proprietor Porter Williams, 'Nothing in itself is world class but the overall experience [of Salt Cay] is world class.'

GETTING THERE

By air Air Turks and Caicos increased their schedule early in 2008 to five days a week between Grand Turk and Salt Cay airport (SLX; ✆ 946 6968, *manned only* *when flights are due*), departing at 6.35am on Monday, 9am on Wednesday, Friday, Saturday and Sunday, and 4.55pm on each of these days, with a flying time of just ten minutes. Ticket costs are as follows:

	Single	Return
Providenciales to Salt Cay	$123	$245
		(or $225 if purchased in advance)
North Caicos to Salt Cay	$146	$292
Middle Caicos to Salt Cay	$156	$310
Grand Turk to Salt Cay	$53	$106

For those in a hurry, it is possible to charter a plane in Providenciales, costing $700 one way, although a cheaper alternative would be to take a scheduled flight to Grand Turk, then charter a boat from there for between $100 and $300 for up to 15 people.

Since February 2007 there has been a periodic direct air freight service by DC-4 between Miami and Salt Cay.

Airlines
Air Turks & Caicos ⤷ 946 6940, 6906; m 241 1009. Charter flights ⤷ 946 4623, 941 5481

By sea A regular ferry run by Salt Cay Charter (m *231 6663*) plies between Grand Turk and Salt Cay on Wednesday, Thursday and Friday, taking about an hour for the journey. The boat leaves Salt Cay in the morning at 7.30am, arriving at Grand Turk's South Dock (just north of the Cruise Ship Terminal) about an hour later. The return journey departs from Grand Turk at 2.30pm on the same day. Extraordinarily, the fare is $12 return for men, but just $8 for women, with freight charged at $1 per box. Unless it is very calm, you may get a bit wet.

GETTING AROUND For the most part, Salt Cay's gravel roads and paths can be explored on foot. The less mobile, and those wishing to get down to the south of the island, however, might want to take one of the motorised **golf buggies** that can be hired from Salt Cay Riders through Sunset Reef Villas (e *sunsetreef@aol.com; www.saltcay.org/golfcart.htm*) for $50–60 per day.

The golf buggies seat either two or four people. They have an accelerator and a brake, the latter only for emergencies as when you lift your foot off the accelerator, they purr quickly to a stop. The only accessory is lights. Springs are not included and when it rains you get extremely wet. But they are very easy to drive and you would have to be drunk, stupid or unbelievably unlucky to have an accident – so long as you remember that livestock have right of way.

Bikes are included with rental of accommodation at Tradewinds. Alternatively, they can be hired from Salt Cay Divers for $10 per day.

WHERE TO STAY Accommodation options on Salt Cay are relatively few, totalling around 70 beds in all with the emphasis on self catering. There is talk of an extensive upmarket development including a deluxe hotel and a golf course, but so far there is no evidence of anyone signing anything.

Hotels and guesthouses
⌂ **Windmills Plantation** (12 rooms) North Beach; ⤷ 946 6962; e windmills@sanctuare.com; www.windmillsplantation.com. At the time of writing,

Windmills has been sold & is temporarily closed, but this review has been left in the anticipation that it will re-open. A genuinely imaginative &

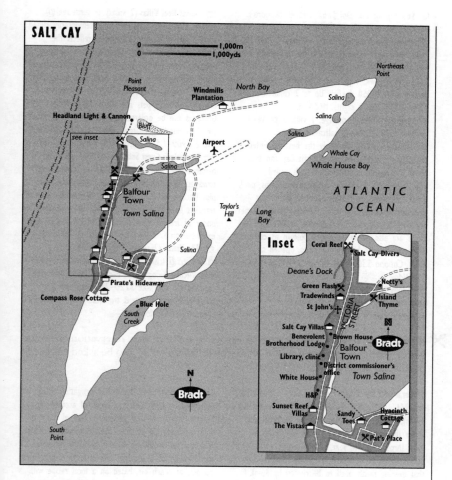

slightly oddball luxury boutique hotel with excellent food. It is partly summed up by Rule 1: No shoes required, & Rule 2: The bar is always open. This leads to barefoot candlelit gourmet dinners with a sufficiency of wine. The hotel stands in an isolated position on a 2½-mile (4km) beach north of Balfour Town. Rooms do not have phones or TVs but they have almost everything else you could want, in some cases including a private plunge pool; there is also a saltwater pool. The hotel has not in the past catered for children & it's fair to say they would almost invariably have been incompatible with the atmosphere. Non-residents were in the past welcome for lunch or dinner, by prior arrangement, with Caribbean/international dishes served. $$$$$

Self-catering villas and apartments

⌂ **Compass Rose Cottage** ✆ 946 6906; e info@saltcay.us; www.saltcay.us. On the beach. Dbl bedroom & sleeping alcove, patio, observation deck, good home entertainment systems, 2 bikes included. Weekly maid service. MCd/Visa. *$1,200–1,400/wk inc transfers; extra person $20/day (max 2).*

⌂ **Hyacinth Cottage** ✆ 946 6906; e scdivers@tciway.tc. 2-bedroom cottage with small kitchen & shower room, deck & garage. *$1,000–1,200/wk for 2 people, $1,000–1,400 for 4. $$$*

⌂ **Pirate's Hideaway** (2 rooms, 1 bungalow) Victoria St, 1 block in from the beach; ✆ 946 6906; e piratequeen3@hotmail.com; www.saltcay.tc. Fairly simple but comfortable rooms; Blackbeard's Quarters (a 4-bedroom bungalow) also has a kitchen. Owner arranges art workshops & rents 4-seater golf buggies for $60/day inc tax. *Dbl $165–175. Blackbeard's $400 for up to 8 people.* $$$

🏠 **Purple Conch Cottage** ✆ US toll free 1 866 790 2667; www.purpleconch@att.net. On the beach. 2 bedrooms with fans, 4 bikes included. 1–2 persons $125/750 day/wk; 4 persons $150/900 day/wk; 6 persons $175/1,050 day/wk. Up to 2 children under 12 free. Min stay 3 nights. MCd/Visa.

🏠 **Salt Cay Villas** (1 cottage, 1 villa, 3 cabanas) ✆ 946 6909; e info@saltcayvilla.com; www.saltcayvilla.com. Probably the best-appointed self-catering accommodation in Salt Cay can take up to 10 people in 2 separate pods called Frangipani villa & cottage. En-suite bedrooms, pool, patio, well-equipped kitchen. Cook & babysitter available. Grocery & laundry services, TV & internet access. 4-seater golf cart available at $60/day. There are also oceanside suites (known as cabanas) with en-suite dbl bedroom & patio, opened in 2008. *Cabana $300/day, cottage $350/day, villa $500/day.* $$$

🏠 **Sandy Toes** US ✆ 1 231 276 9799; www.sandytoesdream@aol.com. Details of accommodation & rates on application.

🏠 **Sunset Reef Villas** (2 villas) e sunsetreef@aol.com. Note: has been sold & is temporarily closed at the time of writing; the review reflects the situation at the time of research. One villa has 1 bedroom with kitchen; the 2nd has 2 bedrooms, living room, kitchen, 2 baths. Both have metered AC, TV, safe, telephone. Laundry facilities $10 per load. Children welcome; pets negotiable. FB $40/day. Groceries can be ordered from Grand Turk or Provo (+ 25% handling charge). *Villa 1 $800–1,300 dbl, villa 2 $900–1,500 dbl, $1,100–1700 quad* $$$

🏠 **Tradewinds Guest Suites** (5 suites) Victoria St, beside Deane's Dock; ✆ 946 6806; e tradewinds@tciway.tc. All en suite with sofa bed in living room, plus kitchen or kitchenette, patio. Metered AC. Bikes & transfers free. Meal & dive packages available. Children under 11 free in parents' room. *Dbl $158–187/day, extra person $20/day pp, all inc tax.* $$$

🏠 **The Vistas** (2 suites) ✆ 946 6906; e scdivers@tciway.tc. Upper & lower floors each with kitchen, living room, bedroom, bath, deck, TV, metered AC. *Top floor $220–260/day, lower $176–204/day, inc tax & transfers inc 10% discount if you take both floors.* $$$

✖ **WHERE TO EAT AND DRINK** It is customary to make dinner reservations by 3pm. This particularly applies out of high season when you may also be asked to specify in advance what you would like to eat.

✖ **Coral Reef Bar & Grill** Deane's Dock; ✆ 946 6906; m 241 1009 ⊕ 7am–late daily (food served until 10pm), inc all holidays. This relaxed seafront café, under the same ownership as Salt Cay Divers, is open throughout the year, serving plenty of fresh fish & conch, good b/fasts & nightly specials (note that evening meals need to be chosen by 3pm). A karaoke night is held every Sat, with a BBQ each Sun at 7pm. Further entertainment comes in the form of horseshoes & volleyball. There's also a TV for dive videos. $$

🍺 **Green Flash Café** Deane's Dock; ⊕ 6.30am–6.30pm Mon–Sat; 2pm–sunset Sun. Under the same ownership as Island Thyme, this relaxed café is right on the harbour. Wed night here is chicken wing night, but most people concentrate on a beer or two & the sunset. For details on the green flash, see box, page 36. $

✖ **Island Thyme** Airport Rd, ✆ 946 6977; m 242 0325; e pwiii@aol.com; www.islandthyme.tc; ⊕ 7am–9pm; closed Wed unless ferry in port, & for at least a month during summer. Complimentary coffee at 7am & complimentary 'Visitors' Guide' & self-guided tour map any time. American owner

Porter Williams lords it over his delightful bistro with evident pride & just a touch of eccentricity. Vibrant Haitian & local paintings – all of them for sale – enliven an already colourful setting, with its blue painted woodwork & cool tiles. The extensive menu comes as a surprise, too. At lunch, expect such goodies as conch pie, based on a local recipe with a twist, or an excellent fish sandwich, or perhaps order a takeaway picnic from $10.95. The creative hand with local ingredients continues into the evening. For a change, Fri is pizza day, & the occasional guest chef adds further character. It's not cheap, but the food is great value. And diners can even surf the net anywhere between here & the dock. Visa/MCd. Recommended. $$$$

🍸 **One Down One to Go Bar** South District; ✆ 946 6901; ⊕ 6.30pm–midnight Mon–Thu & Sat; 6.30pm–whenever Fri. Where the locals go to play dominos or pool & watch big-screen TV.

✖ **Pat's Place** South District, ✆ 946 6919; ⊕ 7–10am, noon–2pm, 7.30–10pm. Set in a traditional house with a cottage-style garden. Does very good cracked conch, but again you should say in advance that you're coming. No credit cards. $$

TWO SECRET RECIPES

PAPAYA SHAKE
Blend thoroughly:

2 cups fresh papaya
crushed ice
sugar syrup, to taste

small tin Carnation evaporated milk
a little water, to thin to taste

IGUANA MARGARITA Ever-smiling Eloisa Dickenson, before she married Halton (also known as Polie; his daughter is district commissioner), used to be the bartender at the renowned but now sadly closed Mount Pleasant Guest House. This was her most popular cocktail.
   Blend together:

Tequila
Triple sec
sugar syrup (make your own by boiling sugar with water for five minutes)
lime juice
(Jamaican) honeydew melon liqueur (there's no substitute for this ingredient).

✕ **Smugglers' Tavern** Pirates' Hideaway, South District. Normally offers good English cooking by reservation only, but not operating at the time of writing.

✕ **Windmills Plantation** North Beach; ✆ 946 6962 ⏰ lunch at 1pm, dinner at 7.30pm, both by prior reservation only. Note: temporarily closed; see page 176. **$$$$$**

SHOPPING Food shopping is limited to three small groceries, all stocking most of the essentials. **Netty's Variety Store** is in North Town, close to Island Thyme (she lives opposite), while **Pat's Groceries** is in South Town, as is **Mr & Mrs Dickenson's Variety Store**. The Dickensons carry a slightly wider range and also offer Mrs Dickenson's papaya juice (see box above), quite the best to be found this side of New York's 86th Street. The opening hours for all three are a bit erratic, but within reason the owners don't mind if you knock on their doors when the shop is closed.

   Serious food or other shopping means a trip to Grand Turk or Provo. Most landlords will arrange an advance order, usually at a 25% handling/transportation charge.

Souvenirs, gifts and sundries

Beachcombers On road to airport. Decorative re-cycled flotsam & jetsam.
H & P Sundries & some chemists items.

Island Thyme Gallery (see above) Jewellery, paintings, papier maché fish & souvenirs
Splash Boutique Deane's Dock. Gifts, island clothing & handcrafts.

OTHER PRACTICALITIES Since 14 April 2004 there has been a small public **library** (⏰ 8.30am–12.30pm Mon–Fri) close to the clinic, offering books, magazines and videos to visitors and residents. The library was opened after an extended campaign by local people, and partly with funds collected by them. It is kept going with volunteer help and interested visitors might consider making a donation of cash or materials. The library offers **internet** access at $3 per half hour, or $5 per hour. Membership is free to islanders, with a $5 donation suggested for visitors.

   There are no **banks** on Salt Cay, though Island Thyme will at its discretion advance cash against a credit card, and most places take travellers' cheques, and no post office; the nearest place for these facilities is Grand Turk. Nevertheless, the island is not entirely free of the trappings of the 21st century. Those who can't leave their laptops behind will be relieved to note that the areas around Island Thyme, Coral Reef and Splash Boutique are all WiFi zones.

Medical facilities A nurse is in attendance at Salt Cay Clinic (*↘ 946 6970;* **m** *242 4960*) from 8am to 1pm Monday to Friday. There is also a dental clinic held here. For anything more serious, patients are transferred to the hospital in Grand Turk. Divers should note that the nearest decompression chamber is on Providenciales. In the event of an **emergency**, here as elsewhere on the islands, phone ↘ 911.

Police Salt Cay's one-man police station can be contacted on ↘ 946 6929.

Religious services There is a choice of four churches on Salt Cay, all in the general area of Deane's Dock. All Sunday services start at 11am and all churches are delighted to welcome visitors.

St John's Anglican Opposite the main salina
Salt Cay Methodist Beyond Netty's

Mt Zion Baptist
Church of God of Prophecy

ACTIVITIES

Diving The underwater topography off Salt Cay's western shores is similar to that off Grand Turk. For the most part lacking the colourful corals that lie further north, the environment is more monochrome, creating a startling backdrop for some of the gaudier reef fish. And while the coral may be less interesting (exceptions include Kelly's Annexe and Turtle Gardens), this is considered to be the better place to see the larger creatures, from turtles and lobsters to rays, barracuda and shark.

Dive sites The island has 15 designated dive sites, strung out along the western shore from the Northwest Wall. All are relatively shallow sites, starting at just 25–35ft (7–10.5m), and leading to the wall that drops almost 7,000ft (2,133m) to the Turks Island Passage.

At the Rockery, a spectacular dive leads to a 60ft (18m) wall renowned for whale sharks, eagle rays and numerous turtles. This, along with Black Coral Canyon, is also the place to spot the slow-growing – and heavily protected – black coral (see page 26). Further north, there are two sites at Northwest Wall, one home to a huge green moray that has been christened Jolly Roger by local divers. Other sites include Kelly's Folly, with its large schools of fish, and the aptly named Turtle Gardens.

The proximity of Salt Cay to the whale migration route means that, between January and April, divers can often hear whale song, although all that is seen of the whales from beneath the waves is usually air bubbles rising to the surface.

For those with an eye for the past, Salt Cay is within striking distance of the wreck of the **HMS** *Endymion*, which lies 7 miles (11km) south of Great Sand Cay in just 40ft (12m) of water. The British ship foundered on the reef without loss of life in 1790, and is now protected as an area of historical interest. Her wooden hull has long since disintegrated, but there are several swim throughs and the presence of eight anchors and a total of 18 coral-encrusted cannons is a powerful draw for divers. Other wrecks on the same site remain unidentified.

Dive operators Salt Cay has one dedicated dive operator. For those who are staying on the island, this gives the enviable option to explore both the island itself and to dive sites further afield, without the prospect of a potentially uncomfortable return to Grand Turk.

All dive operators on Grand Turk offer diving off Salt Cay as well, although their flat-bottomed skiffs can give a bumpy ride so this is only for calm weather. In some cases, a first morning dive off Grand Turk will be followed by a second off Salt Cay. An alternative, offered by Oasis Divers, is a full day at Salt Cay, with two morning dives followed by lunch on the island and time to explore. If you're crossing the channel by boat, keep an eye out for shoals of flying fish.

Salt Cay Divers ✆ 946 6906; m 241 1009; e scdivers@tciway.tc; www.saltcaydivers.tc. American owner Debbie Manos set up her business in 1997, & now has 5 boats, taking 8 divers max per boat. The largest & most powerful of these means that, in addition to Salt Cay's sites, they can comfortably dive off Grand Turk &, weather permitting, visit the wreck of HMS *Endymion*, which is not considered practicable from Grand Turk. The occasional trip to South Caicos, a boat trip of around 1½hrs, is a further option, as are boat charters, sunset cruises & kayaking, & even bike hire. She also runs Splash Boutique (see above). Popular is a day trip incorporating a 2-tank boat dive, lunch & an island tour. *2-tank boat dive $80, Resort course $125; Open Water $395; equipment $20. Whale watching $95 pp ($75 for divers on a package)*

Snorkelling Some of the best snorkelling from the shore at Salt Cay is to be found under the bluff, and around the point called Point Pleasant, to the northwest of the island, where the reef is just 8ft (2.5m) below the surface, attracting plenty of colourful fish. Those on a boat trip would do well to head for Aquarium off the north shore, just five minutes from the dock, at a cost of $10 per person with Salt Cay Divers. A boat ride of 25 minutes, at $45 a head, takes you to Gibb's Cay (see page 175), where you can dive for conch and snorkel with the stingrays. Snorkelling gear is included.

Kayaking Salt Cay offers plenty of scope for kayaking in the mangroves along the coast. There is also a protected 'blue hole' in the South Creek which is ideal for both beginners and experienced kayakers. It's also a great spot for birdwatching. Kayaks can be rented from Salt Cay Divers for $35 per half day.

TOURING THE ISLAND There is only a handful of conventional vehicles on the three-square-mile (7.8km²) island and most people get around the untarred roads either by golf buggy or Shanks's pony. At Island Thyme restaurant and boutique you should be sure to pick up a beautifully comprehensive, complimentary leaflet for self-guided tours, with a detailed description of landmarks.

Much of Salt Cay is protected as an area of historical interest, which encompasses Deane's Dock, the buildings to the west of the Town Salina and the salina itself, as well as Whale Island and Whale House Bay.

There are many buildings of considerable interest in what are rather extravagantly defined as three villages: North Town (or district), Balfour Town and South Town (or district), contiguously linked by Victoria Street that runs between the salt ponds and the sea. The overriding style is naturally enough Bermudian with wide verandas and jalousied windows, often featuring, in the interests of safety, a distinctive separate kitchen.

Singularly imposing on the waterfront is the **White House**, built in 1835 with stone brought as ballast in a salt schooner. It was and still is the property of the Harriott family, 'white gold' merchants of old. Informal tours of the fascinating house whose interior has barely changed at all over nearly 200 years can sometimes be arranged if one of the family is in residence.

Near by, the **Brown House** was erected by a shipwright cousin, Alexander Harriott, who later also inevitably became a salt proprietor. Much of the wood utilised in its construction was salvaged from a shipwreck.

In Balfour Town too, and in dire need of restoration, is the beautiful wooden-framed **Benevolent Brotherhood Lodge** which housed a Masonic-style organisation designed to provide mutual support amongst the islanders, and to allocate combined funds to finance funerals and such matters.

The **District Commissioner's Office** is notable in that the lower floor of the two-storey building at one time served a dual purpose, part jail-cell and part archive storage. Inevitably there came a time when a prisoner succeeded in torching all the documents. Fortunately he was unsuccessful in similtaneously destroying the building.

Beautiful **St John's Anglican Church**, built at the end of the 18th century, is one of the oldest churches in the Turks and Caicos. When the doors are open a sea breeze cools both congregation and pastor.

An excellent example of harmonious early 19th-century Turks Island architecture, Salt Cay's former **Government House,** also known as the **old commissioner's house**, had fallen into a state of disrepair but it has now been leased by the Turks and Caicos National Trust with a view to restoration. Once upon a time this was the seat of local government for the island and 'tea parties were held in the garden with ladies dressed in white gloves and hats'. The intention is to open it as a visitor centre, with various rooms restored, including a Bermudian kitchen. As part of this project, oral and visual histories are being recorded. To contribute to the preservation fund, cheques should be made out to 'The Turks and Caicos Preservation Foundation', preferably including a printed donation form, and posted to The Turks and Caicos Preservation Foundation, c/o Helen Krieble, 6017 N Villard Court, Parker, CO 80134, USA.

To the east, ruins thought to be of a former whale-watching station can be seen on the crest of **Taylor's Hill**. There is no road to the summit but it is well worth the climb on foot for a splendid 360° view taking in Cotton Cay, Whale Cay and many other islets, as well as an opportunity to play detective and speculate on the provenance of a number of symmetrical mounds of stone, each about three feet high, grouped on the hill. No one will be able to tell you how they came to be there. It is simply a Salt Cay mystery. If you are suitably intrigued by these you may also check out what are said to be two pirate graves directly in front of 'Clyde's house', just across the street from Miss Debbie's Splash Boutique. Birdwatchers, though, would do well to head for Whale House Bay, which attracts good numbers of wetland birds.

Salt Cay is a limestone-based island and a number of **underwater caves** are believed to interweave beneath it. Each summer a group of technical divers visits and, employing mixed gases (a potentially hazardous exercise), are attempting to map the system.

A small **blowhole** can be seen – and heard – in the rocks on the southwest coast, just beyond the electricity generator enclosure. At high tide it is fun, as children do in the Pacific islands, to toss a coconut husk, or something similarly biodegradable, into the sea and watch it tossed back up again. To find the blowhole at high tide, walking south from the White House, turn seaward immediately past the electricity facility but short of the island rubbish dump and clamber over the rocks till you hear its roar. With any luck you may even have an island potcake for company.

BOAT TRIPS All boat trips can be organised through Salt Cay Divers, above.

Whale watching With its southerly location, Salt Cay is one of the best islands from which to watch the annual whale migration. Many of these huge creatures pass through the channel between Salt Cay and the more southerly Great Sand Cay, making good, clear sightings more or less guaranteed in season, even from land.

Occasionally it's possible to swim alongside the whales, although visibility is far better from a boat.

Other islands As if Salt Cay were not sufficiently remote, it is possible to charter a boat to visit one of the uninhabited islands within these waters, taking a picnic lunch and snorkelling or diving – perhaps in combination with a visit to the *Endymion*. A popular choice is **Great (or Big) Sand Cay** to the south, a bird sanctuary that is also one of the remaining habitats for the Turks & Caicos iguana. Those in search of a truly Robinson Crusoe experience can even opt to stay overnight, camping under the stars. A day trip, including a picnic, costs $50 per person with Salt Cay Divers, rising to $100 to spend the night, with the boat returning to collect you the following day. Oasis Divers also run trips here from Grand Turk.

Appendix I

ACCOMMODATION

The following is an at-a-glance summary of the various places to stay detailed in this guide, put together as an aid to planning your holiday. For details of each venue, see the page number given.

PROVIDENCIALES

Name	Location	Type	No rooms/ units	Page
Airport Inn	Downtown	medium hotel	12	95
Alexandra	Grace Bay	studios	85	88
Amanyara	Malcolm's Beach	hotel	40	95
Aquamarine Beach Houses	Grace Bay	houses	3	94
Beaches	Grace Bay	all inclusive	453	94
Canterbury	Northwest	suites	45	95
Caribbean Paradise Inn	Grace Bay	medium hotel	17	93
Club Med Turkoise	Grace Bay	all inclusive	290	94
Comfort Suites	Grace Bay	medium hotel	98	93
Coral Gardens	Grace Bay	hotel	30	88
Grace Bay Club	Grace Bay	hotel	21	88
Harbour Club Villas & Marina	South (Turtle Tail)	villas	6	95
Le Vele	Grace Bay	hotel	22	88
Miramar Resort	Turtle Cove	hotel	20	94
Neptune Villas	South (Chalk Sound)	villas	10	95
Nikki Beach Resort	Leeward	suites	48	95
Northwest Point Resort	Northwest	condominiums	49	96
Ocean Club Resort	Grace Bay	hotel	86	89
Ocean Club West	Grace Bay	hotel	88	89
Point Grace Resort	Grace Bay	hotel	30	89
Queen Angel Resort	Turtle Cove	suites	45	94
Reef Residences	Grace Bay	hotel	24	88
Regent Palms	Grace Bay	hotel	72	89
Royal West Indies Resort	Grace Bay	hotel	60	89
Seven Stars	Grace Bay	apartments	114	89
Sibonné	Grace Bay	medium hotel	30	93
South Fleetwood	Grace Bay	cottage/suite	2	94
The Sands at Grace Bay	Grace Bay	condominiums	118	89
The Seagate	Grace Bay	condominiums	4	94
The Somerset	Grace Bay	suites	54	89
The Tuscany	Grace Bay	villas	30	93

Appendix I   ACCOMMODATION

A1

Name	Location	Type	No rooms/ units	Page
Trade Winds Condotel	Grace Bay	suites	18	93
Turks & Caicos Club	Grace Bay	suites	21	93
Turtle Cove Inn	Turtle Cove	hotel	30	95
Villa Renaissance	Grace Bay	suites	44	93
The Villas	Grace Bay	hotel	38	88
Windsong Resort	Grace Bay	condominiums	43	93

WEST CAICOS

Molasses Reef		hotel	125	96

PINE CAY

The Meridian Club		resort	12 rooms, 11 houses	96

DELLIS CAY

Dellis Cay		hotel		96

PARROT CAY

Parrot Cay		hotel/villas	58	96

NORTH CAICOS

Blue Rondo		self catering	2	129
Bottle Creek Lodge	Bottle Creek	villas	3	129
Creek Mouth Guest House	Horse Stable Beach	self catering	2	129
Datai Villa			1	129
Hollywood Beach Suites	Whitby	suites	4	129
Jamilton's Nest		apartments	2	129
La Casita apartments	Whitby	apartment	1	129
La Villa Rose		villa	1	129
Ocean Beach Hotel	Whitby	hotel	10	129
Ocean Front Villas		villas	2	130
Pax Villa	Whitby	villa	1	130
Pelican Beach Hotel	Whitby	hotel	16	130
Royal Reef Resort	Sandy Point	condotel	205	130
St Charles	Horse Stable Beach	condominiums	90	130
Whitby Beach Villa	Whitby	villa	1	130

MIDDLE CAICOS

Blue Horizon	Mudjin Harbour	villas	7	134
Dreamscape Villa	Bambarra Beach	villa	1	134
Eagle's Rest Villas		villas	2	134
Oceanfront Villa	Conch Bar	villa	1	135
Sundial Villa	Bambarra	villa	1	135

SOUTH CAICOS

Caicos Beach Club		condominiums	800	145
East Bay Resort		condominiums	200	145
Ocean Beach Resort		hotel	30	145

AMBERGRIS CAY

Turks & Caicos Sporting Club		members' lodge	4	151

GRAND TURK

Name	Location	Type	No rooms/ units	Page
The Arches		villas	4	164
Bohio Dive Resort		dive lodge	20	164
Cacique Royale		condominiums	116	164
Columbus Landing		condominiums	60	164
Grand Turk Inn	Cockburn Town	hotel	5	162
Island House		self catering	8	164
Manta House	Cockburn Town	self catering	5	162
Osprey Beach Hotel	Cockburn Town	hotel	39	162
Salt Raker Inn	Cockburn Town	hotel	13	162
Turk's Head Mansion	Cockburn Town	hotel	8	162
White Sands Beach Resort		condominiums	16	164

SALT CAY

Name	Location	Type	No rooms/ units	Page
Compass Rose Cottage		self catering	1	177
Hyacinth Cottage		self catering	1	177
Pirate's Hideaway		self catering	3	177
Purple Conch Cottage		self catering	1	177
Salt Cay Villas		self catering	5	178
Sandy Toes		self catering		178
Sunset Reef Villas		villas	3	178
Tradewinds Guest Suites		self catering	5	178
The Vistas		self catering	2	178
Windmills Plantation		hotel	12	

Appendix 2

GLOSSARY

Arawak	Generic term for a group of native peoples originally from northern and western South America, who historically colonised the Caribbean and western Atlantic
archipelago	A group of islands
barbacoa	Taino word meaning a barbecue
Behiques	Taino spiritual healer
Belonger	Local inhabitant with special residential and employment rights
brigantine	A two-masted sailing ship
buccaneer	Originally denoting a cattle rustler, later an alternative term for pirate
cacique	Taino chief
canaoua	Taino word meaning canoe
caravel	A small fast ship of the 15th–17th centuries
Carib	A member of an indigenous people from the north coast of South America
Caribantic	On the borders of the Caribbean Sea and the Atlantic Ocean
casavi	Taino word for cassava, a starchy tropical food
cay	A small island (pronounced 'kee')
corsair	A pirate officially hired by a nation to attack ships of opposing powers; *see privateer*
Devil's or Bermuda Triangle	Area of the western north Atlantic that includes all the Turks and Caicos Islands, in which legend has it there have been a number of mysterious disappearances
duho	Lucayan ceremonial stool
field-road	Trail or path cut through the bush, traditionally used to reach fields of crops, fishing areas, wells or other important sites
green flash	Momentary flash of green light as the sun sinks below the horizon
guano	Seabird excrement used as fertiliser
hamaka	Taino word meaning hammock
hurakan	Hurricane, from Taino 'God of the Storm'
junkanoo	Turcasian carnival, with costume parade and traditional island music from local instruments. Featuring hypnotic dancing, it is typically staged on Boxing Day or New Year's Day. Believed to originate from the 17th century when slaves were given a brief seasonal holiday at that time of year.
Loyalist	Resident of America who remained loyal to Britain during the Revolution
Lucayan	The original inhabitants of the Bahamian archipelago, now extinct
manatee	A sea cow, from Carib *manati*
Ostionan/Ostionoid	Applied to pottery (AD600–900) from Greater Antilles
Palmetto ware	Lucayan pottery deriving from the Bahamas and TCI

petroglyph	A rock carving, generally prehistoric
picaroon	Another term for wrecker/wracker: a salvager of shipwrecks
potcake	Local mongrel dog, generally feral
potsherd	A broken piece of pottery, especially from an archaeological site
privateer	A privately armed individual or ship authorised by a Government to capture enemy vessels
ripsaw	Also known as rake 'n' scrape, the national music of TCI, featuring a saw, and other instruments such as concertina, maracas and guitar
Saladoid pottery	Originating in Venezuela from as early as 2000BC
schooner	Substantial sailing ship with two or more masts
sloop	One-masted sailing ship
tabaco	Taino word for a sort of cigar
Taino	An Arawak people and language, originating from Venezuela; the word means 'noble'. The Tainos colonised the Greater Antilles, followed by the Lucayan Islands – the Bahamas and the Turks and Caicos.
Turks Islander	Person who was born in TCI
Turcasians	Inhabitants of the Turks and Caicos Islands
wracking	Salvaging wrecked ships

Appendix 3

FURTHER INFORMATION

HISTORY AND GENERAL

Bacon, Edward Denny *The Postage Stamps of the Turks Islands* Stanley Gibbons, London, 1917. Covers the first 11 issues of stamps 1867–95.

Keegan, William F *Bahamian Archaeology: Life in the Bahamas and Turks and Caicos Islands Before Columbus* Columbus Media Pub, Nassau, 1997

Keegan, William F *The People who discovered Columbus: Pre-history of the Bahamas (Columbus Quincentanary)* University Press, Florida, 1992

Keegan, William F *Taino Indian Myth and Practice: The Arrival of the Stranger King* University Press, Florida, 2007

Lovelace, S Guy *The Carnival Never Got Started* Vantage Pres, New York, 2005. Autobiographical account of opening a hotel on Salt Cay.

Morison, Samuel Eliot *The European Discovery of America; The Southern Voyages 1492-1616* Oxford University Press, New York, 1974

Palmer, Charles *Living in the Turks and Caicos Islands; From Conchs to the Florida Lottery* Protea Publishing USA, 2001. Autobiography of a fisherman's son growing up in TCI after World War II.

Pusey, J Henry *The Handbook of the Turk and Caicos Islands* Mortimer C DeSouza, Kingston Jamaica, 1897. History and statistics 'from their discovery until the present time'. The author was for 17 years a Baptist missionary in TCI.

Pusey, J Henry *An Elementary Class Book of the Geography and History of the TCI* Eliot Stock, London, 1887

Quasar, Gian *Into the Bermuda Triangle: Pursuing the Truth Behind the World's Greatest Mystery* International Marine/Ragged Mountain Press, Camden Me, 2003

Sadler, H E *Turks Island Landfall: A History of the Turks & Caicos Islands*, 1997. Currently out of print but a copy can be found in some US libraries and in the British Library in London.

Sadler, Nigel (ed) *A Guide to the Turks and Caicos National Museum* Turks and Caicos National Museum, 2001

Sadler, Nigel *Slave History of the Turks & Caicos Islands* Turks & Caicos National Museum, 2004

Saunders, Nicholas J *The Peoples of the Caribbean* ABC, Santa Barbara, California, 2005

Smithers, Amelia, revised by Taylor, Anthony *The Turks and Caicos Islands: Lands of Discovery* Macmillan Caribbean, 2003

Snow, Edward Rouse *Pirates and Buccaneers of the Atlantic Coast* Yankee Publishing Co, Boston, Massachusetts, 1944

Van Tyno, Claude Halstead *The Loyalists in the American Revolution* University Press of the Pacific, Hawaii, 2004 (reprinted from the original 1902 edition)

Wilson, Samuel M *The Archaeology of the Caribbean* Cambridge University Press, 2007. A synthesis of Caribbean pre-history up to the time of the European conquest of the islands.

NATURAL HISTORY

Bradley, Patricia *Birds of the Turks and Caicos Islands* (checklist) National Trust

Correll, Donovan S & Helen B *Flora of the Bahama Archipelago (inc TCI)* J Cramer, Germany, 1982

Ground, Richard *Birds of the Turks and Caicos Islands* National Trust, 2001. Dedicated guide to the islands' birdlife, incorporating 236 colour photographs and coverage of habitats.

Hallett, Bruce *Birds of the Bahamas and the Turks and Caicos Islands* Macmillan Caribbean, 2006

Humann, Paul, and Deloach, Ned *Reef Fish Identification: Florida, Caribbean, Bahamas* New World Publications, Florida, 2007. Superb colour guides to the underwater world. Others in the series cover reef fish behaviour, reef creatures and coral identification.

Morton, Julia F *Medicinal and Other Plants Used by People of North Caicos, TCI* Paper presented at University of Illinois, 1976

Riley, Norman D *A Field Guide to Butterflies of the West Indies* Collins, London, 1975

Spalding, Mark D *World Atlas of Coral Reefs* University of California Press, 2001. With 94 maps and plenty of colour photos, this also enters the realms of reef damage as a result of human intervention.

Wood, Kathleen McNary *Flowers of the Bahamas and the Turks and Caicos Islands* Caribbean Publishing, 2002

DIVING AND SAILING GUIDES

Cummings, Stuart and Susanne, Rosenburg, Steve *Diving and Snorkelling: Turks and Caicos Islands* Lonely Planet, 2001

Pavlidis, Stephen J *The Turks and Caicos Guide: A Cruising Guide to the Turks and Caicos Islands* Seaworthy Publications Inc, USA 1997

Wilson, Mathew *The Bahamas Cruising Guide: With the Turks and Caicos Islands* Nomad Press, 2004

Wood, Lawson *Top Dive Sites of the Caribbean* New Holland Publishers, UK, 1998. Technically out of print, but still available online easily enough.

GENERAL AND PHOTOGRAPHIC GUIDES

Davies, Julia & Phil *Turks & Caicos Islands: Beautiful by Nature* Macmillan Education, 2000. Glossy, coffee-table book aimed at the souvenir market.

World Bibliographic Series Vol 137, Turks & Caicos Clio Press, Oxford, 1991

WEBSITES

www.pomacanthus.com An online guide published in e-book format to the world's coral reefs, designed for snorkellers and divers.

www.tcmuseum.org Grand Turk Museum

www.tcweeklynew.com Online version of the *Turks & Caicos Weekly News*

www.turksandcaicos.tc *The* internet site for factual information, including details of government departments

www.turksandcaicoshta.com Turks and Caicos Hotel and Tourism Association

www.turksandcaicostourism.com Turks and Caicos Tourist Board

Bradt Travel Guides

Africa

Africa Overland	£15.99
Algeria	£15.99
Benin	£14.99
Botswana: Okavango, Chobe, Northern Kalahari	£15.99
Burkina Faso	£14.99
Cape Verde Islands	£13.99
Canary Islands	£13.95
Cameroon	£13.95
Congo	£14.99
Eritrea	£15.99
Ethiopia	£15.99
Gabon, São Tomé, Príncipe	£13.95
Gambia, The	£13.99
Ghana	£15.99
Johannesburg	£6.99
Kenya	£14.95
Madagascar	£15.99
Malawi	£13.99
Mali	£13.95
Mauritius, Rodrigues & Réunion	£13.99
Mozambique	£13.99
Namibia	£15.99
Niger	£14.99
Nigeria	£15.99
Rwanda	£14.99
São Tomé & Principe	£14.99
Seychelles	£14.99
Sudan	£13.95
Tanzania, Northern	£13.99
Tanzania	£16.99
Uganda	£15.99
Zambia	£17.99
Zanzibar	£12.99

Britain and Europe

Albania	£13.99
Armenia, Nagorno Karabagh	£14.99
Azores	£12.99
Baltic Capitals: Tallinn, Riga, Vilnius, Kaliningrad	£12.99
Belarus	£14.99
Belgrade	£6.99
Bosnia & Herzegovina	£13.99
Bratislava	£6.99
Budapest	£8.99
Bulgaria	£13.99
Cork	£6.99
Croatia	£13.99

Cyprus see North Cyprus	
Czech Republic	£13.99
Dresden	£7.99
Dubrovnik	£6.99
Estonia	£13.99
Faroe Islands	£13.95
Georgia	£14.99
Helsinki	£7.99
Hungary	£14.99
Iceland	£14.99
Kiev	£7.95
Kosovo	£14.99
Krakow	£7.99
Lapland	£13.99
Latvia	£13.99
Lille	£6.99
Lithuania	£13.99
Ljubljana	£7.99
Macedonia	£14.99
Montenegro	£13.99
North Cyprus	£12.99
Paris, Lille & Brussels	£11.95
Riga	£6.99
River Thames, In the Footsteps of the Famous	£10.95
Serbia	£14.99
Slovakia	£14.99
Slovenia	£12.99
Spitsbergen	£14.99
Switzerland: Rail, Road, Lake	£13.99
Tallinn	£6.99
Ukraine	£14.99
Vilnius	£6.99
Zagreb	£6.99

Middle East, Asia and Australasia

China: Yunnan Province	£13.99
Great Wall of China	£13.99
Iran	£14.99
Iraq	£14.95
Iraq: Then & Now	£15.99
Kyrgyzstan	£15.99
Maldives	£13.99
Mongolia	£14.95
North Korea	£13.95
Oman	£13.99
Sri Lanka	£13.99
Syria	£14.99
Tibet	£13.99
Turkmenistan	£14.99
Yemen	£14.99

The Americas and the Caribbean

Amazon, The	£14.99
Argentina	£15.99
Bolivia	£14.99
Cayman Islands	£14.99
Colombia	£15.99
Costa Rica	£13.99
Chile	£16.95
Dominica	£14.99
Falkland Islands	£13.95
Guyana	£14.99
Panama	£13.95
Peru & Bolivia: The Bradt Trekking Guide	£12.95
St Helena	£14.99
USA by Rail	£13.99

Wildlife

100 Animals to See Before They Die	£16.99
Antarctica: Guide to the Wildlife	£14.95
Arctic: Guide to the Wildlife	£15.99
Central & Eastern European Wildlife	£15.99
Chinese Wildlife	£16.99
East African Wildlife	£19.99
Galápagos Wildlife	£15.99
Madagascar Wildlife	£15.99
North Atlantic Wildlife	£16.99
Peruvian Wildlife	£15.99
Southern African Wildlife	£18.95
Sri Lankan Wildlife	£15.99

Eccentric Guides

Eccentric America	£13.95
Eccentric Australia	£12.99
Eccentric Britain	£13.99
Eccentric California	£13.99
Eccentric Cambridge	£6.99
Eccentric Edinburgh	£5.95
Eccentric France	£12.95
Eccentric London	£13.99
Eccentric Oxford	£5.95

Others

Your Child Abroad: A Travel Health Guide	£10.95
Something Different for the Weekend	£9.99

WIN £100 CASH!

READER QUESTIONNAIRE

Send in your completed questionnaire for the chance to win £100 cash in our regular draw

All respondents may order a Bradt guide at half the UK retail price – please complete the order form overleaf.

(Entries may be posted or faxed to us, or scanned and emailed.)

We are interested in getting feedback from our readers to help us plan future Bradt guides. Please answer ALL the questions below and return the form to us in order to qualify for an entry in our regular draw.

Have you used any other Bradt guides? If so, which titles? . . . .

. . . .

What other publishers' travel guides do you use regularly? . . . .

. . . .

Where did you buy this guidebook? . . . .

What was the main purpose of your trip to the Turks and Caicos Islands (or for what other reason did you read our guide)? eg: holiday/business/charity etc . . . . . .

. . . .

What other destinations would you like to see covered by a Bradt guide?

. . . .

Age (circle relevant category) 16–25   26–45   46–60   60+

Male/Female (delete as appropriate)

Home country . . . .

Please send us any comments about our guide to the Turks and Caicos Islands or other Bradt Travel Guides . . . .

. . . .

. . . .

. . . .

Bradt Travel Guides
23 High Street, Chalfont St Peter, Bucks SL9 9QE, UK
☎ +44 (0)1753 893444 **f** +44 (0)1753 892333
e info@bradtguides.com
www.bradtguides.com

CLAIM YOUR HALF-PRICE BRADT GUIDE!

Order Form

To order your half-price copy of a Bradt guide, and to enter our prize draw to win £100 (see overleaf), please fill in the order form below, complete the questionnaire overleaf, and send it to Bradt Travel Guides by post, fax or email.

Please send me one copy of the following guide at half the UK retail price

Title	Retail price	Half price
... .	....	....

Please send the following additional guides at full UK retail price

No	Title	Retail price	Total
...	....	....	....
...	....	....	....
...	....	....	....

Sub total ......
Post & packing ......
(£2 per book UK; £4 per book Europe; £6 per book rest of world)
Total ......

Name ....

Address ....

Tel .... Email ....

☐ I enclose a cheque for £ .... made payable to Bradt Travel Guides Ltd

☐ I would like to pay by credit card. Number: ....

Expiry date: ... / ...   3-digit security code (on reverse of card) .....

Issue no (debit cards only) .....

☐ I would like to subscribe to Bradt's monthly enewsletter.

☐ I would be happy for you to use my name and comments in Bradt marketing material.

Send your order on this form, with the completed questionnaire, to:

Bradt Travel Guides TCI1
23 High Street, Chalfont St Peter, Bucks SL9 9QE
☎ +44 (0)1753 893444   **f** +44 (0)1753 892333
e info@bradtguides.com www.bradtguides.com

Index

Page numbers in **bold** indicate major entries; those in *italic* indicate maps